Eating Disorders

Innovative Directions in Research and Practice

Edited by Ruth H. Striegel-Moore and Linda Smolak

American Psychological Association, Washington, DC

Published by
American Psychological Association
750 First Street, NE
Washington, DC 20002
www.apa.org

To order
APA Order Department
P.O. Box 92984
Washington, DC 20090-2984
Tel: (800) 374-2721,
  Direct: (202) 336-5510
Fax: (202) 336-5502,
  TDD/TTY: (202) 336-6123
Online: www.apa.org/books/
Email: order@apa.org

In the U.K., Europe, Africa, and the
  Middle East, copies may be ordered from
American Psychological Association
3 Henrietta Street
Covent Garden, London
WC2E 8LU England

Typeset in Goudy by World Composition Services, Inc., Sterling, VA

Printer: Port City Press, Baltimore, MD
Dust jacket designer: Naylor Design, Washington, DC
Technical/Production Editor: Amy J. Clarke

The opinions and statements published are the responsibility of the authors, and such opinions and statements do not necessarily represent the policies of the American Psychological Association.

Library of Congress Cataloging-in-Publication Data
Eating disorders : innovative directions for research and practice / edited by Ruth H. Striegel-Moore and Linda Smolak.—1st ed.
    p.; cm.
    Includes bibliographical references and indexes.
    ISBN 1-55798-778-5 (CB : acid-free paper)
    1. Eating disorders. I. Striegel-Moore, Ruth H.   II. Smolak, Linda, 1951–   .
    [DNLM: 1. Eating Disorders—diagnosis. 2. Eating Disorders—prevention &
    control. 3. Eating Disorders—therapy. WM 175 E14737 2001]
    RC552.E18 E284 2001
    616.85′26—dc21   00-053113

British Library Cataloguing-in-Publication Data
A CIP record is available from the British Library.

Printed in the United States of America
First Edition

To Klaus Striegel, who was my brother and friend,
and Annette Striegel, the woman he loved.
R. H. S.–M.

To my parents, Marjorie Tyron and
Harry Smolak, whose spirits still guide me.
L. S.

CONTENTS

CONTRIBUTORS

Angela A. Celio, MA, Department of Psychiatry and Behavioral Sciences, Stanford University School of Medicine, Stanford, CA

Majorie Crago, PhD, Department of Family & Community Medicine, College of Medicine, University of Arizona, Tucson

Scott Crow, MD, Department of Psychiatry, University of Minnesota, Minneapolis

Sherrie Selwyn Delinsky, BA, Doctoral Candidate, Department of Psychology, Rutgers University, Piscataway, NJ

Barbara J. Dorian, MD, Centre for Addiction and Mental Health, Sunnybrook and Women's College Health Science Centre, and Department of Psychiatry, University of Toronto, Toronto, Ontario, Canada

Paul E. Garfinkel, MD, Centre for Addiction and Mental Health, Clark Institute of Psychiatry, University of Toronto, Toronto, Ontario, Canada

Vicki Garvin, PhD, private practice, Glastonbury, CT

Leslie J. Heinberg, PhD, Department of Psychiatry & Behavioral Science, School of Medicine, Johns Hopkins University, Baltimore, MD

David B. Herzog, MD, Department of Psychiatry, Harvard University Medical School, Cambridge, MA

Allan Kaplan, MD, Department of Psychiatry, University of Toronto Hospital, Toronto, Ontario, Canada

Michael P. Levine, PhD, Department of Psychology, Kenyon College, Gambier, OH

James E. Mitchell, MD, Department of Neuroscience, School of Medicine & Health Sciences, University of North Dakota, Fargo

Jonas L. Matzon, BA, University of Chicago School of Medicine, Chicago, IL

Sarah K. Murnen, PhD, Department of Psychology, Kenyon College, Gambier, OH

Carol B. Peterson, PhD, Department of Psychiatry, University of Minnesota, Minneapolis

Niva Piran, PhD, CPsych, Department of Adult Education, Community Development & Counseling Psychology, University of Toronto, Toronto, Ontario, Canada

Anne Ruble, BA, Psychiatry Department, College of Medicine, Northwestern University, Chicago, IL

Catherine M. Shisslak, PhD, Department of Family & Community Medicine, College of Medicine, University of Arizona, Tucson

Linda Smolak, PhD, Department of Psychology, Kenyon College, Gambier, OH

Eric Stice, PhD, Department of Psychology, University of Texas at Austin

Ruth H. Striegel-Moore, PhD, Department of Psychology, Wesleyan University, Middletown, CT

C. Barr Taylor, MD, Department of Psychiatry and Behavioral Sciences, Stanford University School of Medical, Stanford, CA

J. Kevin Thompson, PhD, Department of Psychology, University of South Florida, Tampa

Andrew J. Winzelberg, PhD, Department of Psychiatry and Behavioral Sciences, Stanford University School of Medical, Stanford, CA

Stephen A. Wonderlich, PhD, Department of Neuroscience, School of Medicine & Health Sciences, University of North Dakota, Fargo

PREFACE

The impetus for this book was our sense that it was time to take stock of what has been accomplished in the research of eating disorders and to look ahead with the overarching question of What will it take to advance knowledge, not just incrementally but significantly? A major stimulus for this book was our experience of serving on a government task force that had been charged to develop a public health initiative to reduce the burden of eating disorders. A pressing issue was whether the field is ready for prevention. In considering the knowledge base in areas of classification, etiology, treatment, and, of course, prevention, we found that much of the scholarly writing was "playing it safe," a situation that often seemed to contribute to the gaps in information.

In this volume, leading experts in classification, treatment, and prevention of eating disorders have been asked to reflect on the status of the field and to propose bold, new directions for research and interventions. Setting the stage is the opening chapter by Paul Garfinkel and Barbara Dorian, which is based on Garfinkel's lecture when receiving the Academy for Eating Disorder Lifetime Achievement Award. They lay out the key themes to be explored in greater detail in the subsequent three main sections of the book, namely, classification and etiology, treatment, and prevention. Garfinkel and Dorian urge researchers and clinicians not to be complacent with the success that has been achieved to date and point to challenges that remain to be addressed more effectively. These challenges are both academic and political. Major gaps in knowledge remain that require both creative scholarship and financial resources. Moreover, social attitudes of researchers and clinicians as well as of society at large need to be the focus of attention because eating disorders, like other mental disorders, are often not taken seriously or, even worse, stigmatized.

We believe that the contributors to this volume have risen to our challenge and provide eloquent and thoughtful chapters that will be useful for all interested in advancing a constructive research agenda or innovative intervention efforts. We appreciate their candor and willingness to take a risk by not merely summarizing what is known but rather proposing new research ideas, treatment, and prevention programs.

We would like to thank Susan Reynolds, Anne Woodworth, and Amy Clarke at the American Psychological Association for their superb stewardship of this book through all phases of production. Ruth thanks JoAnn Kehoe, administrative assistant in the Psychology Department at Wesleyan University for her dedication to excellence. Ruth also thanks the "power girls" (you know who you are) for their friendship and inspiration. Most of all, Ruth owes a debt of gratitude to Michael Neale for his unwavering support of her in all her roles and for still inviting her to dance. Linda would first like to thank Sonja Gallagher, secretary to the Psychology Department at Kenyon College, who facilitates all her work. Linda would also like to thank her Kenyon colleagues Sarah Murnen and Michael Levine, who simultaneously inspire and support her work. Most especially, she owes a debt of gratitude to Jim Keeler whose patience and kindness make all things possible.

OVERVIEW

INTRODUCTION

RUTH H. STRIEGEL-MOORE AND LINDA SMOLAK

The eating disorders, anorexia nervosa and bulimia nervosa, are characterized by clinically significant disturbances in body image and eating behavior. The core features of anorexia nervosa are cognitive and affective disturbances in body image (e.g., feeling fat even when emaciated, denial of seriousness of one's low weight, morbid fear of weight gain) and the physical consequences of the relentless pursuit of thinness (failure to maintain a minimum adequate body weight and, in girls and women, amenorrhea [the unexpected absence of menstrual periods]). Bulimia nervosa is defined by an overvaluation of weight and shape for one's sense of self-worth and the behavioral symptoms of recurrent binge eating, accompanied by inappropriate compensatory behaviors (e.g., purging, fasting, excessive exercise, use of drugs to compensate for eating binges). Eating disorders were introduced fairly recently into the medical nosology. Anorexia nervosa was first recognized as a mental disorder in the late 19th century; bulimia nervosa, after briefly being considered a variant of anorexia nervosa in the late 1970s, was introduced as a distinct disorder only in 1980. Given this relatively brief history, it is perhaps not surprising that eating disorders are far less researched than other mental disorders of comparable influence on health and adjustment, such as major depression or obsessive–compulsive disorder.

Eating disorders have a peculiar status among mental disorders. Despite extensive evidence that these disorders are associated with significant impairment in health and psychosocial adjustment, there are numerous indications that eating disorders are not taken seriously. Media portrayals tend to glamorize or trivialize these disorders as problems of the "rich and famous" or as "vanity run amok." An advertisement campaign for a popular television show encouraged audiences to see "cool anorexic chicks." An answer not uncommonly heard in response to the screening question "Have you ever been diagnosed to suffer from anorexia nervosa" is "I should be so lucky." Women joke about how they wish they could "catch" anorexia nervosa for a while to help them lose weight. Even though eating disorders and their spectrum variants (captured in the medical nomenclature as "eating disorder not otherwise specified") affect an estimated 10% of female adolescents and women, research funding in this area remains low. Perhaps the most compelling illustration of the inadequate attention paid to eating disorders as a major public health concern is the fact that in the United States, there are no nationally representative data regarding the incidence, prevalence, and basic demographic distribution of eating disorders. Related, because public health directives such as Healthy People 2010, allocation of health services resources, and initiation of prevention efforts are typically justified on the basis of epidemiologic data, eating disorders have not become a public health priority yet.

These challenges notwithstanding, researchers and clinicians working in the field of eating disorders have accumulated an impressive body of knowledge about the clinical presentation and course, assessment, and treatment of eating disorders. Indeed, several journals have devoted special issues to their scholarly review of advances in those areas (e.g., Joiner, 2000; Kashubeck-West & Mintz, in press). What is still needed, however, is a systematic exploration of the predominant theoretical paradigms and research approaches with an emphasis on the question of how the field may be advanced not only incrementally but also exponentially. Researchers are under considerable pressure to approach their work "conservatively" by building on widely accepted paradigms or techniques. We certainly do not mean to suggest that systematic hypothesis testing ought to be abandoned. However, we suggest that cautious editorial or grant review practices tend to make it difficult for researchers to develop novel theoretical concepts or intervention approaches. As a consequence, many invaluable insights and creative ideas about the etiology, treatment, and prevention of eating disorders remain private rather than shared knowledge and do not enter the collective efforts to advance research and clinical practice in the field.

This book aims to address this problem by introducing a collection of scholarly chapters written by researchers who have devoted their careers to reducing the burden of suffering experienced by individuals with an eating disorder. To reduce the burden of suffering, researchers use two major intervention strategies: prevention and treatment. *Preventive* efforts reduce the burden of suffering by lowering the number of individuals who might otherwise experience the onset of a disorder or by decreasing the risk for the development of adverse health consequences associated with these disorders. *Treatment* efforts alleviate the burden of suffering by reducing the severity and duration of the disorder. Advances in treatment and prevention are based in part on the studies of the classification of eating disorders and an appreciation of the risk and protective factors of these disorders.

Contributing authors were asked to focus their chapters on the following questions: How can progress be made in this field? What new paths need to be explored, what methods appear most promising, and what questions have yet to be raised? The book focuses on three major areas: classification and etiology, treatment, and prevention. Not included are topics that have been recently considered in other publications. For example, the issue of the role of genetic factors in the etiology of eating disorders has been discussed extensively in a recent chapter by Strober, Kaye, Lilenfeld, and Bulik (in press) and the biological correlates of eating disorders have been described in a recent article by Ferguson and Pigott (2000). Kashubeck-West and Mintz (in press) offered a state-of-the-art review of diagnostic assessment approaches to eating disorders, and Stein et al. (in press) wrote an excellent integrative review of cognitive–behavior and interpersonal therapies for eating disorders.

The book is organized into four major sections. Following our introductory remarks in this Overview section is a chapter by Paul Garfinkel and Barbara Dorian that lays out a wide-ranging agenda for the future developments needed to improve the understanding of and care for eating disorders. In their chapter, Garfinkel and Dorian anticipate some of the topics discussed in greater depth in subsequent chapters in this book, including issues about diagnosis, mechanisms of risk and protection, and prevention. Garfinkel and Dorian also introduce several topics that have been relatively neglected yet have critical importance to progress in the field, such as changing knowledge and attitudes of health professionals, and the public trust.

The second section, Classification and Etiology, opens with a chapter by David Herzog and Sherry Selwyn Delinksi, who discuss the controversies surrounding the definitions of *anorexia nervosa* and *bulimia nervosa* and examine the complicating factors of crossover (i.e., individuals with anorexia nervosa developing bulimia nervosa or vice versa). They also explore the question of the cultural validity of these definitions. The four remaining chapters in this section focus on risk and protective factors. There is, of course, a substantial existing body of literature on risk and protective factors. In line with the mission of this book, the authors in this section raise new challenges to the way researchers should think about the etiology of eating disorders.

Drawing on Helena Kraemer's (Kraemer et al., 1997) widely acclaimed theoretical framework for evaluating risk, Stice features in his chapter new criteria for identifying risk factors. In the process of presenting these criteria, Stice challenges conventional wisdom as to what constitutes a risk factor for eating disorders. Complementing Stice's chapter is the contribution by Marjorie Crago, Catherine Shisslak, and Anne Ruble, in which the often-neglected topic of protective factors is addressed. The idea that there may be factors that lessen the likelihood that eating disorders will develop, even in the face of risk factors, is critical to the development of prevention programs. In the next chapter, Linda Smolak and Sarah Murnen note that eating disorders disproportionately affect girls and women and are, in fact, one of the most gendered set of disorders in the *Diagnostic and Statistical Manual* (4th ed.; American Psychiatric Association, 1994). They challenge researchers to revisit the question raised almost 20 years ago by Striegel-Moore, Silberstein, and Rodin (1986): "Why women?" Finally, Linda Smolak and Ruth Striegel-Moore seek to shift the way researchers consider the role of ethnicity in the development of eating disorders both in terms of distribution of disorders and in how ethnicity might actually contribute to the onset of particular eating problems.

Section three, Treatment, includes a critical assessment of the status of health services research—a topic not yet widely considered in the field despite its apparent relevance. Yet as Vicki Garvin and Ruth Striegel-Moore rightly point out, health services are influential in who receives what types of treatment today and will be in the future. This is made clear by the other chapters in this section. It is evident that all forms of treatment are trying to respond to the limits established by the health care system, without sacrificing service effectiveness and the client's welfare. The self-help programs described by Vicki Garvin, Ruth Striegel-Moore, Allan Kaplan, and Stephen Wonderlich in chapter 8 present an interesting and novel approach to eating problems, building and improving on earlier forms of such programs. Similarly, Stephen Wonderlich, James Mitchell, Carol Peterson, and Scott Crow outline a new form of cognitive–behavior therapy that draws on the theoretical and empirical advances in cognitive science and extensive clinical experience. This approach represents an important addition to the extant cognitive–behavior therapy paradigm and encourages researchers and clinicians to move in new directions therapeutically. Finally, James Mitchell makes it clear that there is no distinct pharmacological treatment yet for any of the eating disorders. As part of his review, Mitchell outlines new ways to approach the issue of pharmacology and eating disorders. The lack of a pharmacological treatment, although it may be temporary, will present a challenge to health care systems looking for a quick solution to an eating disorder case.

Finally there is the section on Prevention. In some ways, prevention is the culmination of the research on classification, etiology, and treatment, borrowing ideas from all of these fields. The diversity of approaches and the broad challenges in designing prevention programs is in evidence here. Leslie Heinberg, J. Kevin Thompson, and Jonas Matzon start off this section by considering whether appropriate body image dissatisfaction exists and whether such dissatisfaction might in fact be a good thing. They tackle head on the thorny relationship between professionals in the fields of eating disorders prevention and obesity prevention. The issue of coexistence of these two prevention efforts must be resolved before one can expect widely accepted, effective programs in either field. Nowhere is this more evident than in attempts to introduce prevention programs in Black and Hispanic communities. Michael Levine and Niva Piran then introduce an approach to prevention that challenges the very approach of psychology. They emphasize the role of the ecological context rather than of the individual's attitudes and behaviors in preventing eating disorders. Finally, C. Barr Taylor, Andrew Winzelberg, and Angela Celio point the way to using technology in prevention programs. This approach is hailed by some as a cost-effective way to reach a range of girls and women, while others worry about the limited "personal" contact involved. It is likely that both of these positions and Taylor et al.'s program itself will inspire much future research and innovation in prevention.

This idea mirrors the major goal of this volume. The authors present controversial stances, challenges, and suggestions that we hope will generate considerable research and novel intervention efforts. Empirical data, grounded in strong theoretical models and combined with clinical experience, constitute the field's best hope for understanding, and ultimately reducing, the severity and occurrence of the eating disorders.

REFERENCES

American Psychiatric Association. (1994). *Diagnostic and statistical manual of mental disorders* (4th ed.). Washington, DC: Author.

Ferguson, C. P., & Pigott, T. A. (2000). Anorexia and bulimia nervosa: Neurobiology and pharmacotherapy. *Behavior Therapy, 31*, 237–263.

Joiner, T. E. (2000). Special series: Samples from four frontiers of eating disorders research. *Behavior Therapy, 31*, 187–193.

Kashubeck-West, S., & Mintz, L. B. (in press). Eating disorders in women: Etiology, assessment, and treatment. *Journal of Counseling Psychology.*

Kraemer, H. C., Kazdin, A. E., Offord, D. R., Kessler, R. C., Jensen, P. S., & Kupfer, D. J. (1997). Coming to terms with the terms of risk. *Archives of General Psychiatry, 54*, 337–343.

Stein, R. I., Saelens, B. E., Douchinis, J. Z., Lewczyk, C. M., Swenson, A. K., & Wilfley, D. E. (in press). Treatment of eating disorders in women. *Journal of Counseling Psychology.*

Striegel-Moore, R. H., Silberstein, L., & Rodin, J. (1986). Toward an understanding of risk factors for bulimia. *American Psychologist, 41*, 246–263.

Strober, M., Kaye, W. H., Lilenfeld, L. R., & Bulik, C. (in press). Genetics and family studies of anorexia nervosa and bulimia nervosa. In P. Cooper & A. Stein (Eds.), *Feeding problems and eating disorders* (2nd ed.). Chur, Switzerland: Harwood.

1

IMPROVING UNDERSTANDING AND CARE FOR THE EATING DISORDERS

PAUL E. GARFINKEL AND BARBARA J. DORIAN

The eating disorders anorexia nervosa and bulimia nervosa have assumed an increased importance over the past two decades, as clinicians and investigators have recognized their prevalence and alarming rates of morbidity and mortality. At the same time, great strides have been made in providing treatment for patients with these disorders. Future developments may be anticipated in seven areas: treatments, diagnosis, understanding mechanisms, prevention, the consumer movement, changing knowledge and attitudes of health professionals, and the public trust. In this chapter, we consider these seven core areas.

TREATMENTS

Treatments for the eating disorders are hardly recognizable from 30 years ago. This is a consequence of real progress in clinical science. In the 1960s, it was common to have treatment for anorexia nervosa based on a long-term psychoanalytic model, which was ineffective, or on combinations of potentially harmful medications. Today, there is general acceptance of the value of nutritional restoration or stabilization before people with the disorder can meaningfully benefit from psychotherapy. The types of psychotherapy that are useful vary. Cognitive analytic therapy has been shown to be of benefit in anorexia nervosa (Treasure & Ward, 1997a). Work from the Maudsley Hospital (London, England) has documented the value of family therapy for young patients with restricting anorexia (Russell, Dare, Eisler, & LeGrange, 1992). Older patients with anorexia or bulimia benefit from cognitive–behavioral therapy, but this has been much more carefully described for bulimia nervosa. This latter group has also been shown to benefit from interpersonal therapy (Fairburn et al., 1995). Antidepressant drugs, including the serotonin reuptake inhibitors, have also been found to be useful for patients with bulimia, although in controlled studies they have not been demonstrated to be as useful as psychological treatments (Garfinkel & Walsh, 1997). As a result of these advances in understanding and in care, the overall mortality of anorexia nervosa may have been reduced, and more patients are found to be completely well at follow-up (Fichter & Quadflieg, 1999). In comparison, bulimia nervosa has a much lower initial mortality rate and a more variable course in treatment (Keel & Mitchell, 1997).

Clinical science has had a real bearing on these improvements. The randomized controlled trial, first applied to evaluating the efficacy of antibiotics in tuberculosis and pneumococcal pneumonia, quickly led to comparative studies of psychotropic agents in the early 1950s. Progress in psychotherapy research has been greatly enhanced more recently; in the late 1980s, effective treatments were developed through systematic studies of depression. These methods have subsequently been adapted to treatments for bulimia nervosa. Controlled trials of psychotherapy for anorexia nervosa are rare and are much more difficult to conduct, but they are imperative for the field to advance.

Significant in this regard has been the understanding of the egosyntonic nature of the primary symptoms in anorexia nervosa. Recent work on motivational enhancement, adapted from the addictions field, may provide significant benefits to treatment and requires careful evaluation (Treasure & Ward, 1997b). It is also important to develop structured lines of research in the treatment of comorbid states. Whether it is drug dependency or depression, the lack of demonstrable protocols and facilities prepared to undertake combined treatments for comorbid conditions is a serious impediment to enabling the more chronically ill to develop lives with meaning and dignity. Furthermore, trials aimed at the prevention of complications (e.g., osteoporosis) are also warranted.

Most important, it is no longer acceptable to provide care on the basis of the clinician's preferred modality of practice, but rather it is critical to select treatments that are based on the patient's needs and the empiric evidence for treatment efficacy. To achieve this standard of flexible tailored treatments, we must direct our investigations toward a greater understanding of the natural history of these disorders, the explication of underlying mechanisms, comparative treatment trials, and predictors of outcome. Such a systematic program of research will provide the essential building blocks for our therapeutics of the future.

FOCUS ON DIAGNOSIS:
POTENTIAL LOSS OF UNDERSTANDING

The recent focus on diagnosis is a two-edged sword. We now have criteria with good reliability. The first such criteria for anorexia nervosa were proposed by Russell (1979). He emphasized the need for a behavioral disturbance, a psychopathology, and an endocrine disorder. The behavioral disturbance leads to a marked loss of body weight; the psychopathology is characterized by a morbid fear of getting fat; and the endocrine disorder manifests itself clinically by amenorrhea in female patients. These initial criteria have gradually been modified to the current *Diagnostic and Statistical Manual of Mental Disorders* (4th ed. [DSM–IV]; American Psychiatric Association, 1994) and *International Classification of Disease-10* standards, which represent significant advances in diagnostic precision.

There are, however, major difficulties with these criteria. For example, the amount of weight loss necessary for the diagnosis is not known. Ideally, the weight at which an individual becomes caught in the biological syndrome of starvation would be the defining point. Another significant problem with current diagnostic criteria for anorexia nervosa relates to the requirement of amenorrhea in female patients. An epidemiological study by the Toronto Group in Canada found no differences in severity, comorbidity, or family history between patients with anorexia with or without amenorrhea (Garfinkel et al., 1996b).

Russell (1979) described bulimia nervosa over 20 years ago. He defined the syndrome by the powerful, intractable urges to overeat, the consequent compensatory behaviors, and the underlying psychopathology of a morbid fear of fat. Newer criteria have refined these by defining a binge based on the amount of food consumed, discrete eating, and a sense of loss of control, as well as by setting minimal frequency levels for the diagnosis. Although these criteria are improved, the optimal frequency level of the relevant behavior is not known (Garfinkel et al., 1995).

Attempts at distinguishing subtypes of anorexia nervosa date back to Pierre Janet, early in this century, who recognized hysterical and obsessional types. This description was ignored, however, until Peter Dally used it in the late 1960s. Shortly after, Beumont, George, and Smart (1976) began to subtype anorexia nervosa by the presence or absence of vomiting. This categorization was refined a few years later to distinguish subtypes based on the presence or absence of bulimia (Casper, Eckert, Halmi, Goldberg, & Davis, 1980; Garfinkel, Moldofsky, & Garner, 1980). Major differences have been described between these two groups.

Patients with bulimic anorexia have weighed more in the early part of their lives and have more frequently been obese premorbidly. They often come from heavier families with more frequent familial obesity. They are also the group who rely on additional methods of weight control—vomiting or laxative abuse—and they more frequently display other impulsive behavior such as alcohol and street drug use, stealing, and self-mutilation. Patients with bulimic anorexia also display different personality characteristics.

The *DSM–IV* has also separated bulimia nervosa into purging and nonpurging types on the basis of significant differences between these groups (American Psychiatric Association, 1994). More body image disturbance, self-harm behavior, and general psychopathology have been demonstrated in the purging type (C. J. Davis, Williamson, & Goreczny, 1986; Duchman, Williamson, & Strickler, 1986; Mitchell, 1992; Viesselman & Roig, 1985).

Garfinkel et al. (1996a) found that in comparison with nonpurging bulimia patients, the purging group had earlier ages of onset and exceptionally high rates of comorbidity for depression, anxiety disorders, and alcohol abuse. One of the most striking distinguishing characteristics of the purging group was their very high rate of earlier sexual abuse (50%, more than double that of the nonpurging group). These findings exemplify the importance of determining meaningful distinctions between subgroups. Such discriminations may predict differences in complication rates (e.g., purging is associated with electrolyte disturbances) and in treatment needs.

These developments in diagnosis reflect real scientific advances that have a bearing on treatment and outcome. Diagnosis is imperative for clinical practice: It represents a form of communication that permits detailed examination, investigation of approaches to treatment, and delineation of prognosis. Used in a concrete or thoughtless manner, however, it may detract from rather than enhance care.

The *DSM–IV* diagnostic system is a good example of this problem, in that it has contributed to a distortion in the way that psychiatry approaches people and in the extreme can be used as a means of avoiding an in-depth understanding of individuals. The *DSM–IV* has become widely accepted, in large part because of its reliability. It can also describe the diverse aspects of rather complex variables. In this regard, its data-based, atheoretical orientation is a strength. However, the lack of defining theory may also be its major limitation. *DSM–IV* has been developed in such a way that one may make a *DSM* diagnosis while knowing little about the patient as a person and thereby reduce the person to a disorder based on a checklist of signs and symptoms. Awareness of psychological theories of development, unconscious conflict, or the therapeutic process is not needed to make a *DSM* diagnosis. This absence of meaning must be addressed in the therapist's approach to diagnosis and care if the therapist is to retain a humanistic orientation, because it is impossible to treat suffering individuals devoid of an awareness of history, symbolic meaning, conflict, ambivalence, social context, or the primacy of existential concerns.

The writing of one of the world's outstanding philosophers, Sir Isaiah Berlin, provides critical commentary relevant to this dilemma. Berlin displayed a defiance of "a one size fits all" model. Although it was unfashionable, Berlin agreed with Immanuel Kant, who two centuries earlier had said, "out of the crooked timber of humanity no straight thing was ever made." This was not a credo of hopelessness or of cynicism, but a celebration of plurality and of complexity; a recognition that human beings vary and that a proper understanding requires respect for this variability. Berlin was a man who worshipped ideas, but he worshipped them as a humanist who believed in the great man and great woman theory of history. His was not a statement of elitism, but a celebration of the essence of the individual. Essentially, he proclaimed that "we all matter." Our patients, our field, and we, as health professionals, will be enriched by recognizing and valuing this view of strength in diversity.

FURTHER DELINEATION OF MECHANISMS

Although significant improvements in care can evolve from these approaches to treatment and diagnosis, the next breakthrough is dependent on research into mechanisms. Noteworthy in this regard is the work of the Human Genome Project, which will soon provide clinicians with the capacity for an entirely new range of clinical decisions based on a precise knowledge of the subtypes of illness. This advance will then permit the prescription of treatments more specific to the individual. Although some fear that the capacity for precise biological typologies will erode the psychosocial role in understanding and care, it is more likely that the opposite will happen: The ability to delineate more of the biology of the individual will make it possible to identify psychosocial factors with greater precision.

Today, the advancements in both neurobiology and psychosocial sciences are recreating the ferment of 100 years ago when Freud first described the unconscious and the spirochete organism was found to be the cause of neurosyphilis. As in that time, researchers are exploring the complex effects of catastrophic experience and are now prepared scientifically, as well as intellectually and emotionally, to acknowledge the profound consequences of violence and trauma on individuals. Recognition of the mechanisms by which traumatic experience is translated into symptoms and disability will advance the provision of efficacious and humane care to its sufferers.

Culture

One example of improving understanding of mechanisms relates to the recognition of a cultural base for these syndromes. Examining what is currently known about the cultural contributions to bulimia nervosa may indicate how the syndrome may develop in the future.

Current estimates of bulimia nervosa show a prevalence of 1.1% of the female population to have a full syndrome and another 2.3% to have partial syndromes (Garfinkel et al., 1995). It is likely, but not definite, that this represents an increase in frequency. Those studies that permit a longitudinal comparison have found an increased frequency of the disorder in individuals born after 1960 (Kendler et al., 1991). In at least two studies, researchers have also detected a changing age of onset for bulimia nervosa (Garfinkel et al., 1995; Kendler et al., 1991).

At the same time, there has been a change in the distribution of bulimia in relation to anorexia nervosa. Recent studies all demonstrate that bulimia nervosa is about twice as common as anorexia nervosa (Garfinkel et al., 1995, 1996a). This represents a dramatic shift over time. When Bruch reviewed her consultation experiences in 1973, she found that about 25% of the patients with anorexia were bulimic; by 1980 this figure was 50%, and a decade later it was 70% at the Toronto Group's practice. Why this has occurred is not known, but it may relate to the increased frequency of bodily preoccupation and dieting in young women who are also being exposed to extraordinary food availability and to social pressures for consumption.

Sociocultural Factors Affecting Risk

Cultures evolve over time, and it is likely that shifts in cultural values have contributed to the changing frequency of bulimia nervosa. Dieting is particularly important in this regard. Currently, in North America by age 13, 80% of girls and 10% of boys have already begun a weight loss diet (Mellin, Irwin, & Scully, 1992). In a study of dieting London schoolgirls, 38% of the sample were still dieting about 1 year later. About 33% had stopped, and about 20% of the dieters had progressed to an eating disorder, as opposed to only 3% of nondieters (Patton, Johnson-Sabine, Wood, Mann, & Wakeling, 1990). Killen et al. (1994) followed a group of 12-year-old girls over 3 years and found one consistently strong predictor for an eating disorder: the presence of weight concerns. This is similar to earlier findings among 12-year-old girls entering intensive ballet studies (Garner, Garfinkel, Rockert, & Olmstead, 1987).

In Western society, these behaviors are tied to feeling overweight or being out of control with respect to eating. E. Davis and Furnham (1986) studied eating behaviors and body shape concerns of female adolescents. Forty percent considered themselves to be overweight, although only 4% actually were. These studies and others demonstrate the frequency of weight concerns, dieting, and other weight control behaviors and their relationship to the development of an eating disorder. However, although weight concerns and dieting are pervasive in Western society, comparatively few women progress to full-blown eating disorders. Other risk factors must be important in linking weight and shape concerns and dieting to the development of illness.

Some groups have been shown to be particularly vulnerable to developing an eating disorder: people who by career choice have to be thin (dancers or models), people under strong pressures to achieve (e.g., female medical students), and, possibly, some competitive athletes. Women are at heightened risk by virtue of a higher prevalence of certain psychiatric disorders (depression, borderline personality disorder), life experiences (early sexual abuse), and family history (depression, eating disorder, or alcoholism). Obesity is a significant and specific risk factor. Many of these risk factors increase the probability of psychiatric disorder in general and not an eating disorder specifically. Those risk factors primarily related to the production of dieting behaviors and negative self-evaluations seem to be more specifically tied to bulimia nervosa (Fairburn, Welch, Doll, Davies, & O'Connor, 1997).

Examining the rates of bulimia nervosa in different ethnic groups in the same country may help illuminate the cultural factors. African American and Asian American women seem to have had a lower frequency of eating disorders in the United States. Among these minority women, the risk increases for individuals who are heavier, better educated, and more identified with White middle-class culture (Crago, Shisslak, & Estes, 1996). The data on African American women are particularly informative because although they tend to weigh more, they generally have much less body dissatisfaction, fewer weight concerns, and a more positive self-image. These more tolerant attitudes may be considered protective with respect to the development of an eating disorder. However, eating disorders may also be increasing among African Americans. A survey by a popular African American fashion magazine recently found levels of abnormal eating attitudes and body dissatisfaction in African American women that were as high as in White women (Pumariega, Gustavson, & Gustavson, 1994). Dieting behavior has been found to be equal among African American and White women in the United States (Gray, Ford, & Kelly, 1987), and disordered eating behaviors were found to be more prevalent in the African Caribbean population in Britain than among White women (Reiss, 1996).

Recently, Striegel-Moore, Wilfley, Pike, Dohm, and Fairburn (2000) conducted a telephone survey of a large number of American women. African American and White women did not differ on the frequency of recurrent binge eating and vomiting. Cultural beliefs that traditionally have protected ethnic groups against eating disorders may be eroding as adolescents acculturate to mainstream American culture. There in fact may be an enhanced pressure for girls from a nondominant culture to attempt to fit into mainstream North American culture through rigid dieting and adoption of a thin ideal.

A number of interesting comparisons have also been carried out within cultural groups. Nasser (1986, 1994) studied Egyptian students at Cairo University and in high schools and contrasted them with Egyptian students attending London universities. The differences in Eating Attitude Test (EAT) scores were significant: 22% of the London sample were high scorers, compared with only 12% in Egypt, possibly because of the Westernization of the former group. In Israel, Arab school children (15.4%) were less likely to have elevations on the EAT than the Jewish children (27.3%; Apter et al., 1994).

Greek students had higher rates of eating pathology when studying in Munich, Germany, than in Greece (Fichter, Weyerer, Sourdi, & Sourdi, 1983). In different parts of Japan, widely different rates have been reported. Mukai, Crago, and Shisslak (1994) reported an extremely high prevalence (35%) of eating problems in Japan in contrast to Nakamura et al.'s (1999) study (5.4%). This may be, in part, attributable to the fact that the former sample was drawn from a school population in one of the metropolitan areas. Mumford, Whitehouse, and Platts (1991) found that among Lahore girls living in the United Kingdom, those who were most Westernized were most likely to have eating morbidity. In one study, Asian girls living in the United Kingdom had more unhealthy eating attitudes than did White girls (Dolan, 1991). Lucero, Hicks, Bramlette, Brassington, and Welter (1992) found that Asian women had lower levels of eating psychopathology than White women. Recently, Lee and Lee (1999) compared three groups of Chinese high school girls from Hong Kong, Shenzen (a prosperous, rapidly growing area of China), and rural Hunan. The results on the EAT showed a gradient, with highest scores in westernized Hong Kong (10.8%), compared with Shenzen and Hunan (5.2% and 2.5%, respectively), which they interpreted as a consequence of the rapid modernization that has occurred in China throughout the late 1990s. For all of the groups, but particularly for those girls in Hong Kong, body dissatisfaction was the best predictor of fat concern.

Becker, Grinspoon, Klibanski, and Herzog (1999) assessed 63 Fijian schoolgirls whose average age was 17 in 1995, about 1 month after satellites began beaming television signals to the region. Thirty-eight months later, in 1998, she studied another 65 girls who were matched for age, weight, and other characteristics to the original sample. Fifteen percent of the 1998 sample, as opposed to 3% in 1995, had induced vomiting to control weight. In addition, 29% in 1998, as opposed to 13% in 1995, scored as being at risk for an eating disorder. Before 1995, there was little talk of dieting in Fiji, but in the 1998 survey, 69% of the girls said they had been on a diet at some point in their lives. At the time of this follow-up, 74% also said

dings reflect rapid social changes: Traditional
nality over individual achievement; however,
exposed to Western values regarding food, the
individual.

fferent cultures and within one cultural group
ghlight how common bulimia nervosa has be-
is influenced by dieting and by Western social
s also raise further questions about mechanisms.
nization of a society? Does this refer to industri-
rbanization, or does it refer to the role of the
l identity in a global society? What exactly is
t is so important? And can we learn from the
lf of Asians with anorexia really lack a desire
vates them, and what can we learn from this?

he Late 20th Century

an Catholic saints who lived between 1200
ny indulged in states of self-starvation and
possibly developed anorexia nervosa. Although today's women with anorexia
are not likely to be seeking the approval of God or a religious establishment,
in many ways their behavior resembles a distorted form of religious discipline:
The guilt, perfectionism, and preoccupation with self-control are similar—
women purifying themselves by eliminating the taint of material needs.

The historian Brumberg (1998) characterized the body as a "message
board" upon which the demands of popular culture are played out as young
women respond to the incessant and constantly changing media images and
advertisements conveying admired appearances and behaviors that confer
status and esteem. Culture's power in this regard can be seen in its ability
to shift normative behavior and create dramatic changes in the standards
of attractiveness. Slim, bob-haired women of the 1920s represented libera-
tion from Victorian constraints; fashions of the 1950s evoked the yearning
for glamor and the new infatuation with Hollywood role models; today's
starving and piercings, according to Brumberg, signify sexual liberalism
and the erosion of the distinction between public and private worlds as
commercialism has come to dominate modern cultural ideals and values.

The influence of the media is critical to the current bodily preoccupation and excessive dieting among young women. Becker and Hamburg
(1996) argued that the specific images that are presented as ideal are less
important in this regard than the means by which they are rendered so
compelling. It has been hypothesized that individuals develop an active
internal attachment and relatedness to the symbols of culture presented
continuously through television and other media. These symbols then be-

come part of the individual's inner self and object world, and thereby influence private psychological and fantasy life. Consequently it is probable that the media's relation to the eating disorders is mutually, rather than unidirectionally, influential. The media both create and reflect pathogenic values. It was advertising that first enabled women to compare themselves with others and suggested that they should do this in order to remain desirable. The interest in self-cultivation evolved in American culture from the early 1900s when appearance came to be viewed as a window on the person. Since that time, the body has become the site of symbolic work in the projection of a personal image. There has been widespread cultural validation of self-development through perfection of the body that is supported by an ethos directed at self-determination, goal orientation, individualistic striving, and achievement.

The bedrock equation is that of body with image; this objectification of women's bodies has been more intense and of longer duration than the similar equation in men of power and success with control of the body. Consumerism through advertising implies the possibility that the body can be personally created, albeit as a commodity. In this process, women's legitimate desire for food, self-care, and nurturance is negated and replaced by an ongoing sense of insecurity and the deceptive message that internal needs can be satisfied through the creation of a perfect body in harmony with a society that obsessively overvalues thinness. The woman with anorexia epitomizes the extreme negation of all appetite and wanting as well as the determination to seek self-enhancement through the achievement of bodily self-control and regulation of weight.

A clear understanding of why Western society, at this point in history, has developed such an idealized view of thinness is not available (Garfinkel & Dorian, 1997). Likely there are a number of contributors. In some way, it represents an emulation of the values of the higher social classes, but this begs the question as to why people from upper classes disparage fatness and desire thinness. In addition, bodily control has come to represent attainment of personal achievement through control, an attribute that is now highly regarded. The determination to control is fueled by health concerns with respect to fat and a culture of youth based on the myth that under the right circumstances one can remain beautiful and live forever. Such a view predominates in a world that has become narcissistically preoccupied and oriented toward the self. Likely, changing role expectations for women, particularly in the face of ongoing gender discrimination, have also played a significant influence. The phenomenon of dieting and thinness has emerged at a time when women were determined to do more in the world. This has probably had two effects. First, it has probably pushed some women toward external achievement, not for themselves as much as for pleasing others and for the socially desirable responses this produces. Second, the changes in women's roles have actually been enormously conflicting. Although women have been encouraged to achieve more in professional and vocational settings, societal influences have not been to enhance such levels of autonomy in interpersonal relationships or to redress the substantial power imbalances that affect the everyday existence of women.

PRIMARY PREVENTION

Although knowledge of mechanisms has increased, it is not clear how effectively this can be translated into prevention. A number of school-based programs have now been developed and evaluated on the basis of their capacity to influence the precursors of illness, usually the initiation of dieting behaviors (Killen et al., 1993; Moreno & Thelen, 1993; Moriarty, Shore, & Maxim, 1990; Paxton, 1993; Rosen, 1989; Shisslak & Crago, 1990). These programs generally include education about the nature and consequences of the eating disorders, the adverse effects of dieting and other methods of weight control, and skills training to increase resistance to the social pressures to diet. The results have been uniformly disappointing. Although participants' knowledge has been demonstrated to increase, this is not associated with a change in the targeted behaviors.

A typical study from this group is that of Killen et al. (1993). They randomly assigned 995 sixth- and seventh-grade students to 18 sessions of an educational program or to no program and followed the students for 2 years. Knowledge about the impact of dieting and other weight loss measures was enhanced; however, there was no change in dieting behavior. Recently, two studies have reported that such programs may actually do more harm than good. Carter, Stewart, and Fairburn (1998) developed an 8-week intervention; each 45-minute session was aimed to reduce dietary restraint in 12- and 13-year-old school girls. At 6-month follow-up, there was a paradoxical increase in dietary restraint. This pilot study lacked a control group, thus it is possible that the changes observed were part of a normal developmental process or other influences that were not modified by the intervention. Similarly, a peer-led program aimed at reducing eating disorders among college students also had a negative effect (Mann et al., 1997).

Two recent studies have provided some positive findings. Winzelberg et al. (1998) found that a computer-mediated psychoeducational program, rather than traditional group teaching strategies, produced modest but significant benefits to body image as well as disordered eating. Springer, Winzelberg, Perkins, and Taylor (1999) developed an undergraduate body image course that met for 2 hours each week for 10 weeks. Participants displayed improvements in body image and disordered eating. However, because the only postintervention evaluation was done on Week 10, it is not clear how enduring these effects are. This study, however, is encouraging and differed from the others by focusing on body image rather than on eating and weight behaviors.

These studies were early efforts at prevention and may inform future work. Likely, the focus on dieting alone will not be productive. Instead, healthy eating and exercise must be part of a program emphasizing issues of body image and self-esteem development and regulation. These interventions should begin early, ideally for 9-year-old girls, with follow-up sessions periodically. There are also techniques found to be useful in reducing the risk for drug use in adolescents that could be adapted for this purpose. These include changing teacher attitudes, prevention-related messages in the curriculum and in classroom materials, and rules prohibiting certain forms of teasing and peer pressure. Recent work on gender role socialization may also be of value. At the same time, specific interventions for those at high risk—dancers, athletes, and diabetics, for example—or those with partial syndromes should be individually crafted and evaluated.

The fact that culture can so strongly modify these syndromes, that we have learned so much about risks, and that we are beginning to properly design and evaluate studies of prevention signifies that a great deal can be done in this area.

CONSUMER MOVEMENT

In recent years, there has been a dramatic shift in the involvement of patients and their families in the health care delivery system. No longer are we witnessing the delivery of service to passive consumers; patients and their families are now demanding to be part of the planning, governance, and evaluation of treatments. Similarly, clients are beginning to question the research agenda and to want a role in determining which studies are being funded and how they are being conducted. This is a particularly important development for the eating disorders. This partnership of profession and community is actively combating stigma, arguing for a fair share of the health care resource and for improved funding for research.

This change can have an important effect on the prejudice and stigma directed to people with eating disorders. Often, the eating disorders have been treated in a pejorative fashion, by both the public and by physicians. At times, they have been glamorized as the consequence of a life in film or fashion; or they have been characterized as the self-induced problems of spoiled women; or they have been considered to reflect a moral issue, a lack of willpower rather than the serious multidetermined illnesses they are. The evolving public understanding of the eating disorders may also play an important role in changing some of society's current attitudes to body size and female beauty.

CHANGING KNOWLEDGE AND ATTITUDES OF HEALTH PROFESSIONALS

Closely related to the issue of public perception are the attitudes that health professionals display. Clinicians often reflect the broader culture and display the same beliefs and feelings to these patients as does society. Studies of practitioners have shown that more than any other psychiatric disorder, people with bulimia and, in particular, anorexia nervosa, evoke feelings of anger, hostility, stress, and a sense of hopelessness in their therapists and in other caregivers (Kaplan & Garfinkel, 1999). Progress in the care of all people with eating disorders will occur through improved education and support for those clinicians, and when an educated public demand more from the medical profession in reducing stigma among its practitioners.

PUBLIC TRUST

Although we experience the tremendous opportunity and excitement for the future of health care, we must also acknowledge the immense challenges facing us. In North America, there is an extreme misdistribution of services and a growing need to provide care that is sensitive to cultural plurality. Despite the restructuring of hospitals and institutions on the basis of greater efficiency and effectiveness, there is little or no care provided to the population in need in many areas. Economic models of care delivery that punish the less privileged are an important contributor to this problem. The appropriate distribution of treatment in primary care, in general psychiatric care, and in specialized programs requires clarification (Palmer & Treasure, 1999). Current support for research is also weak and reflects an ongoing ignorance of the prevalence and severe morbidity of the eating disorders.

Renewed awareness of the construct of the public trust may begin to reverse that trend through the recognition of the fact that societies and institutions with a humanitarian orientation must give priority to the most seriously ill. There is no doubt that therapeutic advances have encouraged and permitted these developments, as have policy decisions by some governments; however, changes in the academy may also foster this growth. Academic medical centers in Canada are becoming more open to the notion of accountability reflected through a contract with society. In this circumstance, the evolving health needs of the population become an important determinant of the academic center's priorities for research, education, and care.

As knowledge of the frequency and morbidity of the eating disorders becomes known, as knowledge of their true nature alters attitudes, and as new understanding of mechanisms evolves, we can expect educated and sensible clinicians to want to care for these patients, to form a strong alliance with an educated public, and to continue to advocate—for resources for research and care, for prevention, and for the necessity of a humane orientation to all who are suffering.

REFERENCES

American Psychiatric Association. (1994). *Diagnostic and statistical manual of mental disorders* (4th ed.). Washington, DC: Author.

Apter, A., Shah, M., Iancu, I., Abramovitch, H., Weizman, A., & Tanyo, S. L. (1994). Cultural effects on eating attitudes in Israeli sub-populations and hospitalised anorectics. *Genetic Social and General Psychological Monographs, 120,* 83–99.

Becker, A. E., Grinspoon, S. K., Klibanski, A., & Herzog, D. B. (1999). Eating disorders. *New England Journal of Medicine, 340,* 1092–1098.

Becker, A., & Hamburg, P. (1996). Culture, the media, and eating disorders. *Harvard Review of Psychiatry, 4,* 163–170.

Beumont, P. J. V., George, G. C. W., & Smart, D. E. (1976). "Dieters" and "vomiters and purgers" in anorexia nervosa. *Psychological Medicine, 6,* 617–622.

Bruch, H. (1973). *Eating disorders: Obesity, anorexia nervosa and the person within.* New York: Basic Books.

Brumberg J. J. (1998). *The body project: An intimate history of American girls.* New York: Random House.

Carter, J. C., Stewart, D. A., & Fairburn, C. G. (1998). The primary prevention of eating disorders: The dilemma and its denial. *Eating Disorders: The Journal of Treatment and Prevention, 6,* 213–215.

Casper, R. C., Eckert, E. D., Halmi, K. A., Goldberg, S. C., & Davis, J. M. (1980). Bulimia: Its incidence and significance in patients with anorexia nervosa. *Archives of General Psychiatry, 37,* 1030–1035.

Crago, M., Shisslak, C. M., & Estes, L. S. (1996). Eating disturbances among American minority groups: A review. *International Journal of Eating Disorders, 19,* 239–248.

Davis, C. J., Williamson, D. A., & Goreczny, T. (1986). *Body image distortion in bulimia: An important distinction between binge-purgers and binge eaters.* Paper presented at the annual convention of the Association for the Advancement of Behavior Therapy, Chicago.

Davis, E., & Furnham, A. (1986). Body satisfaction in adolescent girls. *British Journal of Medical Psychology, 59,* 279–289.

Dolan, B. (1991). Cross-cultural aspects of anorexia nervosa and bulimia: A review. *International Journal of Eating Disorders, 10,* 67–79.

Duchman, E. G., Williamson, D. A., & Strickler, P. M. (1986). *Dietary restraint and bulimia.* Paper presented at the annual convention of the Association for the Advancement of Behavior Therapy, Chicago.

Fairburn, C. G., Welch, S. L., Doll, H. A., Davies, B. A., & O'Connor, M. E. (1997). Risk factors for bulimia nervosa: A community-based case-control study. *Archives General Psychiatry, 54,* 509–517.

Fairburn, C. G., Welch, S. L., Norman, P. A., Welch, S. L., O'Connor, M. E., Doll, H. A., & Peveler, R. C. (1995). A prospective study of outcome in bulimia nervosa and the long-term effects of three psychological treatments. *Archives General Psychiatry, 52,* 304–312.

Fichter, M., & Quadflieg, N. (1999). Six-year course and outcome of anorexia nervosa. *International Journal of Eating Disorders, 26,* 359–385.

Fichter, M. M., Weyerer, S., Sourdi, L., & Sourdi, Z. (1983). The epidemiology of anorexia nervosa: A comparison of Greek adolescents living in Germany and Greek adolescents living in Greece. In P. L. Darby, P. Garfinkel, D. M. Garner, & D. V. Coscina (Eds.), *Anorexia nervosa: Recent developments in research* (pp. 95–105). New York: Liss.

Garfinkel, P. E., & Dorian, B. J. (1997). Factors that may influence future approaches to the eating disorders. *Journal of Eating and Weight Disorders, 2,* 1–16.

Garfinkel, P. E., Lin, B., Goering, P., Spegg, C., Goldbloom, D., Kennedy, S., Kaplan, A., & Woodside, B. (1995). Bulimia nervosa in a Canadian community sample: Prevalence and comorbidity. *American Journal of Psychiatry, 152,* 1052–1058.

Garfinkel, P. E., Lin, B., Goering, P., Spegg, C., Goldbloom, D., Kennedy, S., Kaplan, A., & Woodside, B. (1996a). Purging and non-purging forms of bulimia nervosa in a community sample. *International Journal of Eating Disorders, 20,* 231–238.

Garfinkel, P. E., Lin, B., Goering, P., Spegg, C., Goldbloom, D., Kennedy, S., Kaplan, A., & Woodside, B. (1996b). Should amenorrhea be necessary for the diagnosis of anorexia nervosa? Evidence from a Canadian community sample. *British Journal of Psychiatry, 168,* 500–506.

Garfinkel, P. E., Moldofsky, H., & Garner, D. M. (1980). The heterogeneity of anorexia nervosa: Bulimia as a distinct subgroup. *Archives of General Psychiatry, 37,* 1036–1040.

Garfinkel, P. E., & Walsh, T. (1997). Drug therapies for the eating disorders. In D. M. Garner & P. E. Garfinkel (Eds.), *Treatments for the eating disorders* (pp. 372–382). New York: Guilford Press.

Garner, D. M., Garfinkel, P. E., Rockert, W., & Olmsted, M. P. (1987). A prospective study of eating disturbances in the ballet. *Psychotherapy and Psychosomatics, 48,* 170–175.

Gray, J., Ford, K., & Kelly, L. (1987). The prevalence of bulimia in a Black college population. *International Journal of Eating Disorders, 6,* 733–740.

Kaplan, A. S., & Garfinkel, P. E. (1999). Difficulties in treating patients with eating disorders: A review of patient and clinical variables. *Canadian Journal of Psychiatry, 44,* 665–670.

Keel, P. K., & Mitchell, J. E. (1997). Outcome in bulimia nervosa. *American Journal of Psychiatry, 154,* 313–321.

Kendler, K. S., MacLean, C., Neale, M., Kessler, R., Heath, A., & Eaves, L. (1991). The genetic epidemiology of bulimia nervosa. *American Journal of Psychiatry, 148,* 1627–1637.

Killen, J. D, Taylor, C. B., Hammer, L. D., Litt, I., Wilson, D. M., Rich, T., Hayward, C., Simmonds, B., Kraemer, H., & Varady, A. (1993). An attempt to modify unhealthful eating attitudes and weight regulation practices of young adolescent girls. *International Journal of Eating Disorders, 13,* 369–384.

Killen, J. D., Taylor, C. B., Hayward, C., Wilson, D. M., Haydel, K. F., Hammer, L. D., Simmonds, B., Robinson, T. N., Litt, I., Varady, A., & Kraemer, H. (1994). Pursuit of thinness and onset of eating disorder symptoms in a community sample of adolescent girls. *International Journal of Eating Disorders, 16,* 227–238.

Lee, S., & Lee, A. M. (1999). Disordered eating in three communities of China: A comparative study of female high school students in Hong Kong, Shenzhen, and rural Hunan. *International Journal of Eating Disorders, 27,* 317–327.

Lucero, K., Hicks, R. A., Bramlette, J., Brassington, G. S., & Welter, M. G. (1992). Frequency of eating problems among Asian and Caucasian college women. *Psychological Reports, 7,* 255–258.

Mann, T., Nolen-Hoeksema, S., Huang, K., Burgard, D., Wright, A., & Hanson, K. (1997). Are two interventions worse than none? Joint primary and secondary prevention of eating disorders in college females. *Health Psychology, 16,* 297–305.

Mellin, L. M., Irwin, C. E., & Scully, S. (1992). Prevalence of disordered eating in girls: A survey of middle-class children. *Journal of American Dietetic Association, 92,* 851–853.

Mitchell, J. E. (1992). Subtyping of bulimia nervosa. *International Journal of Eating Disorders, 4,* 327–332.

Moreno, A., & Thelen, M. H. (1993). Parental factors related to bulimia nervosa. *Addictive Behaviors, 18,* 681–689.

Moriarty, D., Shore, R., & Maxim, N. (1990). Evaluation of an eating disorder curriculum. *Evaluation and Program Planning, 13,* 407–413.

Mukai, T., Crago, M., & Shisslak, C. (1994). Eating attitudes and weight preoccupation among female high school students in Japan. *Journal of Child Psychology and Psychiatry, 33,* 677–688.

Mumford, D. B., Whitehouse, A. M., & Platts, M. (1991). Sociocultural correlates of eating disorders among Asian schoolgirls in Bradford. *British Journal of Psychiatry, 158,* 222–228.

Nakamura, Y. H., Watanabe, A., Honda, K., Niwa, S., Tominaga, K., Shimai, S., & Yamamoto, M. (1999). Problems in female Japanese high school students: A prevalence study. *International Journal of Eating Disorders, 26*, 91–95.

Nasser, M. (1986). Comparative study of the prevalence of abnormal eating attitudes among Arab female students at both London and Cairo universities. *Psychological Medicine, 16*, 621–625.

Nasser, M. (1994). Screening for abnormal eating attitudes in a population of Egyptian secondary school girls. *Social Psychiatry and Psychiatric Epidemiology, 29*, 25–30.

Palmer, R. L., & Treasure, J. (1999). Providing specialized services for anorexia nervosa. *British Journal of Psychiatry, 175*, 306–309.

Patton, G. C., Johnson-Sabine, E., Wood, K., Mann, A. H., & Wakeling, A. (1990). Abnormal eating attitudes in London school girls—a prospective epidemiological study: Outcome at twelve-month follow-up. *Psychological Medicine, 20*, 383–394.

Paxton, S. J. (1993). A prevention program for disturbed eating and body dissatisfaction in adolescent girls: A 1-year follow-up. *Health Education Research: Theory and Practice, 8*, 43–51.

Pumariega, A. J., Gustavson, C. R., & Gustavson, J. C. (1994). Eating attitudes in African-American women: The *Essence* eating disorders survey. *Eating Disorders, 2*, 5–16.

Reiss, D. (1996). Abnormal eating attitudes and behaviours in two ethnic groups from a female British urban population. *Psychological Medicine, 26*, 289–299.

Rosen, J. C. (1989). Cognitive behavior therapy for negative body image. *Behavior Therapy, 20*, 393–404.

Russell, G. F. M. (1979). Bulimia nervosa: An ominous variant of anorexia nervosa. *Psychological Medicine, 9*, 429–448.

Russell, G. F. M., Dare, C., Eisler, I., & LeGrange, D. (1992). Controlled trials of family treatments in anorexia nervosa. In K. A. Halmi (Ed.), *Psychobiology and treatment of anorexia nervosa and bulimia nervosa* (pp. 329–340). Washington, DC: American Psychiatric Press.

Shisslak, C., & Crago, M. (1990). Toward a new model for the prevention of eating disorders. In M. Katzman & S. Wooley (Eds.), *Feminist perspectives on eating disorders* (pp. 419–437). New York: Guilford Press.

Springer, E. A., Winzelberg, A. J., Perkins, R., & Taylor, C. B. (1999). Effects of a body image curriculum for college students on improved body image. *International Journal of Eating Disorders, 26*, 13–19.

Striegel-Moore, R. H., Wilfley, D. E., Pike, K. M., Dohm, F. A., & Fairburn, C. G. (2000). Recurrent binge eating in Black American women. *Archives of Family Medicine, 9*, 83–87.

Treasure, J., & Ward, A. (1997a). Cognitive analytical therapy in the treatment of anorexia nervosa in the practitioner. *Journal of Clinical Psychology and Psychotherapy, 4*, 62–71.

Treasure, J., & Ward, A. (1997b). A practical guide to the use of motivational interviewing in anorexia nervosa. *European Eating Disorders Review, 5,* 102–114.

Viesselman, J. O., & Roig, M. (1985). Depression and suicidality in eating disorders. *Journal of Clinical Psychiatry, 46,* 118–124.

Winzelberg, A. J., Taylor, C. B., Altman, T. M., Eldredge, K. L., Dev, P., & Constantinou, P. S. (1998). Evaluation of a computer-mediated eating disorder intervention program. *International Journal of Eating Disorders, 24,* 339–349.

I

CLASSIFICATION AND ETIOLOGY

American parents often worry about permitting their infants and young children to sleep with them, thinking that it may somehow stunt or distort the child's development. In many, perhaps most, other countries, parents and children typically sleep together. In fact, large extended families may share sleeping quarters. Indeed, these parents might think it cruel to leave a young child alone in a room at night, particularly if the child is distressed. Yet despite these differing cultural belief systems and practices, the children in all of these countries routinely grow up to be healthy adults who contribute to their society.

This small example underscores the fact that there are multiple pathways to healthy development. This principle of developmental psychology also applies to pathological outcomes. Just as no one would claim that one variable "causes" a behavioral problem or disorder, proponents of developmental psychopathology would claim there is not a single combination of variables that creates a particular disorder. This is, of course, as true of eating disorders as it is of any other mental disorders (Rosen, 1996; Smolak & Levine, 1994).

The first part of this book, on classification and etiology, clearly indicates the multitude of possible contributing factors that play a role in the development of anorexia nervosa, bulimia nervosa, binge-eating disorder, eating disorder not otherwise specified (NOS), and the individual symptoms of these disorders. This part begins with David Herzog and Sherry Delinski's (chapter 2) consideration of how eating disorders are classified. This is a crucial issue because, as the authors note, researchers only study what has been defined. As this chapter illustrates, considerable effort has gone into refining the diagnostic criteria of anorexia nervosa and bulimia nervosa, yet this increasing sophistication in definitions has not been paralleled in the important area of eating disorder NOS. It continues to be the case that a majority of patients seeking treatment meet diagnostic criteria for eating disorder NOS, yet this broad and heterogeneous category needs to be defined more clearly if researchers are to make progress in developing treatments for this group. Herzog and Delinski raise many challenges for the field, including the need to establish more clearly the distinctiveness of the various disorders and the meaning of some of the critical symptoms, such as binges. They further suggest new ways one might define and study eating disorders, incorporating some of the new medical technologies. Empirical investigation of these ideas will shape research concerning eating disorders in the 21st century.

Chapters by Eric Stice (chapter 3) and by Marjorie Crago, Catherine Shisslak, and Anne Ruble (chapter 4) then address issues of risk and protective factors. Stice calls for more rigorous standards for risk factor research. Most important, he identifies risk factors that have been documented in prospective and experimental studies. Although some may be disappointed in the length of the list, it is impressive how many risk factors have been so identified. Stice's challenge for imaginative experimental designs is matched by Crago et al.'s call for research in protective factors. Protective factors have clearly been underinvestigated in the area of eating disorders (Striegel-Moore & Cachelin, 1999). Yet it is evident that some girls and women are resilient in the face of substantial pressures to be thin. Crago et al. offer suggestions, based on research in other areas of developmental psychopathology and on the eating disorders risk factor research, that may provide interesting starting points for protective factor research.

The chapters regarding risk and protective factors generally deal with characteristics of the affected individuals or personal vulnerability factors. The remaining two chapters in this part look more closely at the broader context within which eating disorders develop. Linda Smolak and Sarah Murnen (chapter 5) tackle issues of gender, trying to identify what it is about being female that might account for the large and enduring gender difference in rates of eating disorders. Linda Smolak and Ruth Striegel-Moore (chapter 6) then attempt to untangle the conflicting findings regarding ethnicity and eating disorders. In both cases, clearly researchers have oversimplified complex constructs. Both chapters challenge readers to understand specifically what it is about a cultural construct, be it gender or ethnicity, that might contribute to or protect against eating disorders. Only by delineating such specific hypotheses can one advance one's understanding of the cultural milieu in the development of eating disorders.

REFERENCES

Rosen, K. (1996). The principles of developmental psychopathology: Illustration from the study of eating disorders. In L. Smolak, M. P. Levine, & R. H.

Striegel-Moore (Eds.), *The developmental psychopathology of eating disorders* (pp. 3–30). Mahwah, NJ: Erlbaum.

Smolak, L., & Levine, M. P. (1994). Critical issues in the developmental psychopathology of eating disorders. In L. Alexander & D. B. Lumsden (Eds.), *Understanding eating disorders* (pp. 37–60). Washington, DC: Taylor & Francis.

Striegel-Moore, R. H., & Cachelin, F. M. (1999). Body image concerns and disordered eating in adolescent girls: Risk and protective factors. In N. G. Johnson, M. C. Roberts, & J. Worell (Eds.), *Beyond appearance: A new look at adolescent girls* (pp. 85–108). Washington, DC: American Psychological Association.

2

CLASSIFICATION OF EATING DISORDERS

DAVID B. HERZOG AND SHERRIE SELWYN DELINSKY

"We study what we define" (Walsh & Kahn, 1997, p. 369). The explicit diagnostic criteria provided by the American Psychiatric Association's (1980) *Diagnostic and Statistical Manual of Mental Disorders* (3rd ed. [*DSM–III*]) have advanced the understanding of eating disorders. Indeed, classification systems are quite influential; they shape research agendas and participant recruitment, affect the type of treatment and treatment reimbursement that individuals receive, and influence how prevention and intervention plans are conceptualized and implemented. As the ideal classification system is derived empirically, further collection and evaluation of data are needed to validate diagnostic criteria and address controversies within the current system. The most pressing questions for the field at this point concern the validity of binge eating disorder as separate from bulimia nervosa, the proper boundaries between normative concerns and behaviors and true eating disorders, and what constitutes the essence of an eating disorder. In this chapter, we discuss these issues and controversies specific to each disorder and examine the complicating factors of crossover, comorbidity, and culture and how each influences diagnosis.

Following the definition of each eating disorder, diagnosis and research of the currently recognized syndromes have increased dramatically. Cases of anorexia nervosa have been described for over a century, although anorexia nervosa did not receive much recognition until the 1960s and 1970s. In the 1970s, Feighner et al. (1972) and Russell (1979) provided the first explicit, operational diagnostic criteria for anorexia nervosa, which led to its inclusion in the *DSM–III* (American Psychiatric Association, 1980). The original elements of the *anorexia nervosa* diagnosis have changed little over the past two decades; these include marked weight loss, morbid fear of fat, and evidence of an endocrine disorder (amenorrhea). In contrast to anorexia nervosa, the syndrome currently known as *bulimia nervosa* was virtually unknown in the scientific community before 1980. In the late 1970s, the number of individuals presenting with bulimic behaviors rose substantially, some of whom met criteria for anorexia nervosa and others who were at normal body weight. After Russell (1979) named bulimia nervosa as an "ominous variant" of anorexia nervosa and published his seminal work describing the syndrome, the diagnosis and study of bulimia nervosa escalated. A year after Russell operationally defined bulimia nervosa, separate categories for anorexia nervosa and bulimia nervosa first appeared in the *DSM–III* (American Psychiatric Association, 1980). In the early 1990s, scientists began to study a subpopulation of obese people who engaged in regular binge eating but not in inappropriate compensatory behaviors, such as vomiting and laxative use. The recognition of this group led to the provisional diagnosis *binge-eating disorder* in the fourth edition of the *DSM* (*DSM–IV*; American Psychiatric Association, 1994). Consequently, research activity on binge eating disorder has increased dramatically over the past decade.

CURRENT CONTROVERSIES IN THE DIAGNOSIS OF ANOREXIA NERVOSA

The *DSM–IV* criteria for anorexia nervosa appear in Exhibit 2.1. The weight loss criterion (i.e., loss below "minimally normal weight") is the hallmark feature of anorexia nervosa, yet the definition of what constitutes minimally normal weight is not clear. The *DSM–IV* guideline is 15% below expected body weight for adult women. The *DSM–III*, however, required 25% weight loss, indicating the arbitrary nature of the weight loss criterion. This reduction in the weight loss requirement was intended to permit diagnosis of definite cases early in their course and to take into account the younger patient who is still growing (Garfinkel, Kennedy, & Kaplan, 1995). Even the identification of 15% less than expected body weight is questionable because of the wide range of normal expected weights in the population, the lack of data adjusted for pubertal growth in height and weight (Fisher et al., 1995), and the variation of cultural norms for adult female weights (Lee, Chiu, & Chen, 1989). The essential problem with the arbitrary nature of the weight loss cutoff is that few studies have determined when the symptoms of starvation actually supervene or when physiological consequences of weight loss become evident (Garfinkel, Kennedy, & Kaplan, 1995). An examination of the predictive value of various weight criteria on eating disorder outcome, menstrual function, osteoporosis, and other medical complications of anorexia nervosa would make a valuable contribution to establishing the validity of a specific weight loss criterion.

EXHIBIT 2.1
DSM–IV Criteria for Anorexia Nervosa

A. Refusal to maintain body weight at or above a minimally normal weight for age and height (e.g., weight loss leading to maintenance of body weight less than 85% of that expected; or failure to make expected weight gain during period of growth, leading to body weight less than 85% of that expected).
B. Intense fear of gaining weight or becoming fat, even though underweight.
C. Disturbance in the way in which one's body weight or shape is experienced, undue influence of body weight or shape on self-evaluation, or denial of the seriousness of the current low body weight.
D. In postmenarcheal females, amenorrhea, i.e., the absence of at least three consecutive menstrual cycles. (A woman is considered to have amenorrhea if her periods occur only following hormone, e.g., estrogen administration.)

Restricting Type: During the current episode of anorexia nervosa, the person has not regularly engaged in binge eating or purging behavior (i.e., self-induced vomiting or the misuse of laxatives, diuretics, or enemas).

Binge Eating/Purging Type: During the current episode of anorexia nervosa, the person has regularly engaged in binge eating or purging behavior (i.e., self-induced vomiting or the misuse of laxatives, diuretics, or enemas).

Note. From *Diagnostic and Statistical Manual of Mental Disorders* (4th ed. [*DSM–IV*], text revision), by the American Psychiatric Association, 2000, p. 326. Copyright 2000 by the American Psychiatric Association. Reprinted with permission.

It has been argued that weight phobia (fear of weight gain) did not emerge as a feature of anorexia nervosa until the 1930s, when the Western cultural beauty ideal and the practice of extreme fasting became intertwined (Casper, 1983; Russell & Treasure, 1989). However, Lee, Ho, and Hsu (1993) reported that among anorexia nervosa patients in Hong Kong, weight phobia is frequently absent. Consequently, Lee et al. argued, weight phobia should not be an essential criterion of anorexia nervosa because of its cultural (i.e., "artificial") nature. Furthermore, Lee et al. (1993) condemned the Western diagnostic ethnocentrism on which the cognitive component of the anorexia nervosa syndrome is based because it "obstruct[s] meaningful cross-cultural observation and comparison" (p. 1014).

Habermas (1996) argued that the above critiques of cognitive symptoms disregard the psychological nature of anorexia nervosa and threaten its diagnostic specificity. As such, anorexia nervosa becomes a residual category to describe weight loss resulting from food restriction that is not accounted for by any other known disorder. Moreover, research indicates that inclusion of cognitive symptoms in anorexia nervosa diagnostic criteria may be valuable in predicting the severity of course and outcome. Strober, Freeman, and Morrell (1999) compared participants who presented with extreme weight loss but denied weight phobia and body image disturbance (referred to as "atypical" participants) with those who met full criteria for anorexia nervosa. Ten to 15 years after inpatient treatment, the group who denied cognitive symptoms had 19% less chance than the full-criteria group of progressing to chronic morbidity, a faster full recovery rate, and a lower risk of developing binge eating. Additionally, none of these atypical participants later developed weight phobia and body image disturbance.

The clinical utility of the amenorrhea criterion has also been questioned. Amenorrhea (the loss of menses for at least three consecutive cycles) was first included in the *DSM–III–R* (American Psychiatric Association, 1987) to provide evidence of an endocrine disorder. The equivalent requirement for males is considered to be loss of sexual potency or interest. Amenorrhea, it is argued, distinguishes anorexia nervosa from "normal low weight" because it signifies hypothalamic dysfunction and alerts clinicians to possible sequelae such as osteoporosis and infertility. Thus, amenorrhea is a diagnostic criterion and a sign of medical morbidity for anorexia nervosa. Although amenorrhea is common among women who lose substantial body weight and body fat, it also occurs in a minority of women before they achieve significant weight loss (Garfinkel et al., 1996b). Furthermore, data indicate that some patients continue to have menstrual bleeding even at weights that are much lower than the usual standards for minimal normal (Cachelin & Maher, 1998). As for the clinical utility of the criterion, two recent studies (Cachelin & Maher, 1998; Garfinkel et al., 1996b) indicate that amenorrhea does not discriminate between women with full-criteria anorexia nervosa and women with all the features of anorexia nervosa except amenorrhea on measures of eating disorder severity, body image disturbance, depression, or personality disorders. Thus, each of the criteria for anorexia nervosa has been challenged, but there is strong evidence that the essential elements include abnormal weight loss, severely restricted food intake, and cognitive distortions about weight and shape.

CURRENT CONTROVERSIES IN THE DIAGNOSIS OF BULIMIA NERVOSA

The *DSM–IV* criteria for bulimia nervosa appear in Exhibit 2.2. Many revisions to the *DSM* criteria have occurred since bulimia nervosa was introduced in 1980, and overall, the criteria have become more specific (e.g., a cognitive symptom and a frequency minimum were added to the *DSM–III–R*). The prevalence of bulimia nervosa has dropped as a consequence of the diagnosis becoming more restrictive (Ben-Tovim, 1988). Another consequence of these revisions has been that a wider range of patterns that do not meet full criteria fall into the category of eating disorder not otherwise specified (NOS), which is not specific or formally defined.

The diagnosis of bulimia nervosa requires an individual to engage in bingeing behavior; however, controversy remains as to what constitutes a

EXHIBIT 2.2

A. Recurrent episodes of binge eating. An episode of binge eating is character-ized by both of the following:

   (1) eating, in a discrete period of time (e.g., within any 2-hour period), an amount of food that is definitely larger than most people would eat during a similar period of time and under similar circumstances

   (2) a sense of lack of control over eating during the episode (e.g., a feeling that one cannot stop eating or control how much one is eating).

B. Recurrent inappropriate compensatory behavior in order to prevent weight gain, such as self-induced vomiting; misuse of laxatives, diuretics, enemas, or other medications; fasting; or excessive exercise.

C. The binge eating and inappropriate compensatory behaviors both occur, on average, at least twice a week for 3 months.

D. Self-evaluation is unduly influenced by body shape and weight.

E. The disturbance does not occur exclusively during episodes of anorexia nervosa.

Purging Type: During the current episode of bulimia nervosa, the person has regularly engaged in self-induced vomiting or the misuse of laxatives, diuretics, or enemas.

Nonpurging Type: During the current episode of bulimia nervosa, the person has used other inappropriate compensatory behaviors, such as fasting or excessive exercise, but has not regularly engaged in self-induced vomiting or the misuse of laxatives, diuretics, or enemas.

Note. From *Diagnostic and Statistical Manual of Mental Disorders* (4th ed. [*DSM–IV*], text revision), by the American Psychiatric Association, 2000, p. 328. Copyright 2000 by the American Psychiatric Association. Reprinted with permission.

binge and how frequently and for what duration binge eating must occur to meet criteria. The *DSM–IV* defines a *binge* as "eating, in a discrete period of time (e.g., within any 2-hour period), an amount of food that is definitely larger than most people would eat during a similar period of time and under similar circumstances" (American Psychiatric Association, 1994, p. 328). Empirical research on the size of typical binges indicates that there is great variability even within a single individual (Rossiter & Agras, 1990). Studies of objective versus subjective binge episodes suggest that there are no mean-ingful differences in psychopathology based on amount of food alone (Niego, Pratt, & Agras, 1997; Pratt, Niego, & Agras, 1998) except on measures of impulse control (Keel, Meyer, & Fischer, 1999). One study that used cluster analyses to evaluate the current classification system for bulimia nervosa found that the defining features of the group most closely resembling bulimia nervosa did not require binge eating episodes to be objectively large (Hay, Fairburn, & Doll, 1996). It has been suggested that dysphoric mood states, loss of control (Beglin & Fairburn, 1992; Telch & Agras, 1996), and the quality of the binge, rather than the quantity (Garner, Shafer, & Rosen, 1992) should define a binge episode. The assessment of loss of control as a core aspect of binge eating, however, is also problematic. Because of the difficulties involved in differentiating an objective binge from a subjective binge, several researchers have argued that the criterion for "large" be eliminated from the DSM (Agras, 1990).

Frequency of bingeing is a controversial criterion of bulimia nervosa as well. No frequency criterion was mentioned in the DSM–III, but to limit the diagnosis to individuals with more severe symptoms, the twice-weekly for 3 months minimum requirement for bingeing was added in the DSM–III–R. The frequency minimum has been criticized, however, because it was decided arbitrarily rather than derived from empirical research (Garfinkel, Kennedy, & Kaplan, 1995). The implementation of the twice-weekly standard has had an enormous impact on which individuals have been studied and treated to date. Although our knowledge of the clinical characteristics, outcome, and treatment response for this group has become substantial, there is limited information about individuals who binge less than twice weekly. The data available for this group come primarily from community samples and indicate an inconsistent correlation between binge frequency and general outcome. Some research indicates that regular bingeing of less than twice a week occurs in a substantial number of individuals and is associated with a significant level of distress and impairment (Herzog, Norman, Rigotti, & Pepose, 1986; Garfinkel, Lin, et al., 1995). Other researchers, however, have found low rates of infrequent binge eating and no association between binge frequency and degree of psychopathology severity (Fairburn, Peveler, Jones, Hope, & Doll, 1993; Hay, 1998).

Another issue regarding bulimia nervosa symptom criteria surrounds the definition of "inappropriate compensatory behavior." When the purging criterion was added to the DSM–III–R, it included self-induced vomiting, use of laxatives, diuretics, strict dieting or fasting, or vigorous exercise in order to prevent weight gain. DSM–IV, however, modified the purging definition by excluding strict dieting, fasting, and excessive exercise and instituted bulimia nervosa purging and nonpurging subtypes to indicate which types of inappropriate compensatory behaviors accompany binge eating.

EATING DISORDER NOT OTHERWISE SPECIFIED

The DSM–IV criteria for eating disorder NOS appear in Exhibit 2.3. This category (formerly known as atypical anorexia nervosa or bulimia nervosa) consists of individuals with clinically significant disordered eating attitudes and behaviors who do not meet full diagnostic criteria for anorexia nervosa or bulimia nervosa. Eating disorder NOS might describe a patient who falls just short of full criteria (e.g., not having 3 consecutive months of amenorrhea or bingeing once weekly) or one who has a qualitatively

EXHIBIT 2.3
DSM–IV Criteria for Eating Disorder Not Otherwise Specified

The eating disorder not otherwise specified category is for disorders of eating that do not meet the criteria for any specific eating disorder. Examples include:

1. For females, all of the criteria for anorexia nervosa are met except that the individual has regular menses.
2. All of the criteria for anorexia nervosa are met except that, despite significant weight loss, the individual's current weight is in the normal range.
3. All of the criteria for bulimia nervosa are met except that the binge eating and inappropriate compensatory mechanisms occur at a frequency of less than twice a week or for a duration of less than 3 months.
4. The regular use of inappropriate compensatory behaviors by an individual of normal body weight after eating small amounts of food (e.g., self-induced vomiting after the consumption of two cookies).
5. Repeatedly chewing and spitting out, but not swallowing, large amounts of food.
6. Binge-eating disorder: recurrent episodes of binge eating in the absence of the regular use of inappropriate behaviors characteristic of bulimia nervosa.

Note. From *Diagnostic and Statistical Manual of Mental Disorders* (4th ed. [*DSM–IV*], text revision), by the American Psychiatric Association, 2000, p. 330. Copyright 2000 by the American Psychiatric Association. Reprinted with permission.

different clinical picture (e.g., a chronic dieter who constantly monitors her weight and engages in compulsive exercise or restrictive eating or a body builder who is very dissatisfied with his weight and size and exercises for several hours per day). This category thus represents a wide variety of disordered behaviors and cognitions related to weight, shape, appearance, and food, some of which, in combination, may constitute a new syndrome.

Eating disorder NOS is often described as an atypical eating disorder, implying that this group comprises a small minority of eating disorder patients. On the contrary, this diagnosis is common, given to approximately 25%–50% of patients presenting with disordered eating (Bunnell, Shenker, Nussbaum, Jacobson, & Cooper, 1990; Mitrany, 1992). Dancyger and Garfinkel (1995) found 5% prevalence of eating disorder NOS among 1,000 high school students (compared with 1% full anorexia nervosa or bulimia nervosa). Although this prevalence is less than rates reported in epidemiological studies (and may be accounted for by the young age of the study participants), it is consistent with the ratio of 5:1, which has been reported previously (Fairburn & Beglin, 1990). Other community samples of young women have generated similar findings (Hay et al., 1996), and it is estimated that 4%–6% of the general population (both male and female inclusive) has an eating disorder NOS (Hoek, 1995; Shisslak, Crago, & Estes, 1995), as compared with 1%–2% with full syndrome disorders.

Eating disorder NOS usually describes a syndrome that is less severe than anorexia nervosa or bulimia nervosa. However, some researchers have reported no difference in the degree of body dissatisfaction and other cognitive symptoms among women with full criteria anorexia nervosa or bulimia nervosa and eating disorder NOS (Dancyger & Garfinkel, 1995). Additionally, it should be noted that individuals with eating disorder NOS are often significantly affected by their conditions, reporting significant life dissatisfaction and psychosocial impairment, although usually less than that reported by patients with anorexia nervosa or bulimia nervosa (Dancyger & Garfinkel, 1995). Some evidence suggests that eating disorder NOS is highly associated with later development of anorexia nervosa or bulimia nervosa (Herzog, Hopkins, & Burns, 1993).

Overall, eating disorder NOS and atypical disorders are associated with a less malignant course and outcome than those reported for anorexia nervosa or bulimia nervosa. Strober et al. (1999) reported that patients with atypical anorexia nervosa were more likely to recover and recover sooner than full-criteria patients with full anorexia nervosa 10–15 years after inpatient treatment. Hay and Fairburn (1998) similarly suggested that bulimia syndromes exist on a spectrum of clinical severity, based on their findings that participants with eating disorder NOS reported the least severe outcome, compared with bulimia nervosa purging participants (most severe) and nonpurging participants (intermediate severity).

BINGE-EATING DISORDER

Binge-eating disorder, which originally described a distinctive subset of the obese who regularly binge eat but do not purge (Spitzer et al., 1992), was introduced in the *DSM–IV* as a provisional diagnosis requiring further research. Proposed research criteria for binge-eating disorder appear in Exhibit 2.4. Compared with obese patients who do not binge, obese patients with binge-eating disorder report significantly greater distress about eating and weight (Spitzer et al., 1992), psychosocial impairment (Marcus, 1993), and psychopathology including depression (Yanovski, Nelson, Dubbert, & Spitzer, 1993). Binge eating disorder is similar to the other major eating disorders in that individuals with this disorder are significantly more concerned and dissatisfied with their body weight and shape than are weight-matched control individuals without eating disorders (Eldredge & Agras, 1996; Striegel-Moore, Wilson, Wilfley, Elder, & Brownell, 1998; Wilfley, Schwartz, Spurrell, & Fairburn, 2000). Individuals with binge-eating disorder also report lower self-esteem than obese control groups (Striegel-Moore et al., 1998).

Binge-eating disorder, unlike bulimia nervosa, characterizes the group of individuals who do not engage in compensatory behaviors to avoid weight gain and are less likely to be normal weight. The division of bulimia nervosa into purging and nonpurging subtypes has clouded the distinction between

EXHIBIT 2.4
Research Criteria for Binge-Eating Disorder

A. Recurrent episodes of binge eating. An episode of binge eating is characterized by both of the following:
   (1) eating, in a discrete period of time (e.g., within any 2-hour period), an amount of food that is definitely larger than most people would eat during a similar period of time and under similar circumstances
   (2) a sense of lack of control over eating during the episode (e.g., a feeling that one cannot stop eating or control how much one is eating).
B. The binge-eating episodes are associated with 3 (or more) of the following:
   (1) eating much more rapidly than normal
   (2) eating until feeling uncomfortably full
   (3) eating large amounts of food when not feeling physically hungry
   (4) eating alone because of being embarrassed by how much one is eating
   (5) feeling disgusted with oneself, depressed, or very guilty after overeating.
C. Marked distress regarding binge eating is present.
D. The binge eating occurs, on average, at least 2 days a week for 6 months.
E. The binge eating is not associated with the regular use of inappropriate compensatory behaviors (e.g., purging, fasting, excessive exercise) and does not occur exclusively during the course of anorexia nervosa or bulimia nervosa.

Note. From *Diagnostic and Statistical Manual of Mental Disorders* (4th ed. [*DSM–IV*], text revision), by the American Psychiatric Association, 2000, p. 787. Copyright 2000 by the American Psychiatric Association. Reprinted with permission.

it and binge-eating disorder, although most evidence suggests that binge-eating disorder and the purging subtype of bulimia nervosa are, in fact, distinct disorders. Binge eating disorder differs significantly from bulimia nervosa on the basis of eating disorder outcome (Fairburn, 1999), demographic characteristics (Striegel-Moore et al., 1998), and etiology (Raymond, Mussell, Mitchell, de Zwann, & Crosby, 1995). A prospective, community-based study comparing bulimia nervosa and binge-eating disorder over 5 years found that the groups with binge-eating disorder showed more favorable outcome, with a great majority of individuals achieving full recovery in the absence of any treatment (Fairburn, 1999). Individuals with binge-eating disorder are more likely than individuals with bulimia nervosa to be obese (Spitzer et al., 1992), and unlike bulimia nervosa, binge-eating disorder is prevalent in both men and women (Striegel-Moore et al., 1998). Bulimia nervosa tends to have an earlier onset, and patients tend to be younger, thinner (Hay & Fairburn, 1998), and more likely to engage in self-injurious behaviors than are patients with binge-eating disorder (Santonastaso, Ferrara, & Favaro, 1999). Additionally, bulimia nervosa is more frequently precipitated by dieting and weight loss and is more associated with previous episodes of anorexia nervosa than binge-eating disorder, whereas binge eating occurs prior to dieting in binge-eating disorder (Raymond, Mussell, Mitchell, deZwann, & Crosby, 1995), suggesting distinct etiologies for binge-eating disorder and bulimia nervosa.

In summary, the research supports the validity of binge-eating disorder as a separate diagnostic category. However, as the research is not totally consistent, further study of the validity of binge-eating disorder is warranted.

Similar to binge-eating disorder in several ways, night eating syndrome is a disorder that was described in 1955 by Stunkard, Grace, and Wolff and was never subjected to careful clinical study until recently. Characterized by morning anorexia, evening hyperphagia, and insomnia, night eating syndrome occurs more commonly among obese individuals than nonobese individuals. One recent study ($N = 20$) indicates that night eating syndrome differs from bulimia nervosa and binge-eating syndrome in the frequency and size of food ingested at night, with night eating syndrome associated with higher frequency and smaller portions of food (Birketvedt et al., 1999). Additionally, the eating in night eating syndrome is more highly associated with carbohydrate-rich foods, suggesting that it is designed to restore the disrupted sleep of the night eaters (Birketvedt et al., 1999). Individuals with night eating syndrome also display a distinctive neuroendocrine pattern: attenuation of the usual nocturnal rise in melatonin and leptin levels and an elevated level of cortisol throughout the day (Birketvedt et al., 1999).

Further delineation of binge-eating disorder, night eating syndrome, and other distinctive syndromes within eating disorder NOS requires much additional research in the course, biology, treatment, and etiology of these syndromes. Technological innovations such as neuroimaging, neuroendocrine function tests, and genetic testing, among others, should prove to be valuable tools in this research area.

WHAT CONSTITUTES A DIAGNOSIS OF CLINICAL SEVERITY?

As body dissatisfaction and weight concerns become increasingly normative among women in Westernized countries (Rodin, Silberstein, & Striegel-Moore, 1985), it becomes harder to differentiate pathological concern from cultural norms. Dieting and weight dissatisfaction are frequent in younger girls and older women alike (Allaz, Bernstein, Rouget, Archinard, & Morabia, 1998; Field et al., 1999; Heatherton, Nichols, Mahamedi, & Keel, 1995), and there is substantial overlap between levels of body dissatisfaction in dieting or weight-preoccupied women and patients with anorexia nervosa (Garner, Olmsted, Polivy, & Garfinkel, 1984). Defining the parameters of typical versus pathological weight and shape concerns remains a challenge for the field. The intensity of concern and the impact such concern has on an individual's mental and physical health should be foremost in making this determination.

Even behavioral symptoms can be difficult to define along this continuum of normal–abnormal. Binge eating has been reported not only in patients with bulimia nervosa, anorexia nervosa, binge-eating disorder, and obesity but also in normal individuals with no clinical eating disorder (Kinzl, Traweger, Trefalt, Mangweth, & Biebl, 1999). An epidemiological study of 3,000 individuals found that 3.2% engaged in regular binge eating, 1.6% regularly fasted or used strict dieting, and 0.8% purged (Hay, 1998). In college students, the prevalence of these behaviors is much higher: 19% of women and 6% of men reported regular binge eating, 12.4% of women and 3% of men reported regular fasting, and 2.7% of women and 1.3% of men used regular vomiting to control weight (Heatherton et al., 1995).

Unhealthy behaviors and attitudes toward food and weight are quite common, whereas *DSM–IV* eating disorders affect only a small minority of the population. The *DSM–IV* states explicitly that a *mental disorder* is

> a clinically significant behavioral or psychological syndrome or pattern that occurs in an individual and that is associated with present distress (e.g., a painful symptom) or disability (i.e., impairment in one or more important areas of functioning) or with significantly increased risk of suffering death, pain, disability, or an important loss of freedom. (American Psychiatric Association, 1994, p. xxi)

But what qualifies as clinically sufficient impairment to warrant a diagnosis? Eating disorders can be associated with impairment in many domains, ranging from physiological disturbances such as bone loss or cardiac dysfunction to impairment in psychosocial functioning.

TIMING AND CROSSOVER OF EATING DISORDERS

The current diagnostic system relies on formulations of discrete categories, which, in reality, exist along a continuum and vary in severity at any given point in an individual's illness and recovery (Beaumont, Garner, & Touyz, 1994). Garfinkel, Lin, et al. (1995) suggested that nonpurging bulimia nervosa and binge-eating disorder may in some cases represent the same people during different phases of their disorder. Support for this hypothesis comes from a community-based study of binge-eating disorder in which 38% of participants had a history of purging (self-induced vomiting or laxative abuse), with an average duration of purging of 10 months (Peterson et al., 1998). These results indicate that a substantial number of individuals evolved from binge eating and purging to binge eating only.

From 22% to 37% of clinical samples presenting with bulimia nervosa have past histories of anorexia nervosa (Braun, Sunday, & Halmi, 1994; Keel, Mitchell, Miller, Davis, & Crow, 2000), and the common occurrence of crossover among the different disorders may influence classification. Long-term studies indicate that a substantial percentage of individuals with anorexia nervosa develop full-criteria bulimia nervosa at some point during follow-up, with the percentage increasing as the follow-up lengthens. In a retrospective study of treatment-seeking women with anorexia nervosa, 54% developed bulimic symptomatology at some point during the 15.5-year follow-up interval, with the median duration between onset of anorexia nervosa and onset of bulimia nervosa being 2 years (Bulik, Sullivan, Fear, & Pickering, 1997). The majority of individuals developed bulimia nervosa during the first few years after onset of anorexia nervosa, and new cases of bulimia nervosa were increasingly rare 5 years after onset of anorexia nervosa. The factors that predicted the development of bulimia nervosa included the presence of antecedent overanxious disorder, childhood sexual abuse, and recovery from anorexia nervosa (Bulik et al., 1997). In a prospective study of treatment-seeking women followed for 7.5 years, 16% of women with anorexia nervosa restricting type developed full-criteria bulimia nervosa, and 7% of women with bulimia nervosa developed full-criteria anorexia nervosa (Herzog, Flores, et al., 1999). Of note, 14% of the women diagnosed with anorexia nervosa restricting type at intake had histories of prior bulimia nervosa episodes, and 18% of the women diagnosed with bulimia nervosa at intake had histories of prior anorexia nervosa episodes. These data indicate that the diagnostic categories used in studies may represent a phase rather than a temporally stable disorder.

When patients "move" between eating disorders (i.e., change their status as a result of symptom evolution), attempts to isolate unique characteristics of full criteria disorders yield inconsistent results (Pryor, Wiederman, & McGilley, 1996). Despite the frequency of the crossover from one full syndrome to another, little is known about the patterns and predictors of these events or their implications for one's understanding of correlates, risk factors, and consequences. There is a paucity of data about the development of individual symptoms such as bingeing or purging in anorexia nervosa restricting type or weight loss in bulimia nervosa. How long does one have to be a restricting anorexia type to be classified as such? Is any purging behavior permitted in individuals classified as anorexia nervosa restricting type? Further research is needed to determine the timing of onset and course of the disorders and how this timing is related to diagnosis.

SUBTYPING

A major change in the *DSM–IV* was the elimination of dual diagnosis of anorexia nervosa and bulimia nervosa. In the current system, anorexia nervosa "trumps" bulimia nervosa. That is, an individual presenting with both syndromes is classified as anorexia, binge-purge subtype. This change is based on consistent evidence that anorexia nervosa is associated with a more severe outcome and greater medical risk than bulimia nervosa and that combination of both is associated with the most severe risk. One implication of the current subtyping system may be that greater funding for research and treatment will be allocated to anorexia nervosa.

Support for separating purging anorexia from nonpurging anorexia (regardless of whether or not they binge) comes from a large study of treatment-seeking women that revealed significantly more psychopathology in anorexia nervosa purging and in bingeing groups than in anorexia nervosa restricted type without bingeing or purging (Garner, Garner, & Rosen, 1993). Additionally, Garner et al. argued for categorization based on purging because of the association of purging behaviors with medical morbidity. Another study, however, found no differences in levels of psychopathology based on the presence or absence of bingeing and purging in anorexia nervosa when analyses were corrected for duration of illness (Nagata, McConaha, Rao, Sokol, & Kaye, 1997).

The *DSM–IV* subtyping of anorexia nervosa was based on findings that among treatment-seeking women with anorexia nervosa, those with bulimic symptoms are more likely to suffer from comorbid depression, substance abuse, poor impulse control, general emotional distress, and greater psychopathology than restricting anorexia (DaCosta & Halmi, 1992; Garner et al., 1993; Herzog, Keller, Sacks, Yeh, & Lavori, 1992). Research regarding the clinical utility of these subtypes is mixed. Early studies show that the binge-purge subtype is associated with the poorest overall prognosis among patients with anorexia nervosa (Casper, Eckert, Halmi, Goldberg, & Davis, 1980; Garfinkel, Modolfsky, & Garner, 1980; Russell, 1979). Anorexia nervosa binge-purge subtype is associated with higher risk of death and an elevated rate of suicide attempts (Garner et al., 1993; Herzog et al., 1999; Pryor et al., 1996). Another study of treatment-seeking women with anorexia nervosa found that although women with anorexia nervosa binge-purge subtype were more likely to have attempted suicide, there were no differences between subtypes on drug problems, self-injury, satisfaction with sexual activity, age at intake, body mass index at intake, eating disorder outcome, or age of first diet (Pryor et al., 1996).

Some interesting findings about anorexia nervosa subtypes have emerged in a long-term, prospective follow-up study of treatment-seeking women. Despite better outcome for the binge-purge subtype at Year 1, anorexia nervosa subtypes showed similar rates of full recovery, partial recovery, and relapse at 7.5 years of follow-up (Herzog et al., 1996; Herzog, Dorer, et al., 1999). In this same sample, however, nearly all of the participants who died (8 of 9) had a history of bingeing and purging in addition to an intake diagnosis of anorexia nervosa. Differences also emerged between anorexia nervosa restricting type and anorexia nervosa binge-purge subtype groups in terms of psychosocial functioning, with the binge-purge group reporting less overall life satisfaction at baseline and less improvement in global functioning after 5 years than compared with the restricting group.

Only a few studies have examined subtyping of bulimia nervosa, and those studies have reported conflicting findings. Subtyping bulimia nervosa by purging was implemented in the *DSM–IV* because purging with vomiting and laxatives is associated with worse outcome and higher comorbidity and may represent a type of bulimia nervosa that is harder to treat. A large, epidemiological survey study revealed that the purging subtype of bulimia nervosa could be distinguished from nonpurging subtype on a variety of factors, including early age of onset, high rates of affective and anxiety disorders, alcoholism, sexual abuse, and parental discord (Garfinkel et al., 1996a). In contrast, a study of treatment-seeking patients found little support for differentiating between purging and nonpurging bulimia nervosa subtypes, as there were no differences between these groups in terms of severity of eating pathology or rates of comorbid psychopathology (Tobin, Griffing, & Griffing, 1997).

THE ROLE OF CULTURE

The *DSM* classification system is based almost exclusively on research with White Anglo, European, and North American groups. Although studies on other ethnic groups exist, as described briefly in chapter 1, the attention and emphasis on Western groups leaves the question of cultural specificity (i.e., a syndrome is specific to the culture in which it occurs) versus cultural uniformity (i.e., anorexia nervosa is anorexia nervosa no matter where it occurs) largely unaddressed. It has been argued that anorexia nervosa is a culturally bound syndrome, with symptoms attributable to psychosocial stressors, genetic vulnerability, and cultural pressures to be thin (Becker & Kleinman, 2000). However, although cases of anorexia nervosa have been reported predominantly in Great Britain, Europe, North and South America, Japan, China, and some areas of the Middle East, it is very possible that it occurs elsewhere, just in a different form. Future researchers should focus on exploring how body, weight, and food issues are manifested in other cultures and the relationship of those patterns to the Western versions of eating disorders.

FUTURE DIRECTIONS

Considerable progress has occurred in the classification of eating disorders over the past two decades. The resulting *DSM* revisions have generated considerable debate, some of which currently centers around the following:

(a) the validity of binge-eating disorder as separate from bulimia nervosa, (b) the proper boundaries between normative concerns and true eating disorders, and (c) the specific criteria for anorexia nervosa and bulimia nervosa and the complicating factors of crossover and cultural specificity. The 21st century will witness further advances in research that address the above questions and generate new ones. Aided by new techniques in assessment and methodology, neuroendocrine, neuroimaging, and genetic studies will make significant contributions to our understanding of anorexia nervosa and bulimia nervosa phenotypes, their respective subtypes, and other eating disorder categories such as eating disorder NOS and binge-eating disorder. Researchers may use the technological developments to focus on newer areas in the field, such as (a) etiology, including genetic heritability; (b) short-term and long-term outcome, including response to various treatments and assessment of global functioning; (c) medical morbidity, including amenorrhea, infertility, and osteopenia in anorexia nervosa; and (d) related traits, such as impulsivity, perfectionism, and risk aversion. In the future, diagnostic criteria revisions will continue to shape research agendas, and better-defined categories should allow for more specific treatments.

REFERENCES

Agras, W. S. (1990). An empirical test of the *DSM–III–R* definition of binge. *International Journal of Eating Disorders, 9,* 513–518.

Allaz, A. F., Bernstein, M., Rouget, P., Archinard, M., & Morabia, A. (1998). Body weight preoccupation in middle-age and ageing women: A general population survey. *International Journal of Eating Disorders, 23,* 287–294.

American Psychiatric Association. (1980). *Diagnostic and statistical manual of mental disorders* (3rd ed.). Washington, DC: Author.

American Psychiatric Association. (1987). *Diagnostic and statistical manual of mental disorders* (3rd ed., rev.). Washington, DC: Author.

American Psychiatric Association. (2000). *Diagnostic and statistical manual of mental disorders* (4th ed., text revision). Washington, DC: Author.

Becker, A. E., & Kleinman, A. (2000). Anthropology and psychiatry. In B. Sadock & V. Sadock (Eds.), *Kaplan and Sadock's comprehensive textbook of psychiatry* (pp. 463–476). Philadelphia: Lippincott, Williams, & Wilkins.

Beglin, S. J., & Fairburn, C. G. (1992). What is meant by the term "binge"? *American Journal of Psychiatry, 149,* 123–124.

Ben-Tovim, D. I. (1988). *DSM–III,* draft *DSM–III–R,* and the diagnosis and prevalence of bulimia in Australia. *American Journal of Psychiatry, 145,* 1000–1002.

Beaumont, P. J. V., Garner, D. M., & Touyz, S. W. (1994). Diagnoses of eating disorders: What may we learn from past mistakes? *International Journal of Eating Disorders, 16*, 349–362.

Birketvedt, G. S., Florholmen, J., Sundsfjord, J., Osterud, B., Dinges, D., Bilker, W., & Stunkard, A. (1999). Behavioral and neuroendocrine characteristics of the night-eating syndrome. *Journal of the American Medical Association, 282*, 657–663.

Braun, D. L., Sunday, S. R., & Halmi, K. A. (1994). Psychiatric comorbidity in patients with eating disorders. *Psychological Medicine, 6*, 859–867.

Bulik, C. M., Sullivan, P. F., Fear, J., & Pickering, A. (1997). Predictors of the development of bulimia nervosa in women with anorexia nervosa. *Journal of Nervous and Mental Disease, 185*, 704–707.

Bunnell, D. W., Shenker, I. R., Nussbaum, M. P., Jacobson, M. S., & Cooper, P. (1990). Subclinical versus formal eating disorders: Differential psychological features. *International Journal of Eating Disorders, 9*, 357–362.

Cachelin, F. M., & Maher, B. A. (1998). Is amenorrhea a critical criterion for anorexia nervosa? *Journal of Psychosomatic Research, 44*, 435–440.

Casper, R. C. (1983). On the emergence of bulimia nervosa as a syndrome. *International Journal of Eating Disorders, 2*, 3–16.

Casper, R. C., Eckert, E. D., Halmi, K. A., Goldberg, S. C., & Davis, J. M. (1980). Bulimia: Its incidence and clinical importance in patients with anorexia nervosa. *Archives of General Psychiatry, 37*, 1030–1035.

DaCosta, M., & Halmi, K. A. (1992). Classification of anorexia nervosa: Question of subtypes. *International Journal of Eating Disorders, 11*, 305–313.

Dancyger, I. F., & Garfinkel, P. E. (1995). The relationship of partial syndrome eating disorders to anorexia nervosa and bulimia nervosa. *Psychological Medicine, 25*, 1019–1025.

Eldredge, K. L., & Agras, W. S. (1996). Weight and shape overconcern and emotional eating in binge eating disorder. *International Journal of Eating Disorders, 19*, 73–82.

Fairburn, C. (1999, November). *The predictive validity of binge eating disorder.* Paper presented at the annual meeting of the Eating Disorder Research Society, San Diego, CA.

Fairburn, C. G., & Beglin, S. J. (1990). Studies of the epidemiology of bulimia nervosa. *American Journal of Psychiatry, 147*, 401–408.

Fairburn, C. G., Peveler, R. C., Jones, R., Hope, R. A., & Doll, H. A. (1993). Predictors of 12-months outcome in bulimia nervosa and the influence of attitudes to weight and shape. *Journal of Consulting and Clinical Psychology, 61*, 696–698.

Feighner, J. P., Robins, E., Guze, S. B., Woodruff, R. A., Winokur, G., & Munoz, R. (1972). Diagnostic criteria for use in psychiatric research. *Archives of General Psychiatry, 26*, 57–63.

Field, A. E., Camargo, C. A., Taylor, C. B., Berkey, C. S., Frazier, A. L., Gillman, M. W., & Colditz, G. A. (1999). Overweight, weight concerns, and bulimic behaviors among girls and boys. *Journal of the American Academy of Child and Adolescent Psychiatry, 38,* 754–760.

Fisher, M., Golden, N. H., Katzman, D. K., Kreipe, R. E., Rees, J., Schebendach, J., Sigman, G., Ammerman, S., & Hoberman, H. M. (1995). Eating disorders in adolescents: A background paper. *Journal of Adolescent Health, 16,* 420–437.

Garfinkel, P. E., Kennedy, S. H., & Kaplan, A. S. (1995). Views on classification and diagnosis of eating disorders. *Canadian Journal of Psychiatry, 40,* 445–456.

Garfinkel, P. E., Lin, B., Goering, P., Spegg, C., Goldbloom, D., Kennedy, S., Kaplan, A., & Woodside, B. (1995). Bulimia nervosa in a Canadian community sample: Prevalence, co-morbidity, early experiences and psychosocial functioning. *American Journal of Psychiatry, 152,* 1052–1058.

Garfinkel, P. E., Lin, E., Goering, P., Spegg, C., Goldbloom, D. S., Kennedy, S., Kaplan, A. S., & Blake Woodsie, D. (1996a). Purging and nonpurging forms of bulimia nervosa in a community sample. *International Journal of Eating Disorders, 20,* 231–238.

Garfinkel, P. E., Lin, E., Goering, P., Spegg, C., Goldbloom, D. S., Kennedy, S., Kaplan, A. S., & Blake Woodsie, D. (1996b). Should amenorrhea be necessary for the diagnosis of anorexia nervosa? Evidence from a Canadian community sample. *British Journal of Psychiatry, 168,* 500–506.

Garfinkel, P. E., Moldofsky, H., & Garner, D. M. (1980). The heterogeneity of anorexia nervosa: Bulimia as a distinct subgroup. *Archives of General Psychiatry, 37,* 1036–1040.

Garner, D. M., Garner, M. V., & Rosen, L. W. (1993). Anorexia nervosa "restrictors" who purge: Implications for subtyping anorexia nervosa. *International Journal of Eating Disorders, 13,* 171–186.

Garner, D. M., Olmsted, M. P., Polivy, J., & Garfinkel, P. E. (1984). Comparison between weight-preoccupied women and anorexia nervosa. *Psychosomatic Medicine, 46,* 255–260.

Garner, D. M., Shafer, C. L., & Rosen, L. W. (1992). Critical appraisal of the *DSM–III–R* diagnostic criteria for eating disorders. In S. R. Hooper, G. W. Hynd, & R. E. Mattison (Eds.), *Child psychopathology: Diagnostic criteria and clinical assessment* (pp. 261–303). Hillsdale, NJ: Erlbaum.

Habermas, T. (1996). In defense of weight phobia as the central organizing motive in anorexia nervosa: Historical and cultural arguments for a culture-sensitive psychological conception. *International Journal of Eating Disorders, 19,* 317–334.

Hay, P. (1998). The epidemiology of eating disorder behaviors: An Australian community-based survey. *International Journal of Eating Disorders, 23,* 371–382.

Hay, P., & Fairburn, C. (1998). The validity of the *DSM–IV* scheme for classifying bulimic eating disorders. *International Journal of Eating Disorders, 23,* 7–15.

Hay, P. J., Fairburn, C. G., & Doll, H. A. (1996). The classification of bulimic eating disorders: A community-based cluster analysis. *Psychological Medicine, 26,* 801–812.

Heatherton, T. F., Nichols, P., Mahamedi, F., & Keel, P. (1995). Body weight, dieting, and eating disorder symptoms among college students, 1982–1992. *American Journal of Psychiatry, 152,* 1623–1629.

Herzog, D. B., Dorer, D. J., Keel, P. K., Selwyn, S. E., Ekeblad, E., Flores, A. T., Greenwood, D. N., Burwell, R. A., & Keller, M. B. (1999). Recovery and relapse in anorexia and bulimia nervosa. *Journal of the American Academy of Child and Adolescent Psychiatry, 38,* 829–837.

Herzog, D. B., Field, A. E., Keller, M. B., West, J. C., Robbins, W. M., Staley, J., & Colditz, G. A. (1996). Subtyping eating disorders: Is it justified? *Journal of the American Academy of Child and Adolescent Psychiatry, 35,* 928–936.

Herzog, D. B., Flores, A. T., Delinsky, S. S., Greenwood, D. N., Dorer, D. J., & Blais, M. A. (1999). [Prospective crossover rates of anorexia and bulimia nervosa]. Unpublished raw data.

Herzog, D. B., Hopkins, J. D., & Burns, C. D. (1993). A follow-up study of 33 subdiagnostic eating disordered women. *International Journal of Eating Disorders, 14,* 261–267.

Herzog, D. B., Keller, M. B., Sacks, N. R., Yeh, C., & Lavori, P. W. (1992). Psychiatric comorbidity in treatment-seeking anorexics and bulimics. *Journal of the American Academy of Child and Adolescent Psychiatry, 31,* 810–818.

Herzog, D. B., Norman, D. K., Rigotti, N. A., & Pepose, M. (1986). Frequency of bulimic behaviors and associated social maladjustment in female graduate students. *Journal of Psychiatric Research, 20,* 355–361.

Hoek, H. W. (1995). The distribution of eating disorders. In K. Brownell & C. G. Fairburn (Eds.), *Eating disorders and obesity: A comprehensive handbook* (pp. 207–211). New York: Guilford Press.

Keel, P. K., Meyer, S., & Fischer, J. (1999, November). *Importance of size in defining binge-eating episodes in bulimia nervosa.* Paper presented at the annual meeting of the Eating Disorder Research Society, San Diego, CA.

Keel, P. K., Mitchell, J. E., Miller, K. B., Davis, T. L., & Crow, S. J. (2000). Predictive validity of bulimia nervosa as a diagnostic category. *American Journal of Psychiatry, 157,* 136–138.

Kinzl, J. F., Traweger, C., Trefalt, E., Mangweth, B., & Biebl, W. (1999). Binge eating disorder in females: A population-based investigation. *International Journal of Eating Disorders, 25,* 287–292.

Lee, S., Chiu, H. F. K., & Chen, C. (1989). Anorexia nervosa in Hong Kong: Why not more in Chinese? *British Journal of Psychiatry, 154,* 683–688.

Lee, S., Ho, T. P., & Hsu, L. K. G. (1993). Fat phobic and non-fat phobic anorexia nervosa: A comparative study of 70 Chinese patients in Hong Kong. *Psychological Medicine, 23,* 999–1017.

Marcus, M. (1993). Binge eating in obesity. In C. G. Fairburn & G. T. Wilson (Eds.), *Binge eating* (pp. 77–96). New York: Guilford Press.

Mitrany, E. (1992). Atypical eating disorders. *Journal of Adolescent Health, 13,* 400–402.

Nagata, T., McConaha, C., Rao, R., Sokol, M. S., & Kaye, W. H. (1997). A comparison of subgroups of inpatients with anorexia nervosa. *International Journal of Eating Disorders, 22,* 309–314.

Niego, S. H., Pratt, E. M., & Agras, W. S. (1997). Subjective or objective binge: Is the distinction valid? *International Journal of Eating Disorders, 22,* 291–298.

Peterson, C. B., Mitchell, J. E., Engbloom, S., Nugent, S., Pederson Mussell, M., Crow, S. J., & Miller, J. P. (1998). Binge eating disorder with and without a history of purging symptoms. *International Journal of Eating Disorders, 24,* 251–257.

Pratt, E. M., Niego, S. H., & Agras, W. S. (1998). Does the size of a binge matter? *International Journal of Eating Disorders, 24,* 307–312.

Pryor, T., Wiederman, M. W., & McGilley, B. (1996). Clinical correlates of anorexia nervosa subtypes. *International Journal of Eating Disorders, 19,* 371–379.

Raymond, N. C., Mussell, M. P., Mitchell, J. E., de Zwaan, M., & Crosby, R. D. (1995). An age-matched comparison of subjects with binge eating disorder and bulimia nervosa. *International Journal of Eating Disorders, 18,* 135–143.

Rodin, J., Silberstein, L. R., & Striegel-Moore, R. (1985). Women and weight: A normative discontent. In T. B. Sonderegger (Ed.), *Nebraska symposium on motivation* (pp. 267–307). Lincoln: University of Nebraska Press.

Rossiter, E. M., & Agras, W. S. (1990). An empirical test of the *DSM–III–R* definition of binge. *International Journal of Eating Disorders, 9,* 513–518.

Russell, G. (1979). Bulimia nervosa: An ominous variant of anorexia nervosa. *Psychological Medicine, 9,* 429–448.

Russell, G. F., & Treasure, J. (1989). The modern history of anorexia nervosa: An interpretation of why the illness has changed. *Annals of the New York Academy of Sciences, 575,* 13–27.

Santonastaso, P., Ferrara, S., & Favaro, A. (1999). Differences between binge eating disorder and nonpurging bulimia nervosa. *International Journal of Eating Disorders, 25,* 215–218.

Shisslak, C. M., Crago, M., & Estes L. S. (1995). The spectrum of eating disturbances. *International Journal of Eating Disorders, 18,* 209–219.

Spitzer, R. L., Devlin, M., Walsh, B. T., Hasin, D., Wing, R., Marcus, M., Stunkard, A., Wadden, T., Yanovski, S., Agras, S., Mitchell, J., & Nonas, C. (1992). A multisite field trial of diagnostic criteria for binge eating disorder. *International Journal of Eating Disorders, 11,* 191–203.

Striegel-Moore, R. H., Wilson, G. T., Wilfley, D. E., Elder, K. A., & Brownell, K. D. (1998). Binge eating in an obese community sample. *International Journal of Eating Disorders, 23,* 27–38.

Strober, M., Freeman, R., & Morrell, W. (1999). Atypical anorexia nervosa: Separation from typical cases in course and outcome in a long-term prospective study. *International Journal of Eating Disorders, 25,* 135–142.

Stunkard, A. J., Grace, W. J., & Wolff, H. G. (1955). The night-eating syndrome: A pattern of food intake among certain obese patients. *American Journal of Medicine, 19,* 78–86.

Telch, C. F., & Agras W. S. (1996). Do emotional states influence binge eating in the obese? *International Journal of Eating Disorders, 20,* 271–280.

Tobin, D. L., Griffing, A., & Griffing, S. (1997). An examination of subtype criteria for bulimia nervosa. *International Journal of Eating Disorders, 22,* 179–286.

Walsh, B. T., & Kahn, C. B. (1997). Diagnostic criteria for eating disorders: Current concerns and future directions. *Psychopharmacology Bulletin, 33,* 369–372.

Wilfley, D. E., Schwartz, M. B., Spurrell, E. B., & Fairburn, C. G. (2000). Using the eating disorder examination to identify the specific psychopathology of binge eating disorder. *International Journal of Eating Disorders, 27,* 259–269.

Yanovski, S. Z., Nelson, J. E., Dubbert, B. K., & Spitzer, R. L. (1993). Association of binge eating disorder and psychiatric comorbidity in obese subjects. *American Journal of Psychiatry, 150,* 1472–1479.

3

RISK FACTORS FOR EATING PATHOLOGY: RECENT ADVANCES AND FUTURE DIRECTIONS

ERIC STICE

Despite the numerous studies that have been directed at advancing the understanding of the etiology of eating pathology, surprisingly little is known about the risk factors that contribute to the development of anorexia nervosa, bulimia nervosa, and binge-eating disorder. An improved understanding of etiologic processes is crucial because eating disorders are one of the most common psychiatric problems faced by young women, are often chronic, can result in serious medical complications, and are associated with comorbid psychopathology such as mood disorders (Fairburn et al., 1995; Garfinkel et al., 1995; Keller, Herzog, Lavori, Bradburn, & Mahoney, 1992; Whitaker et al., 1990). Eating disorders also have the highest rate of treatment seeking, inpatient hospitalization, and suicide attempts of common psychiatric disorders (Newman et al., 1996). Additionally, there is evidence that eating pathology predicts the onset of obesity (Stice, Cameron, Killen, Hayward, & Taylor, 1999), which results in elevated morbidity and mortality. Insight into the factors that promote eating pathology should facilitate the design of more effective preventive and treatment interventions for this serious mental health problem.

In this chapter, I first define risk factor terminology in support of recent efforts to standardize the nomenclature (Kraemer et al., 1997). Second, prospective and experimental risk factor studies for eating pathology are reviewed. Third, promising multivariate etiologic models for eating pathology are presented, and the research support for each is examined. Next, theoretical and methodological limitations of this literature are discussed. Finally, directions for future research are offered, and a systematic approach to empirically testing etiologic models is outlined.

RISK FACTOR

Terminology

A *risk factor* is a variable that has been shown to prospectively predict a subsequent pathological outcome (e.g., bulimia nervosa; Kraemer et al., 1997). This review focuses on prospective research rather than correlational studies because the latter do not permit an unambiguous interpretation regarding the direction of effects between the variables. It is not possible to differentiate a risk factor from a concomitant or consequence of a disorder in correlational studies. If there is experimental evidence that a manipulation of a risk factor results in a subsequent change in eating pathology, such a variable would be considered a causal risk factor, according to the Kraemer et al. criteria. Thus, experimental studies that attempt to manipulate putative risk factors are also considered. Experimental studies are particularly powerful in etiologic research because they not only document the direction of influence but can also rule out third-variable explanations of an effect (something prospective studies cannot accomplish). A *proxy* risk factor shows a significant prospective relation to a pathological outcome solely because it is correlated with a causal risk factor (Kraemer, Stice, Kazdin, Offord, & Kupfer, in press). However, by definition, a manipulation of a proxy risk factor does not result in a subsequent change in the risk for the outcome.

A variable that accounts for the relation between a predictor and a criterion is referred to as a *mediator*. Thus, *mediation* refers to the mechanism by which a predictor causes change in a criteria, wherein the predictor presumably causes change in the mediator, which in turn causes change in the criteria. Finally, a variable that mitigates the adverse effects of a risk factor is a *protective* factor. Stated differently, a protective factor moderates the effects of a risk factor. The classic example is that social support may reduce the negative impact of stressful events on mental health (i.e., the stress-buffering hypothesis). Note that some refer to variables negatively related to the development of eating pathology as protective factors, but this definition is conceptually unsatisfying because often the only distinction between a risk factor and a protective factor is the way that it is coded. For example, low self-esteem has been considered a risk factor, whereas high self-esteem has been considered a protective factor. Thus, both factors reflect the same construct, and the only distinction between the risk and protective factors is how the variable is coded.

Research

Whereas a host of putative risk factors have been explored in empirical studies, only those that have been supported in at least one prospective or experimental study are reviewed. These types of studies are considered exclusively because they permit inferences regarding the nature of the relations not possible with cross-sectional data. Retrospective studies are not included because this design of study does not permit a demonstration of temporal precedence and retrospective reports have been found to be inaccurate (Henry, Moffitt, Caspi, Langley, & Silva, 1994). It is also important to distinguish between prospective studies indicating that a putative risk factor predicts subsequent onset or increases in eating pathology (e.g., Attie & Brooks-Gunn, 1989; Killen et al., 1996; Leon, Fulkerson, Perry, & Early-Zald, 1995), from those that only document that a putative risk factor is correlated with future eating disturbances (e.g., Joiner, Heatherton, & Keel, 1997; Kendler et al., 1991; Patton, 1988). Only the former demonstrates that a putative risk factor predicts subsequent change in eating pathology and thus establishes temporal precedence. The demonstration of temporal precedence is a necessary prerequisite for attempting to infer causal relations with nonexperimental designs. However, studies that only document that a putative risk factor is correlated with future eating pathology do not provide evidence of temporal precedence because this association may simply be a function of the baseline correlation between the risk factor and eating disturbances. In prospective analyses, researchers must control for initial levels of the outcome to ensure that they are modeling change and establishing temporal precedence. Note that in only 11 of the 23 prospective studies that could be located through an extensive literature review did researchers analyze their data in a way that permitted inferences about temporal precedence.

Adiposity

Elevated adiposity is thought to constitute a risk factor for the development of eating pathology because it fosters social pressure to be thin, body dissatisfaction, dieting, and negative affect (Cattarin & Thompson, 1994). In support of these assertions, body mass prospectively predicted weight-related teasing and body dissatisfaction (Cattarin & Thompson, 1994) as well as the onset of bulimic pathology and binge eating (Killen et al., 1994; Vogeltanz-Holm et al., 2000). However, the relation between body mass and subsequent eating pathology has not been replicated in several longitudinal studies (e.g., Graber, Brooks-Gunn, Paikoff, & Warren, 1994; Keel, Fulkerson, & Leon, 1997; Killen et al., 1996; Stice & Agras, 1998), suggesting that either this relation is not consistent or this effect is small. Thus, there is only modest support for the assertion that body mass is a risk factor for eating pathology. It might be useful in future studies for researchers to examine other aspects of weight history, such as highest past weight or recent weight gain, to assess whether such variables are more consistent predictors of eating pathology.

Sociocultural Pressures To Be Thin

Researchers have postulated that pressure to be thin from family, peers, and mass media promote development of eating disturbances (Levine & Smolak, 1996; Striegel-Moore, Silberstein, & Rodin, 1986). Sociocultural pressure may be related to eating pathology because it fosters an internalization of the thin ideal, body dissatisfaction, dieting, and emotional disturbances. In support of this, perceived pressure to be thin prospectively predicted growth in dieting (Stice, in press; Stice, Mazotti, Krebs, & Martin, 1998) and onset of bulimic pathology (Field, Camargo, Taylor, Berkey, & Colditz, 1999; Stice & Agras, 1998), and weight-related teasing predicted growth in body dissatisfaction (Cattarin & Thompson, 1994). Furthermore, experimental exposure to media-portrayed thin-ideal images resulted in body dissatisfaction and negative affect (e.g., Irving, 1990; Ogden & Mundray, 1998; Richins, 1991; Stice & Shaw, 1994), although some studies suggest that the adverse effects only occur for at-risk participants with initial elevations in thin-ideal internalization and body dissatisfaction (Heinberg & Thompson, 1995; Posavac, Posavac, & Posavac, 1998). In a randomized experiment, researchers also found that a 15-month subscription to a fashion magazine resulted in increased body dissatisfaction, dieting, negative affect, and bulimic symptoms but only for at-risk girls characterized by initial body dissatisfaction, pressure to be thin, and deficits in social support (Stice, Spangler, & Agras, in press). Thus, findings collectively suggest that the negative effects of media exposure are stronger for at-risk individuals. Because the relation between sociocultural pressures and eating pathology has been supported in randomized experiments, sociocultural pressures can be tentatively considered a causal risk factor for eating disturbances.

Thin-Ideal Internalization

Internalization of the thin ideal theoretically increases the risk of eating pathology because it promotes body dissatisfaction, dieting, and negative affect (Stice & Agras, 1998; Thompson, Heinberg, Altabe, & Tantleff-Dunn, 1999). Although few researchers have investigated this construct, internalization of the thin ideal did predict onset of bulimic pathology in one study (Stice & Agras, 1998) as well as future growth in body dissatisfaction, dieting, and negative affect (Stice, in press). Moreover, an experimental reduction of the thin-ideal internalization resulted in decreased body dissatisfaction, dieting, negative affect, and bulimic symptoms (Stice, Mazotti, Weibel, & Agras, 2000), and these findings have been replicated (Stice, Chase, Stormer, & Appel, in press). Whereas the experimental support for the relation between the thin-ideal internalization and eating pathology suggests that this may be a causal risk factor, additional research from independent laboratories would permit greater confidence in this conclusion.

Body Dissatisfaction

Theoretically, body dissatisfaction and weight concerns promote bulimic symptoms because they lead to dieting and negative affect (Heatherton & Polivy, 1992; Stice & Agras, 1998). Consistent with this, body dissatisfaction predicted subsequent growth in dieting (Stice, in press; Stice, Mazotti, et al., 1998) and eating pathology (Attie & Brooks-Gunn, 1989; Stice, in press). Moreover, body dissatisfaction predicted the onset of major depression (Stice, Hayward, Cameron, Killen, & Taylor, 2000) and eating pathology (Field et al., 1999; Graber et al., 1994; Killen et al., 1994, 1996; Stice & Agras, 1998). Indeed, body dissatisfaction has emerged as one of the most robust risk factors for eating disturbances, although some researchers have failed to find this effect (e.g., Leon et al., 1995). Thus, body dissatisfaction can be considered a risk factor for eating disturbances.

Dieting

It has been postulated that dieting increases the risk for binge eating and the onset of bulimia (Garfinkel & Garner, 1982; Polivy, & Herman, 1985). Caloric deprivation is thought to increase the likelihood that an individual will binge eat in an effort to restore a kilocalorie deficit. In addition, transgressions of strict dietary rules may result in overeating because of the abstinence–violation effect, and intense emotional experiences may disrupt dietary inhibition and lead to overeating (Polivy & Herman, 1985). Dieting may also contribute to increased negative affect, which increases the risk for binge eating (Heatherton & Polivy, 1992).

Consistent with the above theory, longitudinal studies indicate that dieting predicts onset of major depression (Stice, Hayward, et al., 2000) and eating pathology (Field et al., 1999; Killen et al., 1994, 1996; Patton, Johnson-Sabine, Wood, Mann, & Wakeling, 1990; Santonastaso, Friederici, & Favaro, 1999; Stice & Agras, 1998; Stice, Killen, Hayward, & Taylor, 1998). However, randomized experiments in which researchers manipulated the dieting of participants produced inconsistent support for the restraint model. Two studies in which researchers manipulated short-term (less than 24 hours) caloric deprivation failed to produce the main effect of dieting on food intake that would be predicted from this model but instead suggest that dieting only results in increased consumption for overweight individuals and unrestrained eaters (Lowe, 1992, 1994).

Only a few experiments examine actual binge eating as an outcome. Telch and Agras (1996b) found that individuals with bulimia nervosa, individuals with binge-eating disorder, or non-eating-disordered controls consumed more calories but did not show greater binge eating after 6 hours of caloric deprivation. Agras and Telch (1998) found that 14 hours of food deprivation resulted in elevated rates of binge eating and increased caloric intake among individuals with a binge-eating disorder. Even more problematic, experiments in which researchers manipulated long-term dieting of overweight individuals indicate that the assignment to a low calorie diet resulted in decreased binge eating and caloric intake (Goodrick, Poston, Kimball, Reeves, & Foreyt, 1998; Telch & Agras, 1993; Wadden, Foster, & Letizia, 1994; Yanovski & Sebring, 1994). For instance, Telch and Agras found that the rates of binge eating declined during the 3-month low-calorie diet phase of the intervention relative to base-line levels. In summary, prospective studies suggest that dieting is positively related to bulimic pathology, experiments in which researchers manipulated short-term caloric deprivation produced inconsistent findings, and long-term caloric deprivation experiments indicate that dieting is negatively related to binge eating.

There are several possible explanations for these inconsistent findings. As the randomized trials rule out third-variable explanations and the longitudinal designs do not, the most likely possibility is that a confounding variable is causing both dieting and binge eating. It has been suggested that a tendency toward caloric overconsumption may cause both dieting and eventual binge-eating onset (Stice et al., 1999). This explanation is consistent with the evidence that dieters gain more weight over time than nondieters (e.g., French, Jeffery, & Wing, 1994; Klesges, Isbell, & Klesges, 1992; Stice et al., 1999). If this is so, self-reported dieting would be a proxy risk factor (Kraemer et al., in press) for bulimic symptoms solely because it is a marker for chronic overconsumption.

An alternative explanation for these discrepant findings is that dieting may have different effects for normal weight versus overweight people; one consistent difference between the two sets of studies is that the randomized trials involved overweight individuals and the longitudinal studies used normative samples. Perhaps individuals with greater adipose tissue reserves are less likely to binge eat, compared with individuals without these reserves, when faced with caloric deprivation because of physiological regulatory processes. Another possible explanation for these inconsistent findings is that going off, rather than on, a diet is the catalyst for increased binge eating. The relaxing of strict dietary rules might leave individuals at risk for overconsumption. It may be that dieters in the naturalistic longitudinal studies discontinue their dieting at some point and experience consequent increases in binge eating. The possible explanations for these inconsistent findings should be explored in future research because the experimental evidence that caloric deprivation results in decreased binge eating is problematic for the restraint model.

In summary, although prospective studies suggest that dieting is a risk factor for eating pathology, results from the experimental studies question this conclusion. Until these inconsistent findings are resolved, it seems premature to draw any firm conclusions regarding the relation of dieting to eating pathology.

Negative Affectivity

It has also been suggested that *negative affectivity*, the propensity to become emotionally distressed, promotes bulimic behavior (McCarthy, 1990; Stice & Agras, 1998). Theoretically, individuals high in negative affectivity binge eat because it provides comfort and distracts them from their aversive emotions. Consistent with this, negative affectivity and negative affect predicted the onset of bulimic pathology (Killen et al., 1996; Stice & Agras, 1998) and growth in bulimic symptoms (Stice, in press), although some studies report null findings (Leon et al., 1995). It is interesting to note that depressive symptoms have not emerged as a significant predictor of future eating pathology (e.g., Keel et al., 1997; Vogeltanz-Holm et al., 2000), suggesting that negative emotionality, rather than depressive symptoms, may play a more important role in the development of eating pathology.

Furthermore, experimentally induced negative affect has been found to trigger increased food consumption among dieters (Baucom & Aiken, 1981; Cools, Schotte, & McNally, 1992; Polivy, Herman, & McFarlane, 1994; Ruderman, 1985; Schotte, Cools, & McNally, 1990) but not among nondieters. However, other researchers have failed to find an effect of negative affect indication on caloric intake among dieters or nondieters (Lowe & Maycock, 1988) or among binge-eating-disordered women or overweight women (Telch & Agras, 1996a). Only one negative affect experiment investigates actual binge eating as an outcome. Agras and Telch (1998) found that a negative affect induction resulted in elevated rates of binge eating among a sample of binge-eating-disordered women. Collectively, findings provide tentative support for the conclusion that negative affect is a causal risk factor for binge eating. Yet the fact that several studies report null findings suggests that the relation between negative affect and eating pathology is not large. Moreover, there was some indication that dieting behaviors and eating-disorder status moderate the effects of negative affect.

Perfectionism

Various theorists have proposed that perfectionism is a risk factor for the development of eating pathology (e.g., Joiner, Heatherton, Rudd, & Schmidt, 1997). In one study, perfectionism was found to predict the onset of bulimic pathology (Killen et al., 1994). However, in other prospective studies, researchers have failed to find support for this relation (Leon et al., 1995; Vohs, Bardone, Joiner, Abramson, & Heatherton, 1999), and in one longitudinal study perfectionism was found to correlate negatively with future eating pathology (Calam & Waller, 1998). Thus, there is only modest support for the assertion that perfectionism is a risk factor for eating pathology. However, as discussed below, there is emerging evidence that perfectionism may interact with other risk factors to predict growth in eating disturbances.

Timing of Puberty

It has been suggested that because puberty results in an increase in adipose tissue for girls, it contributes to the risk for eating pathology (Killen et al., 1992). In support of this, early menarche was positively correlated with body dissatisfaction and eating pathology (Graber, Lewinsohn, Seeley, & Brooks-Gunn, 1997; Killen et al., 1992; Swarr & Richards, 1996) and predicted subsequent eating pathology (Field et al., 1999; Hayward et al., 1997). However, in other studies, researchers failed to find a significant prospective relation between early menarche and subsequent eating pathology (Attie & Brooks-Gunn, 1989; Cattarin & Thompson, 1994; Graber et al., 1994; Keel et al., 1997; Killen et al., 1994; Leon et al., 1995; Smolak, Levine, & Gralen, 1993). This pattern of findings collectively suggests that early menarche is not a consistent or potent risk factor for eating pathology. Perhaps it is deviance from weight norms during a crucial developmental period (early adolescence) that is important. Alternatively, it might be the relative weight gain from prepubertal levels that places certain youth at risk. Finally, as discussed below, early puberty may have to coincide with other stressful life transitions to produce eating pathology (Smolak & Levine, 1996). It would be useful if in future prospective studies researchers would investigate these possible explanations in greater detail.

Externalizing Behaviors

Some researchers have suggested that eating pathology is rooted in poor impulse control (Strober, 1984). Although there is no evidence from the prospective studies reviewed here that impulsivity predicts subsequent eating pathology, aggression, alcohol use, and illicit substance use predict bulimic pathology onset (Killen et al., 1994, 1996; Vogeltanz-Holm et al., 2000). The mechanism of this effect is open to speculation, but elevated aggression and substance use may reflect behavioral impulsivity, which increases the risk for binge-eating onset. In general, there might be some other shared nonspecific risk factor for externalizing problems and eating pathology (i.e., aggression and alcohol use are proxy risk factors for eating pathology because they are correlated with other causal risk factors). Additional research is needed to more fully understand these relations.

Nonestablished Risk Factors for Eating Pathology

It also seems useful to review putative risk factors that have not received support in prospective studies. First, although investigators have suggested that self-esteem is a risk factor for eating pathology (e.g., Williamson et al., 1995), several prospective studies do not find significant relations between self-esteem and subsequent growth in eating pathology (Calam & Waller, 1998; Keel et al., 1997; Vohs et al., 1999). Again, however, there is some evidence that low self-esteem may interact with other risk factors to predict eating disturbances. Second, theorists have suggested that childhood sexual abuse is a risk factor for eating pathology (Fairburn et al., 1998). However, childhood sexual abuse has not emerged as a significant predictor of bulimic pathology in prospective research (Vogeltanz-Holm et al., 2000). Third, there has been speculation about the role of control issues, dysfunctional family systems, and deficits in parental affection in the genesis of eating pathology (Minuchin, Rosman, & Baker, 1978). However, there is no empirical support in the prospective or experimental studies for these assertions (Vogeltanz-Holm et al., 2000). Fourth, theorists have suggested that *interoceptive awareness*, the extent to which one is aware of one's internal experience, and feelings of ineffectiveness are risk factors for eating pathology (Garner, Olmsted, & Polivy, 1983). However, there have been inconsistent findings regarding these factors. For example, interoceptive awareness was negatively related to bulimic pathology onset (Killen et al., 1994) but positively related to increased eating disturbances (Leon et al., 1995). Similarly, ineffectiveness was positively related to bulimic pathology onset (Killen et al., 1996) but negatively related to increased eating pathology (Leon et al., 1995). This pattern of findings suggests the possibility that the effects were due to chance or unstable parameter estimates from models with too many variables. Unfortunately, these "clinical myths" are perpetuated, despite the lack of rigorous scientific evidence. This underscores the need to evaluate putative etiologic risk factors in methodologically sound studies.

Multivariate Models

Numerous multivariate etiologic models have been proposed that attempt to explain how the above risk factors work together to foster the development of eating pathology (Thompson et al., 1999). Some are *mediational*, in that they propose a developmental sequence that links the risk factors, whereas others are interactive in nature. Although many of these models are thoughtful integrations of the literature and theory, few have been tested in a prospective design that provides evidence of temporal precedence for each of the relations in these models. Indeed, this seems to represent one of the most significant gaps in this literature. In this section, I review selected multivariate etiologic models that offer an unique conceptual contribution to the understanding of the development of eating pathology, along with available empirical support from prospective or experimental studies.

Levine and Smolak (1992; Smolak & Levine, 1996) proposed a cumulative stressor model of eating disturbances. The model posits that three developmental features of adolescence—weight gain resulting from puberty, onset of dating, and intensification of academic demands—interact with a slender body ideal to predict the emergence of either nonpathological dieting or eating disturbances (Levine, Smolak, Moodey, Shuman, & Hessen, 1994). The confluence of two or more of these putative risk factors is thought to place unique stress on young girls in regard to body image, dieting, and eating-disordered attitudes (Smolak, Levine, & Gralen, 1993). This model is particularly novel because it incorporates a developmental perspective with attention to potentially important transitions faced by adolescent girls. A prospective test of aspects of this model indicated that girls who experienced the onset of both puberty and dating during the same year showed significantly more growth in body dissatisfaction and eating pathology than girls who did not experience these events simultaneously (Smolak et al., 1993). It is hoped that additional prospective studies will be used to investigate this promising model.

The spiral model of eating disorders also represents a conceptual contribution (Heatherton & Polivy, 1992). The unique feature of this model is that it recognizes the complex reciprocal relations that likely exist between the risk factors in an etiologic model and the evolution of these relations over time. Briefly, the spiral model proposes that body dissatisfaction and low self-esteem lead some individuals to initiate dieting. However, Heatherton and Polivy argued that most diets fail and that this results in a further worsening of self-esteem and general negative affect, which in turn increase the chances of future dietary efforts. They suggested that eventually individuals develop binge eating and begin using compensatory behaviors in an effort to prevent weight gain. Although this model has not been tested in a prospective study, there is longitudinal support for aspects of this model. Specifically, there is evidence that body dissatisfaction predicts increased dieting (Stice, in press; Stice, Mazotti, et al., 1998) and eating pathology (Attie & Brooks-Gunn, 1989; Graber et al., 1994; Killen et al., 1994, 1996; Stice, in press; Stice & Agras, 1998). There is also support for the assertion that dieting predicts onset of depression (Stice, Hayward, et al., 2000) and eating pathology (Killen et al., 1994, 1996; Patton et al., 1990; Stice & Agras, 1998; Stice, Killen, et al., 1998). Furthermore, negative affectivity and negative affect predict future bulimic pathology (Killen et al., 1996; Stice, in press; Stice & Agras, 1998). However, to date, there is no support for the hypothesized relation between self-esteem and the development of dieting or of the reciprocal relation of dieting to both self-esteem and affective disturbance. It is hoped that in future prospective studies, researchers will provide a comprehensive test of this interesting model.

Thompson et al. (1999) also proposed various etiologic models of the development of body image and eating disturbances. For example, they proposed that peer, parental, and media pressures to be thin result in social comparison processes and an internalization of the thin ideal, which all contribute to the development of body dissatisfaction. This body dissatisfaction in turn is thought to give rise to dieting and eventually bulimic pathology. The unique contribution of this model is that it integrates sociocultural factors with more proximal individual difference factors. Although aspects of this model have been supported (see above), it is hoped that the full model will be evaluated in a prospective study that permits a demonstration of the temporal precedence between the constituent factors.

Vohs et al. (1999) proposed that the confluence of perfectionism, body dissatisfaction, and low self-esteem promotes the development of bulimic pathology. They hypothesized that the combination of perfectionism and body dissatisfaction should result in effective weight-control techniques for individuals with high self-esteem but might lead to the development of bulimic pathology for those with low self-esteem. In one of the few prospective tests of an etiologic model, they found that the three-way interaction among these variables predicted change in bulimic symptoms over a 9-month period (Vohs et al., 1999). The interactive nature of this model represents a unique contribution in a field that has been primarily focused on main effects rather than mediation and moderation. Unfortunately, this three-way interactive model explains less than 1% of the variance in change in bulimic symptoms, which is not a substantively meaningful effect size. Thus, despite the novel interactive nature of this model, it is not able to explain the development of bulimic symptoms.

Another etiologic account that has been evaluated in prospective studies is the dual pathway model (Stice, in press). This account proposes that sociocultural pressure to be thin leads to an internalization of the thin ideal and consequent body dissatisfaction. This body dissatisfaction in turn theoretically fosters elevated dieting and negative affect, which in turn increase the risk for bulimic pathology. As such, this model can be considered a synthesis of the sociocultural (Striegel-Moore et al., 1986), dietary restraint (Polivy & Herman, 1985), and affect regulation (McCarthy, 1990) models of eating pathology. In two independent prospective studies, researchers have found that perceived pressure to be thin, thin-ideal internalization, body dissatisfaction, dieting, and negative affect predict the onset of bulimic pathology (Stice & Agras, 1998; Stice, Killen, et al., 1998). However, these researchers were unable to document temporal precedence for the hypothesized mediational relations among the risk factors. A technique for providing prospective tests of all of the linkages in a mediational model, using random regression growth curve models with time-varying covariates, was recently developed and used to evaluate this model (Stice, in press). Initial pressure to be thin and thin-ideal internalization predicted subsequent increases in body dissatisfaction, initial body dissatisfaction predicted increases in dieting and negative affect, and initial dieting and negative affect predicted increases in bulimic symptoms. There was also prospective evidence for nearly all of the hypothesized mediational relations. Although this new analytic technique is more rigorous than other analytic techniques that have been used to test mediational models (e.g., structural equation modeling), a few shortcomings of this strategy still need to be solved. Specifically, this technique does not currently provide a test of the temporal sequencing of change implied by mediational models (i.e., whether the change in the mediator temporally precedes the change in the outcome).

LIMITATIONS OF THE LITERATURE

Methodological

Advances in the understanding of the etiologic processes that give rise to eating pathology have been impeded by the methodological limitations of the risk factor literature. First, the overreliance on cross-sectional designs may be the most important methodological problem. Cross-sectional designs do not permit inferences regarding the nature of the correlations observed. There is no way to differentiate risk factors from concomitants or consequences of eating disorder with such designs. Although cross-sectional studies might arguably have a role in the early phases of exploring whether a variable is related to eating pathology, the vast majority of eating-disorder studies are cross-sectional and therefore do little to advance knowledge. If researchers are going to make more significant headway toward understanding the etiology of eating pathology, more energy will need to be focused on longitudinal studies, randomized experiments with external validity, and strong inference approaches that pit theories against each other. Ideally, such longitudinal studies should involve more than two assessments because the reliability with which one can measure change improves with additional waves of data. Although it may initially appear challenging to use randomized experiments to test etiologic hypotheses, creative applications are possible. For example, Lowe (1992) examined the effects of randomizing dieters to continue or discontinue their dieting. Randomized prevention trials can also be used to reduce one suspected risk factor and assess the effects on change in subsequent eating pathology (Stice, Mazotti, et al., 2000). Strong experimental designs hold the promise of significantly advancing the understanding of etiologic processes because it is possible to rule out third-variable explanations of the effects. Top priority should be given to ecological experiments conducted in the real world because there is always concern that laboratory-based experiments may not generalize. Although prospective and experimental studies are more difficult to conduct, the exponential increase in inferential power make the effort worth the cost.

Second, although numerous multivariate etiologic models have been proposed, most have not been evaluated in rigorous empirical studies. Similarly, there have been relatively few strong tests of mediational and moderational relations among the putative risk factors for eating pathology. There are many proponents of structural equation modeling, yet most applications are cross-sectional and, as such, do not permit inferences regarding the nature of the relations among the variables. There is nothing causal about this type of statistical technique because inferential power is a function of design, not analysis. It is hoped that future research will use more powerful prospective designs that permit a test of all of the linkages in multivariate etiologic models.

On a related note, the meaning behind the correlations among risk factors should be handled thoughtfully. Investigators sometimes dismiss the importance of risk factors that do not show significant unique relations to future eating pathology in multivariate models, even though these same factors show significant bivariate relations. The correlations between risk factors may occur for vastly different reasons. On the one hand, the risk factors may be correlated simply because they assess the same construct or share method or reporter bias. On the other hand, it is possible that the risk factors are correlated because they are related to the outcome in a complex mediational relation. These different possibilities should be explored carefully in prospective studies.

Third, the overreliance on monomethod and monoreporter data represents another limitation. The majority of studies rely on self-report questionnaire data, although some use self-report data from interviews. Increased use of collateral reporters, observational data, and biological measures could significantly advance the understanding of the etiology of eating pathology. As an illustration, it was long accepted that obese individuals do not consume more food than nonobese individuals based on self-report data. The acceptance of this finding by the scientific community stymied the understanding of the etiology of obesity for decades. However, this position was challenged with the advent of objective strategies of assessing caloric intake. Studies with "doubly labeled water" (Schoeller, 1988), an isotope-based technique that accurately measures 24-hour energy expenditure, show that obese individuals vastly underreport their caloric consumption. For example, Prentice et al. (1986) found underreporting rates of caloric intake of 2% for lean participants and 33% for obese participants. Lichtman et al. (1992) found that a group of self-reported "diet-resistant" patients, who claimed they could not lose weight on very-low-caloric diets, underestimated their energy intake by almost 50%. Thus, it is hoped that future studies will make greater use of multimethod and multireporter data.

Fourth, many etiologic studies use developmentally inappropriate samples. For example, it is common to test etiologic hypotheses with college student samples. However, as this developmental period occurs after the peak risk for the onset of eating pathology, such samples are likely to tell the clinical and research community little about the etiology of eating problems. In longitudinal studies, researchers should attempt to span the developmental period during which eating problems emerge (or other outcome of interest). Prospective studies suggest that the peak risk for onset of binge eating and compensatory behaviors occurs between 16 and 18 years of age (Stice, Killen, et al., 1998). However, the belief that etiologic studies need to use preadolescent samples may be unfounded. There is currently little evidence of eating pathology before age 12 (Keel et al., 1997). That the test–retest correlations for eating pathology measures across time are high during adolescence (e.g., Leon et al., 1995) should not be interpreted as indicating that the frequency of these behaviors remains constant. One can have equivalent test–retest correlations when the average frequency is increasing, decreasing, or remaining stable (test–retest correlations largely reflect the consistency of rank ordering over time). Additional research should be directed at understanding the timing of the emergence of eating pathology, so that etiologic (and prevention) studies can target the appropriate age group.

Numerous other methodological issues deserve note. Greater attention should be paid to the magnitude of effects (potency). Accordingly, researchers should routinely report the percentage of variance explained or the relevant index of potency (e.g., odds ratio). In addition, some studies do not use validated measures of eating pathology that have been shown to assess clinically meaningful levels of eating disturbances. Finally, because most etiologic studies focus on predicting bulimic pathology, relatively little is known about the etiology of anorexia nervosa and binge-eating disorder. Given the low base rate of anorexia nervosa, it might be useful for future studies to use high-risk samples (e.g., children of parents with an eating disorder).

Theoretical

Theoretical concerns were also raised by this literature review. Perhaps most important, the experimental evidence that low-calorie diets result in decreased binge eating (e.g., Wadden et al., 1994; Yanovski & Sebring,

1994) is problematic for restraint theory and most of the other etiologic models discussed above. Similarly, the evidence that when obese individuals are randomized to low-calorie diets, versus a no-dieting wait-list condition, they lose weight (Dahlkoetter, Callahan, & Linton, 1979; Epstein, Wing, Koeske, & Valoski, 1984) also directly challenges restraint theory. Future research is needed to explain how dieting can predict the onset of binge eating in prospective studies (e.g., Stice, Killen, et al., 1998) yet result in decreased binge eating and food intake in randomized experiments. As indicated above, it may be that a tendency toward overconsumption causes both dieting and eventual onset of binge eating and thus operates as a third variable that explains the prospective relation between dieting and binge eating. Only a randomized experiment that manipulates dieting in the natural environment and follows participants over time can answer this question. Alternatively, it may be that dieting has different effects for normal weight versus overweight people; one consistent difference between the two sets of studies is that the randomized trials involved overweight individuals and the longitudinal studies used normative samples. This explanation could be tested by an attempt to replicate the effects of the low-calorie diet intervention used in obesity treatment trials with normal weight individuals. A third possible explanation for the inconsistent findings is that going off (rather than on) a diet is the catalyst for increased binge eating. A prospective study in which researchers follow participants who are randomly assigned to different length diets could be used to evaluate this explanation.

The finding that emotional state, rather than the amount of calories consumed, determines whether an individual labels an eating episode as an uncontrollable binge or just overeating (Agras & Telch, 1998) is also theoretically problematic. The evidence that an experimentally based mood manipulation explains more variance in the labeling of a binge than does caloric intake casts doubt on the diagnostic enterprise. Additional research on how to better operationalize binge eating is desperately needed.

There is also a need for a renewed exploration of the factors that moderate the effects of risk factors. Although there have been useful starts in this direction, more attention needs to be directed at an understanding of the factors that mitigate and potentiate the effects of the established risk factors (e.g., body dissatisfaction, dieting, negative affect). However, because moderational effects are particularly difficult to detect statistically in field research, such studies should use larger samples, optimally reliable measurement, and more sensitive analytic approaches.

More theoretical attention should be directed at uncovering new putative risk factors. Even models that include most of the established risk factors only explain a small amount of variance in the development of eating pathology. Potentially promising variables include social support, interpersonal disruptions, feeding avidity, and expectations regarding the effects of eating on mood (e.g., Hohlstein, Smith, & Atlas, 1998), although there are sure to be others.

It would be useful to direct more theoretical attention to the factors that serve to maintain eating pathology (cf. Fairburn, 1997). Binge eating and purging set in motion a powerfully self-perpetuating combination of behaviors, but other factors probably contribute to the maintenance of this cycle (e.g., weight and shape concerns).

SUMMARY AND DIRECTIONS FOR FUTURE RESEARCH

It is hoped that there will be a paradigm shift in the eating-disorder literature, resulting in an increased use of strong inference designs. The widespread use of prospective and experimental studies would greatly advance the understanding of the etiology of eating disorders. These longitudinal studies could be used to provide more rigorous tests of the promising multivariate etiologic models that have been proposed in the literature. Such studies should use multiple reporters and multiple methods in data collection, particularly those that are less subject to distortion. Etiologic studies should also use developmentally appropriate samples that capture the etiologic processes as they unfold.

The following systematic approach to empirically investigate theoretically derived risk factors for eating disorders is offered in the hope that it might promote more rigorous programatic research in this area. The first step would be to establish that there is a correlation between a putative risk factor and eating pathology because one would not want to conduct more costly longitudinal or experimental studies unless this correlation was documented. The second step would be to demonstrate that the putative risk factor predicts future eating pathology in a prospective study. The third step would be to explore the ways that risk factors work together to promote eating pathology, including mediation and moderational relations, with prospective data, so that the temporal precedence of the hypothesized mediational chain could be established. It is important to note, however, that a moderator does not have to show a significant relation to the criterion variable to qualify the direction and strength of the relation between another risk factor and the outcome. The fourth step would be to conduct a randomized laboratory experiment that can assess the nature of the relations with precise experimental control. The fifth step would be to conduct an ecological experiment that reduces the putative risk factor and assesses whether there is a consequent change in the outcome (e.g., with a randomized prevention trial). This experiment would permit the strongest inferences regarding the causal effects of the risk factor. Collectively such a set of studies would definitely establish the nature of the relation between the risk factor and the development of eating pathology.

It is also hoped that there will be a shift away from an exclusive focus on theory confirmation, so that findings that are inconsistent with a model can be openly considered and used to improve the theory (e.g., the experimental evidence that dieting decreases binge eating). Unfortunately, it is all too easy to become wedded to a theory, which makes it difficult to objectively consider incompatible findings. There is also a pressing need to identify new risk factors, mediators, and moderators because the most inclusive models still only explain a small portion of the variance in eating pathology.

REFERENCES

Agras, W. S., & Telch, C. F. (1998). The effects of caloric deprivation and negative affect on binge eating in obese binge-eating disordered women. *Behavior Therapy, 29,* 491–503.

Attie, I., & Brooks-Gunn, J. (1989). Development of eating problems in adolescent girls: A longitudinal study. *Developmental Psychology, 25,* 70–79.

Baucom, D. H., & Aiken, P. A. (1981). Effect of depressed mood on eating among nonobese dieting and nondieting persons. *Journal of Personality and Social Psychology, 41,* 577–585.

Calam, R., & Waller, G. (1998). Are eating and psychosocial characteristics in early teenage years useful predictors of eating characteristics in early adulthood? *International Journal of Eating Disorders, 24,* 351–362.

Cattarin, J. A., & Thompson, J. K. (1994). A three-year longitudinal study of body image, eating disturbance, and general psychological functioning in adolescent females. *Eating Disorders, 2,* 114–125.

Cools, J., Schotte, D. E., & McNally, R. J. (1992). Emotional arousal and overeating in restrained eaters. *Journal of Abnormal Psychology, 101,* 348–351.

Dahlkoetter, J., Callahan, E. J., & Linton, J. (1979). Obesity and the unbalanced energy equation: Exercise versus eating habit change. *Journal of Consulting and Clinical Psychology, 47,* 898–905.

Epstein, L. H., Wing, R. R., Koeske, R., & Valoski, A. (1984). Effects of diet plus exercise on weight change in parents and children. *Journal of Consulting and Clinical Psychology, 52,* 429–437.

Fairburn, C. G. (1997). Eating disorders. In D. M. Clark & C. G. Fairburn (Eds.), *Science and practice of cognitive behaviour therapy* (pp. 209–241). Oxford, England: Oxford University Press.

Fairburn, C. G., Doll, H. A., Welch, S. L., Hay, P. J., Davies, B. A., & O'Connor, M. E. (1998). Risk factors for binge eating disorder: A community-based case-control study. *Archives of General Psychiatry, 55,* 425–432.

Fairburn, C. G., Norman, P. A., Welch, S. L., O'Connor, M. E., Doll, H. A., & Peveler, R. C. (1995). A prospective study of outcome in bulimia nervosa and the long-term effects of three psychological treatments. *Archives of General Psychiatry, 52,* 304–312.

Field, A. E., Camargo, C. A., Taylor, C. B., Berkey, C. S., & Colditz, G. A. (1999). Relation of peer and media influences to the development of purging behaviors among preadolescent and adolescent girls. *Archives of Pediatric Adolescent Medicine, 153,* 1184–1189.

French, S. A., Jeffery, R. W., & Wing, R. R. (1994). Food intake and physical activity: A comparison of three measures of dieting. *Addictive Behaviors, 19,* 401–409.

Garfinkel, P. E., & Garner, D. M. (1982). *Anorexia nervosa: A multidimensional perspective.* New York: Brunner/Mazel.

Garfinkel, P. E., Lin, E., Goering, P., Spegg, C., Goldbloom, D. S., Kennedy, S., Kaplan, A. S., & Woodside, D. B. (1995). Bulimia nervosa in a Canadian community sample: Prevalence and comparison of subgroups. *American Journal of Psychiatry, 152,* 1052–1058.

Garner, D. M., Olmsted, M. P., & Polivy, J. (1983). Development and validation of a multidimensional eating disorder inventory for anorexia nervosa and bulimia. *International Journal of Eating Disorders, 2,* 15–34.

Goodrick, G. K., Poston, W. S., Kimball, K. T., Reeves, R. S., & Foreyt, J. P. (1998). Nondieting versus dieting treatments for overweight binge-eating women. *Journal of Consulting and Clinical Psychology, 66,* 363–368.

Graber, J. A., Brooks-Gunn, J., Paikoff, R. L., & Warren, M. (1994). Prediction of eating problems: An 8-year study of adolescent girls. *Developmental Psychology, 30,* 823–834.

Graber, J. A., Lewinsohn, P. M., Seeley, M. S., & Brooks-Gunn, J. (1997). Is psychopathology associated with the timing of pubertal development? *Journal of the American Academy of Child and Adolescent Psychiatry, 36,* 1768–1776.

Hayward, C., Killen, J. D., Wilson, D. M., Hammer, L. D., Litt, I. F., Kraemer, H. C., Haydel, K. F., Varady, A., & Taylor, C. B. (1997). Psychiatric risk associated with early puberty in adolescent girls. *Journal of the American Academy of Child and Adolescent Psychiatry, 36,* 255–262.

Heatherton, T. F., & Polivy, J. (1992). Chronic dieting and eating disorders: A spiral model. In J. H. Crowther, D. L. Tennenbaum, S. E. Hobfold, & M. A. Parris-Stephens (Eds.), *The etiology of bulimia nervosa: The individual and familial context* (pp. 133–155). Washington, DC: Hemisphere.

Heinberg, L. J., & Thompson, J. K. (1995). Body image and televised images of thinness and attractiveness: A controlled laboratory investigation. *Journal of Social and Clinical Psychology, 14,* 325–338.

Henry, B., Moffitt, T. E., Caspi, A., Langley, J., & Silva, P. A. (1994). On the "remembrance of things past": A longitudinal evaluation of the retrospective method. *Psychological Assessment, 6,* 92–101.

Hohlstein, L. A., Smith, G. T., & Atlas, J. G. (1998). An application of expectancy theory to eating disorders: Development and validation of measures of eating and dieting expectancies. *Psychological Assessment, 10,* 49–58.

Irving, L. M. (1990). Mirror images: Effects of the standard of beauty on the self- and body-esteem of women exhibiting varying levels of bulimic symptoms. *Journal of Social and Clinical Psychology, 9,* 230–242.

Joiner, T. E., Heatherton, T. F., & Keel, P. K. (1997). Ten-year stability and predictive validity of five bulimia-related indicators. *American Journal of Psychiatry, 154,* 1133–1138.

Joiner, T. E., Heatherton, T. F., Rudd, M. D., & Schmidt, N. (1997). Perfectionism, perceived weight status, and bulimic symptoms: Two studies testing a diathesis–stress model. *Journal of Abnormal Psychology, 106,* 145–153.

Keel, P. K., Fulkerson, J. A., & Leon, G. R. (1997). Disordered eating precursors in pre- and early adolescent girls and boys. *Journal of Youth and Adolescence, 26,* 203–216.

Keller, M. B., Herzog, D. B., Lavori, P. W., Bradburn, I. S., & Mahoney, E. M. (1992). The natural history of bulimia nervosa: Extraordinarily high rates of chronicity, relapse, recurrence, and psychosocial morbidity. *International Journal of Eating Disorders, 12,* 1–9.

Kendler, K. S., MacLean, C., Neale, M., Kessler, R., Heath, A., & Eaves, L. (1991). The genetic epidemiology of bulimia nervosa. *American Journal of Psychiatry, 148,* 1627–1637.

Killen, J. D., Hayward, C., Litt, I., Hammer, L. D., Wilson, D. M., Miner, B., Taylor, C. B., Varady, A., & Shisslak, C. (1992). Is puberty a risk factor for eating disorders? *American Journal of Diseases of Children, 146,* 323–325.

Killen, J. D., Taylor, C. B., Hayward, C., Wilson, D., Haydel, K., Hammer, L., Simmonds, B., Robinson, T., Litt, I., Varady, A., & Kraemer, H. (1994). Pursuit of thinness and onset of eating disorder symptoms in a community sample of adolescent girls: A three-year prospective analysis. *International Journal of Eating Disorders, 16,* 227–238.

Killen, J. D., Taylor, C. B., Hayward, C., Haydel, K. F., Wilson, D. M., Hammer, L., Kraemer, H., Blair-Greiner, A., & Strachowski, D. (1996). Weight concerns influence the development of eating disorders: A 4-year prospective study. *Journal of Consulting and Clinical Psychology, 64,* 936–940.

Klesges, R. C., Isbell, T. R., & Klesges, L. M. (1992). Relationship between restraint, energy intake, physical activity, and body weight: A prospective analysis. *Journal of Abnormal Psychology, 101,* 668–674.

Kraemer, H. C., Kazdin, A. E., Offord, D. R., Kessler, R. C., Jensen, P. S., & Kupfer, D. J. (1997). Coming to terms with the terms of risk. *Archives of General Psychiatry, 54,* 337–343.

Kraemer, H. C., Stice, E., Kazdin, A., Offord, D., & Kupfer, D. (in press). How do risk factors work? Mediators, moderators, independent, overlapping, and proxy risk factors. *American Journal of Psychiatry.*

Leon, G. R., Fulkerson, J. A., Perry, C. L., & Early-Zald, M. B. (1995). Prospective analysis of personality and behavioral vulnerabilities and gender influences in the later development of disordered eating. *Journal of Abnormal Psychology, 104*, 140–149.

Levine, M. P., & Smolak, L. (1992). Toward a model of the developmental psychopathology of eating disorders: The example of early adolescence. In J. Crowther, D. Tennenbaum, S. Hoboll, & M. Stephens (Eds.), *The etiology of bulimia nervosa: The individual and familial context* (pp. 59–80). Washington, DC: Hemisphere.

Levine, M. P., & Smolak, L. (1996). Media as a context for the development of disordered eating. In L. Smolak, M. P. Levine, & R. Striegel-Moore (Eds.), *The developmental psychopathology of eating disorders* (pp. 235–257). Mahwah, NJ: Erlbaum.

Levine, M. P., Smolak, L., Moodey, A. F., Shuman, M. D., & Hessen, L. D. (1994). Normative developmental challenges and dieting and eating disturbances in middle school girls. *International Journal of Eating Disorders, 15*, 11–20.

Lichtman, S. W., Pisarska, K., Berman, E. R., Pestone, M., Dowling, H., Offenbacher, E., Weisel, H., Heshka, S., Matthews, D. E., & Heymsfield, S. B. (1992). Discrepancy between self-reported and actual caloric intake and exercise in obese subjects. *New England Journal of Medicine, 327*, 1893–1898.

Lowe, M. (1992). Staying on versus going off a diet: Effects on eating in normal weight and overweight individuals. *International Journal of Eating Disorders, 12*, 417–424.

Lowe, M. (1994). Putting restrained and unrestrained nondieters on short-term diets: Effects on eating. *Addictive Behaviors, 19*, 349–356.

Lowe, M., & Maycock, B. (1988). Restraint, disinhibition, hunger and negative affect eating. *Addictive Behaviors, 13*, 369–377.

McCarthy, M. (1990). The thin ideal, depression, and eating disorders in women. *Behavioral Research and Therapy, 28*, 205–218.

Minuchin, S., Rosman, S. L., & Baker, L. (1978). *Psychosomatic families*. Cambridge, MA: Harvard University Press.

Newman, D. L., Moffitt, T. E., Caspi, A., Magdol, L., Silva, P. A., & Stanton, W. R. (1996). Psychiatric disorder in a birth cohort of young adults: Prevalence, comorbidity, clinical significance, and new case incidence from ages 11 to 21. *Journal of Consulting and Clinical Psychology, 64*, 552–562.

Ogden, J., & Mundray, K. (1998). The effect of the media on body satisfaction: The role of gender and size. *European Eating Disorders Review, 4*, 171–182.

Patton, G. C. (1988). The spectrum of eating disorder in adolescence. *Journal of Psychosomatic Research, 32*, 579–584.

Patton, G. C., Johnson-Sabine, E., Wood, K., Mann, A. H., & Wakeling, A. (1990). Abnormal eating attitudes in London schoolgirls—A prospective epidemiological study: Outcome at twelve month follow-up. *Psychological Medicine, 20*, 383–394.

Polivy, J., & Herman, C. P. (1985). Dieting and binge eating: A causal analysis. *American Psychologist, 40,* 193–204.

Polivy, J., Herman, C. P., & McFarlane, T. (1994). Effects of anxiety on eating: Does palatability moderate distress-induced overeating in dieters? *Journal of Abnormal Psychology, 103,* 505–510.

Posavac, H. D., Posavac, S. S., & Posavac, E. J. (1998). Exposure to media images of female attractiveness and concern with body weight among young women. *Sex Roles, 38,* 187–201.

Prentice, A. M., Black, A. E., Coward, W. A., Davies, H. L., Goldberg, G. R., Murgatroyd, P. R., Ashford, J., Sawyer, M., & Whitehead, R. G. (1986). High levels of energy expenditure in obese women. *British Medical Journal, 292,* 983–987.

Richins, M. L. (1991). Social comparison and the idealized images of advertising. *Journal of Consumer Research, 18,* 71–83.

Ruderman, A. J. (1985). Dysphoric mood and overeating: A test of restraint theory's disinhibition hypothesis. *Journal of Abnormal Psychology, 94,* 78–85.

Santonastaso, P., Friederici, S., & Favaro, A. (1999). Full and partial syndromes in eating disorders: A 1-year prospective study of risk factors among female students. *Psychopathology, 32,* 50–56.

Schoeller, D. A. (1988). Measurement of energy expenditure in free-living humans by using doubly labeled water. *Journal of Nutrition, 118,* 1278–1289.

Schotte, D. E., Cools, J., & McNally, R. J. (1990). Film-induced negative affect triggers overeating in restrained eaters. *Journal of Abnormal Psychology, 99,* 317–320.

Smolak, L., & Levine, M. P. (1996). Adolescent transitions and the development of eating problems. In L. Smolak, M. P. Levine, & R. Striegel-Moore (Eds.), *The developmental psychopathology of eating disorders* (pp. 207–234). Mahwah, NJ: Erlbaum.

Smolak, L., Levine, M. P., & Gralen, S. (1993). The impact of puberty and dating on eating problems among middle school girls. *Journal of Youth and Adolescence, 22,* 355–368.

Stice, E. (in press). A prospective test of the dual pathway model of bulimic pathology: Mediating effects of dieting and negative affect. *Journal of Abnormal Psychology.*

Stice, E., & Agras, W. S. (1998). Predicting onset and cessation of bulimic behaviors during adolescence: A longitudinal grouping analyses. *Behavior Therapy, 29,* 257–276.

Stice, E., Cameron, R., Killen, J. D., Hayward, C., & Taylor, C. B. (1999). Naturalistic weight reduction efforts prospectively predict growth in relative weight and onset of obesity among female adolescents. *Journal of Consulting and Clinical Psychology, 67,* 967–974.

Stice, E., Chase, A., Stormer, S., & Appel, A. (in press). A randomized trial of a dissonance-based eating disorder prevention program. *International Journal of Eating Disorders.*

Stice, E., Hayward, C., Cameron, R., Killen, J. D., & Taylor, C. B. (2000). Body image and eating related factors predict onset of depression in female adolescents: A longitudinal study. *Journal of Abnormal Psychology, 109,* 438–444.

Stice, E., Killen, J. D., Hayward, C., & Taylor, C. B. (1998). Age of onset for binge eating and purging during adolescence: A four-year survival analysis. *Journal of Abnormal Psychology, 107,* 671–675.

Stice, E., Mazotti, L., Krebs, M., & Martin, S. (1998). Predictors of adolescent dieting behaviors: A longitudinal study. *Psychology of Addictive Behaviors, 12,* 195–205.

Stice, E., Mazotti, L., Weibel, D., & Agras, W. S. (2000). Dissonance prevention program decreases thin-ideal internalization, body dissatisfaction, dieting, negative affect, and bulimic symptoms: A preliminary experiment. *International Journal of Eating Disorders, 27,* 206–217.

Stice, E., & Shaw, H. (1994). Adverse effects of the media portrayed thin-ideal on women, and linkages to bulimic symptomatology. *Journal of Social and Clinical Psychology, 13,* 288–308.

Stice, E., Spangler, D., & Agras, W. S. (in press). Exposure to media-portrayed thin-ideal images adversely affects vulnerable girls: A longitudinal experiment. *Journal of Social and Clinical Psychology.*

Striegel-Moore, R. H., Silberstein, L. R., & Rodin, J. (1986). Toward an understanding of risk factors for bulimia. *American Psychologist, 41,* 246–263.

Strober, M. (1984). Stressful life events associated with bulimia in anorexia nervosa. *International Journal of Eating Disorders, 3,* 1–6.

Swarr, A. E., & Richards, M. H. (1996). Longitudinal effects of adolescent girls' pubertal development, perceptions of pubertal timing, and parental relations on eating problems. *Developmental Psychology, 32,* 636–646.

Telch, C. F., & Agras, W. S. (1993). The effects of a very low calorie diet on binge eating. *Behavior Therapy, 24,* 177–193.

Telch, C. F., & Agras, W. S. (1996a). Do emotional states influence binge eating in the obese? *International Journal of Eating Disorders, 20,* 271–279.

Telch, C. F., & Agras, W. S. (1996b). The effects of short-term food deprivation on caloric intake in eating disordered subjects. *Appetite, 26,* 221–234.

Thompson, J. K., Heinberg, L. J., Altabe, M., & Tantleff-Dunn, S. (1999). Future directions: Integrative theories, multidimensional assessments, and multicomponent interventions. In *Exacting beauty: Theory, assessment, and treatment of body image disturbance* (pp. 311–326). Washington, DC: American Psychological Association.

Vogeltanz-Holm, N. D., Wonderlich, S. A., Lewis, B. A., Wilsnack, S. C., Harris, T. R., Wilsnack, R. W., & Kristjanson, A. F. (2000). Longitudinal predictors of binge eating, intense dieting, and weight concerns in a national sample of women. *Behavior Therapy, 31,* 221–235.

Vohs, K. D., Bardone, A. M., Joiner, T. E., Abramson, L. Y., & Heatherton, T. F. (1999). Perfectionism, perceived weight status, and self-esteem interact to predict bulimic symptoms: A model of bulimic symptom development. *Journal of Abnormal Psychology, 108,* 695–700.

Wadden, T. A., Foster, G. D., & Letizia, K. A. (1994). One-year behavioral treatment of obesity: Comparison of moderate and severe caloric restriction and the effects of weight maintenance therapy. *Journal of Consulting and Clinical Psychology, 62,* 165–171.

Whitaker, A., Johnson, J., Shaffer, D., Rapoport, J. L., Kalikow, K., Walsh, B. T., Davies, M., Braiman, S., & Dolinsky, A. (1990). Uncommon troubles in young people: Prevalence estimates of selected psychiatric disorders in a nonreferred adolescent population. *Archives of General Psychiatry, 47,* 487–496.

Williamson, D. A., Netermeyer, R. G., Jackman, L. P., Anderson, D. A., Funsch, C. L., & Rabalais, J. Y. (1995). Structural equation modeling of risk factors for the development of eating disorders symptoms in female athletes. *International Journal of Eating Disorders, 17,* 387–393.

Yanovski, S. Z., & Sebring, N. G. (1994). Recorded food intake of obese women with binge eating disorder before and after weight loss. *International Journal of Eating Disorders, 15,* 135–150.

4

PROTECTIVE FACTORS IN THE DEVELOPMENT OF EATING DISORDERS

MARJORIE CRAGO, CATHERINE M. SHISSLAK,
AND ANNE RUBLE

Protective factors have been defined as those factors that "modify, ameliorate, or alter a person's response to some environmental hazard that predisposes to a maladaptive outcome" (Rutter, 1985, p. 600). There are three general categories of protective factors: individual, family, and community. Protective factors (also sometimes referred to as processes or mechanisms) can be either biological or psychosocial in nature. Protective factors may function in a variety of ways: by decreasing dysfunction directly, interacting with a risk factor to disrupt its effects, disrupting the mediational chain through which the risk factor operates, or preventing the initial occurrence of the risk factor itself (Coie et al., 1993; Kazdin, Kraemer, Kessler, Kupfer, & Offord, 1997; Mrazek & Haggerty, 1994).

Both risk and protective factors may vary depending on whether the disorder is acute or chronic, pure or comorbid, partial or full syndrome, or a community or clinic case (Shisslak & Crago, in press). Some investigators have emphasized that whether a variable is categorized as a risk or protective factor depends on the context in which it occurs because the same variable may function as a risk factor in one situation and as a protective factor in another (Rutter, 1987). Although social support usually functions as a protective factor for various adolescent behavior problems, there are certain situations in which it may function as a risk factor, for example, when the subsystem providing the support is deviant (Buysse, 1997). Also high self-esteem, usually considered protective against a number of disorders, was found to increase rather than decrease the risk of sexually transmitted diseases in a sample of college students (Boney-McCoy, Gibbons, & Gerrard, 1999), and in another study, high self-esteem was found to be a risk factor for behavioral problems in aggressive boys (Hughes, Cavell, & Grossman, 1997). Some investigators have emphasized that age may determine whether a variable functions as a risk or protective factor. For example, marriage is a risk factor for suicide among adolescent girls but is a protective factor among adult women (Kraemer et al., 1997). As Rutter (1987, 1993) pointed out, many definitional problems about what constitutes a risk or protective factor can be avoided if one considers that it is the process or mechanism, not the variable, that determines the function. Thus, it is not enough to merely identify certain factors as having either risk or protective effects with regard to eating disorders. It is equally important to understand the underlying processes or mechanisms by which these factors operate and their relationship to other variables that may have mediating or moderating effects.

The purpose of this chapter is fourfold: (a) to provide a brief summary of general factors found to be protective against a number of emotional and behavioral problems, (b) to discuss these general protective factors in relation to the development of eating disorders, (c) to present a bioecological model that may prove helpful in future studies of protective factors for eating disorders, and (d) to emphasize the importance of including components based on protective factors in prevention programs for eating disorders.

GENERAL PROTECTIVE FACTORS AND RESILIENCE

A decade ago, Rodin, Striegel-Moore, and Silberstein (1990) noted that research on protective factors related to eating disorders was "virtually nonexistent." They suggested that eating disorder researchers might benefit from examining the work of Garmezy (1974) and others who were studying protective factors and resilience in relation to the development of various forms of psychopathology. As noted previously, one of the purposes of this chapter is to apply some of the findings from resilience research on general protective factors to research on protective factors for eating disorders. Both the Institute of Medicine (Mrazek & Haggerty, 1994) and a panel of mental health experts convened by the National Institute of Mental Health (Coie et al., 1993) have concluded that many risk and protective factors are not specific to a single disorder but are common to a number of disorders. These common or general protective factors have been widely studied in research on resilience. Resilience refers to the ability to recover from, or cope successfully with, significant stress or adversity. Whether an individual demonstrates resilience or pathology in response to a stressful situation is dependent on the balance of individual and environmental risk and protective factors operating in his or her life at that time.

Most studies of resilience have focused on children or adolescents living in high-risk environments, such as poverty, crime-ridden neighborhoods, or dysfunctional families. A number of researchers have found that individuals can adjust fairly well to one or two risk factors, but beyond that, the negative effects increase rapidly and the presence of protective factors that can help to buffer these risk mechanisms becomes crucial (Kumpfer, 1999). As Luthar (1993) and others have pointed out, resilience varies across domains, developmental stage, and context. In other words, individuals are not equally resilient at all ages and under all circumstances. Nevertheless, resilient individuals can "teach us better ways to reduce risk, promote competence, and shift the course of development in more positive directions" (Masten & Coatsworth, 1998, p. 205).

A number of general protective factors (individual, family, and community) that are common to a variety of emotional and behavioral problems have been identified in resilience research over the past 25 years (for recent reviews of this research, see Blum, 1998; Kumpfer, 1999; Masten & Coatsworth, 1998; Mrazek & Haggerty, 1994; Stewart, Reid, & Mangham, 1997). The following are some of the individual protective factors that have been identified in resilience research: above-average intelligence, internal locus of control, positive self-esteem, easygoing temperament, problem-solving abilities, social skills, optimism, academic competence, spirituality, and creativity. The family protective factors that have been identified include good relationship with parent or parents, rules and responsibilities within the household, supportive extended family network, prosocial family values, positive role models, and low family stress. Factors in the community that have been found to be protective include positive school experiences, peer friendship networks, responsibilities outside the home, participation in extracurricular activities, and positive relationships with adults outside the family.

Many of the resilience studies mentioned above were cross-sectional in nature, consisting of a comparison of the characteristics of resilient versus nonresilient children or adolescents living in high-risk environments. However, some investigators have conducted longitudinal studies of resilience ranging in length from 10 years (e.g., Masten et al., 1999) to as long as 40 years (e.g., Cederblad, Dahlin, Hagnell, & Hansson, 1994). In some studies, researchers followed a cohort of children from birth until the participants were in their 30s (Werner & Smith, 1992). A number of studies of protective factors and resilience have used individual interviews and large sample sizes. For example, in a study by Tiet et al. (1998), 1,285 children and adolescents between the ages of 9 and 17 and their caretakers were interviewed. Teit et al. found that the most significant protective factors against 30 psychiatric disorders (including eating disorders) were higher intelligence, better family functioning, and higher educational aspirations. Thus, research on general protective factors and resilience has been ongoing for at least 25 years and consists of a number of longitudinal as well as cross-sectional studies, with some studies being based on individual interviews with more than 12,000 adolescents (e.g., Resnick et al., 1997). Although not all of the general protective factors identified in resilience research may prove to protect against the development of eating disorders, this considerable body of research may be helpful to investigators as they begin to design studies for the purpose of identifying protective factors for eating disorders.

PROTECTIVE FACTORS AND EATING DISORDERS

In contrast to the amount of research that has been devoted to risk factors for eating disorders, little research has been focused on identifying protective factors for these disorders (Franko & Orosan-Weine, 1998; Rodin et al., 1990; Shisslak & Crago, in press). One factor for which there is some empirical evidence suggesting protective effects against the development of eating disorders is sports participation. Interestingly, sports participation can function as either a risk or protective factor, depending on certain aspects of the sport and the age of the participant, which is consistent with Rutter's (1987, 1993) contentions. In a meta-analysis of 34 studies of female athletic participation and eating problems, Smolak, Murnen, and Ruble (2000) found that female athletes participating in elite sports or in sports emphasizing thinness had an increased risk of eating problems, whereas participants in nonelite and nonlean sports, especially those in high school, appeared to have fewer eating problems than nonathlete controls. These findings suggest that sports participation can have protective effects, especially among high school girls.

Two recent studies that were not included in the meta-analysis by Smolak et al. (2000) provide further evidence for the protective effects of sports participation in both high school girls (Fulkerson, Keel, Leon, & Dorr, 1999) and college women (Zucker, Womble, Williamson, & Perrin, 1999). Fulkerson et al. (1999) found that female athletes had significantly higher levels of self-efficacy and a less negative view of life than female nonathletes, leading the authors to postulate that athletic participation may enhance self-efficacy and, thereby, serve as a protective factor against the development of eating disorders. Zucker et al. (1999) suggested that various aspects of the athletic environment may contribute to the protective effect of sports participation (e.g., the presence of supportive peer groups and an emphasis on the function and athletic prowess of the female body rather than its aesthetic qualities). Thus far, there have been no studies demonstrating that participation in other activities is protective against the development of eating problems. However, we are currently involved in conducting a 4-year prospective study of girls in Grades 4–12 in which both the risk and protective effects of participation in sports and other activities such as youth clubs, church groups, service organizations, and arts groups will be investigated.

In a study of African American college women, Griffith (1998) reported the following factors to be protective against disordered eating attitudes and behaviors: high self-esteem, assertiveness, having an Africentric world view, and being born in a small city. Griffith's findings regarding acculturation are consistent with previous research indicating that eating disorder risks are higher in African American women who are more acculturated, that is, who are identified with White, middle-class values (Crago, Shisslak, & Estes, 1996).

With regard to self-esteem, a number of cross-sectional studies have provided evidence that self-esteem is generally lower among individuals with eating problems (Shisslak & Crago, in press). However, only Button and his associates (Button, 1990; Button, Loan, Davies, Sonuga-Barke, 1997; Button, Sonuga-Barke, Davies, & Thompson, 1996) have conducted prospective studies in which low self-esteem in British schoolgirls ages 11–12 was predictive of higher levels of eating disturbances 4 years later. One might hypothesize from Button's findings that if low self-esteem is a risk factor for eating disturbances, then high self-esteem may have protective effects against the development of these problems. In addition, high self-esteem has been found to be a general protective factor against a number of other behavioral and emotional problems in the studies of resilience referred to previously.

Kazdin et al. (1997) stressed that it is important to demonstrate that both risk and protective factors precede the outcome of interest. If they do not, then it is more appropriate to refer to them as correlates, concomitants, or consequences of the disorder. Thus, cross-sectional research can provide hypotheses about factors that may protect against a particular disorder, but only longitudinal research can actually demonstrate the protective effects of a particular factor. With regard to life skills such as problem-solving abilities, social skills, and an optimistic attitude (which have been found to be protective factors in resilience research), there have been no longitudinal studies of the protective effects of these factors in relation to eating disorders. However, life skills training has been included in a number of eating disorder prevention programs. In a recent review of these programs, Levine and Piran (1999) reported that 85% of the programs that included a life skills training component were effective compared with a 56% effectiveness rate among those programs that did not include such a component. These findings suggest that life skills training may have protective effects against the development of eating disorders.

A MODEL FOR THE CONCEPTUALIZATION
OF A LIFE SKILLS TRAINING PROGRAM

It is important to design life skills programs that capture and strengthen as many protective factors as possible. A useful model for conceptualizing the relationship of protective factors to the individual and the environment is the bioecological model proposed by Bronfenbrenner and Ceci (1994). The bioecological model describes proximal processes, which can be described as the processes by which development is driven. Proximal processes are patterns of interaction between the person and his or her environment (Bronfenbrenner, 1995). According to the bioecological model, the individual is embedded in a transactional system consisting of individual genetic characteristics and traits (such as intelligence, easygoing temperament, innate athletic ability, and body type) and how these traits are translated into and affected by environmental factors (such as relationship with parents, school experiences, participation in activities, and peer networks). The environment also consists of factors in the greater community, two examples of which are attitudes toward different ethnic groups and media images.

With the realization that individuals differ in their innate talents and abilities as well as their ability to withstand stress, it is important to understand what circumstances allow positive characteristics to find expression (see Bronfenbrenner & Ceci, 1994, for further description). Bronfenbrenner (1995) stated that little is known about these processes and their effects because they have seldom been integrated into research models with concrete hypotheses and analytical models, which result in a number of different outcomes instead of one outcome variable. Proximal processes are empirically testable and may lead to various developmental outcomes, including

> stress and coping style, the acquisition of knowledge and/or skills, the establishment and maintenance of mutually rewarding relationships, the construction and modification of one's own physical, social, and symbolic environment, the direction and control of one's behavior, and the differentiation of perception and response. (Bronfenbrenner & Ceci, 1994, p. 569)

When these proximal processes are weak or absent, an individual's genetically based potential for healthy psychological functioning may remain unrealized. However, as proximal processes increase in magnitude, they become actualized to a greater extent in an additive effect.

The bioecological model asserts that a high level of heritability alone has no real meaning because it can be associated with both high or low levels of functioning depending on the relationships of people both within and between multiple environments (e.g., family, school, and community). Harter, Waters, and Whitesell (1998) described individuals' relational context as the idea that one's sense of worth may vary in different relationships. An important aspect of the bioecological model is its assertion that there is variation even in advantaged environments, which produces a range of positive outcomes. Therefore, life skills programs that bolster protective factors and reduce the risks associated with future stressors may have positive effects even for individuals who are healthy.

Bronfenbrenner and Ceci (1994) stated that the effect of increased levels of proximal processes is manifested in two ways: (a) If proximal processes are indeed mechanisms through which genetic traits are translated into their environmental expression, then increased levels of proximal processes (healthy interaction among the individual, parents, school environment, and community) should result in higher levels of transmission of positive traits; and (b) proximal processes foster the development of effective psychological functioning. Therefore, the interaction between individuals and their environments must be evaluated at all levels to maximize prevention of eating disorders. Researchers need to understand what processes facilitate protective factors such as high self-esteem, mastery, and resiliency to educate parents, teachers, and students to foster these processes in children and adolescents through formal prevention programs or informal individual interactions. Researchers should target their interventions and programs to include not only the individual child or adolescent but also family members, the school environment, peer relationships, and community attitudes such as media messages (Neumark-Sztainer, 1996).

Individual characteristics such as mastery are integral to the utilization of the bioecological model. Troop and Treasure (1997) examined whether helplessness and mastery functioned as risk or protective factors in the childhood of women with and without eating disorders. They found that there was a higher rate of childhood helplessness and a lower rate of childhood mastery in those participants with eating disorders as compared with those without. Thus, mastery experiences may function as protective factors for eating disorders, and methods for enhancing mastery could be incorporated in a life skills program to help ensure a healthy psychological self.

Researchers of the dimensions of social support have examined some of these processes that apply to the prevention of eating disorders and the promotion of protective factors. Stice (1998) found that family and peer modeling of abnormal eating behavior was associated with concurrent bulimic symptoms and predicted onset of bingeing and purging. Wentzel (1998) found that adolescents' supportive relationships with parents, teachers, and peers were related to their motivation at school and their academic goal orientations. Deihl, Vicary, and Deike (1997) found that individuals who were able to maintain positive self-esteem or who had achieved enhanced self-esteem over time had stronger protective variables of supportive peer and family relationships. Piran (1995) contended that prevention programs for eating disorders have not targeted the adults in the lives of children in a satisfactory manner. These individuals should be included in intervention efforts to foster the development of protective factors, which coincides with Bronfenbrenner's (1995) statement that providing parents with easily understood information about proximal processes may create opportunities for conducting further research on their nature, operation, and developmental effects (Piran, 1995).

The attitudes of the community at large, including the media, are also important aspects of the bioecological model. It has been suggested by Levine and Smolak (1996) that a high percentage of adolescent girls (up to 50%) read magazines such as *Seventeen* or *Vogue* on a regular basis and that it is highly likely that there may be a correlation between the reading of such magazines and negative body image and disordered eating. Neumark-Sztainer (1996) suggested that there should be changes in the media, including portrayal of a wider variety of body shapes and role expectations for both genders. Educating students and their families about how photographs of models are made, while emphasizing the unreality of those pictured, may encourage individuals to become more active in criticizing the media and may encourage portrayals of women and men of differing professions, sizes, shapes, and ethnic backgrounds (see also Levine & Piran, this volume, chapter 12).

Thus, the bioecological model may be useful to researchers in both designing life skills programs and future research studies that seek to identify protective factors for eating disorders. According to this model, it is important to address social skills and communication between individuals and their multiple environments, such as family, school, and community. Strengthening individuals' problem-solving skills could be used to address inconsistent and stereotypical messages in media and community attitudes. All of these components are necessary in the development of comprehensive prevention programs for eating disorders that focus on protective factors as well as risk factors.

PROTECTIVE FACTORS AND PREVENTION

One of the objectives of Healthy People 2010 is to develop prevention programs to reduce risk factors and increase protective factors for a variety of negative mental health outcomes in children and adolescents (U.S. Department of Health and Human Services, 1998). As the Institute of Medicine (Mrazek & Haggerty, 1994) and Coie et al. (1993) have pointed out, most risk and protective factors, other than genetic factors, are not specific to a single disorder. Targeting general risk and protective factors that are common to many disorders and dysfunctional states is likely to increase the success of preventive intervention programs as well as help to prevent multiple problems simultaneously (Coie et al., 1993; Durlak, 1998; Masten & Coatsworth, 1998; Mrazek & Haggerty, 1994).

The enhancement of protective factors may be the strategy of choice in cases in which risk factors are difficult to identify or cannot be eliminated entirely once they have been identified (Coie et al., 1993). Moreover, some investigators have suggested that protective factors may have a more profound impact on the lives of children and adolescents growing up under adverse circumstances compared with specific risk factors such as stressful life events (Werner & Johnson, 1999). One advantage of focusing on general protective factors such as life skills is that it should not be difficult to persuade parents, teachers, legislators, and the general public about the benefits of providing life skills training for children and adolescents, especially because this training may help to prevent a number of different problems rather than just eating disorders (Coie et al., 1993). Also, stigmatization of participants is likely to be much less than when the focus of the preventive intervention is on specific risk factors for eating disorders, such as excessive dieting or other unhealthy weight control behaviors.

Resilience is becoming an increasingly popular concept in the field of prevention, and a number of prevention programs aimed at enhancing resilience have been developed (for descriptions of some of these programs, see Blum, 1998; Masten & Coatsworth, 1998; Stewart et al., 1997). However, few of these programs have been subjected to rigorous empirical evaluations. In evaluating these programs, one must assess not only reductions in risk factors but also the degree of change in resilience and protective factors (Durlak, 1998; Kumpfer, 1999). Most longitudinal studies of resilience have focused on examining the characteristics of individuals who not only survived but thrived under adverse circumstances. When asked who had helped them to succeed against the odds, the majority of these resilient individuals gave overwhelming credit to members of their immediate and extended family, neighbors or teachers who functioned as role models for them, and leaders of youth or church groups who mentored them (Werner & Smith, 1992). Social support from this informal network was more highly valued by these individuals than the services of community organizers and mental health professionals. In accordance with these findings, we have emphasized the importance of incorporating mentors and role models in prevention programs for eating disorders (Shisslak, Crago, Renger, & Clark-Wagner, 1998). It should be noted that mentoring is an important part of an eating disorders prevention program currently being implemented by the Harvard Eating Disorders Center (Franko & Orosan-Weine, 1998).

CONCLUSION

There has been little research on protective factors for eating disorders, even though the Institute of Medicine (Mrazek & Haggerty, 1994) and various investigators (e.g., Rutter, 1987) have stressed the importance of incorporating both risk and protective factors in preventive interventions for all mental disorders. According to the Institute of Medicine (Mrazek & Haggerty, 1994, p. 192), "if the number of protective factors can be increased in the individual, family, and community, then resilience is likely to be increased and the disorder may be avoided."

Numerous studies of resilience have been conducted over the past 25 years that have identified a number of general factors found to be protective against the development of a variety of emotional and behavioral problems. It is our contention that eating disorder investigators could benefit from this research by using these findings as a place to begin when designing studies aimed at identifying protective factors for eating disorders. Existing studies of eating disorder risk and protective factors suggest that some of these general factors may indeed be protective against eating disorders as well as other psychological problems (e.g., high self-esteem, sports participation, life skills). However, much more research needs to be done to determine how many other general protective factors may be related to the development of eating disorders. It is also important to identify protective factors that may be specific to eating disorders, such as a positive body image or being a member of a family in which there is not an overemphasis on weight.

General protective factors are more likely to be beneficial in universal (primary) preventive interventions, whereas protective factors found to be specific to a particular disorder may be more appropriate for an indicated (secondary) preventive intervention. In recent meta-analyses of both primary and secondary prevention programs focused on a variety of social, emotional, and behavioral problems in children and adolescents, it was found that most of these programs produced outcomes that were comparable with, or better than, those resulting from established psychological and medical treatment interventions (Durlak & Wells, 1997, 1998). The majority of these programs significantly reduced problems or risk factors and significantly increased competencies (protective factors). It is encouraging to note that the likelihood of negative effects from both types of programs was very small. In a recent review of 31 prevention programs for eating disorders, Levine and Piran (1999) found that 20 of the programs (65%) resulted in a significant positive change in either attitudes or behaviors.

Given the recent controversy concerning the seemingly negative effects of several eating disorder prevention programs (Piran, 1998), it is important that future researchers give serious thought to the possible negative consequences of including components in a primary prevention program that would be more appropriate for a secondary prevention program. For example, symptom-specific education about different methods of purging may pose greater risks than benefits in a primary prevention program, especially in programs targeting younger girls, whereas program components involving protective factors such as self-esteem enhancement or life skills training are unlikely to have harmful effects. Mann et al. (1997) also cautioned that attempting to combine primary and secondary prevention of eating disorders in one program may not only decrease the effectiveness of the program but could also inadvertently promote eating disorder symptoms because the goals and strategies for each type of prevention are different and may oppose each other. In her guidelines for evaluating prevention programs, Piran (1998) emphasized the importance of identifying the goals of the program (primary, secondary, or tertiary prevention) and then examining how the program might best achieve these goals while, at the same time, minimizing the possibility of negative effects.

In this chapter, we have emphasized the importance of taking a holistic approach to prevention as exemplified by the bioecological model proposed by Bronfenbrenner and Ceci (1994), in which the focus is not just on the individual but on various aspects of the environment as well. Because many problems have the same or similar underlying causes, it may be more cost-effective to design prevention programs that are integrated, multifaceted, and aimed at preventing more than one problem rather than developing separate and narrowly focused programs for each problem (Bosworth, 1999). With the growing importance of research in developmental psychopathology and resilience, it seems likely that future preventive interventions for eating disorders will become increasingly multifaceted, targeting multiple risk and protective processes that involve multiple systems (individual, family, peers, school, community, culture). The challenge for future prevention researchers will be how to implement such multisystem programs but, at the same time, be able to evaluate the effectiveness of each of the components for the various systems being targeted.

REFERENCES

Blum, R. W. (1998). Healthy youth development as a model for youth health promotion: A review. *Journal of Adolescent Health, 22,* 368–375.

Boney-McCoy, S., Gibbons, F. X., & Gerrard, M. (1999). Self-esteem, compensatory self-enhancement, and the consideration of health risk. *Personality and Social Psychology Bulletin, 25,* 954–965.

Bosworth, K. (1999). *A vision of protective schools: Linking drug abuse prevention with student success.* Tucson: University of Arizona Press.

Bronfenbrenner, U. (1995). Developmental ecology through space and time: A future perspective. In P. Moen, G. H. Elder, & K. Luscher (Eds.), *Examining lives in context: Perspectives on the ecology of human development* (pp. 619–647). Washington, DC: American Psychological Association.

Bronfenbrenner, U., & Ceci, S. J. (1994). Nature–nurture reconceptualized in developmental perspective: A bioecological model. *Psychological Review, 101*, 568–586.

Button, E. (1990). Self-esteem in girls aged 11–12: Baseline findings from a planned prospective study of vulnerability to eating disorders. *Journal of Adolescence, 13*, 407–413.

Button, E. J., Loan, P., Davies, J., & Sonuga-Barke, E. J. S. (1997). Self-esteem, eating problems, and psychological well-being in a cohort of schoolgirls aged 15–16: A questionnaire and interview study. *International Journal of Eating Disorders, 21*, 39–47.

Button, E. J., Sonuga-Barke, E. J. S., Davies, J., & Thompson, M. (1996). A prospective study of self-esteem in the prediction of eating problems in adolescent schoolgirls: Questionnaire findings. *British Journal of Clinical Psychology, 35*, 193–203.

Buysse, W. H. (1997). Behaviour problems and relationships with family and peers during adolescence. *Journal of Adolescence, 20*, 645–659.

Cederblad, M., Dahlin, L., Hagnell, O., & Hansson, K. (1994). Salutogenic childhood factors reported by middle-aged individuals. *European Archives of Psychiatry and Clinical Neuroscience, 244*, 1–11.

Coie, J. D., Watt, N. F., West, S. G., Hawkins, J. D., Asarnow, J. R., Markman, H. J., Ramey, S. L., Shure, M. B., & Long, B. (1993). The science of prevention: A conceptual framework and some directions for a national research program. *American Psychologist, 48*, 1013–1022.

Crago, M., Shisslak, C. M., & Estes, L. S. (1996). Eating disturbances among American minority groups: A review. *International Journal of Eating Disorders, 19*, 239–248.

Deihl, L. M., Vicary, J. R., & Deike, R. C. (1997). Longitudinal trajectories of self-esteem from early to middle adolescence and related psychosocial variables among rural adolescents. *Journal of Research on Adolescence, 7*, 393–411.

Durlak, J. A. (1998). Common risk and protective factors in successful prevention programs. *American Journal of Orthopsychiatry, 68*, 512–520.

Durlak, J. A., & Wells, A. M. (1997). Primary prevention mental health programs for children and adolescents: A meta-analytic review. *American Journal of Community Psychology, 25*, 115–152.

Durlak, J. A., & Wells, A. M. (1998). Evaluation of indicated preventive intervention (secondary prevention) mental health programs for children and adolescents. *American Journal of Community Psychology, 25*, 775–802.

Franko, D. L., & Orosan-Weine, P. (1998). The prevention of eating disorders: Empirical, methodological, and conceptual considerations. *Clinical Psychology: Science and Practice, 5*, 459–477.

Fulkerson, J. A., Keel, P. K., Leon, G. R., & Dorr, T. (1999). Eating-disordered behaviors and personality characteristics of high school athletes and nonathletes. *International Journal of Eating Disorders, 26,* 73–79.

Garmezy, N. (1974). Children at risk: The search for antecedents of schizophrenia: I. Conceptual models and research methods. *Schizophrenia Bulletin, 8,* 14–90.

Griffith, J. R. (1998). Attitudes toward weight, shape, and eating in African-American college women: A cultural analysis. *Dissertations Abstracts International, 59,* 1367B.

Harter, S., Waters, P., & Whitesell, N. R. (1998). Relational self-worth: Differences in perceived worth as a person across interpersonal contexts among adolescents. *Child Development, 69,* 756–766.

Hughes, J. N., Cavell, T. A., & Grossman, P. B. (1997). A positive view of self: Risk or protection for aggressive children? *Development and Psychopathology, 9,* 75–94.

Kazdin, A. E., Kraemer, H. C., Kessler, R. C., Kupfer, D. J., & Offord, D. R. (1997). Contributions of risk-factor research to developmental psychopathology. *Clinical Psychology Review, 17,* 375–406.

Kraemer, H. C., Kazdin, A. E., Offord, D. R., Kessler, R. C., Jensen, P. S., & Kupfer, D. J. (1997). Coming to terms with the terms of risk. *Archives of General Psychiatry, 54,* 337–343.

Kumpfer, K. L. (1999). Factors and processes contributing to resilience. In M. D. Glantz & J. L. Johnson (Eds.), *Resilience and development* (pp. 179–224). New York: Plenum Press.

Levine, M., & Piran, N. (1999). *Approaches to health promotion in the prevention of eating disorders.* Unpublished manuscript, Kenyon College, Gambier, OH.

Levine, M. P., & Smolak, L. (1996). Media as a context for the development of disordered eating. In L. Smolak, M. P. Levine, & R. Striegel-Moore (Eds.), *The developmental psychopathology of eating disorders* (pp. 235–257). Mahwah, NJ: Erlbaum.

Luthar, S. S. (1993). Annotation: Methodological and conceptual issues in research on childhood resilience. *Journal of Child Psychology and Psychiatry, 34,* 441–453.

Mann, T., Nolen-Hoeksema, S., Huang, K., Burgard, D., Wright, A., & Hanson, K. (1997). Are two interventions worse than none? Joint primary and secondary prevention of eating disorders in college females. *Health Psychology, 16,* 215–225.

Masten, A. S., & Coatsworth, J. D. (1998). The development of competence in favorable and unfavorable environments. *American Psychologist, 53,* 205–220.

Masten, A. S., Hubbard, J. J., Gest, S. D., Tellegen, A., Garmezy, N., & Ramirez, M. (1999). Competence in the context of adversity: Pathways to resilience and maladaptation from childhood to late adolescence. *Development and Psychopathology, 11,* 143–169.

Mrazek, P. J., & Haggerty, R. J. (Eds.). (1994). *Reducing risks for mental disorders: Frontiers for preventive intervention research.* Washington, DC: National Academy Press.

Neumark-Sztainer, D. (1996). School-based programs for preventing eating disturbances. *Journal of School Health, 66,* 64–71.

Piran, N. (1995). Prevention: Can early lessons lead to a delineation of an alternative
model? A critical look at prevention with schoolchildren. *Eating Disorders:
Journal of Treatment and Prevention, 3,* 28–36.

Piran, N. (1998). Prevention of eating disorders: The struggle to chart new territo-
ries. *Eating Disorders: Journal of Treatment and Prevention, 6,* 365–371.

Resnick, M. D., Bearman, P. S., Blum, R. W., Bauman, K. E., Harris, K. M., Jones,
J., Tabor, J., Beuhring, T., Sieving, R. E., Shew, M., Ireland, M., Bearinger,
L. H., & Udry, J. R. (1997). Protecting adolescents from harm: Findings from
the National Longitudinal Study on Adolescent Health. *Journal of the American
Medical Association, 278,* 823–832.

Rodin, J., Striegel-Moore, R. H., & Silberstein, L. R. (1990). Vulnerability and
resilience in the age of eating disorders: Risk and protective factors for bulimia
nervosa. In J. Rolf, A. S. Masten, D. Cicchetti, K. H. Neuchterlein, & S.
Weintraub (Eds.), *Risk and protective factors in the development of psychopathology*
(pp. 361–383). New York: Cambridge University Press.

Rutter, M. (1985). Resilience in the face of adversity: Protective factors in resistance
to psychiatric disorders. *British Journal of Psychiatry, 147,* 598–611.

Rutter, M. (1987). Psychosocial resilience and protective mechanisms. *American
Journal of Orthopsychiatry, 57,* 316–331.

Rutter, M. (1993). Resilience: Some conceptual considerations. *Journal of Adolescent
Health, 14,* 626–631.

Shisslak, C. M., & Crago, M. (in press). Risk and protective factors in the development of eating disorders. In J. K. Thompson & L. Smolak (Eds.), *Body image,
eating disorders, and obesity in children and adolescents: Assessment, treatment and
prevention.* Washington, DC: American Psychological Association.

Shisslak, C. M., Crago, M., Renger, R., & Clark-Wagner, A. (1998). Self-esteem
and the prevention of eating disorders. *Eating Disorders: Journal of Treatment
and Prevention, 6,* 105–117.

Smolak, L., Murnen, S. K., & Ruble, A. E. (2000). Female athletes and eating
problems: A meta-analysis. *International Journal of Eating Disorders, 27,* 371–
380.

Stewart, M., Reid, G., & Mangham, C. (1997). Fostering children's resilience.
Journal of Pediatric Nursing, 12, 21–31.

Stice, E. (1998). Modeling of eating pathology and social reinforcement of the
thin-ideal predict onset of bulimic symptoms. *Behaviour Research and Therapy,
36,* 931–944.

Tiet, Q. Q., Bird, H. R., Davies, M., Hoven, C., Cohen, P., Jensen, P. S., &
Goodman, S. (1998). Adverse life events and resilience. *Journal of the American
Academy of Child and Adolescent Psychiatry, 37,* 1191–1200.

Troop, N. A., & Treasure, J. L. (1997). Setting the scene for eating disorders: II.
Childhood helplessness and mastery. *Psychological Medicine, 27,* 531–538.

U.S. Department of Health and Human Services. (1998). *Healthy People 2010 objectives: Draft for public comment.* Washington, DC: Author.

Wentzel, K. R. (1998). Social relationships and motivation in middle school: The role of parents, teachers, and peers. *Journal of Educational Psychology, 90,* 202–209.

Werner, E. E., & Johnson, J. L. (1999). Can we apply resilience? In M. D. Glantz & J. L. Johnson (Eds.), *Resilience and development* (pp. 259–268). New York: Plenum Press.

Werner, E. E., & Smith, R. S. (1992). *Overcoming the odds: High risk children from birth to adulthood.* Ithaca, NY: Cornell University Press.

Zucker, N. L., Womble, L. G., Williamson, D. A., & Perrin, L. A. (1999). Protective factors for eating disorders in female college athletes. *Eating Disorders: Journal of Treatment and Prevention, 7,* 207–218.

5

GENDER AND EATING PROBLEMS

LINDA SMOLAK AND SARAH K. MURNEN

It has long been evident that anorexia nervosa and bulimia nervosa are gendered disorders, with approximately 90% of those affected being women. Indeed, these disorders show a larger gender difference than most other mental disorders, including depression and Axis II personality disorders (American Psychiatric Association, 1994). That the criteria for diagnosis of anorexia nervosa include a symptom (amenorrhea, the unexpected absence of menstrual periods) applicable only to women further underscores the gendered nature of the disorder.

Even the subthreshold and "normative" behaviors that may lie on a continuum with anorexia nervosa and bulimia nervosa, such as body dissatisfaction and the use of weight loss techniques, are considerably more common among women than men, although the difference is not as pronounced as in anorexia nervosa and bulimia nervosa (Thompson, 1996). Furthermore, these gender differences appear as early as elementary school, when they are evident in various ethnic groups (Smolak & Levine, in press).

There are, however, eating problems that appear to be less dominated by women. Some studies show equal numbers of men and women with binge-eating disorder, whereas others show slightly more women (Johnson & Torgrud, 1996). Body dysmorphic disorder may also frequently affect men. In this disorder, the client is obsessed with a bodily feature that he or she thinks is deformed or ugly but is, in fact, within the normal range. One specific form of this disorder, muscle dysmorphia, may be more common in men than in women (Pope, Olivardia, Gruber, & Borowiecki, 1999).

These prevalence patterns suggest that although eating problems affect both men and women, women are disproportionately affected. Despite the historical longevity and size of these gender differences, there is surprisingly little empirical data showing what it is about being female that contributes to the increased vulnerability to eating disorders. Indeed, as biological explanations of eating problems gain in popularity, the role of the gender differences in etiological explanations seems to be fading. Many books and chapters surveying the field give little or no attention to gender as an etiological factor (e.g., Brownell & Fairburn, 1995; Kaye & Strober, 1999). There are, however, several applicable theoretical models, particularly those offered by feminist writers (e.g., Brown, 1989; Fallon, Katzman, & Wooley, 1994; Frederickson & Roberts, 1997; Piran, 1998; Striegel-Moore, 1994).

In this chapter, we begin by briefly exploring biological explanations of eating disorders, with special attention to those questions researchers need to consider to account for the gender differences. In the bulk of the chapter, we consider experiences and opportunities facing men and women that might account for the gender differences. The focus here is on what feminists have termed the "lived experiences" of women (Frederickson & Roberts, 1997; Piran, 1998) rather than the traditionally defined gender roles.

BIOLOGICAL EXPLANATIONS

There is little doubt that biology plays a role in eating problems and disorders. At the very least, the starvation associated with anorexia nervosa and the purging that is part of bulimia nervosa alter a variety of aspects of biochemistry, including levels of neurotransmitters and hormones (Kaye & Strober, 1999). It has long been known that individual symptoms of anorexia nervosa, bulimia nervosa, and binge-eating disorder, such as bingeing and obsession with food, can be associated with calorie restriction (Keys, Brozek, Henschel, Mickelson, & Taylor, 1950; Polivy & Herman, 1985). The biochemical changes associated with starvation or chaotic eating probably underlie these associations.

It is much less clear what biochemical factors may predate anorexia nervosa, bulimia nervosa, or binge-eating disorder and hence serve as potential etiological factors. The relative rarity of anorexia nervosa and bulimia nervosa make prospective biochemical research on eating disorders expensive. Therefore, researchers have typically relied on comparing the biochemical profiles of women who have recovered from eating disorders with those who have never been diagnosed. Any differences between these two groups are assumed to reflect preexisting differences (Kaye & Strober, 1999). There are several problems inherent in this assumption. First is the difficulty and variation in defining *recovered*. How long should someone be symptom free before being considered recovered? What counts as symptom free? Second, the duration of the effects of eating disorders themselves on biochemistry is unknown. Particularly in the case of long-lasting cases of anorexia nervosa or bulimia nervosa, it is possible that some effects are more or less permanent. These questions of long-term effects are empirical questions that must be investigated before accepting current methodological assumptions.

Should a biochemical etiological factor be discovered, we will be left with one of two questions. We must either answer why the biochemical factor occurs more commonly in women than in men or answer why it is expressed as an eating disorder more commonly in women. In addition, given that the symptoms of eating disorders are remarkably similar for men and women, an explanation of the male cases that do exist is imperative. Similar problems would be faced by an argument for a genetic etiological factor. Currently, it is difficult to argue for or against a specific genetic factor in anorexia nervosa or bulimia nervosa (Fairburn, Cowen, & Harrison, 1999). Should one be uncovered, however, it will be important to explain why the genetic vulnerability is more common in women or at least why the vulnerability is expressed more commonly as an eating disorder in women than in men.

A biochemical or genetic vulnerability for eating disorders may involve a nonspecific personality characteristic that is expressed as an eating problem in some people rather than a predisposition specifically for an eating disorder. There are several putative risk factors that may have a biochemical or genetic base, including depression, negative affect, impulsivity, low self-esteem, and harm avoidance (Cloninger, 1987; Kaye & Strober, 1999; Strober, 1991). There are well-documented individual differences in many of these factors as early as infancy. However, they rarely show gender differences, much less gender differences even approaching those seen in eating disorders (e.g., Bates, 1987; Lemery, Goldsmith, Klinnert, & Mrazek, 1999). Thus, it is important to explain why a biologically based personality factor that does not show gender differences, at least in early development, is an main etiological factor in a gendered disorder (Smolak & Levine, in press).

It is possible, of course, that other factors shape the biological vulnerability into a particular disorder. For example, Martin et al. (2000) reported significant relationships for girls between temperament, including negative affect, measured in preschool and elementary school and drive for thinness scores assessed in early adolescence but no comparable relationships among the boys. Thus, it is possible that the vulnerability inherent in certain temperament characteristics is expressed differently in adolescent boys than adolescent girls. Again, the process of how a possibly nonspecific biological factor is ultimately expressed as a specific, gendered disorder requires explanation.

Finally, it is important to note that individual differences in neurochemical (and even neurological) functioning are not necessarily innate. Instead, the environment, including trauma, and its accompanying coping style at any age can significantly influence the structure and function of the brain and hence future coping styles (Perry, Pollard, Blakley, Baker, & Vigilante, 1995). Similarly, there is at least suggestive evidence that dieting producing moderate weight loss may affect 5-HT (serotonin) levels by significantly reducing L-tryptophan levels in women but not in men (I. Anderson, Parry-Billings, Newsholme, Fairburn, & Cohen, 1990; Walsh, Oldman, Franklin, Fairburn, & Cowen, 1995). That reduced serotonin appears to be associated with carbohydrate craving and overeating (and, perhaps, binge eating) as well as a depressive affect makes this finding particularly provocative (Kaye & Strober, 1999). Furthermore, because this effect appears to be restricted to women and because dieting is more common among women than men, it may explain some of the gender differences in eating problems and disorders. Most notably, dieting may be less of a risk factor for individuals with binge-eating disorder than for those with anorexia nervosa or bulimia nervosa (Stice, Nemeroff, & Shaw, 1996); researchers might investigate this as a contribution to the smaller gender difference in binge-eating disorder.

GENDER ROLES AND EATING PROBLEMS

Traditional Gender Roles

Even before a child's birth, adults hold gendered expectations of personality (e.g., activity), play preferences, and physical characteristics (e.g., strength; see Huston, 1983, for a review). These expected differences are all part of *gender roles*—societally defined and sanctioned expectations about the behaviors, attitudes, and characteristics associated with being male versus being female. These gender roles, referred to as masculinity and femininity, are separate, continuous dimensions that exist in varying degrees in all people rather than a dichotomy describing exclusive groups. The feminine gender role may be described as "communal," focusing on characteristics and behaviors that foster interpersonal relationships, whereas the masculine gender role is more "agentic," emphazing assertiveness and independence (Eagly & Wood, 1999). Such gender roles may be related to eating disorders. Some theorists (e.g., Bruch, 1978; Silverstein & Perlick, 1995) have suggested that girls and women suffering from anorexia nervosa or bulimia nervosa are trying to reject the adult female role. Others (e.g., Boskind-Lodahl, 1976) have argued that women with eating disorders show more feminine traits, such as high passivity and need for approval.

The research findings looking at the relationships between gender role measures and eating problems, particularly anorexia nervosa and bulimia nervosa, are inconsistent. In fact, they are so inconsistent that some reviewers (Lancelot & Kaslow, 1994; Timko, Striegel-Moore, Silberstein, & Rodin, 1987) have concluded that there is no relationship. Using a meta-analysis, Murnen and Smolak (1998) documented small but significant relationships, such that (a) high femininity was associated with an increased risk of eating problems and (b) high masculinity scores were correlated with a decreased risk of eating disorders.

The masculinity and femininity effects reported by Murnen and Smolak (1998) were marked by substantial heterogeneity. Differences in definitions of eating disorders and in sample characteristics (e.g., clinical vs. nonclinical) accounted for some of the heterogeneity of findings. Nonetheless, it seems somewhat surprising that gender role is not more strongly and consistently related to eating problems. One possible explanation for this is that commonly used measures, such as the Bem Sex Roles Inventory (BSRI; Bem, 1974) and the Personal Attributes Questionnaire (PAQ; Spence & Helmreich, 1978), do not adequately capture current gender roles.

Superwomen

The last third of the 20th century was marked by rapid and substantial changes in the feminine gender role. Women were, for example, no longer expected to simply be nurturant and family oriented. They were also expected to participate in the workforce and establish careers. Hence, during this time, the percentage of U.S. women in college, professional schools (e.g., law and medicine), and certain careers (e.g., law) grew so much that women now constitute a majority in these venues. Similarly, women increasingly showed at least some independence from men, as indicated by the growth of divorce, single-parent families, and single-person households. Femininity as defined on the BSRI and PAQ does not capture or even allow for these changes.

Several researchers, beginning with Steiner-Adair (1986), have suggested that the dominant feminine role modeled for today's girls and college women is the "superwoman." This image of women suggests that women should be able to "have it all": good career, happy marriage, healthy children, an active social life, and good looks. It is important to note that those who adopt this role are not intrinsically motivated to achieve in these multiple areas (Murnen, Smolak, & Levine, 1994). Instead, they are seeking social approval and extrinsic reward.

There are three reasons that the superwoman role might be expected to be related to eating problems. First, all of its components seem to require thinness for success. Thus, women who are thinner are more likely to be hired and promoted, more likely to have dates, and more likely to meet the cultural definition of attractive (Yuker & Allison, 1994). Thus, the superwoman role emphasizes thinness. Second, the role encourages unrealistic and perhaps even perfectionistic striving. Perfectionism has long been associated with eating problems (e.g., Striegel-Moore, Silberstein, & Rodin, 1986). Although the empirical work concerning perfectionism has yielded mixed results, perhaps future research taking into account the context of the perfectionism (i.e., the superwoman role) will help to clarify the issue. Finally, the superwoman role encourages independence from family, friends, and even one's spouse (Hart & Kenny, 1997). This "loss of connection" may leave girls and women feeling isolated and out of control, characteristics that may facilitate eating problems. For example, feelings of isolation have been associated with binge eating (Arnow, Kenardy, & Agras, 1995).

Although the research is not extensive, the data do suggest that high school girls and college women who endorse the superwoman role have a higher rate of eating problems (Hart & Kenny, 1997; Murnen et al., 1994; Steiner-Adair, 1986, 1989; Thorton, Leo, & Alberg, 1991; Timko et al., 1987). It is not achievement striving per se that is problematic; rather the lack of intrinsic self-confidence and motivation and the loss of connection in combination with attempting to achieve in multiple roles are associated with an increased risk of eating problems (Hart & Kenny, 1997).

WOMEN'S LIVED EXPERIENCES AND EATING PROBLEMS

Feminists (e.g., Kahn & Yoder, 1989) have criticized the gender role approach to examining eating disorders to be focusing on personality characteristics inherent in individual women rather than on the sociocultural forces that may discourage some options for women while facilitating other paths. Although there are many potential sociocultural forces to consider, we opt to focus on three: (a) the culture of thinness as evidenced in the media, parental pressure, and peer pressure; (b) sexual harassment and sexual abuse that may contribute to both body shame and loss of voice; and (c) limitations on female achievement that may raise conflicts with intimacy, focus girls on a good body as the key to success, and, again, limit girls' voices.

Culture of Thinness

In a study of middle school girls, Levine, Smolak, and Hayden (1994) identified a group (12.5% of the total sample) who reported frequent use of magazines as a source of body shape information and who also had parents and peers who were invested in losing weight, that is, girls who lived in a "subculture of dieting." Compared with the other middle school girls, these girls reported significantly greater body dissatisfaction and investment in thinness, more use of weight management techniques, and more disturbed eating. Some of these effects were substantial. The subculture-of-dieting girls scored 2.5 times higher on the children's version of the Eating Attitude Test (Maloney, McGuire, Daniels, & Specker, 1989) compared with the other girls ($\eta^2 = .86$). Thus, receiving the message that thinness is important from a variety of socialization agents is associated with an increased risk of eating problems (Levine et al., 1994).

Society's message about the ideal body shape and the importance of attaining it appears to be stronger for girls than for boys. Comparisons of the best-selling men's and women's magazines indicate that there are more ads and articles concerning dieting, body shape, and food in women's magazines (Andersen & DiDomenico, 1992; Nemeroff, Stein, Diehl, & Smilack, 1994). Furthermore, research indicates, for example, that boys do not pay the same consequences as girls do in terms of dating and educational opportunities for failing to meet society's ideals (Yuker & Allsion, 1994). Although there may be a growing pressure on boys to be muscular, which may be related to the development of body dysmorphic disorder in some men (Pope et al., 1999), boys have not yet begun to absorb this sociocultural message to the extent girls adopt the thinness ideal (Smolak, Levine, & Thompson, in press).

There is little doubt that the women presented in television and movies and as fashion models are unusually thin (see, e.g., Gilbert & Thompson, 1996; and Levine & Smolak, 1996, for reviews). However, virtually all American girls and women are exposed to this image, and only a minority develop clinical or subthreshold eating disorders. How can the media be blamed?

There are at least two answers to this question. First, the majority of women do suffer from eating problems, most notably body dissatisfaction and calorie-restrictive dieting (Rodin, Silberstein, & Striegel-Moore, 1985). Although these problems are well below clinical levels, they still may cost time, money, and, at least occasionally, opportunities to participate in certain activities because of body shame. The frequency of body dissatisfaction and dieting among girls and women suggests that a broadly available message is being sent to women about their bodies. Although rates of dieting and body dissatisfaction may vary across ethnic groups, girls are always more dissatisfied than boys (Smolak & Levine, in press). Furthermore, high school girls engage in "fat talk," disparaging remarks about their own and others' body shape to be accepted (Nichter, 2000). This too suggests a perceived cultural message, perhaps even a cultural imperative, that girls dislike their bodies and should attempt to change them.

Second, for some girls and women, the message is reinforced by family and peers. Research suggests that even among elementary school children, parental remarks about weight and shape are associated with children's body dissatisfaction and weight loss attempts (Smolak, Levine, & Schermer, 1999; Striegel-Moore & Kearney-Cook, 1994). This may be more true for girls than boys (Smolak et al., 1999), perhaps because the combination of messages from media, peers, and parents may be more common and stronger for girls. Peer messages, in the form of girlfriends' discussion of weight and weight loss techniques or weight-related teasing, may be influential during adolescence (Paxton, 1999).

The research examining the relationship of cultural influences to eating problems tends to be correlational, using measures taken concurrently. Smolak and Levine (1996) suggested that girls and women with eating problems use a "thinness schema" to process weight and shape information. More specifically, these girls and women have come to associate success with thinness and to believe that thinness is an achievable goal. Thus, the direction and nature of the relationship between sociocultural pressures to be thin and eating problems require additional research. The question is whether the cultural messages somehow help form this processing schema or whether they simply refine, strengthen, and maintain it.

Sexual Harassment and Sexual Abuse

Sexual harassment and sexual abuse are also gendered experiences in terms of frequency and effects (O'Donohue, Downs, & Yeater, 1998). There is a long-standing debate in the eating disorders literature about the etiological role of child sexual abuse (for reviews, see Kearney-Cooke & Striegel-Moore, 1994; Wooley, 1994). The debate is fueled in part by the finding that many forms of psychopathology appear to be related to child sexual abuse (Kendall-Tackett, Williams, & Finkelhor, 1993) and that eating disorders tend to be comorbid with many of these disorders, including borderline personality disorder and depression. Hence, some researchers argue that child sexual abuse is a nonspecific risk factor for eating problems (Wonderlich, Brewerton, Jocic, Dansky, & Abbott, 1997).

The relationship of child sexual abuse to several forms of psychopathology should not deter eating disorders researchers and clinicians (Kearney-Cooke & Striegel-Moore, 1994). Abuse may reflect poor family interactions and even familial psychopathology. Inadequate self-development may be both a precursor and an outcome of abuse. The differential development of victims may demonstrate the roles of temperament, coping strategies, and social support in recovery from a trauma. In other words, victims may constitute a high-risk group for eating disorders (Smolak & Murnen, in press). By studying this group prospectively, we may ultimately tease apart factors that lead to eating disorders with or without comorbidity.

Although child sexual abuse is not a trauma unique to girls, it is probably more common in girls than in boys. Furthermore, the nature of the trauma probably differs for boys and girls (Kendall-Tackett et al., 1993). Similarly, sexual harassment victims may be either boys or girls, although girls are in general the more frequent targets (e.g., Bryant, 1993). Furthermore, girls report more distress in the face of sexual harassment. For example, elementary school girls were more likely than boys to think that sexual harassment would be frightening, despite the lack of threat in the vignettes to which the children were responding (Murnen & Smolak, 2000). Indeed, in one scenario presented to the children, the target child's clothing was commented on by a child of the other sex. Boys tended to take such comments from girls as compliments, with nearly 76% of the boys saying the comment would make the boy in the vignette feel good. Only 12% of the girls thought the comment from the boy in the story was a compliment; in fact, almost 10% said the girl in the scenario would be afraid (Murnen & Smolak, 2000).

The well-known American Association of University Women Study of Adolescents (Bryant, 1993) similarly documents differential reactions by gender. For example, girls were nearly five times more likely than boys to be afraid at school and three times more likely to feel less confident following sexual harassment (Bryant, 1993). Indeed, one third of the harassed girls did not want to attend school, and nearly one third did not want to speak in class because of sexual harassment (Bryant, 1993).

There is also evidence that sexual harassment is related to body esteem problems among elementary and high school girls as well as college women (Larkin, Rice, & Russell, 1999; Murnen & Smolak, 2000; Piran, 1998). There are several possible explanations for this link. Perhaps the lowered confidence associated with sexual harassment spills over into body esteem. Or girls may hope to change their bodies to reduce harassment, either by meeting the "feminine ideal" (Brumberg, 1997) or by becoming "invisible" (Chernin, 1981). Girls' reluctance to speak up about sexual harassment (Bryant, 1993) seems to support the latter argument. It also indicates a loss of voice (Taylor, Gilligan, & Sullivan, 1995). Thus, the shame and anger associated with harassment is turned inward, an approach encouraged by the social norm that discourages girls' and women's expression of anger (Taylor et al., 1995).

It is noteworthy that child sexual abuse and sexual harassment may both serve to silence women (Sheffield, 1995). Indeed, objectification (i.e., equating women with their sexualized bodies) may generally be associated with a loss of voice. Experimental data show that women who are judged to be sexy and attractive are also seen as less competent and knowledgeable so that their opinions are more likely to be dismissed (Matschiner & Murnen, 1999). Loss of voice (i.e., an inability to express, even to oneself, one's wishes, needs, and opinions) has been associated with an increased risk of eating problems. For example, Smolak and Fairman (1999) reported that lower levels of voice were associated with more dieting, more emotional eating, and more binge eating among college women more so than among college men.

Although the precise mechanisms by which child sexual abuse and sexual harassment affect eating behaviors and body esteem remain unclear, it is evident that both are preventable. Simply increasing knowledge about sexual harassment policies among employees has been shown to be associated with lower rates of sexual harassment (O'Donohue et al., 1998). Furthermore, Piran (1998, 1999) emonstrated that changes in administrative responses to sexual harassment at an elite ballet school are related to lower levels of student eating disorders. Piran's findings, while not conclusive, serve to encourage prevention researchers to consider trying to alter the school environment rather than focusing exclusively on the individual students.

Achievement Opportunities

Researchers have long argued that issues concerning achievement might contribute to the development of eating problems in women (for a review, see Gilbert & Thompson, 1996). These arguments have often focused on the conflict between the maternal, nurturant role and the career-oriented, independent role (e.g., Silverstein & Perlick, 1995). More recently, theorists have suggested that it is the lack of achievement opportunities, rather than a conflict created by such options, which contributes to eating disorders (e.g., Shisslak, Crago, Renger, & Clark-Wagner, 1998). More specifically, many young girls may see attractiveness as their best path to success so that they make a rational choice to pursue a thin, model-like body. Because weight control techniques, including dieting (Polivy & Herman, 1985) and exercise (Davis, Kennedy, Ravelski, & Dionne, 1994), may actually trigger eating disorders in some girls, this choice may eventually career out of control, resulting in eating pathology.

Achievement opportunities continue to be gendered in the United States. For example, for the 1997–1998 academic year, over 2.5 million girls participated in high school sports, whereas over 3.7 million boys participated ("Gender equity in sports high school participation," 2000). Furthermore, men earned more money in 19 of the 20 job categories listed by the Bureau of Labor Statistics for the third quarter of 2000 (Bureau of Labor Statistics, 2000). In the one category (mechanics and repairers) in which women's salaries are higher, men made 92% of women's income. However, women executives and managers made 66% of male executives' salaries (Bureau of Labor Statistics, 2000). Visible people in power, be it government, sports, or business, are more likely to be men. Often the most recognizable women are those known more for their looks (e.g., supermodels, actresses) than their skills or abilities.

Higher self-esteem is associated with fewer eating problems (Shisslak et al., 1998). Self-esteem may be enhanced by participation in a variety of activities, including volunteer work or sports, and by active mentoring (Allen, Philliber, Herrling, & Kuperminc, 1997; Shisslak et al., 1998). Facilitating girls' participation in activities that take the focus off a thin appearance may help reduce eating problems. This may help explain why participation in nonelite high school sports may serve as a protective factor against eating problems (Smolak, Murnen, & Ruble, 2000). In addition, such activities may give girls a place or a means to express themselves, thereby improving their levels of voice. Indeed, Taylor et al. (1995) noted the lack of participation in self-enhancing activities, to the point of dropping out of previously valued activities, among girls with low voice.

OBJECTIFICATION THEORY

The culture of thinness, child sexual abuse and sexual harassment, and lack of achievement opportunities for girls all point to gendered aspects of American culture that contribute to the gender differences in eating problems. The mechanisms by which these factors affect the body image and eating habits of girls and women have often been poorly defined. Although various theoretical perspectives have been offered (see, e.g., Gilbert & Thompson, 1996), objectification theory (Fredrickson & Roberts, 1997) appears to present a parsimonious explanation for these and other gendered risk factors for the development of eating problems. Indeed, one of the common threads uniting the culture of thinness, sexual harassment, and limited achievement opportunities is that women are defined primarily as bodies in all three.

Objectification theory (Fredrickson & Roberts, 1997) begins with the premise that the dominant, White male culture in the United States treats men's and women's bodies differently. Specifically, compared with men's bodies, women's bodies are much more likely to be "looked at, evaluated, and always potentially objectified" (Fredrickson & Roberts, 1997, p. 175). This happens in face-to-face interactions with both familiar and unfamiliar people. It is evident in the way women are posed in advertisements (Kilbourne, 1994). Women's roles in pornography, movies, and television demonstrate that they are to be "looked at" rather than to "act." Furthermore, the looking is sexualized, sending the message that men may "possess" women's bodies (see Fredrickson & Roberts, 1997). This societal tendency to treat the female body as a sexual object begins when girls are quite young. About three quarters of the third- through fifth-grade elementary school girls in Murnen and Smolak's (2000) study reported experiencing sexual harassment. Retrospective reports have also indicated that harassment begins for many girls in elementary school (Bryant, 1993). By adolescence, sexual harassment becomes normative for girls (Bryant, 1993), and date rape is added to the already extant threat of child sexual abuse (Unger & Crawford, 1996). As was noted earlier, even young girls are aware that certain types of looking or comments by boys and men may be threatening (Bryant, 1993;

Murnen & Smolak, 2000). Thus, objectification serves as a way to limit women's roles and behaviors, keeping them in their restricted and restrictive societal place.

In addition to learning that their bodies may "invite" danger, girls learn that attractiveness is a key to success. As was discussed earlier, girls who are judged to be thin and attractive are more likely to get dates, get into college, and get job promotions. Thus, girls and women learn that people are watching and judging them, people who have the power to make the girls' lives happy or difficult. This socialization process may lead girls and women to internalize the gaze of the other and hence to "treat *themselves* as objects to be looked at and evaluated" (Fredrickson & Roberts, 1997, p. 177, emphasis in original). After all, the goal of socialization is to get the developing child to adopt the values and behaviors society values in an adult of their gender (race, age, etc.). It should not be surprising, then, that girls learn to believe that looks are important and to perform the behaviors that will give them the societally defined desirable appearance, even if it is at a cost to their own health or, ironically, safety.

Not all women internalize the objectification to the same extent (Fredrickson & Roberts, 1997). Context determines how frequently a particular girl or woman experiences objectification. Some women resist the social standard. Nonetheless, even those who fight the "ideal" and refuse to subscribe to it do so in hopes that it will elicit a nonobjectifying reaction from other people. In some ways, then, even these women have internalized the objectification and are using it as a strategy to judge how others will treat them.

Internalization of a societal standard means at least two things have happened: The person is aware of the standard, and he or she has come to believe that achieving that standard is important. When achieving a standard is important to an individual, the person's ability to measure up can affect self-esteem (Harter, 1986). Failure to achieve at the desired level, then, may result in shame and anxiety (Fredrickson & Roberts, 1997). The standard of beauty that self-objectification involves is extraordinarily difficult to achieve. Only extraordinary efforts have even a remote chance at making most women fit the standard. The effects of this inconsistency between the desired look and reality is evident in the "normative discontent" (Rodin et al., 1985) most American women feel with their bodies.

Objectification theory, then, suggests why women focus so strongly on their bodies. Furthermore, objectification theory demonstrates why this focus is a negative one for many women and may even contribute to eating disorders for some. Most important, objectification theory raises the possibility of prevention of these problems if boys and girls can be taught that the equation of women with their bodies is inappropriate (Fredrickson & Roberts, 1997).

Objectification theory is predicated on the argument that women are more likely to be treated as objects and men as actors. This objectification is then internalized, leading to shame, anxiety, and potentially psychopathology. In today's American society, such objectification is more likely to happen to women because they are lower in social status. But what happens in situations in which men are objectified and treated as if they are primarily bodies to be looked at and evaluated by people of higher status? Do men also show symptoms of body image and eating problems?

Two situations seem relevant here. First, men (and women) who become interested in bodybuilding are at risk for developing distorted body images, eating problems, steroid (and food supplement) abuse, and body dysmorphic disorder (Pope et al., 1999; Thompson, Heinberg, Altabe, & Tantleff-Dunn, 1999). Bodybuilders are indeed judged on their appearance and on the size and definition of their muscles. Bodybuilding competitions resemble beauty pageants in that the contestants dress in bathing suits and are asked to pose for the judges. There is an increasing emphasis on this body type as desirable (Pope et al., 1999). Those people who internalize this message, then, may experience self-objectification.

Gay male culture places a greater emphasis on appearance than does heterosexual male culture. A man's shape and clothing influences his ability to date and engage in sexual behavior (Bordo, 1999). Gay men are more likely to be looked at and evaluated on the basis of looks, that is, objectified, than are heterosexual men (because heterosexual women rank personality above looks in a mate; Thompson et al., 1999). Again, research suggests that gay men are at greater risk than heterosexual men for eating problems (Beren, Hayden, Wilfley, & Grilo, 1996).

CONCLUSION

Eating disorders, particularly anorexia nervosa and bulimia nervosa, are clearly more common among women than men. Yet researchers and theorists have given seemingly decreasing attention to the role of gender in the development of these problems. It is a challenge to operationalize gender and its effects. Gender tends to operate on a societal level, whereas behavior tends to be analyzed by psychologists at the level of the individual. This, in conjunction with the reluctance to acknowledge sexism in society in general and psychology in particular, has contributed to a de-emphasizing of gender as a factor in eating disorders.

In this chapter, we have argued that the lived experiences of girls and women account for much of the gender difference in eating problems. These lived experiences include growing up in a culture that emphasizes an unrealistically thin body type as the societal ideal, limited achievement opportunities, and sexual abuse and harassment as normative experiences. Objectification theory was presented as a means of understanding how these lived experiences might translate to eating problems. The emphasis, then, is on societal definitions and treatment of girls and women. Rather than conceptualizing eating problems as primarily an individual pathology, our perspective focused on the sociocultural pressures that lead to these problems.

Much research needs to be done to evaluate the position presented in this chapter. Very little research exists, for example, on girls' experience of sexual harassment, how they learn its meaning, and how that meaning is translated into body dissatisfaction. More research is also needed on why some girls absorb the objectification messages more thoroughly than do others. Are there protective factors that mitigate against some girls absorbing the message? It is intriguing, for example, that African American women seem to use messages from the dominant culture less in self-definition compared with Asian American or White women (Crocker, Luhtanen, Blaine, & Broadnax, 1994). Similarly, would increased opportunities for girls to achieve in areas that are not appearance based decrease the likelihood that they will internalize the objectification? Would critiquing societal norms and influences and discussing their impact on girls as individuals serve as a prevention of eating disorders technique (Friedman, 1998)?

There is much to be gained from this and related research. Although it is a difficult process, attitudes about appearance and body satisfaction can be changed. In addition, behaviors that people direct toward one another in public places can also be altered. This is clear from the successful campaigns that have significantly reduced smoking, drunk driving, and public displays of racism. In schools, children can be taught to conceptualize gender differently (Bigler & Liben, 1992); teachers and school personnel can work together to change the school environment (Piran, 1999; Smolak, 1999). By understanding objectification theory, people have myriad opportunities for instituting such changes.

REFERENCES

Allen, J., Philliber, S., Herrling, S., & Kuperminc, G. (1997). Preventing teen pregnancy and academic failure: Experimental evaluation of a developmentally based program. *Child Development, 64*, 729–742.

American Psychiatric Association. (1994). *Diagnostic and statistical manual of mental disorders* (4th ed.). Washington, DC: Author.

Andersen, A., & DiDomenico, L. (1992). Diet vs. shape content of popular male and female magazines: A dose-related relationship to the incidence of eating disorders. *International Journal of Eating Disorders, 11*, 283–287.

Anderson, I., Parry-Billings, M., Newsholme, E., Fairburn, C., & Cowen, P. (1990). Dieting reduces plasma tryptophan and alters brain 5-HT in women. *Psychological Medicine, 20,* 785–791.

Arnow, B., Kenardy, J., & Agras, W. S. (1995). The Emotional Eating Scale: The development of a measure to assess coping with negative affect by eating. *International Journal of Eating Disorders, 18,* 79–90.

Bates, J. (1987). Temperament in infancy. In J. D. Osofsky (Ed.), *Handbook of infant development* (2nd ed., pp. 1101–1149). New York: Wiley.

Bem, S. (1974). The measurement of psychological androgyny. *Journal of Consulting and Clinical Psychology, 42,* 155–162.

Beren, S. E., Hayden, H. A., Wilfley, D. E., & Grilo, C. M. (1996). The influence of sexual orientation on body dissatisfaction in adult men and women. *International Journal of Eating Disorders, 20,* 135–141.

Bigler, R., & Liben, L. (1992). Cognitive mechanisms in children's gender stereotyping: Theoretical and educational implications of a cognitive-based intervention. *Child Development, 63,* 1351–1363.

Bordo, S. (1999). *The male body: A new look at men in public and in private.* New York: Farrar, Straus & Giroux.

Boskind-Lodahl, M. (1976). Cinderella's stepsisters: A feminist perspective on anorexia nervosa and bulimia. *Signs: Journal of Women in Culture and Society, 2,* 35–41.

Brown, L. (1989). Fat oppressive attitudes and the feminist therapist: Directions for change. *Women and Therapy, 8,* 19–30.

Brownell, K., & Fairburn, C. (1995). *Eating disorders and obesity: A comprehensive handbook.* New York: Guilford Press.

Bruch, H. (1978). *The golden cage: The enigma of anorexia nervosa.* Cambridge, MA: Harvard University Press.

Brumberg, J. (1997). *The body project: An intimate history of American girls.* New York: Random House.

Bryant, A. (1993). Hostile hallways: The AAUW Survey on Sexual Harassment in America's Schools. *Journal of School Health, 63,* 355–357.

Bureau of Labor Statistics. (2000). *Median weekly earnings of full-time wage and salary workers by occupation and sex* [Report]. Retrieved on November 26, 2000 from the World Wide Web, ftp://ftp.bls.gov/pub/special

Chernin, K. (1981). *The obsession: Reflections on the tyranny of slenderness.* New York: Harper & Row.

Cloninger, C. (1987). A systematic method for clinical description and classification of personality variants. *Archives of General Psychiatry, 44,* 573–588.

Crocker, J., Luhtanen, R., Blaine, B., & Broadnax, S. (1994). Collective self-esteem and psychological well-being among White, Black and Asian college students. *Personality and Social Psychology Bulletin, 20,* 503–513.

Davis, C., Kennedy, S., Ravelski, E., & Dionne, M. (1994). The role of physical activity in the development and maintenance of eating disorders. *Psychological Medicine, 24,* 957–967.

Eagly, A., & Wood, W. (1999). The origins of sex differences in human behavior: Evolved dispositions versus social roles. *American Psychologist, 54,* 408–423.

Fairburn, C., Cowen, P., & Harrison, P. (1999). Twin studies and the etiology of eating disorders. *International Journal of Eating Disorders, 26,* 349–358.

Fallon, P., Katzman, M., & Wooley, S. (1994). *Feminist perspectives on eating disorders.* New York: Guilford Press.

Frederickson, B., & Roberts, T. (1997). Objectification theory: Toward understanding women's lived experiences and mental health risks. *Psychology of Women Quarterly, 21,* 173–206.

Friedman, S. (1998). Girls in the 90s: A gender-based model for eating disorder prevention. *Patient Education and Counseling, 33,* 217–224.

Gender equity in high school sports participation [Report]. (2000). Retrieved on January 24, 2000 from the World Wide Web, http://www.bailiwick.lib.uiowa.edu/ge/statistics.htm Participation Index

Gilbert, S., & Thompson, J. K. (1996). Feminist explanations of the development of eating disorders: Common themes, research findings, and methodological issues. *Clinical Psychology: Science and Practice, 3,* 183–202.

Hart, K., & Kenny, M. (1997). Adherence to the super woman ideal and eating disorder symptoms among college women. *Sex Roles, 36,* 461–478.

Harter, S. (1986). Processes underlying the construction, maintenance, and enhancement of the self-concept in children. In J. Suls & G. Greenwald (Eds.), *Psychological perspectives on the self* (Vol. 3, pp. 137–180). Hillsdale, NJ: Erlbaum.

Huston, A. (1983). Sex-typing. In E. M. Hetherington (Ed.), *Handbook of child psychology: Vol. 4. Socialization, personality, and social development* (4th ed., pp. 387–467). New York: Wiley.

Johnson, W., & Torgrud, L. (1996). Assessment and treatment of binge eating disorder. In J. K. Thompson (Ed.), *Body image, eating disorders, and obesity: An integrative guide for assessment and treatment* (pp. 321–344). Washington, DC: American Psychological Association.

Kahn, A., & Yoder, J. (1989). The psychology of women and conservatism: Rediscovering social change. *Psychology of Women Quarterly, 13,* 417–432.

Kaye, W., & Strober, M. (1999). Neurobiology of eating disorders. In D. Charney, E. Nestler, & W. Bunney (Eds.), *Neurobiological foundations of mental illness* (pp. 891–906). New York: Oxford University Press.

Kearney-Cooke, A., & Striegel-Moore, R. (1994). The treatment of childhood sexual abuse in anorexia nervosa and bulimia nervosa: A feminist psychodynamic approach. *International Journal of Eating Disorders, 15,* 305–320.

Kendall-Tackett, K., Williams, L., & Finkelhor, D. (1993). Impact of sexual abuse on children: A review and synthesis of recent empirical studies. *Psychological Bulletin, 113,* 164–180.

Keys, A., Brozek, J., Henschel, A., Mickelson, D., & Taylor, H. (1950). *The biology of human starvation* (Vol. 1). Minneapolis: University of Minnesota Press.

Kilbourne, J. (1994). Still killing us softly: Advertising and the obsession with thinness. In P. Fallon, M. Katzman, & S. Wooley (Eds.), *Feminist perspectives on eating disorders* (pp. 395–418). New York: Guilford Press.

Lancelot, C., & Kaslow, N. (1994). Sex role orientation and disordered eating in women: A review. *Clinical Psychology Review, 14,* 139–157.

Larkin, J., Rice, C., & Russell, V. (1999). Sexual harassment and the prevention of eating disorders: Educating young women. In N. Piran, M. P. Levine, & C. Steiner-Adair (Eds.), *Preventing eating disorders: A handbook of interventions and special challenges* (pp. 194–207). Philadelphia, PA: Brunner/Mazel.

Lemery, K., Goldsmith, H., Klinnert, M., & Mrazek, D. (1999). Developmental models of infant and childhood temperament. *Developmental Psychology, 35,* 189–204.

Levine, M. P., & Smolak, L. (1996). Media as a context for the development of disordered eating. In L. Smolak, M. P. Levine, & R. Striegel-Moore (Eds.), *The developmental psychopathology of eating disorders: Implications for research, prevention, and treatment* (pp. 235–257). Mahwah, NJ: Erlbaum.

Levine, M. P., Smolak, L., & Hayden, H. (1994). The relation of sociocultural factors to eating attitudes and behaviors among middle school girls. *Journal of Early Adolescence, 14,* 471–490.

Maloney, M., McGuire, J., Daniels, S., & Specker, B. (1989). Dieting behavior and eating attitudes in children. *Pediatrics, 84,* 482–489.

Martin, G., Wertheim, E., Prior, M., Smart, D., Sanson, A., & Oberklaid, F. (2000). A longitudinal study of the role of childhood temperament in the later development of eating concerns. *International Journal of Eating Disorders, 27,* 150–163.

Matschiner, M., & Murnen, S. (1999). Hyperfemininity and influence. *Psychology of Women Quarterly, 23,* 631–642.

Murnen, S., & Smolak, L. (1998). Femininity, masculinity, and disordered eating: A meta-analytic approach. *International Journal of Eating Disorders, 22,* 231–242.

Murnen, S., & Smolak, L. (2000). The experience of sexual harassment among grade-school students: Early socialization of female subordination? *Sex Roles, 43,* 1–17.

Murnen, S., Smolak, L., & Levine, M. P. (1994). *Development of a scale to measure adherence to the "superwoman" construct.* Unpublished manuscript, Kenyon College, Gambier, OH.

Nemeroff, C., Stein, R., Diehl, N., & Smilack, K. (1994). From the Cleavers to the Clintons: Role choices and body orientation as reflected in magazine article content. *International Journal of Eating Disorders, 16,* 167–176.

Nichter, M. (2000). *Fat talk*. Cambridge, MA: Harvard University Press.

O'Donohue, W., Downs, K., & Yeater, E. (1998). Sexual harassment: A review of the literature. *Aggression and Violent Behavior, 3*, 111–128.

Paxton, S. (1999). Peer relations, body image, and disordered eating in adolescent girls: Implications for prevention. In N. Piran, M. P. Levine, & C. Steiner-Adair (Eds.), *Preventing eating disorders: A handbook of interventions and special challenges* (pp. 134–147). Philadelphia: Brunner/Mazel.

Perry, B., Pollard, R., Blakley, T., Baker, W., & Vigilante, D. (1995). Childhood trauma, the neurobiology of adaptation, and "use-dependent" development of the brain: How "states" become "traits." *Infant Mental Health Journal, 16*, 271–291.

Piran, N. (1998). A participatory approach to the prevention of eating disorders in a school. In W. Vandereycken & G. Noordenbos (Eds.), *The prevention of eating disorders* (pp. 173–186). London: Athlone.

Piran, N. (1999). Eating disorders: A trial of prevention in a high risk school setting. *Journal of Primary Prevention, 20*, 75–90.

Polivy, J., & Herman, P. (1985). Dieting and bingeing: A causal analysis. *American Psychologist, 40*, 193–201.

Pope, H., Olivardia, R., Gruber, A., & Borowiecki, J. (1999). Evolving ideals of male body image as seen through action toys. *International Journal of Eating Disorders, 26*, 65–72.

Rodin, J., Silberstein, L., & Striegel-Moore, R. (1985). Women and weight: A normative discontent. In T. Sonderegger (Ed.), *Nebraska Symposium on Motivation: Vol. 32. Psychology and gender* (pp. 267–308). Lincoln: University of Nebraska Press.

Sheffield, C. (1995). Sexual terrorism. In J. Freeman (Ed.), *Women: A feminist perspective* (pp. 1–21). Mountain View, CA: Mayfield.

Shisslak, C., Crago, M., Renger, R., & Clark-Wagner, A. (1998). Self-esteem and the prevention of eating disorders. *Eating Disorders: The Journal of Treatment and Prevention, 6*, 105–117.

Silverstein, B., & Perlick, D. (1995). *The cost of competence: Why inequality causes depression, eating disorders, and illness in women*. New York: Oxford University Press.

Smolak, L. (1999). Elementary school curricula for the primary prevention of eating problems. In N. Piran, M. P. Levine, & C. Steiner-Adair (Eds.), *Preventing eating disorders: A handbook of interventions and special challenges* (pp. 85–104). Philadelphia: Brunner/Mazel.

Smolak, L., & Fairman, B. (1999). *Gender and voice: Relationships to depression and eating disorders*. Manuscript submitted for publication, Kenyon College, Gambier, OH.

Smolak, L., & Levine, M. P. (1996). Adolescent transitions and the development of eating problems. In L. Smolak, M. P. Levine, & R. Striegel-Moore (Eds.),

The developmental psychopathology of eating disorders: Implications for research, prevention, and treatment (pp. 207–234). Mahwah, NJ: Erlbaum.

Smolak, L., & Levine, M. P. (in press). Body image in children. In J. K. Thompson & L. Smolak (Eds.), *Body image, eating disorders, and obesity in youth: Theory, assessment, treatment, and prevention*. Washington, DC: American Psychological Association.

Smolak, L., Levine, M. P., & Schermer, F. (1999). Parental input and weight concerns among elementary school children. *International Journal of Eating Disorders, 25,* 263–271.

Smolak, L., Levine, M. P., & Thompson, J. K. (in press). The use of the Sociocultural Attitudes Towards Appearance Questionnaire with middle school boys and girls. *International Journal of Eating Disorders.*

Smolak, L., & Murnen, S. (in press). A meta-analytic examination of the relationship between sexual abuse and eating problems. *International Journal of Eating Disorders.*

Smolak, L., Murnen, S., & Ruble, A. (2000). Female athletes and eating problems: A meta-analytic approach. *International Journal of Eating Disorders, 27,* 371–380.

Spence, J., & Helmreich, R. (1978). *Masculinity and femininity: Their psychological dimensions, correlates, and antecedents.* Austin: University of Texas Press.

Steiner-Adair, C. (1986). The body politic: Normal female adolescent development and the development of eating disorders. *Journal of the American Academy of Psychoanalysis, 14,* 95–114.

Steiner-Adair, C. (1989). Developing the voice of the wise woman: College students and bulimia. *Journal of College Student Psychotherapy, 3,* 151–165.

Stice, E., Nemeroff, C., & Shaw, H. (1996). A test of the dual pathway model of bulimia nervosa: Evidence for restrained-eating and affect-regulation mechanisms. *Journal of Social and Clinical Psychology, 15,* 340–363.

Striegel-Moore, R. (1994). A feminist agenda for psychological research on eating disorders. In P. Fallon, M. Katzman, & S. Wooley (Eds.), *Feminist perspectives on eating disorders* (pp. 438–454). New York: Guilford Press.

Striegel-Moore, R., & Kearney-Cooke, A. (1994). Exploring parents' attitudes and behaviors about their children's physical appearance. *International Journal of Eating Disorders, 15,* 377–385.

Striegel-Moore, R., Silberstein, L., & Rodin, J. (1986). Toward an understanding of risk factors for bulimia. *American Psychologist, 41,* 2246–263.

Strober, M. (1991). Family-genetic studies of eating disorders. *Journal of Clinical Psychiatry, 52,* 9–12.

Taylor, J., Gilligan, C., & Sullivan, A. (1995). *Between voice and silence: Women and girls, race and relationship.* Cambridge, MA: Harvard University Press.

Thompson, J. K. (1996). Body image, eating disorders, and obesity: An emerging synthesis. In J. K. Thompson (Ed.), *Body image, eating disorders, and obesity: An integrative guide for assessment and treatment* (pp. 1–20). Washington, DC: American Psychological Association.

Thompson, J. K., Heinberg, L., Altabe, M., & Tantleff-Dunn, S. (1999). *Exacting beauty: Theory, assessment, and treatment of body image disturbance*. Washington, DC: American Psychological Association.

Thorton, B., Leo, R., & Alberg, K. (1991). Gender role typing, the superwoman ideal, and the potential for eating disorders. *Sex Roles, 25*, 469–484.

Timko, C., Striegel-Moore, R., Silberstein, L., & Rodin, J. (1987). Femininity/masculinity and disordered eating in women: How are they related? *International Journal of Eating Disorders, 6*, 701–712.

Unger, R., & Crawford, M. (1996). *Women and gender: A feminist psychology* (2nd ed.). New York: McGraw-Hill.

Walsh, A., Oldman, A., Franklin, M., Fairburn, C., & Cowen, P. (1995). Dieting decreases plasma tryptophan and increases prolactin response to d-fenfluramine in women but not in men. *Journal of Affective Disorders, 33*, 89–97.

Wonderlich, S., Brewerton, T., Jocic, Z., Dansky, B., & Abbott, D. (1997). Relationship of childhood sexual abuse and eating disorders. *Journal of the American Academy of Child and Adolescent Psychiatry, 36*, 1107–1115.

Wooley, S. (1994). Sexual abuse and eating disorders: The concealed debate. In P. Fallon, M. Katzman, & S. Wooley (Eds.), *Feminist perspectives on eating disorders* (pp. 171–211). New York: Guilford Press.

Yuker, H., & Allison, D. (1994). Obesity: Sociocultural perspectives. In L. Alexander & D. Mott (Eds.), *Understanding eating disorders* (pp. 243–270). Washington, DC: Taylor & Francis.

6

CHALLENGING THE MYTH OF THE GOLDEN GIRL: ETHNICITY AND EATING DISORDERS

LINDA SMOLAK AND RUTH H. STRIEGEL-MOORE

Sociocultural theorists (e.g., Huon & Strong, 1998; Piran, 1999; Smolak & Levine, 1996; Stice, 1994; Striegel-Moore & Smolak, 2000; J. K. Thompson, Heinberg, Altabe, & Tantleff-Dunn, 1999) have long argued that cultural influences contribute substantially to body image disturbances and eating disorders. A broad set of cultural factors have been implicated in the development of eating disorders, including power inequities between men and women, gender roles and stereotypes, and cultural beliefs and practices regarding the body, food, and eating (Rodin, Silberstein, & Striegel-Moore, 1985). Of these, most research attention has been given to cultural beliefs and practices regarding the body and to gender roles. This reflects the assumption that beliefs about attractiveness, body shape, and gender roles lead people to define themselves in terms of body shape and, hence, put them at risk for eating disorders. These beliefs are seen as rooted in and socialized by cultural forces.

Preferences concerning weight and shape appear to be learned. Ideal body shape becomes thinner as children get older (Gardner, Sorter, & Friedman, 1997). In addition, the preferred body shape has varied across history (Bordo, 1993, 1999; Brumberg, 1997). It also appears to vary across cultures and even across ethnic groups within the United States (Douchinis, Hayden, & Wilfley, in press; Striegel-Moore & Smolak, 2000).

To date, the primary reason for studies of ethnic differences in body image and disordered eating has been to test sociocultural hypotheses of eating disorders. If the sociocultural perspective is correct, then we should expect ethnic group differences in the prevalence and type of eating problems if there are ethnic group differences in risk and protective factors. A second reason for advancing research in this area is to identify intervention and treatment needs in diverse populations. Until recently, eating disorders have been a neglected problem among ethnic minority girls and women because they were assumed not to exist in these populations (Striegel-Moore & Smolak, 2000). It has long been held, for example, that anorexia nervosa occurs nearly exclusively among upper-class White girls. With the advent of population-based studies, the view of eating disorders as limited to affluent White women and girls is changing: Such studies identify eating disorders among lower-class women and among ethnically diverse populations. Finally, research on ethnic group differences has implications for prevention efforts. On the one hand, if some ethnic groups are "protected" against the development of eating disorders, then aspects of those cultures might be incorporated into prevention programs. On the other hand, there must be programs to address the special needs of ethnic minority groups in terms of eating problems.

The major goal of this chapter is to explore avenues that might lead to a better evaluation of these three issues: the sociocultural perspective of eating disorders, intervention and treatment needs of diverse populations, and prevention. We begin with some definitional issues, followed by a brief overview of the documented differences (and similarities) in body image and eating problems among American ethnic groups. This is followed by a discussion of risk and protective factors that may be shared by or unique to different ethnic groups. Special attention is given to the importance of specifying potentially influential cultural features. Finally, implications of these issues for treatment and prevention are discussed.

CULTURE, ETHNICITY, AND MINORITY STATUS

Culture is a broad term, describing how individuals expect to behave and interact and how that information is passed on to children. Culture is a complex, multidimensional social context that includes shared institutions, values, norms, and language. It provides a social–cognitive framework for people to use to interpret their experiences and their world (McLoyd, 1999). Culture should not be viewed as just a distant, general context within which development occurs. Rather, culture is translated into proximal influences that directly influence development and behavior. Because culture is multidimensional, any attempt to understand cultural influences on development and behavior must include the "unpacking" of culture (Garcia Coll & Magnuson, 1999; McLoyd, 1999). We must seek to identify which components of a culture's values and socialization practices might affect the behavior of interest.

Ethnicity is a narrower term. Ethnic groups occur within a culture. Members of an ethnic group share a culture of origin, and perhaps a language, that differs from the dominant culture. However, the ethnic group's culture may include elements of the dominant culture as well as the culture of origin. Ethnicity may be related to race but incorporates culture with race, providing a greater context for understanding development (Harris & Kuba, 1997). In this chapter, we use the term *ethnic minority group* as defined by Phinney (1996) to refer to populations in the United States who are members of nondominant groups of non-European descent. Hence, this chapter focuses on American ethnic minority groups, including those of Latina (Central or Latin America), Asian, Native (or American Indian), and African or Black Caribbean descent. All of these groups are embedded in "American culture." At present and since the founding of the United States in 1776, European Americans have dominated American culture. Their values concerning, for example, gender, family, and work roles have frequently been accepted as normative. Although it is expected that some time during the 21st century, European Americans will no longer constitute a demographic majority, they will continue to be the single largest ethnic group. This, combined with historical tradition, is likely to facilitate their continued influence on the culture and the continued status of the other American ethnic groups as minorities for some time to come.

When one observes differences between European Americans and any of the ethnic minority groups in the United States, then, the first question to consider is whether the differences are attributable to the specific aspects of the ethnic minority group's culture or to the experiences associated with minority status (or to some interaction of the two). Issues pertaining to minority status have been largely ignored in the eating disorders literature. Such issues might include limited educational and career opportunities and resulting class differences, exposure to racial epithets and caricatures, and race- or ethnicity-based sexual harassment (Larkin, 1994/1997). For some ethnic minority groups, additional issues arise from their immigrant status, including culture shock, language difficulties, and in some groups the sequelae of traumatic experiences associated with political or religious persecution in their home country. Cultural stereotypes of ethnic minorities do vary somewhat. For example, Latina and Black children are often stereotyped as lazy or unintelligent and hence may not be given as much classroom support by their teachers (Sadker & Sadker, 1993). Asians, however, may face the "model minority" stereotype, carrying with it the expectation of perfectionism and low emotionality. Although these are different stereotypes, either may facilitate eating disorders by lowering self-esteem and voice among ethnic minority adolescent girls (Taylor, Gilligan, & Sullivan, 1995).

Thus, we need to carefully examine the roots of any ethnic difference in eating problems or their risk and protective factors. Particularly in terms of designing intervention or prevention programs, it is important to identify which risk or protective factors come from the ethnic culture, which come from the dominant culture (to which the ethnic minority members are exposed), and which result from discrimination. Furthermore, general terms for ethnic minority groups, such as *Asian American* or *Latina*, may mask heterogeneity within those groups. For example, although Chinese and Japanese Americans may be stereotyped as "model" minorities who have enjoyed substantial educational and economic success within the United States, this stereotype appears less applicable to more recent Cambodian and Vietnamese refugees. Whether such within-ethnicity differences are important for eating disorders remains to be seen.

ETHNIC GROUP DIFFERENCES IN EATING DISORDER SYMPTOMS AND SYNDROMES

Anorexia nervosa and bulimia nervosa were first described on the basis of the clinical presentation of European or European American patients. These case studies provide the foundation for the disorders' definitions in the medical nomenclatures, such as the *Diagnostic and Statistical Manual of Mental Disorders* (4th ed.; American Psychiatric Association, 1994). Although the specific diagnostic criteria have been revised several times since each disorder was first introduced (see Herzog & Delinski, chapter 2, this volume), none of these modifications were concerned with whether the definitions were appropriate for non-European or non-European American populations. Although the appropriateness of the body disturbance criterion for anorexia nervosa has been questioned regarding certain cultures (e.g., Chinese or Japanese culture), the applicability of particular criteria to ethnic minority groups in the United States has not yet been discussed. Relatedly, because studies typically use only the existing criteria for studying prevalence and clinical significance of eating disorders, clinically significant behavioral or attitudinal disturbances within different ethnic groups may go unrecorded.

Even when applying existing diagnostic criteria, case reports and initial survey studies make it clear that no ethnic group is completely immune to developing an eating disorder (for reviews, see Crago, Shisslak, & Estes, 1996; and Douchinis et al., in press; see also Striegel-Moore, Garvin, Dohm, & Rosenheck, 1999). To date, most studies of ethnic group differences in prevalence of eating disorders focus on the syndromes of anorexia nervosa and bulimia nervosa or the symptoms that define these disorders, particularly body dissatisfaction and dieting for weight loss. In a study of a large sample of Black and White American adults, researchers found comparable prevalence rates of binge-eating disorder in Black and White women (Smith, Marcus, Lewis, Fitzgibbon, & Schreiner, 1998). At present, there are no nationally representative data regarding the prevalence of eating disorders among minority populations. Indeed, there are no nationally representative data concerning the exact prevalence of bulimia nervosa and binge-eating disorder for any U.S. population. Only regional samples, albeit large epidemiological samples, have provided prevalence data of bulimia nervosa, and these have comprised basically White female participants (e.g., Garfinkel et al., 1995; Kendler et al., 1991; Lewinsohn, Hops, Roberts, Seeley, & Andrews, 1993). These epidemiological studies show that anorexia nervosa is very rare and that bulimia nervosa, although more common than anorexia nervosa, also is a relatively rare disorder (for a review, see van Hoeken, Lucas, & Hoek, 1998). Consequently, very large samples are needed to determine ethnic differences in anorexia or bulimia nervosa.

A majority of studies examining ethnic differences focus on symptoms of eating disorders, especially on body image disturbances. For example, Douchinis et al. (in press) recently cataloged 63 empirical comparisons of childhood and adolescent eating problems (including dieting, body dissatisfaction, and eating disorders symptoms) among various ethnic groups. Of these, 30 studies focus on body image. This emphasis on body image may contribute to a distorted view regarding the extent of disordered eating among minority populations. For example, although Black women appear to be less likely to report body dissatisfaction than White women, rates of binge eating appear to be equal in the two groups, and Black women may actually fast and abuse diuretics more frequently (Striegel-Moore, Wilfley, Pike, Dohm, & Fairburn, 2000). The importance of these eating disorder symptoms among Black women is underscored by the findings of significant associations of binge eating with other psychiatric symptoms and increased body mass index (BMI; Striegel-Moore et al., 2000). Given the high rates of obesity among Black girls and women (Kuczmarski, Flegal, Campbell, & Johnson, 1994), it is crucial that symptoms such as binge eating be fully understood.

Similarly, the available research tends to focus on Black girls and women in relation to their White peers. Other ethnic groups have been underrepresented in the literature. This is illustrated in the literature review by Douchinis et al. (in press): Of the 63 reported comparisons, 44 involve Blacks, 30 include Latinas, 13 consider Asians, and 21 include American Indians (several comparisons involved more than one ethnic group). Clearly, these groups are not interchangeable. They do not report eating problems and disorders at equal rates. For example, in a study of Minnesota adolescents, frequent dieting was reported by 23.6% of the Latina, 21.5% of the White, 20.6% of the American Indian, 17.4% of the Asian, and 13.6% of the Black girls. Binge eating was most common among the Asian (33.6%), followed by the White (30.6%), American Indian (29%), Latina (25.2%), and Black (23%) girls (French et al., 1997). Such differences have not always been replicated. However, it is reasonable, on the basis of extant data, to suggest that Asian and Latina women differ from Black women as frequently as they differ from White women on measures of eating problems.

The failure to gather comprehensive data regarding eating disorder symptoms and syndromes in ethnically diverse samples has contributed to the misperception that ethnic minority girls and women do not experience symptoms or syndromes of eating disorders. The challenge, then, is to collect better descriptive data that includes not only dieting and body dissatisfaction but also purging, bingeing, emotional eating, and refusal to eat normally for reasons other than weight loss.

This challenge is greater than it may initially seem. There are questions as to how to measure eating problems in different ethnic groups. First, there is the issue of whether available measures of eating problems are valid for use with various groups. These measures were developed and validated with primarily or exclusively White samples. There have been some attempts to demonstrate the validity of these measures within various ethnic and cultural groups. The National Heart, Lung, and Blood Institute (NHLBI) Growth and Health Study Research Group (1992) found that internal consistency of the Eating Disorder Inventory (Garner & Olmsted, 1984) subscales Body Dissatisfaction, Drive for Thinness, and Bulimia was satisfactory among a large sample of Black girls. For example, Cronbach's alpha coefficients for Body Dissatisfaction ranged from .92 (age 11) to .93 (age 18) in White girls and from .86 (age 11) to .90 (age 18) in Black girls. Cronbach's alpha coefficients for the Bulimia subscale ranged from .78 (age 11) to .79 (age 18) in White girls and from .72 (age 11) to .70 (age 18) in Black girls (personal communications, R. Striegel-Moore, March 2000). Researchers have also found evidence of psychometric validity when the Eating Attitude Test has been translated into other languages for use in other cultures, although there are some problems (e.g., Lee, Lee, & Leung, 1998).

However, this approach still leaves the question of whether these measures actually address the entire range of eating problems and attitudes faced by various ethnic groups. More specifically, the question remains whether these measures have cultural validity (McLoyd, 1999). First, are they measuring all relevant eating symptoms? For example, studies show that Black girls are much more likely than White girls to want to gain weight (e.g., Schreiber et al., 1996). Many body dissatisfaction scales do not take such desires into account nor do they ask about potentially unhealthy methods (e.g., overeating) to achieve the body ideal. Second, do the symptoms always carry the same meaning? Waller and Matoba (1999) reported that negative eating attitudes were less correlated with emotional eating among Japanese women living in Japan than among Japanese or British women living in the United Kingdom. As Miller (1999) urged, psychological research needs to gain more in-depth knowledge of the specific cultural groups under investigation by using methods conducive to this goal, including ethnographic studies and focus groups.

In addition to these measurement issues, there is the issue of demand characteristics. Part of being a member of a minority group, independent of the basis for that categorization, is that one has lower status. This, in turn, means that one's well-being, and perhaps even survival, depend on being able to "read" members of the majority group. This may explain, for example, why women are more adept than men at reading social cues (Miller, 1986). In terms of eating disorder research with ethnic minority girls, this aspect of lower status has an interesting implication, particularly when a White researcher is involved in data collection. Demand characteristics, in which the participant is guessing the wishes of the researcher, may come into play. Parker et al. (1995) reported that there were no ethnic group differences when they surveyed Black and White girls concerning dieting. However, in focus groups, differences emerged such that the Black girls reported more body satisfaction and less dieting. One reason for this discrepancy was that the Black girls apparently answered the surveys according to what they thought the White researchers expected adolescent girls to do. It is not uncommon in psychological research to find effects of the race or ethnicity of the people collecting the data. Thus, researchers need to be careful to reduce demand characteristics that might trigger an acute awareness of status among girls and women from ethnic minority groups.

Such methodological caveats apply not only to research attempting to ascertain the prevalence of eating problems but also to studies trying to assess potential risk and protective factors in the development of eating disorders. Indeed, they may be even more important in this research because people may seek to protect the identity and integrity of their communities from the judgment of White academicians and clinicians.

PROTECTIVE AND RISK FACTORS
IN ETHNIC GROUP DIFFERENCES

Traditionally, research examining race and ethnicity has focused on group *differences*, involving comparison of various groups. Sometimes the comparison is across ethnic groups. But, most commonly, minority ethnic groups are compared with the majority group. This is problematic for several reasons. One of the most important is that it sets the majority group, in this case White girls and women, as the standard and then proceeds under the assumption that development and pathology in all other groups should be identical to that standard. Such an approach overlooks the obvious: Growing up in a different culture raises the possibility of different influences. Peers may be of greater influence in some cultures than others (Chen,

Greenberger, Lester, Dong, & Guo, 1998). Definitions of maturity may differ, with some cultures emphasizing independence and other cultures focusing on communality. Acceptability of emotional expression may differ. It is clear that gender roles differ. All of these suggest that the relative meaning and importance of social influences may vary.

Furthermore, the group comparison approach ignores the potential role of minority status per se. Current popular models of eating problems do not deal with bicultural identity development, for example. Nor do they consider the role of racial discrimination. Finally, these studies fail to consider the stresses and challenges associated with immigration. Studies that look at within-group processes are needed to try to identify how eating problems might develop within different ethnic groups.

Thus, this section addresses two major questions. The first is whether there are aspects of a particular culture that either protect the girls and women from developing eating problems or, conversely, place them at increased risk. The risk and protective factors discussed in this section are those that have been identified in research using primarily White girls. This approach may neglect some influences and symptoms that operate only in certain ethnic minority communities. The second is whether there are risk factors involving minority status in the United States that might not operate among White girls. Hence, these factors may have been ignored in current models of the etiology of eating problems and disorders.

General Risk Factors

Thin Body Ideal

It has been hypothesized that one pathway to developing an eating disorder involves the internalization of Western culture's beauty ideal of a thin body and that women and girls who adopt this ideal and yet fail to achieve it experience body image dissatisfaction. As suggested by the influential restraint model (Polivy & Herman, 1993), the body dissatisfaction leads to weight loss efforts which, in turn, are hypothesized to result in binge eating (see also Stice, chapter 3, this volume). Therefore, researchers have examined ethnic differences in the body shape ideal and (not always in the same study) the experience of weight or shape dissatisfaction. Consistently, they have shown that the body ideal held in the African American community is heavier and less narrowly defined than that of the European American community and that Black women report less weight dissatisfaction than White women (for reviews, see Manns & Murnen, 2000; and Striegel-Moore & Smolak, 1996). Moreover, Black women have been reported to experience less social pressure about being overweight (Striegel-Moore, Wilfley, Caldwell, Needham, & Brownell, 1996). Similarly, Latina women report larger ideal body sizes than do White women (Winkleby, Gardner, & Taylor, 1996). This greater flexibility in the definition of an acceptable body shape may contribute to a lower prevalence of eating disorders in which restrictive eating is a major risk variable.

The cultural ideal of thinness may be particularly personally relevant to those girls or women who experience familial or peer pressure to conform to this ideal. Teasing and peer comments have frequently been shown to be correlates of eating problems (e.g., Cattarin & Thompson, 1994; Levine, Smolak, & Hayden, 1994) and have been reported in case control studies to be associated with specific risk for developing bulimia nervosa and binge-eating disorder (Fairburn et al., 1998; Fairburn, Welch, Doll, Davies, & O'Connor, 1997; Striegel-Moore, Dohm, Fairburn, Pike, & Wilfley, 1999). The importance and meaning of peer relationships may vary by culture. Mukai (1996) reported that peer influence may not become more important than maternal influence until mid high school among Japanese girls. This at least appears to be later than for European American girls (e.g., Attie & Brooks-Gunn, 1989). Whether this timing difference is important remains to be seen, but it may at least have implications for prevention programs. The McKnight Risk Factor Study (2000) reports that levels of peer concerns about weight and shape were lower among Latina and African American than European American adolescents. In another study, researchers found that Latina adolescents indicated that their perceptions of whether they were overweight were more strongly influenced by their weight in relation to the weight of their peers than by their weight in relation to health-based standards (Hall, Cousins, & Power, 1991). Thus, peer influences may play more of a role for White than for Black or Latina adolescents, and the role of peers for Asian adolescents may differ from all other groups.

Obesity

Obesity is a major health problem among ethnic minority women (Kuczmarski et al., 1994). Perhaps related to the level of acceptance of diverse body types, Black and Latina women and girls are typically heavier than are White women and girls (see Striegel-Moore & Smolak, 2000). Among girls, this difference in BMI is first evident around age 9, when pubertal development begins (Rosner, Prineas, Loggie, & Daniels, 1998). BMIs of Asian American girls tend to be more comparable with those of White girls (Rosner et al., 1998), although individual studies of specific Asian communities sometimes find that Asian Americans have lower BMIs. BMI consistently emerges as a predictor of body dissatisfaction and dieting in the eating disorder literature, even among adolescents of various ethnic groups (Robinson et al., 1996; Striegel-Moore, 1993). For example, in a sample of girls ages 11 to 16 years, Striegel-Moore et al. (2000) found that in both Black and White girls, body dissatisfaction and drive for thinness increased with increasing body weight. This effect of increasing BMI on body dissatisfaction or drive for thinness was more pronounced, however, among the White than among the Black girls. In a study that compares Black and White women who were dieting to lose weight, Black women reported a later onset of dieting than White women (Striegel-Moore et al., 1996). It is possible that White women are particularly at risk for diet-induced eating disorders because they are more likely to initiate dieting during the developmental period of puberty, when dieting may be particularly harmful.

In case control studies of bulimia nervosa and binge-eating disorder, childhood obesity was shown to be a risk factor for developing an eating disorder (Fairburn et al., 1997, 1998). In adult samples, BMI is correlated with binge-eating severity, and binge-eating disorder has been found to be overrepresented in the obese community (Smith et al., 1998; Yanovski, 1993). Thus, BMI differences might contribute to some ethnic group differences in eating disorders.

There are, of course, myriad risk and protective factors that may differ by ethnicity. Although even in childhood girls show more eating problems than boys in a variety of ethnic groups (see Smolak & Levine, in press, for a review), there are gender role differences across ethnic groups that might contribute to varying rates of different problems (Striegel-Moore & Smolak, 1996). Levels of perfectionism, need for social approval, and family relationships may vary by ethnicity in ways that have implications for the development of eating disorders. For example, Striegel-Moore et al. (2000) found higher self-reported perfectionism in Black girls compared with White girls. At this point, it is important to do the descriptive research to examine these and other differences as well as the research looking at the relationships between putative risk factors and eating problems within ethnic groups.

All risk factors do not necessarily vary by ethnic group. Indeed, several reseachers have found considerable similarity in the correlates of eating problems within various ethnic groups. For example, Wilfley et al. (1996) found that sociocultural factors, including weight and shape comments and teasing, were correlated with body dissatisfaction in both Black and White women. However, Black women continued to report lower levels of body dissatisfaction, suggesting that these potential influences may not be as strong for Black women as for White women. In a study of White, Black, Latina, American Indian, and Asian American adolescents, Story, French, Resnick, and Blum (1995) showed that across all ethnic groups, poor body image was the strongest correlate of a variety of eating problems, including dieting, purging, and binge eating, although the relationships were not significant in all groups, perhaps because of a lack of power.

Thus, several researchers have found remarkable similarity across American ethnic groups in the correlates of eating disorders. However, such results need to be interpreted cautiously. First, these are all concurrent correlations. It is possible that relationships among aspects of eating problems are similar once the problem has emerged and consolidated but that the etiological causes of the problems differ. Second, the results do not always report the strength of the relationships. It is possible that a set of factors is more important in one ethnic group than for another (e.g., Chen et al., 1998). Finally, developmental psychopathology theorists have noted that there are multiple pathways to the same outcome (Rosen, 1996). It is possible, then, that although some pathways are shared across ethnic groups, there are other pathways that are unique to or at least more common in particular ethnic groups. This leads to the question of whether there are risk factors that might be unique to ethnic minority groups.

Factors Unique to Ethnic Minority Girls and Women

There are at least two issues faced by ethnic minority girls and women that might affect the development of eating problems: acculturation and discrimination. Both of these may be associated with negative affect, an important risk factor for bulimia nervosa and binge-eating disorder (Stice, 1998; Striegel-Moore, 1993).

Acculturation

Acculturation is one aspect of forming a bicultural identity. The term *acculturation* is generally used to refer to adoption of the value and belief systems of the majority culture. Researchers have long held that in addition to the problems facing all girls, ethnic minority girls must face the challenge of living in two cultures, their culture of origin and the majority culture. They must find a way to form a personal identity that acknowledges and incorporates this challenge. Thus, they must form an ethnic identity. There are a variety of ways to achieve this, ranging from rejection of the majority culture (separated) to attempts to blend the two cultures (e.g., blended or alternating bicultural) to rejection of the culture of origin (assimilated; Phinney & Devich-Navarro, 1998). Although girls from the ethnic majority also have an ethnicity, they are not routinely faced with integrating their ethnic traditions with those of another ethnic group. Indeed, many European Americans do not truly think of themselves as having an ethnic identity (Phinney & Devich-Navarro, 1998). They simply consider themselves "Americans." The limited use of the term "European American" compared with "African American," "Asian American," "Mexican American," or "Native American" underscores which group's "culture" is the one that serves as the standard.

In the field of eating disorders, the issue of acculturation has been applied in two contradictory ways. First, some researchers have argued that greater acculturation results in an increased risk of eating problems (Harris & Kuba, 1997). This argument is grounded in early research indicating that as girls moved from non-Western to Western cultures, their risk for eating disorders increased. The underlying assumption, then, is that the Western culture is more facilitative of the development of eating disorders.

This assumption may well be true for some non-Western cultures, particularly, perhaps, for those cultures in which media are less saturating and food deprivation is still an issue. However, it is not clear that eating problems are equally rare in all non-Western cultures. Indeed, there is evidence of rates of eating disorders comparable with those of the United States in several Asian countries, including Japan, Taiwan, India, and Hong Kong (King & Bhugra, 1989; Mukai, Crago, & Shisslak, 1994; Nakamura et al., 1999). The assumption that adoption of European American values is conducive to the development of eating disorders needs to be refined. In fact, researchers do sometimes find that high acculturation is a risk factor for some ethnic minority girls (e.g., Latinas) but not for other groups (e.g., Asian Americans; see Gowen, Hayward, Killen, Robinson, & Taylor, 1999; and Robinson, Change, Haydel, & Killen, in press). It is imperative that researchers identify cultural values concerning body ideal, gender role, appearance, and other factors that may contribute to eating problems. This enables specific testable hypotheses as well as the more accurate generation of appropriate risk factor models within each ethnic group. Again, then, we see evidence that it is not reasonable to treat all ethnic minority groups as equivalent.

To further confuse the issue, in the second way in which acculturation is applied, some researchers have argued that lower acculturation (i.e., adherence to traditional culture of origin values) increases the risk of eating problems (e.g., Lake, Staiger, & Glowinski, 2000). These researchers suggest that retaining the traditional cultural values places the girl at odds with the majority culture, and this stress then contributes to the development of eating disorders.

There is evidence supporting both of these positions as well as research that fails to find a substantial effect of acculturation (Cachelin, Veisel, Striegel-Moore, & Barzegarnzazri, in press; Davis & Katzman, 1999; Gowen et al., 1999; Robinson et al., in press). It is noteworthy that effects of acculturation seem to be somewhat more consistently documented among Latina and African American girls and women than among Asian girls and women, although there is some inconsistency within all groups. In part, the inconsistent results may be due to the different populations studied and the various definitions and ways of measuring acculturation.

The challenge is to identify how a particular culture's values get translated to proximal influences that may affect the development of eating symptoms and disorders. This information can then be used to hypothesize which forms of acculturation and bicultural identity, if any, may increase or decrease the risk for a particular ethnic group. Broad hypotheses about acculturation are not likely to be applicable to all groups, because acculturation likely carries different meanings in different ethnic groups.

More sophisticated models of acculturation and bicultural identity taking into account the social meaning of acculturation within a particular group (and at a particular time and place) are needed. Furthermore, new models must more clearly investigate and acknowledge ethnic group differences not only in body ideal but also in culturally valenced mediators, such as gender roles or the acceptability of expressing anger. These factors affect how levels of acculturation might be related to types and prevalence of eating disorders. Only when such complex models are developed can we develop reasonable hypotheses concerning the impact of acculturation on eating disorders.

Discrimination

Prejudice and discrimination against racial and ethnic groups still exist. One dramatic example of this is that in 1995 the Federal Bureau of Investigation (FBI) recorded 4,831 incidents of racially motivated hate crimes involving 6,438 victims (FBI, 2000). In 1999, 28,819 employment-related racial discrimination complaints were received by the U.S. Equal Employment Opportunity Commission (2000). In addition, in a small interview study, 81.3% of the African American, 45.9% of the Mexican American, and 27.8% of the Japanese American adolescents reported being the victim of discriminatory treatment. In addition, 38.9% of the Japanese American, 29.2% of the Mexican American, and 6.3% of the African American teens reported being the targets of verbal racial slurs (Phinney & Chavera, 1995).

Such events may be related to documented differences in academic and career achievement. For example, in 1996, high school completion rates were 81% for White, 73% for Black, and 55.2% for Latina adolescents (National Center for Education Statistics, 2000). In the third quarter of 2000, Black and Latina workers earned significantly less than did White male workers. For example, among all full-time workers, Latina women earned approximately 57% of what White men earned. The disparity among young workers, ages 16–24 years, was not as great but was still considerable. In this category, Latina women made 82% of White men's salaries (U.S. Bureau of Labor Statistics, 2000).

What does this mean for ethnic minority women and eating problems? It should be noted that individual effects of racial and ethnic discrimination are poorly understood (Phinney & Chavera, 1995). There certainly are individual differences in people's reactions to discrimination; some respond actively, others angrily, others passively (Phinney & Chavera, 1995). Such differences in reactions may be mediated by culture as translated by parents, teachers, and other socialization agents. African American parents, for example, seem to spend more time teaching their children how to "get along" in the face of racial discrimination than do Japanese American or Mexican American parents (Phinney & Chavera, 1995). As is true with coping styles generally, the meaning of these coping styles probably depends on other factors, such as a sense of control in the situation or the presence of other stressors and hassles. Nonetheless, we might expect that some styles of coping with discrimination, particularly in the presence of other factors, might increase the risk of eating problems.

On the basis of data from a small, but rich, set of interviews, B. Thompson (1994) argued that racial discrimination does play a role in eating problems. When women and girls of color feel that they cannot stop, control, or at least respond to the discrimination, they report negative affect (Larkin, 1994/1997; B. Thompson, 1994). Such lack of control may be rooted in limited social support especially from those in authority, poor job options, or threats of retaliation. In any case, the negative affect may be reflected in at least two ways relevant to eating disorders. First, it may take the form of body dissatisfaction (Larkin, 1994/1997). This is possible, for example, when the racial slurs are directed at the woman's body.

The second possible relationship between the negative affect associated with discrimination and eating problems is evident in binge eating. Both theory and empirical data indicate that negative affect is a common trigger of binge eating. Indeed, some women who develop binge-eating disorder and bulimia nervosa did not diet prior to the onset of the disorder; instead, they came to their disorder through bingeing in response to negative affect (Arnow, Kenardy, & Agras, 1995; Stice, 1998). Evidence now suggests that binge eating is indeed a serious problem among at least African American girls and women (McKnight Risk Factor Study, 2000; Striegel-Moore et al., 2000). Furthermore, given the high rates of obesity and depression among Latina girls and women (e.g., McKnight Risk Factor Study, 2000; Roberts & Sobhan, 1992), it is reasonable to argue that Latinas, too, may suffer high rates of binge eating. Given the relationship between binge eating and obesity (Telch & Agras, 1994), this seems like a particularly important link to investigate.

In chapter 5 in this volume, Smolak and Murnen argue that gender discrimination might contribute to eating problems. Their arguments appear to have analogies in racial discrimination. First, harassment and abuse may lead to self-silencing, which may in turn mediate the relationship among discrimination, negative affect, and binge eating. Second, limited opportunities for achievement may lead to self-silencing. Taylor et al. (1995), for example, reported that as girls from ethnic minority groups lost the support of their teachers and families for academic achievement, they also lost their confidence and direction. Such loss of voice appeared to be associated with depressive symptoms and perhaps eating problems. Similarly, Orenstein (1994) found that the self-esteem of Latina girls seemed to be dramatically affected by the lack of support for their academic achievement, beginning in middle school.

Eating disorders research has been remiss in considering broad sociocultural factors such as racial discrimination. This is understandable. The nature and effects of such broad influences are difficult to assess. Yet, it is possible that the experiences of discrimination, as well as bicultural identity development, are among the factors creating the ethnic group differences in eating problems. Such variables may help us understand, for example, why binge-eating disorder and anorexia nervosa show different prevalence patterns across ethnic groups. These are challenging opportunities for future research. They are also particularly exciting opportunities because of their potential link to intervention and prevention efforts.

INTERVENTION AND PREVENTION WITH ETHNIC MINORITY GROUPS

Most programs designed to prevent eating problems, whether they are universal or targeted in nature, have been aimed at and evaluated with predominantly or exclusively White samples. Similarly, as is true of the field of clinical psychology generally, treatment programs have not typically been sensitive to ethnicity issues.

There are at least three issues that are relevant: (a) Are eating disorders being properly diagnosed among ethnic minorities? (b) Are treatment programs sensitive to special needs of ethnic minority eating disorders clients? (c) Are prevention programs inclusive enough to positively affect girls of color? It is beyond the scope of this chapter to fully address these issues. Instead, we aim to raise some questions that might be considered in future research.

The diagnostic question actually has two elements. One was addressed briefly earlier in the chapter: Are current assessment tools appropriate for use with various ethnic groups? Such discussions may provide clues for eating disorders specialists wishing to evaluate the usefulness of current assessment tools. The second question perhaps encapsulates the purpose of this chapter: Are eating disorders among women of color often misdiagnosed or underdiagnosed (Crago et al., 1996; Striegel-Moore et al., 2000)? Has the myth that only White women suffer from eating disorders led clinicians to assume that warning signs in women of color add up to something other than eating disorders? How well informed are clinicians about eating disorders among women of color? In particular, are primary care physicians and medical personnel, who are often the first line of defense in diagnosing eating problems, aware of these ethnicity issues?

As with assessment techniques, there is a large literature noting the underutilization of mental health services by ethnic minority members. Again, this literature may serve as a guide to clinicians wishing to be more culturally sensitive in their treatment approaches. At this time, however, we also need research documenting the effectiveness of various treatment approaches with ethnic minority groups. Currently, there is virtually no research assessing whether the treatment approaches that appear to be effective with European American girls and women (e.g., cognitive–behavioral therapy) are equally effective with other ethnic groups. To date, there are too few minority participants in clinical trials to be able to answer this question. In addition, treatment seeking may vary across ethnic groups, and acculturation may affect the likelihood of seeking help (Cachelin et al., in press).

Finally, many of the current eating disorders prevention programs are aimed at a broad school audience (see Levine & Piran, chapter 12, this volume). Yet, it is not clear that they are routinely culturally sensitive (Nichter, Vuckovic, & Parker, 1999; Smolak, 1999). Again, one of the first issues that needs to be addressed is the identification of specialized needs of ethnic groups. It may be that some components of prevention programs can and should be quite similar for all audiences. For example, ending weight-related teasing is a goal that might apply to all ethnic groups (Wilfley et al., 1996); however, African American girls may be less interested in discussing weight loss techniques as a problem and more interested in discussing their usefulness in reducing obesity (Nichter et al., 1999).

Finally, researchers need to evaluate delivery techniques to ascertain whether, for example, classroom curricula, computer-based programs, or discussion groups might be viable for use with ethnic minority girls. Researchers also need to examine the materials used in and the personnel delivering prevention programs to understand how these might affect the effectiveness of the programs with girls of color.

REFERENCES

American Psychiatric Association. (1994). *Diagnostic and statistical manual of mental disorders* (4th ed.). Washington, DC: Author.

Arnow, B., Kenardy, J., & Agras, W. S. (1995). The Emotional Eating Scale: The development of a measure to assess coping with negative affect by eating. *International Journal of Eating Disorders, 18,* 79–90.

Attie, I., & Brooks-Gunn, J. (1989). Development of eating problems in adolescent girls. *Developmental Psychology, 25,* 70–79.

Bordo, S. (1993). *Unbearable weight: Feminism, Western culture, and the body.* Berkeley: University of California Press.

Bordo, S. (1999). *The male body: A new look at men in public and private.* New York: Farrar, Straus, & Giroux.

Brumberg, J. (1997). *The body project: An intimate history of American girls.* New York: Random House.

Cachelin, F., Veisel, C., Striegel-Moore, R., & Barzegarnzazri, E. (2000). Disordered eating, acculturation, and treatment seeking in a community sample of Hispanic, Asian, Black, and White women. *Psychology of Women Quarterly, 24,* 244–253.

Cattarin, J., & Thompson, J. K. (1994). A three-year longitudinal study of body image, eating disturbance, and general psychological functioning in adolescent females. *Eating Disorders: The Journal of Treatment and Prevention, 2,* 114–125.

Chen, C., Greenberger, E., Lester, J., Dong, Q., & Guo, M. (1998). A cross-cultural study of family and peer correlates of adolescent misconduct. *Developmental Psychology, 34,* 770–781.

Crago, M., Shisslak, C. M., & Estes, L. S. (1996). Eating disturbances among American minority groups. *International Journal of Eating Disorders, 19,* 239–248.

Davis, C., & Katzman, M. A. (1999). Perfection as acculturation: Psychological correlates of eating problems in Chinese male and female students living in the United States. *International Journal of Eating Disorders, 19,* 239–248.

Douchinis, J., Hayden, H., & Wilfley, D. (in press). Obesity, body image, and eating disorders in ethnically diverse children and adolescents. In J. K. Thompson & L. Smolak (Eds.), *Body image, eating disorders, and obesity in youth: Theory, assessment, treatment, and prevention.* Washington, DC: American Psychological Association.

Fairburn, C. G., Doll, H. A., Welch, S., Hay, P. J., Davies, B. A., & O'Connor, M. E. (1998). Risk factors for binge eating disorder: A community-based, case-control study. *Archives of General Psychiatry, 55,* 425–432.

Fairburn, C. G., Welch, S. L., Doll, H. A., Davies, B. A., & O'Connor, M. E. (1997). Risk factors for bulimia nervosa: A community-based case-control study. *Archives of General Psychiatry, 54,* 509–517.

Federal Bureau of Investigation. (2000). *Uniform crime reports: Hate crime—1995.* Retrieved January 27, 2000 from the World Wide Web: http://www.fbi.gov/ucr/hatecm.htm#race

French, S. A., Story, M., Neumark-Sztainer, D., Downes, B., Resnick, M., & Blum, R. (1997). Ethnic differences in psychosocial and health behavior correlates of dieting, purging, and binge eating in a population-based sample of adolescent females. *International Journal of Eating Disorders, 22,* 315–322.

Garcia Coll, C., & Magnuson, K. (1999). Cultural influences on child development: Are we ready for a paradigm shift? In A. Masten (Ed.), *Cultural processes in child development: The Minnesota symposia on child psychology* (Vol. 29, pp. 1–24). Mahwah, NJ: Erlbaum.

Gardner, R., Sorter, R., & Friedman, B. (1997). Developmental changes in children's body images. *Journal of Social Behavior and Personality, 12,* 1019–1036.

Garfinkel, P. E., Lin, E., Goering, P., Spegg, C., Goldbloom, D. S., Kennedy, S., Kaplan, A. S., & Woodside, D. B. (1995). Bulimia nervosa in a Canadian community sample: Prevalence and comparison of subgroups. *American Journal of Psychiatry, 152,* 1052–1058.

Garner, D. M., & Olmsted, M. P. (1984). *The Eating Disorder Inventory manual.* Odessa, FL: Psychological Assessment Resources.

Gowen, L. K., Hayward, C., Killen, J. D., Robinson, T. N., & Taylor, C. B. (1999). Acculturation and eating disorder symptoms in adolescent girls. *Journal of Research on Adolescence, 9,* 67–83.

Hall, S. K., Cousins, J. H., & Power, T. G. (1991). Self-concept and perceptions of attractiveness and body size among Mexican-American mothers and daughters. *International Journal of Obesity, 15,* 567–575.

Harris, D., & Kuba, S. (1997). Ethnocultural identity and eating disorders in women of color. *Professional Psychology: Research and Practice, 28,* 341–347.

Huon, G., & Strong, K. (1998). The initiation and maintenance of dieting: Structural models for large-scale longitudinal investigations. *International Journal of Eating Disorders, 23,* 361–370.

Kendler, K. S., MacLean, C., Neale, M., Kessler, R., Heath, A., & Eaves, L. (1991). The genetic epidemiology of bulimia nervosa. *American Journal of Psychiatry, 148,* 1627–1637.

King, M., & Bhugra, D. (1989). Eating disorders: Lessons from a cross-cultural study. *Psychological Medicine, 19,* 955–958.

Kuczmarski, R. J., Flegal, K. M., Campbell, S. M., & Johnson, C. L. (1994). Increasing prevalence of overweight among adults: The National Health and Nutrition Examination Surveys, 1960–1991. *Journal of the American Medical Association, 272,* 205–211.

Lake, A., Staiger, P., & Glowinski, H. (2000). Effect of Western culture on women's attitudes to eating and perceptions of body shape. *International Journal of Eating Disorders, 27,* 83–89.

Larkin, J. (1997). *Sexual harassment: High school girls speak out.* Toronto, Ontario, Canada: Second Story Press. (Original work published 1994)

Lee, S., Lee, A. M., & Leung, T. (1998). Cross-cultural validity of the Eating Disorders Inventory: A study of Chinese patients with eating disorders in Hong Kong. *International Journal of Eating Disorders, 23,* 177–188.

Levine, M. P., Smolak, L., & Hayden, H. (1994). The relation of sociocultural factors to eating attitudes and behaviors among middle school girls. *Journal of Early Adolescence, 14,* 472–491.

Lewinsohn, P. M., Hops, H., Roberts, R. E., Seeley, J. R., & Andrews, J. A. (1993). Adolescent psychopathology: I. Prevalence and incidence of depression and other *DSM–III–R* disorders in high school students. *Journal of Abnormal Psychology, 102,* 133–144.

Manns, L., & Murnen, S. (2000, March). *Are African-American women less at risk for disordered eating? A meta-analytic review.* Paper presented at the annual meeting of the Association for Women in Psychology, Salt Lake City, UT.

McKnight Risk Factor Study. (2000, May). *Ethnic group differences in disordered eating attitudes and behaviors and related risk factors.* Paper presented at the Ninth International Conference on Eating Disorders, New York.

McLoyd, V. (1999). Cultural influences in a multicultural society: Conceptual and methodological issues. In A. Masten (Ed.), *Cultural processes in child development: The Minnesota Symposia on Child Psychology* (Vol. 29, pp. 123–136). Mahwah, NJ: Erlbaum.

Miller, J. (1999). Cultural psychology: Implications for basic psychological theory. *Psychological Science, 10,* 85–91.

Miller, J. B. (1986). *Toward a new psychology of women* (2nd ed.). Boston: Beacon Press.

Mukai, T. (1996). Mothers, peers, and perceived pressure to diet among Japanese adolescent girls. *Journal of Research on Adolescence, 6,* 309–324.

Mukai, T., Crago, M., & Shisslak, C. (1994). Eating attitudes and weight preoccupation among female high school students in Japan. *Journal of Child Psychology and Psychiatry and Allied Disciplines, 35,* 677–688.

Nakamura, K., Hoshino, Y., Watanabe, A., Honda, K., Niwa, S., Tominaga, K., Shimai, S., & Yamamoto, M. (1999). Eating problems in female Japanese high school students: A prevalence study. *International Journal of Eating Disorders, 26,* 91–96.

National Center for Education Statistics. (2000). *Dropout rates in the United States: 1996.* Retrieved January 28, 2000 from the World Wide Web: http://www .nces.ed.gov/pubs98/dropout/ch06t13a.html

National Heart, Lung, and Blood Institute Growth and Health Study Research Group. (1992). Obesity and cardiovascular disease risk factors in Black and White girls: The NHLBI Growth and Health Study. *American Journal of Public Health, 82,* 1613–1621.

Nichter, M., Vuckovic, N., & Parker, S. (1999). The Looking Good, Feeling Good Program: A multi-ethnic intervention for healthy body image, nutrition, and physical activity. In N. Piran, M. P. Levine, & C. Steiner-Adair (Eds.), *Preventing eating disorders: A handbook of interventions and special challenges* (pp. 175–193). Philadelphia: Brunner/Mazel.

Orenstein, P. (1994). *Schoolgirls: Young women, self-esteem, and the confidence gap.* New York: Doubleday.

Parker, S., Nichter, Mi., Nichter, Ma., Vuckovic, N., Sims, C., & Ritenbaugh, C. (1995). Body image and weight concerns among African American and White adolescent females: Differences that make a difference. *Human Organization, 54,* 103–114.

Phinney, J. (1996). When we talk about American ethnic groups, what do we mean? *American Psychologist, 51,* 918–927.

Phinney, J., & Chavera, V. (1995). Parental ethnic and socialization and adolescent coping with problems related to ethnicity. *Journal of Research on Adolescence, 5,* 31–54.

Phinney, J., & Devich-Navarro, M. (1998). Variations in bicultural identification among African American and Mexican American adolescents. *Journal of Research on Adolescence, 7,* 3–32.

Piran, N. (1999). The reduction of preoccupation with body weight and shape in schools: A feminist approach. In N. Piran, M. P. Levine, & C. Steiner-Adair (Eds.), *Preventing eating disorders: A handbook of interventions and special challenges* (pp. 148–159). Philadelphia: Brunner/Mazel.

Polivy, J., & Herman, C. P. (1993). Etiology of binge eating: Psychological mechanisms. In C. Fairburn & G. T. Wilson (Eds.), *Binge eating: Nature, assessment, and treatment* (pp. 173–205). New York: Guilford Press.

Roberts, R., & Sobhan, M. (1992). Symptoms of depression in adolescence: A comparison of Anglo, African, and Hispanic Americans. *Journal of Youth & Adolescence, 21,* 639–651.

Robinson, T., Change, J., Haydel, K., & Killen, J. (in press). Overweight concerns, body dissatisfaction and desired body shape among 3rd grade children: The impact of ethnicity, socioeconomic status and acculturation. *Journal of Pediatrics.*

Robinson, T. N., Killen, J. D., Litt, I. F., Hammer, L. D., Wilson, D. M., Haydel, K. F., Hayward, C., & Taylor, C. B. (1996). Ethnicity and body dissatisfaction: Are Latina and Asian girls at increased risk for eating disorders? *Journal of Adolescent Health, 19,* 384–393.

Rodin, J., Silberstein, L. R., & Striegel-Moore, R. H. (1985). Women and weight: A normative discontent. In T. B. Sonderegger (Ed.), *Nebraska Symposium on Motivation* (pp. 267–308). Lincoln: University of Nebraska Press.

Rosen, K. (1996). The principles of developmental psychopathology: Illustration from the study of eating disorders. In L. Smolak, M. P. Levine, & R. H. Striegel-Moore (Eds.), *The developmental psychopathology of eating disorders: Implications for research, prevention, and treatment* (pp. 3–30). Mahwah, NJ: Erlbaum.

Rosner, B., Prineas, R., Loggie, J., & Daniels, S. R. (1998). Percentiles for body mass index in U.S. children 5 to 17 years of age. *Journal of Pediatrics, 132,* 211–222.

Sadker, M., & Sadker, D. (1993). *Failing at fairness: How American schools cheat girls.* New York: Scribner's.

Schreiber, G. B., Robins, M., Striegel-Moore, R., Obarzanek, E., Morrison, J. A., & Wright, D. J. (1996). Weight modification efforts reported by Black and White preadolescent girls. *Pediatrics, 98,* 63–70.

Smith, D. E., Marcus, M. D., Lewis, C., Fitzgibbon, M., & Schreiner, P. (1998). Prevalence of binge eating disorder, obesity, and depression in a biracial cohort of young adults. *Annals of Behavioral Medicine, 20,* 227–232.

Smolak, L. (1999). Elementary school curricula for the primary prevention of eating problems. In N. Piran, M. P. Levine, & C. Steiner-Adair (Eds.), *Preventing eating disorders: A handbook of interventions and special challenges* (pp. 85–104). Philadelphia: Brunner/Mazel.

Smolak, L., & Levine, M. P. (1996). Adolescent transitions and the development of eating problems. In L. Smolak, M. P. Levine, & R. H. Striegel-Moore (Eds.), *The developmental psychopathology of eating disorders: Implications for research, prevention, and treatment* (pp. 207–234). Mahwah, NJ: Erlbaum.

Smolak, L., & Levine, M. P. (in press). Body image in children. In J. K. Thompson & L. Smolak (Eds.), *Body image, eating disorders, and obesity in youth: Theory, assessment, treatment, and prevention.* Washington, DC: American Psychological Association.

Stice, E. (1994). Review of the evidence for a sociocultural model of bulimia nervosa and an exploration of the mechanisms of action. *Clinical Psychology Review, 14,* 633–661.

Stice, E. (1998). Relations of restraint and negative affect to bulimic pathology: A longitudinal test of three competing models. *International Journal of Eating Disorders, 23,* 243–260.

Story, M., French, S. A., Resnick, M. D., & Blum, R. W. (1995). Ethnic/racial and socioeconomic differences in dieting behaviors and body image perceptions in adolescents. *International Journal of Eating Disorders, 18,* 173–179.

Striegel-Moore, R. (1993). Etiology of binge eating: A developmental perspective. In C. Fairburn & G. T. Wilson (Eds.), *Binge eating: Nature, assessment, and treatment* (pp. 144–172). New York: Guilford Press.

Striegel-Moore, R., Dohm, F., Fairburn, C., Pike, K., & Wilfley, D. (1999, November). *Risk factors for binge eating disorder.* Paper presented at the annual meeting of the Eating Disorder Research Society, San Diego, CA.

Striegel-Moore, R. H., Garvin, V., Dohm, F. A., & Rosenheck, R. A. (1999). Eating disorders in a national sample of hospitalized female and male veterans: Detection rates and comorbidity. *International Journal of Eating Disorders, 25,* 405–414.

Striegel-Moore, R. H., & Smolak, L. (1996). The role of race in the development of eating disorders. In L. Smolak, M. P. Levine, & R. H. Striegel-Moore (Eds.), *The developmental psychopathology of eating disorders* (pp. 259–284). Mahwah, NJ: Erlbaum.

Striegel-Moore, R. H., & Smolak, L. (2000). The influence of ethnicity on eating disorders in women. In R. Eisler & M. Hersen (Eds.), *Handbook of gender, culture, and health* (pp. 227–254). Mahwah, NJ: Erlbaum.

Striegel-Moore, R. H., Wilfley, D. E., Caldwell, M. B., Needham, M. L., & Brownell, K. D. (1996). Weight-related attitudes and behaviors of women who diet to lose weight: A comparison of Black dieters and White dieters. *Obesity Research, 4*, 109–116.

Striegel-Moore, R. H., Wilfley, D., Pike, K., Dohm, F., & Fairburn, C. (2000). Recurrent binge eating in Black American women. *Archives of Family Medicine, 9*, 83–87.

Taylor, J., Gilligan, C., & Sullivan, A. (1995). *Between voice and silence: Women and girls, race and relationship*. Cambridge, MA: Harvard University Press.

Telch, C. F., & Agras, W. S. (1994). Obesity, binge eating and psychopathology: Are they related? *International Journal of Eating Disorders, 15*, 53–61.

Thompson, B. W. (1994). *A hunger so wide and so deep: American women speak out on eating problems*. Minneapolis: University of Minnesota Press.

Thompson, J. K., Heinberg, L., Altabe, M., & Tantleff-Dunn, S. (1999). *Exacting beauty: Theory, assessment, and treatment of body image disturbance*. Washington, DC: American Psychological Association.

U.S. Bureau of Labor Statistics (2000). *Median usual weekly earning of full-time wage and salary workers by age, race, Hispanic origin, and sex, third quarter 2000 averages, not seasonally adjusted*. Retrieved November 21, 2000 from the World Wide Web http://www.bls.gov/news.release/wkyeng.t02.htm

U.S. Equal Employment Opportunities Commission. (2000). *Race-based charges FY1992–FY1999*. Retrieved on November 21, 2000 from the World Wide Web http://www.eeoc.gov/stats/race.html

van Hoeken, D., Lucas, A. R., & Hoek, H. W. (1998). Epidemiology. In H. W. Hoek, J. T. Treasure, & M. A. Katzman (Eds.), *Neurobiology in the treatment of eating disorders* (pp. 97–126). New York: Wiley.

Waller, G., & Matoba, M. (1999). Emotional eating and eating psychopathology in nonclinical groups: A cross-cultural comparison of women in Japan and the United Kingdom. *International Journal of Eating Disorders, 26*, 333–340.

Wilfley, D., Schreiber, G., Pike, K., Striegel-Moore, R., Wright, D., & Rodin, J. (1996). Eating disturbance and body image: A comparison of a community sample of adult Black and White women. *International Journal of Eating Disorders, 20*, 377–387.

Winkleby, M. A., Gardner, C. D., & Taylor, C. B. (1996). The influence of gender and socioeconomic factors on Latina/White differences in body mass index. *Preventive Medicine, 25*, 203–211.

Yanovski, S. Z. (1993). Binge eating disorder: Current knowledge and future directions. *Obesity Research, 1*, 306–318.

II

TREATMENT

The nature of psychological treatment is changing. College physicians are hard pressed to find nearby inpatient programs for their most troubled students. Private practice psychologists bemoan the limited amount of time they are given to effectively help clients. Research suggests that eating disorder patients do not receive as much care as would be consistent with recently updated treatment guidelines (Striegel-Moore, Leslie, Petrill, Garvin, & Rosenheck, 2000). Government representatives struggle to find legislative remedies to ensure fair, cost-effective treatment. The impact of managed care is everywhere.

This part begins with an important chapter by Vicki Garvin and Ruth Striegel-Moore (chapter 7) in which they document such changes and their potential effect on eating disorder practitioners and clients. They outline not only how managed care has affected services but also what types of data are available and what data are needed to help ensure better treatment for clients. Their research agenda will be crucial in improving and monitoring the care available to Americans diagnosed with eating disorders.

Necessity is the mother of invention, and one necessity created by managed care is shorter, less-expensive treatment options. In chapter 8, Vicki Garvin, Ruth Striegel-Moore, Allan Kaplan, and Stephen Wonderlich look at one such option: professionally developed self-help interventions. They point out important differences between these self-help programs and those that were popular in the 1960s and 1970s. They also consider the strengths and weaknesses of these programs, noting the research questions that need to be addressed before such programs can be comfortably recommended.

In chapter 9, Stephen Wonderlich, James Mitchell, Carol Peterson, and Scott Crow consider how cognitive–behavior therapy (CBT) might be made more effective. CBT is arguably the single best therapy currently available to treat eating disorders. Yet it falls far short of helping all clients. Wonderlich et al. propose a new paradigm for CBT, incorporating the heretofore missing elements of interpersonal relationships and emotional functioning. Their program, which is still being developed, offers numerous opportunities for research evaluation that will be helpful not only to those using this program but also in the development of other treatment options.

Finally, the enormous success of pharmacological treatments with other psychiatric disorders, including depression that is so often comorbid with eating disorders, has led many to wonder whether drug therapy might be efficacious with eating disorders. In chapter 10, James Mitchell considers this question, exploring a variety of drugs that have been tried in the treatment of eating disorders. He points out what still needs to be discovered to identify more effective drug therapies, emphasizing how they might be combined with other treatment options to best offer relief from eating disorders.

REFERENCE

Striegel-Moore, R. H., Leslie, D., Petrill, S. A., Garvin, V., & Rosenheck, R. (2000). One-year use and cost of inpatient and outpatient services among female and male patients with an eating disorder: Evidence from a national database of health insurance claims. *International Journal of Eating Disorders, 27*, 381–389.

7

HEALTH SERVICES RESEARCH FOR EATING DISORDERS IN THE UNITED STATES: A STATUS REPORT AND A CALL TO ACTION

VICKI GARVIN AND RUTH H. STRIEGEL-MOORE

Bulimia nervosa and anorexia nervosa are relatively rare but serious eating disorders, associated with significant impairments in physical, psychological, and social functioning (Becker, Grinspoon, Klibanski, & Herzog, 1999). In the past 15 years, there have been great strides in developing evidence-based treatments (see Mitchell, chapter 10, this volume; and Peterson & Mitchell, 1999), yet research suggests that many individuals with eating disorders do not seek or are not being identified and referred for treatment (Hoek, 1991; Ogg, Millar, Pusztai, & Thom, 1997; Whitehouse, Cooper, Vize, Hill, & Vogel, 1992). Moreover, recent changes in the financing and delivery of health care in the United States have resulted in limited insurance coverage for eating disorder care, which, in turn, has reduced access to needed services (Academy for Eating Disorders, 1998; Hill & Maloney, 1997; Wooley, 1993).

At present, relatively little is known about health services in the United States for people with eating disorders. By *health services*, we are referring to data on the type, distribution, and accessibility of behavioral and medical health services; the type, distribution, and training of providers; and the use, benefits, and costs of these services (Olfson & Pincus, 1994). This chapter brings together research in the areas of epidemiology, develop-

This work was supported by a supplemental career reentry award funded jointly by the Office of Research of Women's Health of the National Institutes of Health and the National Institute of Mental Health (RO1 MH52348-01A1).

mental psychopathology, and treatment outcome to provide a status report on health services in the United States for eating disorders. First, we review epidemiological studies of the prevalence and comorbidity of anorexia nervosa, bulimia nervosa, and eating disorders not otherwise specified. These studies provide the foundation for identifying potential users of eating disorder care and the scope of needed services. Second, we investigate the factors that facilitate or create barriers to treatment seeking. Third, we examine the types of services used and the factors associated with service use and treatment compliance. Fourth, we consider the handful of studies with data on service providers for eating disorders. On the basis of these studies, we generate hypotheses about how provider characteristics may be related to case identification, treatment referral, and treatment outcome. Finally, we summarize studies in which researchers have examined the cost of eating disorder services. We raise questions about how cost could be defined and encourage researchers to consider cost in the context of treatment outcome.

EPIDEMIOLOGICAL STUDIES OF EATING DISORDERS

The first step in identifying potential users of health care is to obtain frequency estimates and basic demographic correlates of the disorder in the community. To date, in the United States four community-based, epidemiological studies provide information about eating disorders in adults (17 years or older): the Epidemiological Catchment Area Study (ECA; Robins et al., 1984), the Virginia Twin Study (Kendler et al., 1991; Walters & Kendler, 1995), the Stanford Study (Bruce & Agras, 1992), and the National Women's Study (Dansky, Brewerton, Kilpatrick, & O'Neil, 1997). In addition, two epidemiological studies were used to ascertain the prevalence of eating disorders in adolescents: the New Jersey Adolescent Study (M. Whitaker et al., 1990) and the Oregon Adolescent Depression Study (Lewinsohn, Hops, Roberts, Seeley, & Andrews, 1993).

These studies show that younger populations have higher rates of eating disorders than older populations (because of cohort effects and because onset occurs during adolescence and early adulthood) and that eating disorders are relatively uncommon (lifetime prevalence estimates for women range from less than 0.5% for anorexia nervosa to about 3.0% for bulimia nervosa). Several U.S. population groups have been understudied, yet they represent potential users of eating disorder health care. These understudied populations include the following groups.

1. With the exception of the ECA (carried out over 2 decades ago, before bulimia nervosa was introduced into the psychiatric

nomenclature), there is no study that includes a nationally representative sample of men. Although results from a community-based Canadian study (Garfinkel et al., 1995, 1996) show that men are much less at risk for both anorexia nervosa and bulimia nervosa than are women, eating disorders do occur in a small subset of men, and research is needed regarding their specific health service needs. Moreover, preliminary studies of binge-eating disorder suggest that men are relatively more likely to develop binge-eating disorder than anorexia nervosa or bulimia nervosa, yet to date the prevalence of binge-eating disorder among male populations is unknown.

2. Minority populations are either absent or severely underrepresented in epidemiologic studies of eating disorders. Case and survey studies show that members of ethnic minority groups are also vulnerable to eating disorders (Striegel-Moore & Smolak, 2000; Striegel-Moore, Wilfley, Pike, Dohm, & Fairburn, 2000), and research is needed on the clinical characteristics and service needs of people of color with eating disorders. This is particularly important because in community studies, researchers have already established that self-disclosure, help seeking, and access to health services can differ by ethnicity (Vessey & Howard, 1993).

3. Additional data are needed on both ends of the age spectrum. Although eating disorders are far more common in young adults, eating disorders also occur in middle-aged women (Hay, 1998). Similarly, although eating disorders are rare in young children, the sequelae are serious (Bryant-Waugh & Lask, 1995; Childress, Brewerton, Hodges, & Jarrell, 1993). Children may also have particular difficulty accessing needed health services, given their dependence on adults and the large number of children without health insurance.

4. The recognition of anorexia nervosa and bulimia nervosa as spectrum disorders (Garfinkel et al., 1995, 1996; Kendler et al., 1991; Walters & Kendler, 1995) raises the issue about the availability of health services for people who suffer from disordered eating but do not meet full diagnostic criteria. In the present U.S. health care system, these individuals may not qualify for "medically necessary" treatment.

5. Only the Stanford Study (Bruce & Agras, 1992) provides epidemiological data on eating disorder not otherwise specified, although eating disorder not otherwise specified is estimated to affect more individuals than anorexia nervosa and

bulimia nervosa combined (Striegel-Moore & Marcus, 1995). Data on the clinical presentation and health service needs of this group are clearly needed.

Epidemiological studies also show that both adolescent girls and adult women with anorexia nervosa and bulimia nervosa have high rates of comorbid psychiatric disorders, such as depression, generalized anxiety disorder, alcoholism, phobias, panic disorder, and posttraumatic stress disorder (Dansky et al., 1997; Kendler et al., 1991; Lewinsohn et al., 1993; Walters & Kendler, 1995; A. Whitaker, 1992). Men with eating disorders also have high rates of psychiatric comorbidity (Carlat, Camargo, & Herzog, 1997). However, men with eating disorders may evidence certain comorbidities not typically found among women, such as organic disorders or schizophrenia (Striegel-Moore, Garvin, Dohm, & Rosenheck, 1999). The implications of these findings for service use and treatment outcome remain to be explored.

At present, there are no comparable epidemiological studies examining medical comorbidity. However, clinic-based studies show that people with eating disorders evidence menstrual and reproductive irregularities, cardiovascular problems, gastrointestinal disturbance, fluid and electrolyte imbalance, dental erosion, bone density problems, infertility, and obesity (Pike & Striegel-Moore, 1997). Documenting in a community sample the range of medical disorders associated with eating disorders would be an invaluable addition to the current debate over economic parity in benefit coverage for medical and mental disorders.

From a health services perspective, these comorbidity studies point to the following research concerns. First, although it is clear that eating disorders typically present in the context of another psychiatric disorder, presently relatively little is known about how comorbidity is related to case detection, referral, and prognosis. Are there certain co-occurring conditions, for example, alcohol and substance abuse, that have a high public cost (e.g., reduced work productivity) and relatively high visibility that make it more likely for a person with a comorbid eating disorder to be identified for treatment? Conversely, are there other patterns of comorbidity, for example, the relatively rare presentation of eating disorders and psychotic disorder (Striegel-Moore et al., 1999), that are likely to go underidentified and undertreated? Second, the range of medical comorbidity in eating disorders needs to be examined in a community-based study. At present, little is known about the implications of medical comorbidity for case identification, treatment seeking, and treatment referral. For example, research is needed to determine whether case identification may be improved by training medical practitioners (e.g., gynecologists) with high proportions of young female patients to recognize the known medical correlates of eating disorders or to administer screening instruments to their patients (see also Becker et al., 1999). Third, the multiple comorbidity of eating disorders raises issues about the focus and sequencing of treatment services. At present, there are no research-based guidelines to help clinicians decide which disorder should be treated first or if the disorders can be addressed simultaneously. Relatedly, it is unknown how productive treatment approaches are that focus solely on the eating disorder. Fourth, as comorbidity is associated with greater functional impairment, the identification of comorbidity can provide the documentation required by managed care companies to justify intensive, long-term, or multimodal health services.

DETERMINANTS AND BARRIERS TO TREATMENT SEEKING

In his recent report on mental health, the U.S. Surgeon General noted that "effective, well-documented treatments exist for most mental disorders, *yet nearly half of all Americans who have a severe mental illness fail to seek treatment* (Satcher, 1999, p. 1, emphasis added). It is not clear just how many Americans with eating disorders remain unidentified and untreated or what factors contribute to identification and treatment referral. European studies also suggest that treatment seeking is low among individuals with an eating disorder (e.g., Hoek, 1991).

Given the large number of sufferers who are not receiving treatment, it is imperative to investigate factors associated with service use. In general psychiatric samples, person factors, such as demographic characteristics (Olfson & Pincus, 1994) and clinical manifestation (e.g., severity), have been found to be related to probability of use, number of visits, and referral to specialty treatment (Kessler et al., 1999; Wu, Kouzis, & Leaf, 1999).

Preliminary studies suggest that individuals with anorexia nervosa are more likely to have received treatment than individuals with bulimia nervosa (A. Whitaker, 1992; Yager, Landsverk, & Edelstein, 1989). For example, a 1984 survey of 5,596 high school boys and girls shows that students with anorexia nervosa (83.3%) were more likely to have received professional services than those with bulimia nervosa (27.8%; A. Whitaker, 1992). At present, eating disorder researchers know little about other person factors that facilitate or impede treatment seeking. In a sample of obese individuals, Sansone, Sansone, and Wiederman (1998) reported that increasing body mass index was associated with greater health care use, primarily because of increased morbidity. In a related study, Fitzgibbon, Stolley, and Kirschenbaum (1993) found that obese people who sought treatment reported greater psychopathology and more binge eating than nontreatment seekers. Clinical experience suggests that denial and shame are associated with delayed help seeking, but to date, there have been no systematic studies of the association between personality factors or attitudes toward help seeking and health care use for people with eating disorders.

These studies raise several concerns that could be addressed by health service researchers. First, research is needed about the rates of treatment seeking in the United States. Recent European studies suggest that rates of treatment seeking are especially low for bulimia nervosa (e.g., Fairburn, Welch, Doll, Davies, & O'Connor, 1997). Second, given the hypothesized association between early detection–treatment and improved outcome, it is important to investigate factors that are associated with delayed help seeking. These would include demographic factors (Olfson & Pincus, 1994; Vessey & Howard, 1993), clinical features (e.g., duration of disorder, partial syndrome status, psychiatric comorbidity; Fairburn, Welch, Norman, O'Connor, & Doll, 1996; Wu et al., 1999), and attitudes that influence treatment seeking. As discussed later in this chapter, research on these personal characteristics needs to be complemented by research on institutional and service provider factors that may impede case identification and treatment seeking.

TYPES OF SERVICES AND SERVICE USE

For those individuals with eating disorders who do seek treatment, relatively little is known about the types of psychiatric and medical services being used. Over 15 years ago, researchers began to study psychiatric service use (Johnson, Stuckey, Lewis, & Schwartz, 1982; Yager et al., 1989), but unfortunately, these preliminary investigations were never followed up. Likewise, we could find no current, comprehensive description of medical service use, although clinical experience suggests that individuals with eating disorders are high consumers of medical care. Similarly, little is known about the range of pharmacological interventions offered to individuals with anorexia nervosa and bulimia nervosa. Despite significant progress in drug therapies (see Mitchell, chapter 10, this volume) and psychotherapies (Peterson & Mitchell, 1999), it is not known to what extent practitioners in the community are actually using these empirically validated pharmacotherapies and psychotherapies. Relatedly, although practice guidelines are available (American Psychiatric Association, 2000), it is not known to what extent current service patterns conform to these guidelines.

One recent study has begun to address this research gap. Using a large national insurance database, which contained claims for 1,902,041 male patients and 2,005,760 female patients, Striegel-Moore, Leslie, Petrill, Garvin, and Rosenheck (2000) identified patients with an eating disorder and examined the amount of treatment they received. Eating disorder treatment of any kind was found to be very rare, confirming what specialists have long suspected: Eating disorders tend to go undetected, untreated, or both. For those individuals who did receive treatment, neither the average number of inpatient days for anorexia nervosa nor outpatient sessions for bulimia nervosa met the American Psychiatric Association's (2000) practice guidelines for recommended duration of care. Male patients with eating disorders appeared to be at a double disadvantage: They were less likely to receive treatment than female patients, and those who did were likely to receive less care (Striegel-Moore, Leslie, et al., 2000). As demonstrated by this study, institutional databases can provide descriptive data on frequency and duration of psychiatric service use that are greatly needed.

A handful of new studies provides data that can ultimately guide decisions about sequencing of care, level of care (e.g., inpatient, day treatment, outpatient), and duration of treatment. Research on *treatment sequencing* (i.e., the optimal provision and timing of services for an eating disorder and the comorbid conditions) is in the early stages. Preliminary studies suggest that for obese people with binge-eating disorder, outcome is improved if treatment for the binge eating precedes attempts at weight loss (Telch & Agras, 1994). However, for common psychiatric comorbidities (e.g., mood, anxiety, and substance abuse disorder), we do not know under what conditions simultaneous treatments enhance or detract from effectiveness. Indeed, as Mitchell, Maki, Adson, Ruskin, and Crow (1997) showed, clinical trials often screen out potential patients on the basis of certain comorbid conditions.

With respect to level of care and duration of treatment, recent studies suggest that the initial provision of more expensive, intensive inpatient treatment for anorexia nervosa is associated with reduced relapse and therefore reduced overall personal, social, and financial costs in the long term. Studies examining the factors predictive of readiness for step down from inpatient to day treatment offer promising new models for relating level of care and compliance with discharge criteria to treatment outcome (Commerford, Licinio, & Halmi, 1997; Howard, Evans, Quintero-Howard, Bowers, & Andersen, 1999).

Researchers are also beginning to investigate the health care benefits of *stepped care* approaches for eating disorders: the initial provision of brief, less intensive, relatively inexpensive care, followed by increasingly longer, more intensive, and more costly treatments (e.g., Treasure et al., 1996). Research is needed to determine the potential financial savings realized by minimal interventions as well as the financial and subjective costs in delaying more intensive treatment for those individuals who do not respond to brief interventions (see also Garvin, Striegel-Moore, Kaplan, & Wonderlich, chapter 8, this volume).

Service use, whether in the context of a stepped care or an alternative service delivery model, is only viable if people are willing to engage in this kind of program. To date, researchers have found that engagement and compliance are particularly low for drug trials, the stricter regimes for anorexia nervosa, and computerized cognitive–behavior therapy (CBT) self-help programs (for a review, see Treasure & Schmidt, 1999). For bulimia nervosa, higher dropout rates are associated with comorbid borderline personality disorder, self-harm, and substance abuse. For anorexia nervosa, dropout rates from inpatient treatment have been related to age at admission, duration of illness, educational level, social class, and parental sabotage and emotional reactivity. More could be learned about the subjective appraisals, such as degree of perceived control or level of confidence in treatment providers, which are related to the perceived acceptability of program participation.

Ideally, treatment seeking and treatment compliance would be examined in the context of clinical outcome studies. For anorexia nervosa, there are formidable challenges in conducting randomized clinical trials (RCT). As Mitchell, Peterson, and Agras (1999) reviewed, difficulties include problems with informed consent (especially for adolescent patients), poor motivation of participants (typically resulting in high dropout rates), the need for multiple interventions (complicating randomization), and inequities in insurance coverage (biasing the samples because of differential access to inpatient hospitalization).

For bulimia nervosa, there are considerably more data on treatment outcome. RCTs show that about half of participants with bulimia nervosa will experience a significant symptom reduction after a 16- to 20-week course of either CBT or interpersonal psychotherapy (Peterson & Mitchell, 1999). However, there is concern about the representativeness of participants in the clinical trials. Mitchell et al. (1997) found that compared with the general population of women with bulimia nervosa, participants in clinical trials were younger, weighed less, and reported less substance use involvement. Dissemination studies are needed to assess whether efficacious treatments will generalize to community practice settings with their more diverse populations.

Our review highlights the need to comprehensively document the range of medical, psychological, and pharmacological treatments for eating disorders currently provided in the diverse U.S. health care environment. As a first step, researchers could characterize the type, duration, frequency, and theoretical orientation of services. Toward this end, the Academy of Eating Disorders is currently conducting a survey of practitioners, which is intended to provide much-needed data on the intervention strategies and services currently offered in actual practice settings (S. Wonderlich, personal communication, November 20, 1999). Second, given current pressures toward mental health cost containment, researchers can further examine the benefits and costs of treatment sequencing and stepped care. Third, more needs to be learned about both the personal factors (e.g., motivation) and service factors (e.g., duration of treatment) associated with treatment engagement and compliance. Fourth, the identification of the participants who do not improve over the course of treatment trials could facilitate more appropriate referrals, ultimately improving outcome and reducing overall cost.

HEALTH CARE ADMINISTRATION AND SERVICE PROVIDERS

Over the past decade, the administration and financing of U.S. health care have changed dramatically. In mental health care there are three new trends: an increased reliance on bachelor's-level and master's-level therapists, decreased access to specialist therapists, and an increased percentage of individuals treated by outpatient rather than inpatient therapists (Newell & Saltzman, 1997). Moreover, staff at managed care companies (rather than physicians providing the care) or primary care physicians (with little training in mental health) are increasingly responsible for the authorization of psychiatric services. Researchers in the United States have not yet investigated how these changes affect case identification, referral, and treatment outcome for eating disorders.

European studies show an association between provider characteristics and the identification of eating disorders. Specifically, these studies all show that nonspecialist clinicians were likely to fail to detect eating disorders (Hoek, 1991; Ogg et al., 1997; Whitehouse et al., 1992). An exploratory study reports that the presence of a female physician, larger practices, higher levels of training, and a professional connection with a tertiary care center were associated with higher referral rates to specialty care for patients with eating disorders (Hugo, Reid, Kendrick, & Lacey, 1997).

Therapist factors, such as role modeling, identification, and the ability to manage the vicissitudes of the patient–therapist relationship, are also known to affect treatment outcome (Luborsky, McLellan, Diguer, Woody, & Seligman, 1997). In the United States, managed care companies increasingly move toward standardized and manualized treatments and easily quantified predictors, these therapist or relationship factors are likely to be minimized by the health care industry. It is imperative that the therapist's contribution becomes an empirical question, not a political or economic question. For example, researchers could study how factors such as confidence in the therapist or level of interpersonal comfort with the therapist are related to treatment outcome in guided self-help programs.

Preliminary evidence suggests that the growth of managed care is associated with shorter lengths of inpatient treatment for individuals with anorexia nervosa and a reduction in treatment for all individuals with eating disorders (reviewed in Kaye, Kaplan, & Zucker, 1996). This trend is alarming, given that insufficient treatment duration has been shown to contribute to poor outcome and higher rates of relapse in patients with anorexia nervosa (Howard et al., 1999; Via, Kaye, Pavetto, & Crossan, 1997). The current practice of administering and financing mental health services separately from physical health (through mental health "carve outs") makes it difficult to document comprehensively the negative medical outcomes (e.g., infertility, osteoporosis) of inadequate treatment of mental disorders because data for medical and psychiatric conditions are now maintained in separate databases.

Our brief review suggests several areas for future research. First, studies are needed of how provider characteristics affect case identification, service use, and treatment outcome of eating disorders. For example, how do the provider's demographic characteristics, level of training, or years of experience relate to the type and outcome of treatment? Second, researchers can investigate how the administrative and financial policies specific to the different managed care companies affect case identification, referral, and treatment. Are rates of identification higher for health plans that allow the insured person to choose her or his provider or cover the costs of specialty care? Is outcome worse for individuals whose health plan imposes severe restrictions on the type or intensity of care? Third, researchers could examine how service factors, such as the availability of general practice versus specialty centers, or medical versus psychiatric inpatient units, relate to the identification, referral, and treatment of eating disorders.

COST OF SERVICES

Researchers have only recently included cost–benefit and cost-effectiveness analysis in the evaluation of treatments for eating disorders. These studies raise complex ethical, methodological, and political issues.

Koran et al. (1995) conducted an exploratory post hoc study that compared the cost-effectiveness of five treatments for bulimia nervosa, which included CBT, medication treatment with desipramine, and combined CBT and desipramine therapy. They were careful to point out the complexities involved in the measurement and interpretation of cost effectiveness:

> First, the most cost-effective treatment may not be the most effective treatment. Second, the outcome of a cost-effectiveness analysis depends strongly on when the evaluation data are collected. ... Third, the outcome measure will strongly influence the analysis. ... Fourth, the cost-effectiveness balance for an individual patient may vary considerably from the average cost-effectiveness balance for a treatment group. ... Finally, the results of a cost-effectiveness analysis can be strongly influenced by the patient's stage of illness at treatment entry, by age and treatment history, and by such variables as the quality of the patient's social support system. (Koran et al., 1995, p. 19)

Using a similar research design, Mitchell et al. (1999) compared the costs of individual CBT, group CBT, and medication (fluoxetine) treatment for bulimia nervosa. Mitchell et al. emphasized that treatment effectiveness is a complex outcome variable that can be defined narrowly (e.g., reduction in bingeing) or more broadly (e.g., improvement in quality of life or work productivity). The definition of outcome strongly influences the interpretation of the treatment's cost effectiveness. Similarly, cost can be narrowly and most easily defined as professional fees or could include such hard-to-measure costs as expenditures for training and supervision.

Several experts have investigated the relationship among level of care, duration of treatment, treatment outcome, and cost effectiveness. Hill and Maloney (1997) reported that patients with anorexia nervosa who were discharged while still underweight experienced worse outcomes and higher rates of rehospitalization. Via et al. (1997) found that the initial provision of lengthy, relatively expensive treatment for anorexia nervosa resulted in long-term monetary savings because of improved outcome. Howard et al. (1999) demonstrated that inpatients with anorexia nervosa with poor prognostic indicators, such as longer duration of illness or lower body mass index at the time of inpatient admission, require longer inpatient stays, which are initially more expensive but ultimately reduce recidivism and overall costs in the long term.

For bulimia nervosa, the relationships among health service use, outcome, and cost are also complicated. Based on a review of 88 studies that include follow-up assessment with bulimic participants at least 6 months postpresentation, Keel and Mitchell (1997) concluded that treatment interventions may speed eventual recovery in the first 5 years postintervention; however, after the 5-year mark, "no difference in recovery rates exists between a sample of women who received early and consistent intervention and women whose treatment varied in the community or who received no treatment at all" (p. 320). Does this indicate that in the first 5 years treatment is cost effective? Does this mean that if recovery is speeded up, then the significant (and expensive) medical comorbidity of bulimia nervosa is reduced? If after 10 years all groups had similar recovery rates, how should this be interpreted by insurance companies that currently only provide and reimburse for "medically necessary" treatment? What is the time frame for establishing "medical necessity": 1 year, 5 years, 10 years? Finally, this provocative study highlights that there was a subset of women with a chronic course. What are the treatment options and costs for these women, who are potentially recurrent consumers of health care?

More research is needed regarding the cost of not providing care. For example, Ogg et al. (1997) found that patients with eating disorders, compared with controls, consulted their general practitioner significantly more in the 5 years prior to the diagnosis of an eating disorder. These consultations were for a variety of psychological, gastrointestinal, and gynecological complaints, which presumably were the costly medical and financial consequences of the undetected and untreated eating disorder. Not yet documented empirically are the social costs (Kessler & Frank, 1997; Ustun, 1999) associated with untreated eating disorders (e.g., divorce, loss of work productivity). It is clear that in determining costs for treating eating disorders, one must assess the medical, psychological, and social costs of not treating the eating disorder. Appropriate medical and psychological interventions, even those requiring high initial expenditures, may result in significant cost savings over time.

These preliminary studies point to several promising avenues for future research. First, researchers need to develop comprehensive definitions of cost. Second, because eating disorders are shown to be cyclical and may require a lengthy time period for recovery, cost-effectiveness studies need to include a time frame significantly longer than the 1-year enrollment period typically used by insurance companies. Third, the medical, psychological, and social costs of providing no treatment, delayed treatment, or insufficient treatment of an eating disorder need to be measured. Fourth, it is essential that cost be related to treatment effectiveness. Here, again, it is critical that clinical researchers knowledgeable about eating disorders contribute to the definition of cost and effectiveness.

CONCLUSION

Researchers working in the areas of epidemiology, developmental psychopathology, and treatment outcome have provided informative data on the prevalence, course, and prognosis of bulimia nervosa and anorexia nervosa. Building on this research base, researchers have found that it is now possible to investigate the complex health service needs of individuals suffering from eating disorders. To accomplish this goal requires new data, collaborative research efforts, and broadened research designs. To further identify who needs what kinds of eating disorder services, researchers should obtain additional data on male patients, people of color, children and young adolescents, middle-aged and older adults, people with eating disorder not otherwise specified, and medical and psychiatric comorbidity. However, in view of the low base rates for eating disorders and, consequently, the need for extremely large samples to obtain representative prevalence rates, it is not economical to pursue large epidemiological studies that focus solely on anorexia nervosa, bulimia nervosa, or eating disorder not otherwise specified. Instead, collaborative studies of general psychiatric epidemiology (examining the range of Axis I and Axis II disorders) could provide data on prevalence, specific risk factors, general risk factors, comorbidity, and developmental course.

Data on cross-sectional and longitudinal comorbidity would be particularly useful for informing the timing of preventive interventions and the sequencing of multiple treatments. Long-term trend data can be used to determine whether the need for specific health services is increasing or decreasing, while also enabling researchers to sort out the determinants of the trends (e.g., true incidence changes, environmental causes, methodological artifacts; Pawluck & Gorey, 1998). If conducted in collaboration with researchers investigating health service use, such studies also could determine who is being referred for which kinds of treatments and, conversely, who remains unidentified and untreated. For example, older patients may use different types of treatments compared with younger patients. Determining the demographic, psychiatric, and medical profiles associated with delayed use or nonuse would aid in the identification of barriers to case detection and referral.

Researchers should also identify the range of providers and services currently available for eating disorder care (Pincus et al., 1999). Toward this end, Wonderlich, Mussel, and Mitchell (S. Wonderlich, personal communication, November 20, 1999) are planning to survey members of the Academy of Eating Disorders, a multidisciplinary organization of eating disorder specialists, asking detailed questions about theoretical orientation, intervention strategies, practice setting, training, and caseload. When administered to a representative sample of providers, such surveys can provide valuable data on the range of eating disorder services available in the diverse health care environment of the United States and help determine the extent to which community practitioners use the treatments tested in clinical trials.

For separate research endeavors to contribute optimally to the same knowledge base, researchers should ideally use similar diagnostic criteria and operationalize major variables in similar ways. Mitchell (personal communication, November 13, 2000) provided valuable direction by encouraging researchers to use a standard assessment protocol and to submit their data into a common database. This would greatly facilitate the comparison of participants across study sites, thereby contributing to systematic data collection on diagnosis, health service use, and treatment outcome.

With a common research language and methodology, it would be possible to link health services use data (e.g., service users, providers, and treatments) to treatment outcome research. This broadened research scope requires the collaboration of epidemiologists, health service researchers, and treatment outcome researchers. It is imperative that clinical researchers join the current debate about cost and treatment effectiveness. Otherwise, there is the considerable danger that insurance companies, focused on the bottom line, will develop increasingly stringent definitions of cost (e.g., severe functional impairment, with no consideration of subjective cost), with correspondingly limited definitions of improvement (e.g., a return to 90% ideal body weight for a patient with anorexia and no consideration of resources for self-care and social competencies).

Managed care companies already collect considerable data on patients, service providers, treatment course, and treatment outcome. We call on epidemiological, clinical, and health services researchers to evaluate these data and to provide compelling rationales for what additional data should be collected. For example, it is becoming increasingly common for insurance companies to provide and finance services for behavioral health in "mental health carve outs." This means that data for mental health services are collected by an administrative company or unit that is separate from the administrative unit responsible for collecting comparable data about medical services. However, as noted above, to obtain an accurate and comprehensive picture of service use and cost for eating disorders, which typically occur in the context of significant medical comorbidity and medical service use, one must consider the costs for both behavioral and medical services. Similarly, individual and social costs—what Ustun (1999) defined as "loss of life years in terms of productivity as well as social functioning" (p. 1316)—should be taken into account.

In summary, it is time for eating disorder researchers to collaborate with epidemiologists and health service researchers in defining the heterogeneous groups that suffer from eating disorders, specifying the range of psychiatric and medical comorbidity, and identifying barriers to treatment seeking and engagement. We want to bridge the gap between science and service (between efficacy and effectiveness studies) and help develop inclusive, socially responsible definitions of cost and treatment effectiveness. The resulting dialogue will add important voices to the current health services debate.

REFERENCES

Academy for Eating Disorders. (1998). *Position statement on equity in insurance coverage for eating disorders.* New York: Author.

American Psychiatric Association. (2000). Practice guidelines for eating disorders. *American Journal of Psychiatry, 157,* 1–37.

Becker, A. E., Grinspoon, S. K., Klibanski, A., & Herzog, D. B. (1999). Eating disorders. *New England Journal of Medicine, 340,* 1092–1098.

Bruce, B., & Agras, W. (1992). Binge eating in females: A population-based investigation. *International Journal of Eating Disorders, 12,* 365–373.

Bryant-Waugh, R., & Lask, B. (1995). Eating disorders in children. *Journal of Child Psychology and Psychiatry, 36,* 191–202.

Carlat, D., Camargo, C., & Herzog, D. (1997). Eating disorders in males: A report on 135 patients. *American Journal of Psychiatry, 154,* 1127–1132.

Childress, A. C., Brewerton, T. D., Hodges, E. L., & Jarrell, M. P. (1993). The Kids' Eating Disorders Survey (KEDS): A study of middle school students. *Journal of the American Academy of Child and Adolescent Psychiatry, 32,* 843–850.

Commerford, M., Licinio, J., & Halmi, K. (1997). Guidelines for discharging eating disorder inpatients. *Eating Disorders, 5,* 69–74.

Dansky, B., Brewerton, T., Kilpatrick, D., & O'Neil, P. (1997). The National Women's Study: Relationship of victimization and posttraumatic stress disorder to bulimia nervosa. *International Journal of Eating Disorders, 22,* 213–228.

Fairburn, C., Welch, S., Doll, H., Davies, B., & O'Connor, M. (1997). Risk factors for bulimia nervosa: A community-based case-control study. *Archives of General Psychiatry, 54,* 509–517.

Fairburn, C., Welch, S., Norman, P., O'Connor, & Doll, H. (1996). Bias and bulimia nervosa: How typical are clinic cases? *American Journal of Psychiatry, 153,* 386–391.

Fitzgibbon, M., Stolley, M., & Kirschenbaum, D. (1993). Obese people who seek treatment have different characteristics than those who do not seek treatment. *Health Psychology, 12,* 342–345.

Garfinkel, P., Lin, E., Goering, P., Spegg, C., Goldbloom, D., Kennedy, S., Kaplan, A., & Woodside, D. (1995). Bulimia nervosa in a Canadian community sample: Prevalence and comparison of subgroups. *American Journal of Psychiatry, 152,* 1052–1058.

Garfinkel, P., Lin, E., Goering, C., Spegg, C., Goldbloom, D., Kennedy, S., Kaplan, A., & Woodside, D. (1996). Should amenorrhoea be necessary for the diagnosis of anorexia nervosa? *British Journal of Psychiatry, 168,* 500–506.

Hay, P. (1998). The epidemiology of eating disorder behaviors: An Australian community-based survey. *International Journal of Eating Disorders, 23,* 371–382.

Hill, K., & Maloney, M. (1997). Treating anorexia nervosa patients in the era of managed care. *Journal of the American Academy of Child and Adolescent Psychiatry, 36,* 1632–1633.

Hoek, H. (1991). The incidence and prevalence of anorexia nervosa and bulimia nervosa in primary care. *Psychological Medicine, 21,* 455–460.

Howard, W., Evans, K., Quintero-Howard, C., Bowers, W., & Andersen, A. (1999). Predictors of success or failure of transition to day hospital treatment for inpatients with anorexia nervosa. *American Journal of Psychiatry, 156,* 1697–1702.

Hugo, P., Reid, F., Kendrick, A., & Lacey, J. (1997, November). *Factors associated with referral to an eating disorders service.* Paper presented at the meeting of the Eating Disorder Research Society, Albuquerque, NM.

Johnson, C., Stuckey, M., Lewis, L., & Schwartz, D. (1982). Bulimia: A descriptive survey of 316 cases. *International Journal of Eating Disorders, 2,* 3–16.

Kaye, W., Kaplan, A., & Zucker, M. (1996). Treating eating-disorder patients in a managed care environment. *Psychiatric Clinics of North America, 19,* 793–810.

Keel, P., & Mitchell, J. (1997). Outcome in bulimia nervosa. *American Journal of Psychiatry, 154,* 313–321.

Kendler, K., MacLean, C., Neale, M., Kessler, R., Heath, A., & Eaves, L. (1991). The genetic epidemiology of bulimia nervosa. *American Journal of Psychiatry, 148,* 1627–1637.

Kessler, R., & Frank, R. (1997). The impact of psychiatric disorders on work loss days. *Psychological Medicine, 27,* 861–873.

Kessler, R., Zhao, S., Katz, S., Kouzis, A., Frank, R., Edlund, & Leaf, P. (1999). Past-year use of outpatient services for psychiatric problems in the National Comorbidity Survey. *American Journal of Psychiatry, 156,* 115–123.

Koran, L., Agras, W., Rossiter, E., Arnow, B., Schneider, J., Telch, C., Raeburn, S., Bruce, B., Perl, M., & Kraemer, H. (1995). Comparing the cost effectiveness of psychiatric treatments for bulimia nervosa. *Psychiatry Research, 58,* 13–21.

Lewinsohn, P., Hops, H., Roberts, R., Seeley, R., & Andrews, J. (1993). Adolescent psychopathology: I. Prevalence and incidence of depression and other *DSM–III–R* disorders in high school students. *Journal of Abnormal Psychology, 102,* 133–144.

Luborsky, L., McLellan, A., Diguer, L., Woody, G., & Seligman, D. (1997). The psychotherapist matters: Comparison of outcomes across twenty-two therapists and seven patient samples. *Clinical Psychology—Science & Practice, 4,* 53–65.

Mitchell, J., Maki, D., Adson, D., Ruskin, B., & Crow, S. (1997). The selectivity of inclusion and exclusion criteria in bulimia nervosa treatment studies. *International Journal of Eating Disorders, 22,* 243–252.

Mitchell, J., Peterson, C., & Agras, S. (1999). Cost effectiveness of psychotherapy for eating disorders. In N. E. Miller & K. M. Magruder (Eds.), *Cost-effectiveness of psychotherapy* (pp. 270–278). New York: Oxford University Press.

Newell, A., & Saltzman, G. (1997). The impact of managed mental health care on women. *Journal of the American Medical Women's Association, 52,* 69–74.

Ogg, E., Millar, H., Pusztai, E., & Thom, A. (1997). General practice consultation patterns preceding diagnosis of eating disorders. *International Journal of Eating Disorders, 22,* 89–93.

Olfson, M., & Pincus, H. (1994). Outpatient psychotherapy in the United States: I. Volume, costs, and user characteristics. *American Journal of Psychiatry, 151,* 1281–1288.

Pawluck, D., & Gorey, K. (1998). Secular trends in the incidence of anorexia nervosa: Integrative review of population-based studies. *International Journal of Eating Disorders, 23,* 347–352.

Peterson, C. B., & Mitchell, J. E. (1999). Psychosocial and pharmacological treatment of eating disorders: A review of research findings. *Journal of Clinical Psychology, 55,* 685–697.

Pike, K., & Striegel-Moore, R. (1997). Disordered eating and eating disorders. In S. J. Gallant, G. P. Keita, & R. Royak-Schaler (Eds.), *Health care for women* (pp. 97–114). Washington, DC: American Psychological Association.

Pincus, H., Zarin, D., Tanielian, T., Johnson, J., West, J., Pettit, A., Marcus, S., Kessler, R., & McIntyre, J. (1999). Psychiatric patients and treatment in 1997: Findings from the American Psychiatric Practice Research Network. *Archives of General Psychiatry, 56,* 441–449.

Robins, L., Helzer, J., Weissman, M., Orvaschel, H., Gruenberg, E., Burke, J., & Regier, D. (1984). Lifetime prevalence of specific psychiatric disorders in three sites. *Archives of General Psychiatry, 41,* 949–958.

Sansone, R., Sansone, L., & Wiederman, M. (1998). The relationship between obesity and medical utilization among women in a primary care setting. *International Journal of Eating Disorders, 23,* 161–167.

Satcher, D. (1999). *Mental health: A report of the Surgeon General.* Retrieved December 14, 1999 from the World Wide Web: http://www.mentalhealth.org/specials/surgeongeneralreport/pressrelease.htm

Striegel-Moore, R., Garvin, V., Dohm, F., & Rosenheck, R. (1999). Psychiatric comorbidity of eating disorders in men: A national study of hospitalized veterans. *International Journal of Eating Disorders, 25,* 399–404.

Striegel-Moore, R., Leslie, D., Petrill, S., Garvin, V., & Rosenheck, R. (2000). One-year use and cost of inpatient and outpatient services among female and male patients with an eating disorder: Evidence from a national database of health insurance claims. *International Journal of Eating Disorders, 27,* 381–389.

Striegel-Moore, R., & Marcus, M. (1995). Eating disorders in women: Current issues and debates. In A. L. Stanton & S. J. Gallant (Eds.), *Women's health book* (pp. 445–487). Washington, DC: American Psychological Association.

Striegel-Moore, R., & Smolak, L. (2000). The influence of ethnicity on eating disorders in women. In R. Eisler & M. Hersen (Eds.), *Handbook of gender, culture, and health* (pp. 227–254). Mahwah, NJ: Erlbaum.

Striegel-Moore, R., Wilfley, D., Pike, K., Dohm, F., & Fairburn, C. (2000). Recurrent binge eating in Black American women. *Archives of Family Medicine, 9,* 83–87.

Telch, C., & Agras, S. (1994). Obesity, binge eating and psychopathology: Are they related? *International Journal of Eating Disorders, 15,* 53–61.

Treasure, J., & Schmidt, U. (1999). Beyond effectiveness and efficiency lies quality in services for eating disorders. *European Eating Disorders Review, 7,* 162–178.

Treasure, J. , Schmidt, U., Troop, N., Tiller, J., Todd, G., & Turnbull, S. (1996). Sequential treatment for bulimia nervosa incorporating a self care manual. *British Journal of Psychiatry, 168,* 94–98.

Ustun, T. (1999). The global burden of mental disorders. *American Journal of Public Health, 89,* 1315–1318.

Vessey, J., & Howard, K. (1993). Who seeks psychotherapy? *Psychotherapy, 30,* 546–553.

Via, M., Kaye, W., Pavetto, C., & Crossan, P. (1997, November). *Short-term savings and long-term consequences in the treatment of anorexia nervosa*. Paper presented at the meeting of the Eating Disorder Research Society, Albuquerque, NM.

Walters, E., & Kendler, K. (1995). Anorexia nervosa and anorexic-like syndromes in a female twin sample. *American Journal of Psychiatry, 152,* 64–71.

Whitaker, A. (1992). An epidemiological study of anorectic and bulimic symptoms in adolescent girls: Implications for pediatricians. *Pediatric Annals, 21,* 752–759.

Whitaker, M., Johnson, J., Shaffer, D., Rapoport, J., Kalikow, K., Walsh, T., Davies, M., Braiman, S., & Dolinsky, A. (1990). Uncommon troubles in young people: Prevalence estimates of selected psychiatric disorders in a non-referred adolescent population. *Archives of General Psychiatry, 47,* 487–496.

Whitehouse, A., Cooper, P., Vize, C., Hill, C., & Vogel, L. (1992). Prevalence of eating disorders in three Cambridge general practices: Hidden and conspicuous morbidity. *British Journal of General Practice, 42,* 57–60.

Wooley, S. (1993). Managed care and mental health: The silencing of a profession. *International Journal of Eating Disorders, 14,* 387–401.

Wu, L., Kouzis, A., & Leaf, P. (1999). Influence of comorbid alcohol and psychiatric disorders on utilization of mental health services in the National Comorbidity Survey. *American Journal of Psychiatry, 156,* 1230–1236.

Yager, J., Landsverk, J., & Edelstein, C. (1989). Help seeking and satisfaction with care in 641 women with eating disorders. *Journal of Nervous and Mental Disease, 177,* 632–637.

8

THE POTENTIAL OF PROFESSIONALLY DEVELOPED SELF-HELP INTERVENTIONS FOR THE TREATMENT OF EATING DISORDERS

VICKI GARVIN, RUTH H. STRIEGEL-MOORE, ALLAN KAPLAN,
AND STEPHEN A. WONDERLICH

In the United States in the 1960s, proponents of the community mental health movement advocated individual empowerment, self-care, and peer support (Dumont, 1974). Spokespeople for the antipsychiatry movement claimed that people were not "psychiatrically ill" but suffering from social and political oppression (Scheff, 1975; Szasz, 1970). Mental health services, previously developed by professionals in secondary and tertiary care settings, were now designed and organized by laypeople in community settings. The self-help movement of the 1960s and 1970s championed the person: as expert (replacing the professional), as resource to self and others (replacing the institution as the provider of support), and as decision maker (replacing the medical and psychiatric system as definer of problems and solutions).

Despite the diversity of the self-help groups in the 1960s, they generally shared common features. Self-help groups were promoted to enhance self-esteem, share information and experiences, develop political awareness, and provide and receive support. Typically, the commitment was mutual and evolving; that is, the group continued to develop and refine its own agenda and purpose. The group structure was explicitly egalitarian, often with shared or rotating leadership and small nonhierarchical working groups. Relationships within the group were identified and explored, with the aim of enhanc-

This work was supported by a supplemental career reentry award funded jointly by the Office of Research of Women's Health of the National Institutes of Health and the National Institute of Mental Health (RO1 MH52348-01A1).

ing growth for each participant. To help oneself would necessarily involve helping the other, who simultaneously would reciprocate the help received (e.g., Dumont, 1974; Katz, 1981).

During the 1980s and early 1990s, the self-help industry continued to grow (for reviews, see Rosen, 1987, 1993). Academic psychologists became increasingly involved in authoring self-help texts and designing self-help interventions. Self-help books, videotapes, and audiocassettes became widely available, addressing a growing range of concerns, including self-esteem, sexual dysfunction, overeating, and phobias. During the 1970s and 1980s, self-identified sufferers continued to meet in groups, provide peer and family support, engage in political advocacy, and develop and distribute self-help materials. Mental health professionals also increasingly reported incorporating self-help materials into their clinical practices (Marx, Gyorky, Royalty, & Stern, 1992).

Despite this proliferation of self-help interventions, the broadened scope of problems addressed, and the emergence of novel forms of service delivery (e.g., videotape, audiocassette), most self-help programs were not supported by published empirical research (for reviews, see American Psychological Association, 1978; Glasgow & Rosen, 1978; and Rosen, 1993). Controversy developed over the desirability and ethics of promoting self-help interventions. Advocates for self-help rallied behind the words of George Miller (1969), past president of the American Psychological Association, who encouraged mental health professionals to "give psychology away" (p. 1074) by helping people to help themselves. Critics worried about the "commercialization of psychotherapy" and the failure to submit self-help programs to rigorous empirical study (Apfel, 1996; Ellis, 1993; Riessman & Caroll, 1995; Rosen, 1987, 1993).

Today there is a dizzying array of self-help products and services, which can be classified as "pure self-help" (a self-care program with no professional assistance) or "guided self-help" (a self-care program facilitated by a lay or professional therapist). As the boom in the self-help industry continues, how can consumers select the self-help product most suited to their needs? How can they evaluate the effectiveness of vastly different services, all of which are identified as self-help? Clearly, there is a difference among a "do-it-yourself" book purchased at a local bookstore, self-help through participation with a long-standing mutual support group with a public record of process and success, and participation in a self-help intervention designed and administered by a mental health professional in a tertiary care setting.

In this chapter, we (a) examine the current research and health care context to identify factors that promote renewed interest in self-help models and (b) review a newly emerging subset of self-help interventions derived from treatment protocols developed from randomized clinical trials (RCTs). Through case examples, we examine 14 self-help and guided self-help interventions that were designed by eating disorder specialists for women with bulimia nervosa and binge-eating disorder. We conclude by developing a research agenda to further investigate the safety and efficacy of these new self-help interventions.

CURRENT CONTEXT FOR SELF-HELP

Within the past decade there has been renewed interest in developing self-help interventions. Proponents in the 1990s, adopting the language of the self-help movement of the 1960s, are again advocating self-help because it can be nonstigmatizing, empowering, and broadly accessible (for reviews, see Apfel, 1996; and Riessman & Carroll, 1995). However, this echoing of the rallying catchwords that supported self-help in the 1960s may serve to obscure what is unique about the current self-help revival. As we discuss below, self-help in the 1990s was fueled by three new developments: the proliferation of treatment outcome studies, advances in electronic communication, and economic pressure from the insurance industry.

Developments in Treatment Outcome Research

During the past 20 years scientists have been conducting RCTs to establish the efficacy of treatments for a variety of psychiatric disorders, including anxiety, mood, and eating disorders (Task Force on Promotion and Dissemination of Psychological Procedures, 1995). The aim of this research is to determine whether a specific treatment intervention works under controlled, experimental conditions. Although there is still debate over what qualifies as a "well-established" or "probably efficacious" treatment (Kazdin, 1996), there are now well-researched treatment protocols informed by psychodynamic, interpersonal, behavioral, and cognitive–behavior theory. Researchers are increasingly publishing these protocols in the form of treatment manuals, thus encouraging standardization, replication, and dissemination (Sanderson & Woody, 1995). Drawing on this tradition of RCTs, mental health service researchers can now examine the related question of treatment effectiveness: Does this particular intervention work in actual clinical practice settings?

Clinical researchers have also been exploring the "specific" and "nonspecific" components that contribute to positive treatment outcomes (e.g., Beutler, Machado, & Neufeldt, 1994; Garfield, 1997; Lambert & Bergin, 1994). An important research question has been how the active components of intensive, long-term therapies can be incorporated into brief, focused, solution-oriented, and minimal interventions (e.g., Crits-Christoph & Barber, 1991; Sifneos, 1987).

Technological Advances

With advances in computer technology and electronic communication, the treatment protocols developed from RCTs can now be made more widely available. The development of CD-ROMs, the availability of affordable personal computers, and increased Internet access make it possible to widely disseminate interventions at relatively low cost. Still to be addressed are issues of dissemination: Not all socioeconomic and ethnic groups have equal access to electronic resources. Moreover, not only empirically validated treatment protocols can be easily and inexpensively disseminated via the Internet and CD-ROM. The potential to develop homepages and to participate in on-line chat groups makes it possible for unidentified people without particular training or expertise to provide information and advice to a potentially large number of anonymous users. Electronic communication thus raises complicated ethical and regulatory concerns. For example, how do we distinguish between sharing ideas, providing psychoeducation, and offering on-line psychotherapy?

Cost Containment in the Health Care Industry

The promotion of relatively brief, low-cost interventions is also supported by insurance companies that have an economic stake in limiting professional services and reducing the length and cost of treatment. Self-help interventions could contain costs by reducing the number of individuals who enter intensive, expensive treatment; by serving as an adjunct to traditional therapy, thereby reducing the overall length of traditional treatment; and by providing effective relapse prevention, therefore reducing costly recidivism. Payers of health care may have a special interest in guided self-help programs that employ bachelor's-level and master's-level professionals, who are paid less than doctoral-level psychologists and psychiatrists.

In view of the current health care crisis in the United States, it is virtually certain that there will be a continued interest in using self-help treatments in the future. Ideally, these interventions would provide quality care for more people for less money. Realistically, given economic pressures, there is the risk that these interventions will be prematurely disseminated without sufficient empirical study.

At present, with diverse products and services identified as self-help, it is not clear how to define self-help or guided self-help. Does the emphasis on self assume that the problem, the cure, or both are located within the self? Does this imply that pure self-help has no interpersonal or relational features? What does *guided* mean: guided by peers, by recovered fellow sufferers, or by mental health specialists?

PROFESSIONALLY DEVELOPED SELF-HELP AND GUIDED SELF-HELP FOR EATING DISORDERS: A NEW PARADIGM

To address these questions and to help differentiate among the various forms of self-help, we now examine one specific subset of minimal interventions: self-help and guided self-help programs developed by eating disorder specialists for women with eating problems. We focus on those interventions that have explicitly been modeled on treatment protocols developed in the course of RCTs. First, these interventions can teach one about the benefits and limitations of adapting the features of well-researched, relatively intensive therapies to briefer interventions. Second, feasibility studies and field trials piloting these new modes of self-help are well documented in the eating disorder research literature. On the basis of our PsycLIT and Medline search covering the last 7 years, we found 14 reports of self-help interventions for women with bulimia nervosa or binge-eating disorder. Third, all of these interventions explicitly identify themselves as self-help or guided self-help, thereby implicitly invoking the self-help language of the 1960s consumer-oriented social protest movement. This provides an opportunity to compare how these new interventions relate to the self-help, consciousness-raising, and support groups of that period. Fourth, the majority of self-help interventions for eating disorders, like the majority of manualized treatments in general, are based on cognitive–behavior principles (Sanderson & Woody, 1995). We hope to critique and extend this literature by applying what has already been learned from the extensive empirical literature on short-term focal psychodynamic psychotherapy (e.g., Crits-Cristoph & Barber, 1991; Davanloo, 1990; Luborsky, 1990; Sifneos, 1987).

Table 8.1 summarizes the major features of these 14 newly developed self-help interventions for bulimia nervosa and binge-eating disorder. With respect to structure, these programs are typically brief and time limited, with the majority meeting in tertiary care settings. Although the participant is still self-referred, membership is no longer open. Eligibility or screening criteria are developed by the guiding institution and include the establishment of an eating disorder diagnosis, as specified in the *Diagnostic and Statistical Manual of Mental Disorders* (4th ed. [*DSM–IV*]; American Psychiatric Association, 1994) or the *International Classification of Diseases* (*ICD*; U.S. Department of Health and Human Services, 1990). Some programs also report explicit exclusion criteria, such as history of self-harm or current suicidal behavior.

Once enrolled in the self-help program, participants engage in brief, problem-focused treatment, typically informed by cognitive–behavior principles. Current treatment protocols are standardized and manualized, generally following a cumulative, sequential approach. Participants progress through

TABLE 8.1
Pure Self-Help (PSH) and Guided Self-Help (GSH) Interventions for Bulimia Nervosa (BN) and Binge-Eating Disorder (BED)

Study	Participants		Type of intervention			Characteristics of intervention		
	N	Diagnosis	Individual/group	PSH/GSH	Structure	Duration	Professional	Setting
Carter & Fairburn (1998)	72	BED (DSM–IV)	I	3 conditions: PSH, GSH, Wait-list	PSH (no sessions) GSH 6–8 sessions; 25 min./session	12 weeks	Nonspecialist therapist	Not specified
Cooper et al. (1994)	18	BN (DSM–III–R)	I	GSH	6–12 sessions; 25 min./session	4–6 months	Social worker	Secondary
Cooper et al. (1996)	82	BN (DSM–III–R)	I	GSH	8 sessions; 25 min./session	4–6 months	Social worker	Secondary
Grave (1998)	17	BN (DSM–IV)	I	GSH	8 sessions; 20 min./session	4 months	Psychiatrist	Tertiary
Hartley (1995)	9	Eating disorder (unspecified)	G	GSH	12 sessions; 90 min./session	6 months	PhD psychologist	Not specified
Mitchell et al. (in press)	91	BN (DSM–III–R)	I	4 conditions: placebo only, fluoxetine only, self-help and placebo, self-help and fluoxetine	14 reading and homework assignments	16 weeks	N/A	Eating disorder specialty center
Peterson et al. (in press)	60	BED (DSM–IV)	G	3 conditions: GSH–therapist, GSH–peer PSH	14 sessions; 60 min./session	8 weeks	PhD psychologist	Tertiary
Rathner et al. (1993)	19	BN (DSM–III–R)	G	GSH	60 sessions	15 months	PhD psychologist	Tertiary
Schmidt et al. (1993)	28	BN or atypical BN (ICD-10)	I	PSH	N/A	4–6 weeks	N/A	Tertiary

Study	N	Diagnosis	Therapy	Self-help	Conditions	Duration	Provider	Setting
Thiels et al. (1998)	62	BN (DSM–II–R)	I	GSH	2 conditions: Manual and 8 CBT sessions; CBT-16 sessions	16 weeks	2 psychologists, 1 health scientist	Polytechnic
Treasure et al. (1994)	81	BN or atypical BN (ICD-10)	I	PSH	3 conditions: PSH, CBT, wait-list	8 weeks	N/A	Tertiary
Treasure et al. (1996)	110	BN or atypical BN (ICD-10)	I	PSH and CBT	3 conditions: PSH, CBT, wait-list	8–16 weeks	N/A	Tertiary
Waller et al. (1996)	11	BN (DSM–IV)	I	GSH	8 sessions; 20 min./session	2 months	4 GPs, 1 nurse	Primary
Wells et al. (1997)	9	BED (DSM–IV)	I	GSH	8 sessions; 30 min./session	3 months	MA psychologist	University

Note. I = Individual therapy; G = group therapy; DSM = *Diagnostic and Statistical Manual for Mental Disorders* (3rd ed. rev. *[DSM–III–R]*; 4th ed. *[DSM–IV]*); ICD-10 = *International Classification of Diseases*; N/A = not applicable; CBT = cognitive–behavior therapy.

predesignated stages, which take precedence over a focus on the treatment relationship and open-ended exploratory work. For example, a participant might pursue the following mandated sequence: develop a behavioral record of eating patterns, regularize eating, analyze and correct eating-related disordered cognitions, learn generalized problem solving, and develop relapse prevention skills. After program completion, outcome is typically assessed in terms of a reduction in eating-related pathology (e.g., reduction in bingeing, vomiting, and purging) and, in some studies, reduction in general psychiatric symptomatology. Although several programs measure changes in subjective well-being and role functioning, significant changes are not expected in these areas. The explicit goal is symptom reduction, not relationship enhancement, improved coping, increased self-esteem, or broadened political awareness, even though these goals may also be realized.

Even from this brief summary, it is clear that these new interventions represent a significant departure from the self-help interventions typical of the 1960s. The person-to-person mutual support of earlier self-help groups, with an emphasis on giving and receiving, has been replaced by a more traditional hierarchical professional–patient relationship. Eating disorder specialists now identify the problem, design the treatment protocol, determine membership criteria, and define positive outcome. The problem, which is assumed to reside within the individual, who is now thought of as a patient, is conceptualized in traditional medical terms. In the 1960s, in contrast, the problem was not located in the individual but in oppressive social, political, and economic institutions. In the self-help tradition of the 1960s, individuals with eating disorders might have rejected medical treatment in favor of social and political advocacy or mutual support.

These new (pure or guided) self-help interventions for eating disorders, with their focus on diagnosing and treating the person, implicitly embrace an individual pathology model. However, these interventions also adopt the language of personal empowerment that emerged from 1960s social activism. It is not yet clear how these newly developed interventions can usefully draw on each of these traditions and what contradictions may emerge. For example, can diagnosis and assessment be comprehensive, as required by RCTs, and nonstigmatizing and collaborative, as advocated by liberal activists? Can the success of brief interventions be measured using the same outcome criteria used in RCTs? We now turn to an explicit consideration of these kinds of dilemmas as we develop a research agenda for further investigating assessment, treatment matching, treatment modality, the therapist–client relationship, risk management, and outcome criteria and evaluation.

Assessment and Treatment Matching

Self-help advocates in the 1960s, espousing egalitarian values and determined not to pathologize the individual, explicitly opposed screening participants for membership. Open membership was in itself a political response to elitism and, as such, identified as part of the cure. In contrast, current proponents of self-help now assume that there is an underlying problem (conceptualized, for instance, as an eating disorder) and that people with this disorder can be accurately identified and treated. From this set of assumptions, it follows that current self-help researchers require comprehensive preintervention assessments to determine appropriate inclusion and exclusion criteria for participation.

To identify individuals who have the disorder, all of the self-help interventions for eating disorders require the establishment of a *DSM–IV* or *ICD* eating disorder diagnosis. It is not yet known, however, whether people with subthreshold diagnoses (e.g., who binge eat but do not meet the twice per week frequency criterion), who represent a large group of sufferers (e.g., Garfinkel et al., 1995), could also benefit from these self-help interventions. It is also not clear how comorbid psychopathology may complicate the eating disorder and influence treatment outcome. At present, fewer than half of the self-help interventions for eating disorders include an assessment of comorbid Axis I disorders and Axis II personality functioning. Preliminary findings suggest that the following factors may be associated with poor outcome in self-help interventions for eating disorders: more frequent bingeing (Turnbull et al., 1997), a history of anorexia nervosa or a comorbid personality disorder (Cooper, Coker, & Fleming, 1996), greater weight and shape concerns (Troop et al., 1996), greater depression (Rathner, Bonsch, Maurer, Walter, & Sollner, 1993), significant obesity, concurrent major life events, and multiple psychiatric problems, including personality disorders (Waller et al., 1996). This suggests when evaluating outcome of self-help, researchers need to go beyond the definition of disorder and investigate factors, such as duration of eating problem, severity of eating problem, type of eating problem, and psychiatric and medical comorbidity.

Ideally, assessment not only yields relevant diagnostic information but also identifies participants who are motivated to engage in treatment. Just because an individual expresses interest in pursuing self-help and meets diagnostic criteria for an eating disorder does not necessarily mean that self-help is the appropriate intervention. From the research literature on short-term psychodynamic therapy, several factors emerge as good prognostic indicators: verbal fluency, above-average intelligence, rapport with the therapist, ability to formulate a focused presenting problem, history of at least one meaningful interpersonal relationship, history of at least one major accomplishment (e.g., in school, at work, with family), and motivation for change (including curiosity, psychological mindedness, willingness to be actively engaged, and realistic expectations; Malan, 1992; Sifneos, 1992). These prognostic indicators should be included in future outcome studies of self-help interventions.

Researchers could also investigate at what point in the history of the eating disorder self-help treatment will be most effective. It is often assumed that people with recent onset of the disorder will most benefit, but to date, there has been no empirical study to determine how the chronicity of the disorder influences treatment outcome. It is also not known at what point in the history of treatment seeking self-help interventions will be most beneficial. The stepped care model assumes that participants move along a continuum from brief, less intensive, less costly treatment to increasingly intensive, expensive, and specialized treatment. Presently, however, the self-help interventions for bulimia nervosa or binge-eating disorder are typically investigated as independent treatments (for an exception, see Treasure et al., 1996). We do not yet know if they serve best as the only step in treatment, as the first and potentially priming step in a sequence of treatments, as an adjunct to more traditional treatment, or as a final step in relapse prevention.

Finally, it is important to acknowledge that current self-help interventions, such as treatments for eating disorders in general (Mitchell, Maki, Adson, Ruskin, & Crow, 1997), have been studied using a highly selective, predominantly White female patient population. None of the 14 self-help interventions included a sizable number of women of color or men of any race, although epidemiological studies indicate that a significant minority of these populations meet DSM–IV criteria for binge-eating disorder (Spitzer et al., 1993; Striegel-Moore, Wilfley, Pike, Dohm, & Fairburn, 2000). Ideally, self-help interventions for eating disorders would build on the self-help traditions and values that have already emerged spontaneously in particular local communities or social groups (Neighbors, Braithwaite, & Thompson, 1995).

Treatment Modality and Mode of Service Delivery

The self-help interventions for eating disorders use a variety of treatment modalities (e.g., pure vs. guided, individual vs. group) and modes of service delivery (e.g., self-help book, in-person contact, videotaped presentation, telephone session). The number of possible combinations presents a formidable challenge for treatment outcome research. Today, relatively little is known about the relationship between treatment modality and mode of service delivery and client satisfaction, engagement in treatment, and symptom reduction. To date, in only two studies have researchers compared pure and guided self-help (Carter & Fairburn, 1998; Peterson et al., in press). We are not aware of any researchers who have compared individual and group formats.

Virtually nothing is known about the "ecology" (Anderson & Strupp, 1996) of guided self-help interventions. Self-help interventions in the 1990s seem to be oddly context free, as if the self-help book, audiocassette, or videotape is merely a means of conveying the treatment, with no formative impact on the treatment itself. In contrast, leaders of the 1960s community mental health movement explicitly argued that treatment setting and modality constituted the treatment. They believed that the goals of self-determination, autonomy, and empowerment would develop from supportive, egalitarian residential and community settings and be thwarted in traditional institutional settings. Similarly, group work, which was viewed as facilitating interpersonal involvement and mutuality, was thought to be intrinsically more growth promoting than individually based treatment.

We now have an opportunity to evaluate these assumptions empirically. Researchers can compare residential and university–medical settings as well as individual and group administrations of guided self-help, in terms of their effect on variables such as locus of control, competency, and help-seeking behavior. In addition, it is important to investigate how therapist factors, such as level of therapist training (using bachelor's-, master's-, and doctoral-level therapists), are associated with treatment engagement, satisfaction, and outcome.

These evaluations should be conducted in actual practice environments, not confined to the research laboratory. Ultimately, researchers may be able to develop self-help and guided self-help protocols that reflect the unique needs of particular settings (e.g., rural areas, college campuses, sports facilities). Factors such as access to technological equipment, availability of backup services, literacy level, and the local culture of self-care could then be included.

The Therapist–Client Relationship

Self-help groups in the 1960s explicitly acknowledged and attempted to mobilize the growth potential of relationships. Present interventions, in contrast, even those that include a guided component, typically do not identify or fully use the interpersonal opportunities inherent in the intervention. The hierarchical professional–client relationship, which now characterizes many self-help interventions, may contribute to obscuring the interpersonal aspects of participation. The rhetoric of *self*-help, with its explicit focus on the self, furthers the misconception that self-help only involves the individual. Yet even in their present form, self-help interventions for eating disorders provide a relational context, even if the intervention is not explicitly designed to be relational. For example, our pilot study found that participants in guided self-help reported developing a relationship with and feelings toward their lay therapist, host institution, and written materials. Several participants expressed intense envy and competitiveness toward women portrayed in clinical vignettes (Garvin, Striegel-Moore, & Wells, 1998).

Whereas self-help groups in the 1960s attempted to maximize the potential for mutual support, role modeling, and identification, current proponents of self-help have only begun to systematically study how to use these kinds of interpersonal opportunities. Blake, Turnbull, and Treasure (1997) and Treasure and Ward (1997), building on the transtheoretical stages of change model (Prochaska, Norcross, & DiClemente, 1994), have made an important contribution by highlighting how motivation for guided self-care treatment, rather than residing solely in the individual, can be mobilized and enhanced through interpersonal interactions. After identifying the stage of participant readiness (e.g., in terms of precontemplation, contemplation, action), the therapist then offers the client the interpersonal approach (e.g., psychoeducation, advice, support) most appropriate for mobilizing interest and motivation for subsequent guided self-help.

Additional approaches for studying and mobilizing the interpersonal aspects of self-help are elaborated in the research literature on short-term psychodynamic treatment. There is already extensive research on engaging the client, challenging resistances, and modulating the intensity of the therapist–participant relationship (e.g., Davanloo, 1992; Malan, 1992). Data on the interpersonal style and resources of self-help participants could be used to further refine inclusion–exclusion criteria. For example, it would be helpful to quantify a participant's ability to develop rapport with the therapist, without developing an overly intense, dependent, or distorted relationship that could not be sufficiently addressed within the limitations of a brief self-help intervention.

If one fails to acknowledge interactions between the lay therapist and client or between one self-help group member and another, one may overlook interpersonal variables that are related to problematic symptoms or behaviors and, if addressed, may enhance treatment outcome. Faludi (1991) and Jordan (1996) suggested that an exclusive emphasis on the isolated individual, when the individual is female, may represent an antifeminist backlash, blaming the victim while depriving her of the relational context and potential for connection that may be particularly supportive of female development.

Ironically, interpersonal or therapist factors may turn out to be a critical component of self-help. As Strupp (1995) suggested, it may be nonspecific or common factors, such as support, role modeling, and empathic listening, that are most crucial to therapy outcome, hardest to measure, and most likely to be minimized by the health care industry. Given the mounting pressures toward standardization, electronic communication, and reduced cost, it is imperative that the value of the therapeutic relationship become an empirical question, not a political or economic question (Beutler et al., 1994; Garfield, 1997; Strupp & Anderson, 1997).

Ongoing Risk Management and Supervision

If we as mental health professionals fail to acknowledge the interpersonal aspects of self-help interventions, we may fail to comply with the professional standards that regulate and protect these relationships. To the extent that self-help interventions are perceived as minimal or supportive, we may further overlook treatment safeguards. The adoption of the self-help banner of the 1960s, which implicitly invoked the antipsychiatry indictment of paternalistic, invasive, and controlling treatment, should not blind us to the need for ongoing risk management. Researchers need to not only refine screening criteria but also develop ongoing risk assessment protocols to evaluate when the program is not working or when a participant's condition is deteriorating. Referral decision trees and relationships with backup emergency services should be developed. Supervision needs to be particularly extensive when the therapists are less-experienced lay therapists. Training for short-term psychodynamic therapy, for example, requires extensive training beyond the usual graduate and licensing requirements (Malan & Osimo, 1992). If payers of health care are hoping to reduce costs by employing less highly compensated providers, the costs of ongoing supervision (or of increased lawsuits) needs to be recognized.

The new self-help programs for eating disorders also introduce new modes of service delivery. Electronic communication promises many benefits, including wide dissemination of services at relatively low cost. However, electronic communication also raises serious concerns about compliance with the ethical standards for clinical practice promulgated by various professional organizations, including the American Psychiatric Association (1995) and the American Psychological Association (1992). Clinical researchers need to investigate how services delivered with electronic communication can comply with the established ethical standards for advertising, boundaries of competence, confidentiality, and basis for scientific and professional judgments (American Psychological Association, 1996).

Electronic communication also presents unique ethical challenges, which do not apply to the more traditional therapies. For example, self-help through the Internet allows for the therapist and client to be in different states. Under what circumstances does electronic communication provide a sufficient basis for professional decision making? To what extent can the confidentiality of the relationship be protected from computer hackers? How is it possible for an out-of-state therapist to provide adequate backup and referral in the case of an emergency?

As eating disorder researchers begin the next phase of self-help dissemination trials, they face additional challenges with respect to treatment effectiveness and treatment safeguards. As noted earlier, dissemination studies can address how the setting—for example, primary care, college campus, and private residence—affects engagement in treatment, treatment satisfaction, and treatment outcome. But researchers also need to explore how introducing self-help interventions into new settings may require the development of new treatment safeguards. At present, most self-help interventions for eating disorders are administered in academic medical care settings, in which human participant research guidelines guarantee considerable attention to informed consent and prevention of harm. As self-help interventions are disseminated more broadly, researchers should examine how to safeguard informed consent, confidentiality, and the provision of quality services. This is particularly problematic for pure self-help interventions, which do not include access to a trained professional.

Outcome Criteria and Program Evaluation

From their emergence from RCTs, self-help interventions for eating disorders inherited traditional psychiatric outcome criteria: reduction in specific and general psychiatric symptomatology, changes in role functioning, and changes in subjective well-being. In our view, conceptualizing outcome exclusively in terms of specific and general disease indicators overlooks the potential educational, supportive, and interpersonal benefits of eating disorder self-help interventions. We therefore suggest expanding positive outcome to include increased knowledge of the eating problem, decreased social isolation and increased social support, changes in help-seeking behavior, broadened coping skills, improved self-esteem, and increased motivation for further treatment (Garvin et al., 1998). With one exception (Carter & Fairburn, 1998), these domains were not included as positive outcomes in the interventions we reviewed, yet these outcomes are consistent with the aims of the support groups of the 1960s and with the possibilities inherent in short-term treatment.

The effectiveness of a specific program can also include the participants' subjective evaluation of their intervention experience. However, to date, only two of the self-help programs for eating disorders report using a formal evaluation. In our view, participants should be systematically asked what was most helpful, least helpful, and harmful about each treatment component and how to improve various program features. These data can then be used to identify which features appeal to which participants, while also providing valuable feedback to improve program accessibility and acceptability. Treating the participant as a collaborator rather than a passive recipient of services is also more consistent with the egalitarian values advocated by earlier proponents of self-help.

In evaluating the impact of a self-help intervention, we suggest that positive outcome cannot be understood as a uniform concept. Instead of asking whether this particular program was successful, it may be more informative to ask at what level was this particular program successful. Did it address the level of morale, the level of symptom reduction, or the level of character change? Who are the various stakeholders: the client, the professional, the family, the employer, or the insurance company? What level of change would satisfy the different stakeholders (Strupp, 1996)?

Evaluating intervention outcome in terms of the requirements of the various stakeholders can help clarify the benefits and the realistic limitations of self-help. For example, improvement in a participant's sense of hopefulness can be expected from a short-term intervention such as self-help. As a corollary, it would be unlikely to expect change at the level of character structure from a brief intervention; this would be more consistent with the aims and opportunities provided by more intensive, long-term treatment. But should changes in morale be considered a success? The answer depends on the stakeholder. An employer may be satisfied with remoralization: A less despairing employee is generally more productive. The insurance company may be satisfied: Remoralization requires far less time, expense, and professional involvement than does character change. However, the professional may be less satisfied: More intensive work is typically more interesting, rewarding, and consistent with personal values regarding quality of life. What about the participant? Her or his definition of success is probably the hardest to predict because it depends on her or his experience and current conflicts and expectations. Identifying the different criteria for success for the different stakeholders could thus provide a more comprehensive approach to identifying self-help intervention outcome.

CONCLUSION

Treatment outcome studies and RCTs have produced treatment protocols that now are ready for dissemination, especially as CD-ROM and Internet access become increasingly available. With mounting pressure from the insurance industry to contain the cost of mental health care, this virtually ensures continued interest in developing and marketing self-help interventions. Potentially, these interventions offer significant advantages: Self-help can be brief, inexpensive, and widely disseminated. However, there is the danger that self-help will be prematurely embraced as a quick fix to the current health care crisis. Although self-help interventions have been available for many decades, the current approach to self-help discussed in this chapter represents a significant departure from earlier self-help interventions. It is not yet clear who is best served by these self-help interventions, at what point in the course of the disorder, and at what point in treatment seeking. Investigators are just beginning to examine how self-help approaches may be used in conjunction with well-established treatments to enhance treatment effects, shorten treatment time, decrease overall costs, and reduce recidivism (see Mitchell et al., in press; and Treasure et al., 1996). For this new breed of self-help services, extensive research is needed to learn more about selection criteria, treatment matching, risk management, and outcome evaluation.

This lengthy research agenda not only highlights that researchers are still at the beginning stages of program development but also clarifies several paradoxes that may be intrinsic to minimal interventions. The more standardized the treatment, the easier and cheaper it is to disseminate. However, the more general the treatment, the more likely it is that such intervention will not meet individual needs. Furthermore, brief interventions may require sophisticated, time-consuming assessments as well as costly training and ongoing specialist supervision. How does one reconcile extensive costly assessment and expert involvement with the aims of brief, inexpensive, short-term treatment? Does thorough diagnostic assessment diminish autonomy and increase stigmatization, therefore abrogating just those values championed by the self-help movement of the 1960s? Comprehensive assessment and ongoing supervision may be essential to provide a safe context for minimal interventions, yet these are just the services the payers of health care are least likely to reimburse.

We highlight these competing tensions to identify contradictions that may be inherent in trying to create a short-term self-help treatment that incorporates all the advantages of RCTs. Some tradeoffs may be inevitable. We do hope, however, that these dilemmas can be identified, debated openly within the research community, and submitted to empirical study.

REFERENCES

American Psychiatric Association. (1994). *Diagnostic and statistical manual of mental disorders* (4th ed.). Washington, DC: Author.

American Psychiatric Association. (1995). *The principles of medical ethics*. Washington, DC: Author.

American Psychological Association. (1978). *Task force on self-help therapies*. Washington, DC: Author.

American Psychological Association. (1992). Ethical principles of psychologists and code of conduct. *American Psychologist, 47,* 1597–1612.

American Psychological Association. (1996). *Services by telephone, teleconferencing, and Internet.* Washington, DC: Author.

Anderson, T., & Strupp, H. (1996). The ecology of psychotherapy research. *Journal of Clinical and Consulting Psychology, 64,* 776–782.

Apfel, R. (1996). "With a little help from my friends I get by": Self-help books and psychotherapy. *Psychotherapy, 59,* 309–321.

Beutler, L., Machado, P., & Neufeldt, S. (1994). Therapist variables. In A. Bergin & S. Garfield (Eds.), *Handbook of psychotherapy and behavior change* (pp. 229–269). New York: Wiley.

Blake, W., Turnbull, S., & Treasure, J. (1997). Stage and processes of change in eating disorders: Implications for therapy. *Clinical Psychology and Psychotherapy, 4,* 186–191.

Carter, J., & Fairburn, C. (1998). Cognitive behavioral self-help for binge eating disorder: A controlled effectiveness study. *Journal of Counseling and Clinical Psychology, 66,* 616–623.

Cooper, P., Coker, S., & Fleming. C. (1994). Self-help for bulimia nervosa: A preliminary report. *International Journal of Eating Disorders, 16,* 401–404.

Cooper, P., Coker, S., & Fleming, C. (1996). An evaluation of the efficacy of supervised cognitive behavioral self-help for bulimia nervosa. *Journal of Psychosomatic Research, 40,* 281–287.

Crits-Christoph, P., & Barber, J. (Eds.). (1991). *Handbook of short-term dynamic psychotherapy.* New York: Basic Books.

Davanloo, H. (1990). *Unlocking the unconscious.* Chichester, England: Wiley.

Davanloo, H. (1992). *Short-term dynamic psychotherapy.* Northvale, NJ: Aronson.

Dumont, M. (1974). Self-help treatment programs. *American Journal of Psychiatry, 131,* 631–635.

Ellis, A. (1993). The advantages and disadvantages of self-help therapy materials. *Professional Psychology: Research and Practice, 24,* 335–339.

Faludi, S. (1991). *Backlash: The undeclared war against American women.* New York: Doubleday.

Garfield, S. (1997). The therapist as a neglected variable in psychotherapy research. *Clinical Psychology: Science and Practice, 4,* 40–43.

Garfinkel, P. E., Lin, E., Goering, P., Spegg, C., Goldbloom, D. S., Kennedy, S., Kaplan, A. S., & Woodside, D. B. (1995). Bulimia nervosa in a Canadian community sample: Prevalence and comparison of subgroups. *American Journal of Psychiatry, 152,* 1052–1058.

Garvin, V., Striegel-Moore, R., & Wells, A. (1998). Participant reactions to a cognitive–behavioral guided self-help program for binge eating: Developing criteria for program evaluation. *Journal of Psychosomatic Research, 44,* 407–412.

Glasgow, R., & Rosen, G. (1978). Behavioral bibliotherapy: A review of self-help behavior therapy manuals. *Psychological Bulletin, 85,* 1–23.

Grave, R. (1998). Guided self-help for bulimia nervosa in a specialist setting: A pilot study. *Eating and Weight Disorders, 2,* 169–172.

Hartley, P. (1995). Changing body image through guided self-help: A pilot study. *Eating Disorders, 3,* 165–174.

Jordan, J. (1996, May). [Featured speaker]. Women's Growth in Connection: Theory and Clinical Applications [Workshop], Elmcrest Hospital, Portland, CT.

Katz, A. (1981). Self help and mutual aid. *Annual Review of Sociology, 7,* 129–155.

Kazdin, A. (Ed.). (1996). Validated treatments: Multiple perspectives and issues— Introduction to the series. *Clinical Psychology, 3,* 216–217.

Lambert, M., & Bergin, A. (1994). The effectiveness of psychotherapy. In A. Bergin & S. Garfield (Eds.), *Handbook of psychotherapy and behavior* (4th ed., pp. 143–189). New York: Wiley.

Luborsky, L. (1990). Theory and technique in dynamic psychotherapy: Curative factors and training therapist to maximize them. *Psychotherapy and Psychosomatics, 53,* 50–57.

Malan, D. (1992). Criteria for selection. In H. Davanloo (Ed.), *Short-term dynamic psychotherapy* (pp. 169–189). Northvale, NJ: Aronson.

Malan, D. H., & Osimo, F. (1992). *Psychodynamics, training and outcome in brief Psychotherapy.* Oxford, England: Butterworth-Heineman.

Marx, J., Gyorky, Z., Royalty, G., & Stern, T. (1992). Use of self-help books in psychotherapy. *Professional Psychology: Research and Practice, 23,* 300–305.

Miller, G. (1969). Psychology as a means of protecting human welfare. *American Psychologist, 24,* 1063–1075.

Mitchell, J., Fletcher, L., Hanson, K., Mussell, M., Seim, H., Al-Banna, M., Wilson, M., & Crosby, R. (in press). The relative efficacy of fluoxetine and manual-based self-help in the treatment of outpatients with bulimia nervosa. *Journal of Clinical Psychopharmacology.*

Mitchell, J., Maki, D., Adson, D., Ruskin, B., & Crow, S. (1997). The selectivity of inclusion and exclusion criteria in bulimia nervosa treatment studies. *International Journal of Eating Disorders, 22,* 243–252.

Neighbors, H., Braithwaite, R., & Thompson, E. (1995). Health promotion and African-Americans. *Science of Health Promotion, 9,* 281–287.

Peterson, C., Mitchell, J., Engbloom, S., Nugent, S., Mussell, M., & Miller, J. (in press). Group cognitive–behavioral treatment of binge eating disorder: A comparison of therapist-led vs. self-help formats. *International Journal of Eating Disorders.*

Prochaska, J., Norcross, J., & DiClemente, C. (1994). *Changing for good: The revolutionary program that explains the six stages of change and teaches you how to free yourself from bad habits.* New York: Morrow.

Rathner, G., Bonsch, C., Maurer, G., Walter, M., & Sollner, W. (1993). The impact of a "guided self-help group" on bulimic women: A prospective 15-

month study of attenders and non-attenders. *Journal of Psychosomatic Research, 37*, 389–396.

Riessman, F., & Carroll, D. (1995). *Redefining self-help: Policy and practice.* San Francisco: Jossey-Bass.

Rosen, G. (1987). Self-help treatment books and the commercialization of psychotherapy. *American Psychologist, 42*, 46–51.

Rosen, G. (1993). Self-help or hype? Comments on psychology's failure to advance self-care. *Professional Psychology: Research and Practice, 24*, 340–345.

Sanderson, W., & Woody, S. (1995). *Manuals for empirically validated treatments: A project of the Task Force on Psychological Interventions.* Washington, DC: Division of Clinical Psychology, American Psychological Association.

Scheff, T. (Ed.). (1975). *Labeling madness.* Englewood Cliffs, NJ: Prentice Hall.

Schmidt, U., Tiller, J., & Treasure, J. (1993). Self-treatment for bulimia nervosa: A pilot study. *International Journal of Eating Disorders, 13*, 273–277.

Sifneos, P. (1987). *Short-term dynamic psychotherapy: Evaluation and technique* (2nd ed.). New York: Plenum Medical Book.

Sifneos, P. (1992). Motivation for change. In H. Davanloo (Ed.), *Short-term dynamic psychotherapy* (pp. 93–98). Northvale, NJ: Aronson.

Spitzer, R., Yanovski, S., Wadden, J., Wing, R., Marcus, M., Stunkard, A., Devlin, M., Mitchell, J., & Hasin, D. (1993). Binge eating disorder: Its further validation in a multi-site study. *International Journal of Eating Disorders, 13*, 137–154.

Striegel-Moore, R. H., Wilfley, D. E., Pike, K. M., Dohm, F., & Fairburn, C. G. (2000). Recurrent binge eating in Black American women. *Archives of Family Medicine, 9*, 83–87.

Strupp, H. (1995). The psychotherapist's skills revisited. *Clinical Psychology: Science and Practice, 2*, 70–74.

Strupp, H. (1996). The tripartite model and the Consumer Reports Study. *American Psychologist, 51*, 1017–1024.

Strupp, H., & Anderson, T. (1997). On the limitations of therapy manuals. *Clinical Psychology, 4*, 76–82.

Szasz, T. (1970). *Ideology and insanity: Essays on the psychiatric dehumanization of man.* New York: Anchor Books.

Task Force on Promotion and Dissemination of Psychological Procedures. (1995). Training in and dissemination of empirically validated psychological treatments: Report and recommendations. *The Clinical Psychologist, 48*, 3–23.

Thiels, C., Schmidt, U., Treasure, J., Garthe, R., & Troop, N. (1998). Guided self-change for bulimia nervosa incorporating use of a self-care manual. *American Journal of Psychiatry, 155*, 947–953.

Treasure, J., Schmidt, U., Troop, N., Tiller, J., Todd, G., Keilen, M., & Dodge, E. (1994). First step in managing bulimia nervosa: Controlled trial of a therapeutic manual. *British Medical Journal, 308*, 686–689.

Treasure, J., Schmidt, U., Troop, N., Tiller, J., Todd, G., & Turnbull, S. (1996). Sequential treatment for bulimia nervosa incorporating a self-care manual. *British Journal of Psychiatry, 168,* 94–98.

Treasure, J., & Ward, A. (1997). A practical guide to the use of motivational interviewing in anorexia nervosa. *European Eating Disorders Review, 5,* 105–124.

Troop, N., Schmidt, U., Tiller, J., Todd, G., Keilen, M., & Treasure, J. (1996). Compliance with a self-care manual for bulimia nervosa: Predictors and outcome. *British Journal of Clinical Psychology, 35,* 435–438.

Turnbull, S., Schmidt, U., Troop, N., Tiller, J., Todd, G., & Treasure, J. (1997). Predictors of outcome for two treatments for bulimia nervosa: Short and long term. *International Journal of Eating Disorders, 21,* 17–22.

U.S. Department of Health and Human Services. (1990). *International classification of diseases* (9th ed.). Washington, DC: Author.

Waller, D., Fairburn, C., McPherson, A., Kay, R., Lee, A., & Novwell, T. (1996). Treating bulimia nervosa in primary care: A pilot study. *International Journal of Eating Disorders, 19,* 99–103.

Wells, A., Garvin, V., Dohm, F., & Striegel-Moore, R. H. (1997). Telephone-based guided self-help for binge eating disorder. *International Journal of Eating Disorders, 21,* 341–346.

9

INTEGRATIVE COGNITIVE THERAPY FOR BULIMIC BEHAVIOR

STEPHEN A. WONDERLICH, JAMES E. MITCHELL,
CAROL B. PETERSON, AND SCOTT CROW

The most widely studied psychotherapeutic approach for the treatment of bulimia nervosa is cognitive–behavior therapy (CBT), with more than 20 controlled trials (for reviews, see Peterson & Mitchell, 1995; and Wilson & Fairburn, 1998). CBT has been shown to be superior to minimal or wait-list control treatments in terms of reducing the frequency of binge eating and purging behavior, with reasonable maintenance of change at 6 months and 1-year follow-up (e.g., Agras et al., 1994; Agras, Schneider, Arnow, Raeburn, & Telch, 1989; Fairburn, Jones, Peveler, Hope, & O'Connor, 1993). However, some studies suggest that CBT has distinct limitations in the treatment of bulimia nervosa, with 50%–60% of patients failing to abstain from bingeing and purging behaviors (e.g., Fairburn et al., 1995). Increasingly, there have been calls for more effective psychotherapeutic treatments for bulimia nervosa (e.g., Wilson, 1996).

Paralleling the observation of a need for new treatments for bulimia nervosa has been the development and study of new conceptual models for bulimia nervosa. Cognitive–behavior approaches to the treatment of bulimia nervosa are frequently based on conceptual models that imply that low self-esteem triggers concerns about appearance, which result in dieting behavior as a means of overcoming perceived appearance-related problems (e.g., Fairburn & Cooper, 1989). These models further suggest that dieting or food restriction ultimately precipitate binge eating in response to prolonged periods of caloric deprivation. Thus, proximal antecedents for bingeing behavior typically include dieting behavior, whereas more distal antecedents include self-esteem deficits.

More recently, explanatory models of bulimic behavior have invoked emotional states as proximal antecedent conditions for binge-eating behavior (e.g., Heatherton & Baumeister, 1991; Meyer, Waller, & Waters, 1998;

173

Striegel-Moore & Smolak, 2000). Rather than focusing on hunger-related binge eating, these models imply that bulimic behavior may be an effort to regulate or escape from negative affect. In support of such models, recent empirical evidence suggests that negative mood induction and subliminal presentation of emotional cues may be strong precipitants of binge eating (e.g., Meyer & Waller, 1999; Telch & Agras, 1996). Furthermore, naturalistic studies suggest that negative mood states may be better predictors of binge-eating episodes than normal meal consumption (e.g., Davis, Freeman, & Garner, 1988). These data imply that treatment approaches that emphasize affect regulation in bulimic individuals may be worthy of further development.

DEVELOPMENT OF INTEGRATIVE COGNITIVE THERAPY

Integrative cognitive therapy (ICT) is an extension of standard CBT for patients with bulimia nervosa, with a theoretical and clinical emphasis on several areas that have not been considered primary factors or treatment targets in current protocols for bulimia (e.g., Fairburn, Marcus, & Wilson, 1993). These include enhancing motivation for treatment and expanding the focus on self-oriented cognition, interpersonal relationships and interpersonal schemas, emotional responding, and cultural factors, all of which may increase the risk for developing and maintaining the disorder.

Although ICT incorporates these concepts and associated treatment principles have been included in the such treatment, we believe that ICT generally adheres to the basic principles of cognitive therapy. Clark (1995) suggested that the following principles characterize CBT: (a) Individuals actively participate in the construction of their psychological reality, (b) cognition influences or mediates both affect and behavior, (c) cognition is knowable and accessible, (d) cognitive change is central to human change process, and (e) cognitive therapy adopts a present time frame. Although we believe that ICT generally conforms to these fundamental principles, it is clearly informed by more recent developments in cognitive science and cognitive psychotherapy. Before presenting the fundamental ideas associated with ICT, we review some of the major themes in contemporary cognitive theory that have influenced our thinking.

THE EVOLUTION OF COGNITION: THEORY, EMPIRICAL STUDIES, AND THERAPY

Although many consider the cognitive revolution in psychology to be a phenomenon of the 1970s, continued advances in the cognitive sciences over the past few decades have been substantial and cut across theory, empirical studies, and psychotherapeutic implications. For example, there has been a dramatic increase in empirically based studies of a growing number of cognitive constructs. In the literature on depression, experimental studies of cognition substantially influence our knowledge about depressive disorders. Several authors have recently identified what they consider to be the most useful contemporary cognitive approaches to the study of depression, including the following: the examination of neural networks, capacity limitation in cognitive systems, automatic and effortful information processing, selective processing of information, levels of information processing, top-down versus bottom-up information processing, processing information outside of awareness, interpersonal schemas, availability and accessibility of cognitions, narrative-based approaches to self-representation, priming studies, and personal vulnerability–adversity correspondence (Ingram, Miranda, & Segal, 1998; Segal & Muran, 1993). Furthermore, Safran and Segal (1996) suggested that the study of these cognitive constructs may have a significant impact on psychotherapeutic treatment of the depressive disorders. Although some of these cognitive constructs have received preliminary investigation in eating disorders (for reviews, see Meyer et al., 1998; and Vitousek & Ewald, 1993), we believe that further study of these constructs may enhance existing causal models of the eating disorders and associated model-based treatments.

Accompanying these empirical discoveries in the cognitive sciences has been an increase in the criticisms of traditional cognitive therapy. Despite continued demonstrations of at least moderate efficacy of CBT, various cognitive therapists have suggested that significant alterations should be made to standard cognitive therapy (e.g., Guidano, 1987; Mahoney, 1991; Meichenbaum, 1993; Safran & Segal, 1996). In one of the most detailed criticisms of cognitive therapy, Clark (1995) summarized the objections to traditional cognitive therapy and suggested they fall into four categories: (a) a limited view of emotional responding, (b) an inadequate consideration of interpersonal factors, (c) insufficient attention to the therapist–client relationship, and (d) an overemphasis on conscious controlled cognitive processing.

In response to these and other criticisms, numerous authors have discussed how CBT may be modified and refined to address its perceived current limitations (e.g., Hollon, Shelton, & Davis, 1993; Robins & Hayes, 1993; Safran & Segal, 1996; Segal, Lowe, & Rokke, 1999). These suggestions may be roughly grouped into four categories. First, a number of authors have suggested that rather than focusing on automatic thoughts or peripheral schema, CBT should be more focused on affectively laden core schemas. They argued that by addressing such "deeper" cognitive structures, CBT may produce a broader range of behavioral change (e.g., Robins & Hayes,

1993; Safran, 1990a, 1990b). Second, CBT should extend its emphasis to interpersonal and affective issues (e.g., Greenberg & Safran, 1980, 1987; Safran & Segal, 1996; Young, 1990). By extending the exploration of core schemas to interpersonal relationships rather than focusing only on self-schematic information, this modification would highlight the significance of interpersonal behavior on cognitive functioning and allow the inclusion of cognitive–interpersonal cycles into the domain of CBT (Leahy, 1996; Ryle, 1985; Safran & Segal, 1996). Third, there should be an increased emphasis on long-standing aspects of the patient's underlying belief system and associated developmental issues (e.g., Guidano & Liotti, 1983; Robins & Hayes, 1993; Young, 1990). Finally, several authors have also suggested that CBT extend its exploration into the domain of the patient–therapist relationship (e.g., Robins & Hayes, 1993; Safran & Segal, 1996). By doing so, the domain of cognitive exploration is broadened through the immediate accessibility of the behaviors that are occurring within the therapeutic relationship.

As we consider the large number of theoretical and empirical advancements in the cognitive sciences, we are optimistic that these can fruitfully be applied to the understanding and treatment of eating disorders. Indeed, some of these ideas have already been considered in the treatment of anorexia nervosa (e.g., Garner, Vitousek, & Pike, 1997) and body image disturbance (Kearney-Cooke & Striegel-Moore, 1997). We have developed a model of bulimic behavior underlying ICT and our current version of ICT, with several of these more contemporary cognitive concepts in mind. Although we consider this work preliminary and likely to undergo modification, we are optimistic that several of the constructs in our model and approaches in our treatment may ultimately enhance the understanding of bulimic behavior and the associated clinical response.

AN INTEGRATIVE COGNITIVE MODEL OF BULIMIA NERVOSA

The model of etiology and maintenance of bulimia nervosa that underlies ICT, previously reviewed and presented by Wonderlich, Peterson, Mitchell, and Crow (2000), is multifactorial and attempts to integrate an array of interpersonal, cognitive–affective, cultural, and biological factors that are thought to increase the risk of developing and maintaining behaviors associated with bulimia nervosa (see Figure 9.1). It is different from other cognitive or interpersonal models of bulimia nervosa (see Agras, 1991; and Fairburn, 1997) in that there is a greater emphasis on cultural factors, self-oriented cognition, interpersonal schemas, interpersonal patterns, and emotional experiences.

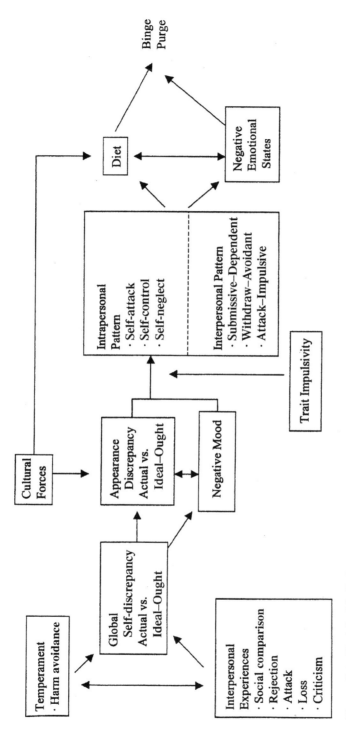

Figure 9.1. Model of bulimia nervosa. From "Integrative Approaches to Treating Eating Disorders" (p. 260), by S. A. Wonderlich, C. Peterson, J. E. Mitchell, and S. Crow. In K. J. Miller and J. S. Mizes (Eds.), *Comparative Treatments of Eating Disorders.* Copyright 2000 by Springer Publishing Company, Inc., New York 10012. Reprinted with permission.

Temperament

The model posits that individuals with bulimia display a temperament characterized by a propensity to avoid change and situations that are perceived as threatening or harmful to their self-esteem. The model relies heavily on the theoretical work of Cloninger (1987) and other psychobiological personality theorists (e.g., Tellegen, 1985), some of whose work has been previously applied to eating disorders (e.g., Brewerton, Hand, & Bishop, 1993; Bulik, Sullivan, Weltzin, & Kaye, 1995; Waller et al., 1993). Empirical reports testing Cloninger's model consistently reveal that individuals with bulimia show elevated harm avoidance (e.g., Brewerton et al., 1993; Waller et al., 1993), but novelty seeking is not consistently shown to be associated with bulimia nervosa (e.g., Berg, Crosby, Wonderlich, & Hawley, 2000). Although a propensity to pursue novel and exciting stimuli may be present in some of these individuals, in our model this temperamental variable is posited to be primarily present in one subtype of individuals with bulimia, characterized by impulsivity and substance use (see Lilenfeld et al., 1997, for a discussion of such subtypes).

Environmental Experiences

The model posits that individuals with bulimia are likely to experience an array of events or circumstances in their lives that threaten or interfere with attachment processes. For example, individuals with bulimia are more likely to have been adopted (Holden, 1991), to have experienced physical or sexual abuse in childhood (e.g., Welch & Fairburn, 1994; Wonderlich, Brewerton, Jocic, Dansky, & Abbott, 1997), and to have parental histories of psychopathology, including depression and substance abuse (e.g., Fairburn, Welch, Doll, Davies, & O'Connor, 1997). Furthermore, considerable research indicates that adolescents and adults with bulimia perceive their relationships with their parents and their overall family environments as conflictual, disengaged, and nonnurturant (e.g., Kendler et al., 1991; Strober & Humphrey, 1987; Wonderlich, 1992). Supporting these descriptions, observational studies of these individuals' families in the laboratory suggest that their relationships are best described as disengaged, conflictual, and lacking in effective communication (e.g., Humphrey, 1989). Furthermore, evidence suggests that individuals with eating disturbances display unstable attachments (e.g., Cole-Detke & Kobak, 1996). This model implies that such experiences, along with any other experience that threatens these individuals' feelings of interpersonal security and self-esteem (e.g., criticism, teasing, and social comparison), are emotionally significant for individuals with bulimia, especially given their temperamental sensitivity to harm.

Self-Discrepancy

Consistent with recent risk factor studies (e.g., Fairburn et al., 1997), the model posits that negative self-evaluation is associated with bulimia nervosa and is the consequence of the previously described problematic interpersonal–attachment experiences. However, the model predicts that it is not simply negative self-evaluation (i.e., negative self-representation) that is most precisely causal in individuals with bulimia. Instead, according to the model, these individuals perceive a deficit in themselves, which reflects a discrepancy between their perceived actual self-concept and a comparative ideal standard that they apply to themselves or they believe others apply to them. These ideas are derived from self-discrepancy theory (e.g., Higgins, 1987) and its application to depression (e.g., Strauman, 1989) and to eating-disordered behaviors (e.g., Strauman & Glenberg, 1994; Strauman, Vookles, Berenstein, Chaiken, & Higgins, 1991). Specifically, self-discrepancy theory postulates various domains of the self, including the *actual* self (a mental representation of the attributes or features the individual believes he or she actually possesses), the *ideal* self (a representation of the attributes that the individual or significant other would ideally like him or her to possess), and the *ought* self (a representation of the attributes that the individual or a significant other believes is his or her obligation or duty to possess; e.g., Strauman et al., 1991).

Central to the current theory are Strauman's findings (e.g., Strauman et al., 1991; Strauman & Glenberg, 1994) suggesting that actual self-ideal discrepancies are related to negative mood and, more important, body dissatisfaction, body size overestimation, and bulimic symptoms. It is further hypothesized that such body dissatisfaction, as a specific facet of self-concept, may exacerbate negative affective states, including depression (e.g., Joiner, Wonderlich, Metalsky, & Schmidt, 1995). Furthermore, Altabe and Thompson (1996) conducted a series of experiments that suggest that actual versus ideal discrepancy, in terms of appearance, functions as a true cognitive schema that can influence information processing and affect negative mood. Together, these findings suggest that discrepancies between the actual self and ideal self elicit negative affect, body dissatisfaction, and body size overestimation, which in turn interact with one another.

Negative Mood

Considerable evidence suggests that individuals with bulimia experience intense states of aversive self-awareness and a propensity for negative affectivity (e.g., Johnson & Larson, 1982; Ruderman & Grace, 1987). The model posits that such negative affectivity and aversive self-awareness are precipitated by the previously described self-related discrepancy. Consistent with escape theory (Heatherton & Baumeister, 1991), we predict that individuals with bulimia experience prolonged states of aversive, self-oriented preoccupation focused on their perceived self-deficits and the implication of such deficits for their interpersonal security. Our model predicts that in individuals with bulimia, the magnitude of such negative affectivity will be positively correlated with a magnitude of self-discrepancies.

Interpersonal Factors and Cognitive Style

Bowlby (1969) and emotion theorists (e.g., Buck, 1980; Greenberg & Safran, 1987) have described the motivational relationship between emotional states and action dispositions. Recent cognitive–behavior accounts of bulimia nervosa emphasize emotional factors less than cognitive factors in the onset and maintenance of the disorder (e.g., Fairburn, Marcus, & Wilson, 1993; Wilson & Fairburn, 1993). The model posits two broad categories of behavior that are thought to occur in individuals with bulimia to regulate negative affective experience related to self-discrepancy: specific interpersonal patterns and cognitive styles.

More important, in numerous empirical studies researchers have found that individuals with bulimia exhibit problematic interpersonal relationships (e.g., Johnson & Larson, 1982) and long-term social adjustment problems (e.g., Norman & Herzog, 1984). These individuals also reported experiencing less support from existing interpersonal relationships compared with individuals with no eating disorders, and they perceive themselves as having higher degrees of social conflict and less social competence than control individuals (e.g., Grisset & Norvell, 1992). Furthermore, individuals with bulimia reportedly form more dependent relationships (e.g., Jacobson & Robbins, 1989), develop insecure attachments (Cole-Detke & Kobak, 1996), and experience problems with intimacy (e.g., Pruitt, Kappius, & Gorman, 1992).

To reduce negative affect related to self-discrepancy, the model posits that individuals with bulimia emit specific repetitive interpersonal patterns across a variety of relationships. Some evidence indicates that interpersonal patterns seen in individuals with bulimia are strongly related to negative mood (e.g., Wonderlich & Swift, 1990b), suggesting that such relationship styles may be an effort to manage negative affect. Influenced heavily by Benjamin's (1974, 1993) model of social behavior, we imply through our model that these interpersonal patterns are oriented toward avoiding interpersonal rejection or abandonment. The two primary patterns posited to be associated with bulimia nervosa in the model are a submission pattern and a withdrawal pattern, which parallel Bowlby's (1969) original thinking about two forms of anxious attachment: ambivalent and avoidant. In the *submission* pattern, the individual with bulimia is likely to appease and satisfy key attachment figures in an effort to avoid rejection and associated negative emotional experience. For similar reasons, the *withdrawal* pattern may develop when relationships are perceived as threatening to attachment status and associated self-esteem, and the individual sees no way to reduce the relational problem through engagement in relationships.

Although moderator variables are not well defined in this version of the model, trait impulsivity is thought to moderate the relationships between self-discrepancy-related negative affect and interpersonal patterns and cognitive styles. This is consistent with findings from recent field studies that trait impulsivity moderates the association between bulimic behavior and both dietary restraint and negative mood (Steiger, Lehoux, & Gauvin, 1999; Wonderlich, 1999). Specifically, it is hypothesized that highly impulsive individuals with bulimia are more likely to display an interpersonal attack pattern in their relationships with key attachment figures. Such a pattern is most common when these individuals perceive the attachment figures as withdrawing or unavailable to them. The pattern is based on the fundamental interpersonal idea that such individuals engage in hostile control behaviors to prevent the withdrawal of significant others (e.g., Benjamin, 1993).

In addition to these interpersonal patterns, our model highlights specific cognitive styles as another means of attempting to regulate negative affect associated with self-discrepancy. Three specific cognitive styles are predicted: self-control, self-attack, and self-neglect. Some individuals with bulimia may engage in extreme efforts to control their self and attain perfection to reduce their self-discrepancy and associated negative affects. Others may rely on a more hostile pattern of self-control in which they attack themselves for their self-discrepancy. Still others may attempt to avoid the discrepancy through self-neglect and engage in more reckless unpredictable behaviors; this is particularly true with highly impulsive individuals. It is important to note that such cognitive styles are used by the individual with bulimia in an effort to manage the underlying negative mood that is ultimately linked to his or her fundamental self-discrepancy.

Dieting and Interpersonal Distress

The interpersonal patterns and cognitive styles adopted by the individual with bulimia are predicted to have two particular effects in the model. First, the extreme interpersonal patterns (i.e., submission, withdrawal, and attack) are likely to result in heightened interpersonal distress, which only intensifies existing negative affect. Furthermore, the cognitive style that the individual with bulimia develops (self-attack, self-control, self-neglect) within a specific context (i.e., appearance focused) may increase the likelihood of attempting to reduce appearance-related discrepancy through the pursuit of thinness and dieting. Such extreme dieting reflects an interesting amalgam of self-control and self-neglect as the individual with bulimia attempts to perfect the self (self-control) while also neglecting fundamental nutritional needs (self-neglect).

The combination of extreme dieting and its associated psychological and physiological dysregulatory effects, in conjunction with the heightened negative emotional states produced by the maladaptive interpersonal patterns and extreme cognitive styles, is posited to increase the likelihood of binge and purge behavior. Consistent with Heatherton and Baumeister's (1991) escape theory, bingeing and purging behaviors are posited to provide a transitory avoidance of increasing negative affective states by the individual with bulimia. Furthermore, by focusing on more immediate issues such as food consumption and purging, the individual is able to avoid more meaningful underlying issues related to self-discrepancy and the negative effects of interpersonal and cognitive coping styles.

AN OVERVIEW OF THE TREATMENT

Because of the theoretical relevance of cultural factors, self-oriented cognition, interpersonal schemas, emotional reactions, and interpersonal relationships in this model of bulimia nervosa, these variables become a focus in the current treatment protocol. However, direct behavioral change of bulimic symptomatology is also encouraged and relies on cognitive and behavior techniques previously used in the treatment of bulimia nervosa (e.g., Fairburn, Marcus, et al., 1993; Mitchell et al., 1990). The longitudinal structure of the therapy is outlined below.

Phase I: Enhancing Motivation and Psychoeducation, Sessions 1–3

In the early sessions of treatment, there is an emphasis on educating the patients about their disorder, including readings in a patient workbook. There is also an emphasis on conducting a collaborative interview with the patients to identify general discrepancies between their current behavior and broader goals (e.g., Miller & Rollnick, 1991). This is typically done by reviewing the history of their bulimia and the social and interpersonal context in which it developed. Relying heavily on techniques from motivational interviewing (Miller & Rollnick, 1991), these early sessions are used to explore and enhance the patients' motivation for treatment. Clearly, the first step in treatment is to establish a nonauthoritative therapeutic relationship that provides a safe context in which the patients may examine their behavior and consider the implications of change. In this way, the therapeutic relationship differs from that established in some forms of CBT for bulimia nervosa.

Initially, the therapy may focus on general areas of self-discrepancy for the patients, but it shifts during the first few sessions toward a more specific exploration of any discrepancy that the patients hold between their actual physical appearance and their desired physical appearance. Consistent with work on self-discrepancy theory (e.g., Higgins, 1987; Strauman et al., 1991) and its application to appearance (e.g., Altabe & Thompson, 1996), there is an effort to delineate cognitions about the perceived actual appearance and the relationship of these cognitions to comparative appearance standards (i.e., ideal, ought). Relying in part on homework worksheets, the therapist examines the patient's standards for body shape and weight, which provide a context for an exploration and discussion of cultural factors that may affect the patients' (especially women's) perceptions of ideal body shape and weight. This treatment approach places a heavy emphasis on the potential role that cultural factors may have played in the patient's unrealistic standards for appearance and associated decision to diet—a point that has been made by various clinicians and theoreticians (e.g., Steiner-Adair, 1986; Striegel-Moore, 1993). The therapist provides the patient with information about cultural factors related to weight, body shape, dieting, and eating disorders. This is the significant emphasis in the first few sessions of the treatment.

More important, however, the therapy must remain focused on the patients' emotional reaction to the self-discrepancy between the way they actually perceive their body shape, their idealized body shape, and the pressure they feel to attain it. This emotion-focused aspect of the treatment is thought to be essential in assisting the patients to cope effectively with fear associated with behavior change and recovery. The therapist is encouraged to acknowledge and explore the patients' feelings as they occur in the session. This is consistent with a variety of client-centered and experiential psychotherapies (e.g., Greenberg, Ford, Alden, & Johnson, 1993; Greenberg & Korman, 1993; Safran & Segal, 1996). Therapist interventions may appropriately consist of such questions as "Can you say what the feeling is like for you when you are not at your ideal weight?" This is then followed by a series of questions or statements that deepen or clarify the emotional response (e.g., "It is frightening" or "It is hard to even think about it"). Also the therapist may assess how the patients would feel if they were at their ideal weight. By exploring the emotional significance of such discrepancies, the therapist clarifies motivational forces that may maintain the eating disorder symptoms and remains appropriately empathic as the patients face the limits of their weight control strategy.

In summary, the following goals are established for Phase 1:

1. Establish a treatment relationship that clearly includes the patient as a significant collaborator in her or his treatment and identifies discrepancies between behavior and broad goals.
2. Begin to develop an understanding of the discrepancy between the patient's perception of her or his actual and desired physical appearance.
3. Remain sensitive to the patient's emotional state as the patient discusses discrepancies in her or his life and demonstrate how such feeling may be linked to self-discrepancies. This serves as a basic strategy throughout the therapy.
4. Highlight and emphasize how cultural factors may influence the patient's decisions about dieting and begin to educate her or him about realistic and healthy weight goals.
5. Begin self-monitoring of food intake.

Phase II: Normalization of Eating and Associated Coping Skills, Sessions 4–8

Phase II, which generally runs from Session 4 through Session 8, relies on the direct encouragement of behavioral change in the area of eating and meal planning. Similar to other treatments for bulimia nervosa (e.g., CBT), patients are encouraged to eat three meals a day with snacks. Eating a variety of foods is encouraged; introducing feared foods is also part of this intervention. Although similar to other approaches in terms of normalizing eating patterns as a necessary condition from a nutritional and biological standpoint, the consumption of meals is also construed as a form of appropriate self-care (i.e., opposite of a self-neglecting cognitive style), which the patient deserves and should pursue.

During this phase of treatment, meal planning skills and specific coping skills are introduced to help the patients achieve the behavioral goal of normalization of eating. Another major goal for Phase II is to help the patients begin to identify antecedents or precipitants of their binge eating, food restriction, or other eating disorder behaviors. This is conducted in the context of helping the patients to identify high-risk situations, so that they may develop effective coping strategies, which is a goal for Phase II of treatment. The treatment assumes that much of the reluctance that patients exhibit when asked to increase food intake is based on fear and anxiety rather than oppositional defiance or characterologic resistance. Consistent with recent "dialectical" treatment strategies used with other populations (e.g., Linehan, 1993), a primary coping skill, which is taught, is the identification, expression, and tolerance of emotional states, while the therapist also works with the patient to learn other skills that may help moderate the feeling state. Specific self-regulatory behavioral skills that have been used to decrease physiological arousal and anxiety (e.g., Foa & Wilson, 1991), such as breathing skills and relaxation, are introduced to help reduce anxiety associated with direct exposure to feared stimuli (e.g., food, weight gain, or loss of control). Furthermore, at this point in the treatment, other behavioral techniques, such as shaping, graded exposure, stimulus control, and self-reinforcement, are encouraged. The essential principle in developing coping skills in Phase II is to assist the patient to structure time and food consumption through the meal plan and to manage negative emotional states associated with change in general and meal consumption specifically.

In summary, the following goals are established for Phase II:

1. Continue self-monitoring of food intake.
2. Continue to identify and modify self-discrepancy regarding appearance (especially in terms of unrealistic standards).
3. Begin formal meal planning phase with emphasis on organization of nutritionally adequate meals and snacks.
4. Encourage the identification and expression of the patient's emotional states associated with increased eating and teach coping skills to assist the patient in completing the meal planning assignment and consumption of regular meals.

Phase III: Interpersonal Patterns and Schemas, Sessions 9–18

In Phase III, there is a clear shift in treatment toward a focus on interpersonal and cognitive (intrapsychic) factors that are posited in the model to be relevant for the development and maintenance of bulimia nervosa. Furthermore and central to this treatment, Phase III focuses on attempting to identify how such cognitive and interpersonal factors serve as efforts to overcome the individual's fundamental self-discrepancies. Simply put, this phase of treatment focuses on identifying and modifying the cognitive and interpersonal patterns that the individual has developed in an effort to manage the negative mood associated with his or her underlying self-discrepancy.

The therapist attempts to complete several basic tasks in Phase III of treatment. They are not necessarily completed sequentially and may overlap during the treatment. First, the therapist conducts an interpersonal analysis. In this portion of Phase III, the therapist and patient review specific interpersonal transactions that either precede bulimic symptoms or precede negative emotional states. Analysis of such interpersonal transactions is conducted in accord with Benjamin's (1974, 1993) circumplex model of interpersonal behavior, which has been studied frequently in individuals with bulimia (e.g., Humphrey, 1989; Wonderlich & Swift, 1990a, 1990b; Wonderlich, Klein, & Council, 1996). The therapist focuses on identifying with the patients their basic patterns when relating to another person. This may include such prototypic patterns as submission–dependency, withdrawal–avoidance, or attack–impulsivity. In this portion of the assessment, it is critical for the therapist to identify the relationship between affective states and such interpersonal patterns, as it is assumed that interpersonal patterns serve as a means of managing negative affect. The goal is to identify the salient and repetitive means by which the patient manages or avoids affect and interpersonal situations.

A second task in Phase III of the treatment is to identify the patients' cognitive (intrapsychic) style. This refers to how the patients focus their attention on themselves or attempt to regulate their self, including such prototypic cognitive patterns as trying to control or restrain the self (i.e., self-control), criticizing the self (i.e., self-attack), or not attending to the needs of self (i.e., self-neglect). Again, the goal in this analysis is to identify the patient's repetitive and most salient style of self-directed behaviors.

The third major task in Phase III of the treatment is for the therapist to work with the patients to understand the linkage between their underlying self-discrepancy and their compensatory interpersonal patterns and cognitive styles and then begin to modify these patterns. This may include interventions intended to directly modify self-discrepancy through changing unrealistic standards associated with the ideal self and ought self, or it may focus on enhancing positive perceptions of the actual self, both of which reduce discrepancy. Additionally, there may be an opportunity to assist the patient to make direct interpersonal and cognitive style changes. For example, there is a significant emphasis placed on developing healthy assertive patterns of behavior with others and attempting to adopt a more self-accepting cognitive style that includes tolerance of inadequacies and deficiencies.

In brief therapies for bulimic behavior (i.e., 20 sessions or less), it is difficult to target cognitive structures beyond self-discrepancy, interpersonal patterns, and cognitive styles. However, in longer treatments, the therapist may choose to more fully delineate and modify the patient's interpersonal schema. Safran (1990a, 1990b) proposed the notion of an interpersonal schema, which can be defined as a generic representation of self–other interactions and is based on actual interpersonal experiences. In other words, the therapist attempts to identify the patient's interpersonal rules, or "scripts" (e.g., Leahy, 1996), and their developmental origins, which guide and direct everyday interpersonal and cognitive behavior. Obviously, it is difficult to sufficiently address these topics in brief treatments.

In summary, Phase III of the treatment attempts to facilitate several skills:

1. Identify repetitive cognitive styles.
2. Identify repetitive interpersonal patterns.

3. Identify the connection between self-discrepancy and interpersonal patterns and cognitive styles.
4. Identify underlying interpersonal schemas or rules for interpersonal behavior that the patient has learned (usually only possible in longer term treatments).

Phase IV: Relapse Prevention and Lifestyle Management

The final phase of the treatment focuses on consolidating improvements and preventing relapse. This process requires the therapist and patient to review the patient's progress in the treatment, especially identifying interventions that were particularly helpful and effective. In addition, cognitive–behavior techniques (e.g., Fairburn, Marcus, et al., 1993; Marlatt & Gordon, 1985) are implemented to facilitate continued recovery and prevent relapse—a significant risk following improvement in bulimic symptoms (e.g., Olmsted, Kaplan, & Rockert, 1994). Final sessions should also include discussions of the patient's feelings and thoughts about ending treatment.

An essential component in the end of the treatment is to educate the patient about the nature of relapse to prevent its occurrence. Specifically, the therapist should emphasize the distinction between a "lapse" and a "relapse" to prevent the patient from overgeneralizing the importance of a minor slip, a process that can lead to symptomatic deterioration. In addition, the patient is asked to consider various relapse scenarios and to formulate coping strategies using skills developed in treatment. The patient also identifies her or his own potential cognitive, interpersonal, and behavioral triggers of lapses and relapses and develops plans to get back on track should these occur.

Finally, the patient reviews the changes she or he has made in treatment and develops a maintenance plan to facilitate continued improvement. As part of the maintenance plan, components of a healthy lifestyle are identified and implemented. In addition, the therapist encourages the patient to discuss feelings and thoughts about ending the treatment.

In summary, Phase IV of the treatment includes the following components:

1. Learn about the nature of relapse and review coping strategies that can be used to prevent it from occurring.
2. Identify risk factors or relapse and plan ways of getting back on track if symptoms worsen.
3. Review progress made in treatment.
4. Develop a maintenance plan for continued improvement and healthy lifestyle.
5. Discuss thoughts and feelings about ending treatment.

SUMMARY AND CONCLUSION

We have described a psychotherapeutic treatment for bulimia nervosa that modifies traditional CBT through the incorporation of ideas from contemporary cognitive science, interpersonal and emotion theory, and sociocultural models of bulimic behavior. We were motivated to develop a model of bulimic behavior that was relatively complex and dynamic in its depiction of causal relationships in bulimia nervosa. In describing his belief that behavioral disorders are best conceptualized by such complex and comprehensive models, Haynes (1992) stated that limited causal models "promote intervention programs with limited effectiveness or applicability" (p. 21). We believe that developing and empirically testing complex cognitive models may provide important new findings that may inform the next generation of treatments for bulimia nervosa.

Although the model that underlies ICT continues to evolve and is in need of precise and specific empirical tests, particularly regarding the mediational and moderational relationships among self-discrepancy, affect, interpersonal patterns, cognitive styles, and bulimic behavior, we believe it incorporates constructs that may further illuminate bulimic behavior. Furthermore, we continue to refine the treatment principles based on this model. Although we have conducted some interesting pilot cases, we continue to generate as many questions as answers regarding the development of a new treatment for bulimia nervosa. Many of our questions pertain to specific treatment parameters, such as intensity, content, format, and length. The following questions reflect some of our current thinking about these issues.

1. How much can be truly accomplished in 20 sessions? Motivational interviewing, psychoeducation, meal planning, addressing interpersonal patterns, and relapse prevention is a lot to tackle in 20 weeks. Which pieces of this treatment are most essential, and what is the best order of these components?
2. Does shifting cognitive exploration from automatic thoughts about shape and weight (i.e., CBT) to a broader range of thoughts and underlying schemas associated with both interpersonal and food-related issues (i.e., ICT) offer a meaningful content change? We wonder if the highly motivated individual with bulimia could not use either approach to effectively attain recovery. However, for individuals who show severe and "habitual" binge–purge episodes, does the content matter, especially when there is a 20-session limit? Is there value to using resources, such as the hospital, to interrupt the behaviors and conduct exposure and response prevention (e.g., Wilson,

1996), or should an entirely different approach focusing more on self-regulation rather than eating behavior be pursued (e.g., Linehan, 1993)?

3. Is it meaningful to initiate active behavior change for an individual with bulimia who is in the "precontemplative" or "early contemplative" stages of change? In other words, does the aggressive application of cognitive–behavior technology to the precontemplative individual not only predict treatment failure but also an iatrogenically determined "learned helplessness" or hopelessness phenomenon? How can one enhance motivation?

4. Are there other approaches, whose intensity and invasiveness vary somewhere between office visits in the clinic and hospitalization, which may support and facilitate change in the individual with bulimia in her or his everyday environment? Should one consider the possible role of extending or intensifying therapy through the application of new technology, such as palm top computers, email, and Internet access?

5. Can ICT be applied in a self-help format, and how might this be integrated into more complex stepped-care models of treatment for bulimia nervosa?

6. Should researchers conduct more thorough assessments of concurrent characteristics of the patient, such as personality functioning (e.g., impulsivity) or comorbid psychopathology, and then create specific modules, which could be attached to a core treatment for the eating disturbance, to address these issues? Alternatively, is it possible that ICT may be more effective for the anxious, perfectionistic patient than for the impulsive, disregulated patient?

ICT is in the very early stages of development, and its developers are more prone to ask questions than provide answers. We hope this open forum of inquiry will allow researchers to consider new ideas that will ultimately enhance the treatment of bulimic behavior.

REFERENCES

Agras, W. S. (1991). Nonpharmacologic treatments of bulimia nervosa. *Journal of Clinical Psychiatry, 52*(Suppl), 29, 33.

Agras, W. S., Schneider, J. A., Arnow, B., Raeburn, S. D., & Telch, C. F. (1989). Cognitive–behavioral and response-prevention treatments for bulimia nervosa. *Journal of Consulting and Clinical Psychology, 57,* 215–221.

Agras, W. S., Rossiter, E. M., Arnow, B., Telch, C. F., Raeburn, S. D., Bruce, B., & Koran, L. (1994). One-year follow-up of psychosocial and pharmacologic treatments for bulimia nervosa. *Journal of Clinical Psychiatry, 55,* 179–183.

Altabe, M., & Thompson, J. K. (1996). Body image: A cognitive self-schema construct? *Cognitive Therapy and Research, 20,* 171–193.

Benjamin, L. S. (1974). Structural analysis of social behavior. *Psychological Review, 81,* 392–425.

Benjamin, L. S. (1993). *Interpersonal treatment of personality disorders.* New York: Guilford Press.

Berg, M. L., Crosby, R. D., Wonderlich, S. A., & Hawley, D. (2000). The relationship of temperament and perceptions of nonshared environment in bulimia nervosa. *International Journal of Eating Disorders, 28,* 148–154.

Bowlby, J. (1969). *Attachment and loss: Vol. 1. Attachment.* New York: Basic Books.

Brewerton, T. D., Hand, L. D., & Bishop, E. R., Jr. (1993). The tridimensional personality questionnaire in eating disorder patients. *International Journal of Eating Disorders, 14,* 213–218.

Buck, R. (1980). Nonverbal behavior and the theory of emotion: The facial feedback hypothesis. *Journal of Personality and Social Psychology, 38,* 811–824.

Bulik, C. M., Sullivan, P. F., Weltzin, T. E., & Kaye, W. (1995). Temperament in eating disorders. *International Journal of Eating Disorders, 17,* 251–261.

Clark, D. A. (1995). Perceived limitations of standard cognitive therapy: A consideration of efforts to revise Beck's theory and therapy. *Journal of Cognitive Psychotherapy: An International Quarterly, 9,* 153–172.

Cloninger, C. R. (1987). A systematic method for clinical description and classification of personality variants. *Archives of General Psychiatry, 44,* 573–588.

Cole-Detke, H., & Kobak, R. (1996). Attachment processes in eating disorder and depression. *Journal of Consulting and Clinical Psychology, 64,* 282–290.

Davis, R., Freeman, R. J., & Garner, D. M. (1988). A naturalistic investigation of eating behaviour in bulimia nervosa. *Journal of Consulting and Clinical Psychology, 56,* 273–279.

Fairburn, C. G. (1997). Eating disorders. In D. M. Clark & C. G. Fairburn (Eds.), *Science and practice of cognitive behaviour therapy.* Oxford, England: Oxford University Press.

Fairburn, C. G., & Cooper, P. (1989). Eating disorders. In K. Hawton, P. M. Salkozskis, J. Kirk, & D. M. Clark (Eds.), *Cognitive behaviour therapy for psychiatric problems* (pp. 227–314). New York: Oxford University Press.

Fairburn, C. G., Jones, R., Peveler, R. C., Hope, R. A., & O'Connor, M. (1993). Three psychological treatments for bulimia nervosa: A comparative trial. *Archives of General Psychiatry, 48,* 463–469.

Fairburn, C. G., Marcus, M. D., & Wilson, G. T. (1993). Cognitive–behavioral therapy for binge eating and bulimia nervosa: A comprehensive treatment manual. In C. G. Fairburn & R. Wilson (Eds.), *Binge eating: Nature, assessment, and treatment* (pp. 361–404). New York: Guilford Press.

Fairburn, C. G., Norman, P. A., Welch, S. L., O'Connor, M. E., Doll, H. A., & Peveler, R. C. (1995). A prospective study of outcome in bulimia nervosa and the long-term effects of three psychological treatments. *Archives of General Psychiatry, 52,* 304–312.

Fairburn, C. G., Welch, S. L., Doll, H. A., Davies, B. A., & O'Connor, M. E. (1997). Risk factors for bulimia nervosa: A community based case-control study. *Archives of General Psychiatry, 54,* 509–517.

Foa, E., & Wilson, R. (1991). *Stop obsessing: How to overcome your obsessions and compulsions.* New York: Bantam.

Garner, D. M., Vitousek, K. M., & Pike, K. M. (1997). Cognitive–behavioral therapy for anorexia nervosa. In D. M. Garner & P. E. Garfinkel (Eds.), *Handbook of treatment for eating disorders* (2nd ed., pp. 94–144). New York: Guilford Press.

Greenberg, L., Ford, C., Alden, L., & Johnson, S. (1993). In-session change in emotionally focused therapy. *Journal of Consulting and Clinical Psychology, 61,* 1–7.

Greenberg, L. S., & Korman, L. (1993). Assimilating emotion into psychotherapy integration. *Journal of Psychotherapy Integration, 3,* 249–265.

Greenberg, L. S., & Safran, J. D. (1980). Encoding, information processing and cognitive behaviour therapy. *Canadian Psychologist, 21,* 59–66.

Greenberg, L. S., & Safran, J. D. (1987). *Emotion in psychotherapy.* New York: Guilford Press.

Grisset, N. I., & Norvell, N. K. (1992). Perceived social support, social skills, and quality of relationships in bulimic women. *Journal of Consulting and Clinical Psychology, 60,* 293–299.

Guidano, V. F. (1987). *Complexity of the self.* New York: Guilford Press.

Guidano, V. F., & Liotti, G. (1983). *Cognitive processes and emotional disorders.* New York: Guilford Press.

Haynes, S. N. (1992). *Models of causality in psychopathology.* New York: Macmillan.

Heatherton, T. F., & Baumeister, R. F. (1991). Binge eating as escape from self awareness. *Psychological Bulletin, 110,* 86–108.

Higgins, E. T. (1987). Self-discrepancy: A theory relating self and affect. *Psychological Review, 94,* 319–340.

Holden, N. L. (1991). Adoption and eating disorders: A high risk group. *British Journal of Personality and Social Psychology, 158,* 829–833.

Hollon, S. D., Shelton, R. C., & Davis, D. D. (1993). Cognitive therapy for depression: Conceptual issues and clinical efficacy. *Journal of Consulting and Clinical Psychology, 61,* 270–275.

Humphrey, L. L. (1989). Observed family interactions among subtypes of eating disorders using structural analysis of social behavior. *Journal of Consulting and Clinical Psychology, 57,* 206–214.

Ingram, R. E., Miranda, J., & Segal, Z. V. (1998). *Cognitive vulnerability to depression.* New York: Guilford Press.

Jacobson, R., & Robbins, C. J. (1989). Social dependency and social support in bulimic and nonbulimic women. *International Journal of Eating Disorders, 8,* 665–670.

Johnson, C., & Larson, R. (1982). Bulimia: An analysis of moods and behavior. *Psychosomatic Medicine, 44,* 341–351.

Joiner, T. E., Jr., Wonderlich, S., Metalsky, G. I., & Schmidt, N. B. (1995). Body dissatisfaction: A feature of bulimia, depression, or both? *Journal of Social and Clinical Psychology, 14,* 339–355.

Kendler, K. S., MacLean, C., Neale, M., Kessler, R., Heath, A., & Eaves, L. (1991). The genetic epidemiology of bulimia nervosa. *American Journal of Psychiatry, 148,* 1627–1637.

Kearney-Cooke, A., & Striegel-Moore, R. (1997). The etiology and treatment of body image disturbance. In D. M. Garner & R. E. Garfinkel (Eds.), *Handbook of treatment for eating disorders* (2nd ed., pp. 295–306). New York: Guilford Press.

Leahy, R. (1996). *Cognitive therapy basic principles and applications.* Northvale, NJ: Aronson.

Lilenfeld, L. R., Kaye, W. H., Greeno, C. G., Merikangas, K. R., Plotnicov, K., Pollice, C., Rao, R., Strober, M., Bulik, C. M., & Nagy L. (1997). Psychiatric disorders in women with bulimia nervosa and their first-degree relatives: Effects of comorbid substance dependence. *International Journal of Eating Disorders, 22,* 253–264.

Linehan, M. M. (1993). *Cognitive–behavioral treatment of borderline personality disorder.* New York: Guilford Press.

Mahoney, M. J. (1991). *Human change processes.* New York: Basic Books.

Marlatt, G. A., & Gordon, J. R. (Eds.). (1985). *Relapse prevention: Maintenance strategies in the treatment of addictive behaviors.* New York: Guilford Press.

Meichenbaum, D. (1993). Changing conceptions of cognitive–behavior modification: Retrospect and prospect. *Journal of Consulting and Clinical Psychology, 6,* 202–204.

Meyer, C., & Waller, G. (1999). The impact of emotion upon eating behaviour: The role of subliminal visual processing of threat cues. *International Journal of Eating Disorders, 25,* 319–326.

Meyer, C., Waller, G., & Waters, A. (1998). Emotional states and bulimic psychopathology. In J. W. Hoek, J. L. Treasure, & M. A. Katzman (Eds.), *Neurobiology in the treatment of eating disorders* (pp. 271–289). New York: Wiley.

Miller, W. R., & Rollnick, S. (1991). *Motivational interviewing: Preparing people to change addictive behavior.* New York: Guilford Press.

Mitchell, J. E., Pyle, R. L., Eckert, E. D., Hatsukami, D., Pomeroy, C., & Zimmerman, R. (1990). A comparison study of antidepressants and structured intensive group psychotherapy in the treatment of bulimia nervosa. *Archives of General Psychiatry, 47,* 149–157.

Norman, D. K., & Herzog, D. B. (1984). Persistent social maladjustment in bulimia: A one-year follow-up. *American Journal of Psychiatry, 143,* 444–446.

Olmsted, M. P., Kaplan, A., & Rockert, W. (1994). Rate and prediction of relapse in bulimia nervosa. *American Journal of Psychiatry, 151*, 738–743.

Peterson, C. B., & Mitchell, J. E. (1995). Cognitive–behavior therapy. In G. O. Gabbard (Ed.), *Treatments of psychiatric disorders, second edition* (Vol. 2, pp. 2103–2127. Washington, DC: American Psychiatric Press.

Pruitt, J. A., Kappius, R. E., & Gorman, P. W. (1992). Bulimia and fear of intimacy. *Journal of Clinical Psychology, 48*, 472–476.

Robins, C. J., & Hayes, A. M. (1993). An appraisal of cognitive therapy. *Journal of Consulting and Clinical Psychology, 61*, 205–214.

Ruderman, A. J., & Grace, P. S. (1987). Bulimics and restrained eaters: A personality comparison. *Addictive Behaviors, 13*, 359–368.

Ryle, A. (1985). Cognitive theory, object relations and the self. *British Journal of Medical Psychology, 58*, 1–7.

Safran, J. D. (1990a). Towards a refinement of cognitive therapy in light of interpersonal theory: I. Theory. *Clinical Psychology Review, 10*, 87–105.

Safran, J. D. (1990b). Towards a refinement of cognitive therapy in light of interpersonal theory: II. Practice. *Clinical Psychology Review, 10*, 107–121.

Safran, J. D., & Segal, Z. V. (1996). *Interpersonal process in cognitive therapy.* Northvale, NJ: Aronson.

Segal, Z. V., Lowe, M. A., & Rokke, P. D. (1999). Cognition and emotion research and the practice of cognitive–behavioural therapy. In T. Dalgleish & M. Power (Eds.), *Handbook of cognition and emotion* (pp. 705–726). New York: Wiley.

Segal, Z. V., & Muran, J. C. (1993). A cognitive Perspective on self-representation in depression. In Z. Segal & S. Blatt (Eds.), *The self in emotional distress: Cognitive and psychodynamic perspectives* (pp. 131–163). New York: Guilford Press.

Steiger, H., Lehoux, P. M., & Gauvin, L. (1999). Impulsivity, dietary control and the urge to binge in bulimic syndromes. *International Journal of Eating Disorders, 23*, 261–274.

Steiner-Adair, C. (1986). The body politic: Normal female adolescent development and the development of eating disorders. *Journal of the American Academy of Psychoanalysis, 14*, 95–114.

Strauman, T. J. (1989). Self-discrepancies in clinical depression and social phobia: Cognitive structures that underlie emotional disorders? *Journal of Abnormal Psychology, 98*, 5–14.

Strauman, T. J., & Glenberg, A. M. (1994). Self-concept and body-image disturbance: Which self-beliefs predict body size overestimation? *Cognitive Therapy and Research, 18*, 105–125.

Strauman, T. J., Vookles, J., Berenstein, V., Chaiken, S., & Higgins, E. T. (1991). Self-discrepancies and vulnerability to body dissatisfaction and disordered eating. *Journal of Personality and Social Psychology, 61*, 946–956.

Striegel-Moore, R. H. (1993). Etiology of binge eating: A developmental perspective. In C. G. Fairburn & G. T. Wilson (Eds.), *Binge eating: Nature, assessment and treatment* (pp. 144–172). New York: Guilford Press.

Striegel-Moore, R. H., & Smolak, L. (2000). The influence of ethnicity on eating disorders in women. In R. M. Eisler & M. Hersen (Eds.), *Handbook of gender, culture, and health* (pp. 227–253). Mahwah, NJ: Erlbaum.

Strober, M., & Humphrey, L. L. (1987). Familial contributions to the etiology and course of anorexia nervosa and bulimia. *Journal of Consulting and Clinical Psychology, 55*, 654–659.

Telch, C. F., & Agras, W. S. (1996, November). *The effects of acute caloric deprivation and induced negative mood on binge-eating in subjects with binge eating disorder.* Poster presented at the meeting of the Eating Disorders Research Society, Pittsburgh, PA.

Tellegen, A. (1985). Structures of mood and personality and their relevance to assessing anxiety, with an emphasis on self-report. In A. H. Tuma & J. D. Maser (Eds.), *Anxiety and the anxiety disorders* (pp. 681–706). Hillsdale, NJ: Erlbaum.

Vitousek, K., & Ewald, L. (1993). Self-representation in eating disorders: A cognitive perspective. In Z. Segal & S. Blatt (Eds.), *The self in emotional distress: Cognitive and psychodynamic perspectives* (pp. 221–257). New York: Guilford Press.

Waller, D. A., Petty, F., Hardy, B. W., Gullion, C. M., Murdock, M. V., & Rush, A. J. (1993). Tridimensional personality questionnaire and serotonin in bulimia nervosa. *Psychiatry Research, 48*, 9–15.

Welch, S. L., & Fairburn, C. G. (1994). Sexual abuse and bulimia nervosa: Three integrated case control comparisons. *American Journal of Psychiatry, 151*, 402–407.

Wilson, G. T. (1996). Treatment of bulimia nervosa: When CBT fails. *Behaviour Research and Therapy, 34*, 197–212.

Wilson, G. T., & Fairburn, C. G. (1993). Cognitive treatments for eating disorders. *Journal of Consulting and Clinical Psychology, 61*, 261–269.

Wilson, G. T., & Fairburn, C. G. (1998). Treatments for eating disorders. In P. E. Nathan & J. M. Gorman (Eds.), *Treatments that work* (pp. 501–530). New York: Oxford University Press.

Wonderlich, S. A. (1992). Relationship of family and personality factors in bulimia nervosa. In J. H. Crowther, D. L. Tannenbaum, S. E. Hobfoll, & M. A. Stephens (Eds.), *The etiology of bulimia nervosa: The individual and familial context* (pp. 170–196). Washington, DC: Hemisphere.

Wonderlich, S. A. (1999, April). *Personality and eating disorders.* Paper presented at the Fourth London International Conference on Eating Disorders, London, England.

Wonderlich, S. A., Brewerton, T. D., Jocic, Z., Dansky, B. S., & Abbott, D. W. (1997). Relationship of childhood sexual abuse and eating disorders. *Journal of the American Academy of Child and Adolescent Psychiatry, 36*, 1107–1115.

Wonderlich, S. A., Klein, M., & Council, J. (1996). Relationship of social perceptions and self-concept in bulimia nervosa. *Journal of Consulting and Clinical Psychology, 64*, 1231–1238.

Wonderlich, S. A., Peterson, C., Mitchell, J. E., & Crow, S. (2000). Integrative approaches to treating eating disorders. In J. S. Mizes & K. J. Miller (Eds.). *Comparative treatments of eating disorders* (pp. 258–282). New York: Springer.

Wonderlich, S. A., & Swift, W. J. (1990a). Borderline versus other personality disorders in the eating disorders. *International Journal of Eating Disorders, 9*, 629–638.

Wonderlich, S. A., & Swift, W. J. (1990b). Perceptions of parental relationships in eating disorder subtypes. *Journal of Abnormal Psychology, 99*, 353–360.

Young, J. E. (1990). *Cognitive therapy for personality disorders: A schema-focused approach*. Sarasota, FL: Professional Resource Exchange.

10

PSYCHOPHARMACOLOGY OF EATING DISORDERS: CURRENT KNOWLEDGE AND FUTURE DIRECTIONS

JAMES E. MITCHELL

In this chapter, I attempt three tasks: (a) to critically review the extant literature on controlled treatments with psychopharmacological agents in treating patients with anorexia nervosa, bulimia nervosa , and binge-eating disorder; (b) to discuss the role of pharmacotherapy in the treatment of these disorders, which is for the most part ancillary to other therapies; and (c) to offer some ideas for further research in this area, suggesting research directions that might have a significant impact on the clinical care of these groups of patients.

Before reviewing the literature, I offer a few preliminary comments. First, although anorexia nervosa has been a disorder of interest for a much longer period of time than bulimia nervosa or binge-eating disorder, the treatment literature on anorexia nervosa remains limited because of several factors: (a) Patients with anorexia nervosa usually require a multiplicity of interventions, and it is exceedingly difficult to design trials that meaningfully control for all treatment variables simultaneously; (b) these patients by definition do not appreciate the severity of their illness and are therefore often uncooperative with the requirements of randomized treatment trials; (c) many anorexia nervosa patients are adolescents, and therefore human participant issues commonly limit the designs one can implement; and (d) anorexia nervosa is a relatively rare condition, and it is difficult to accumulate the requisite number of participants at any one clinical site. This problem has led to the use of multicenter trials.

A second point concerns the nature of the published studies. In terms of the controlled-treatment literature, studies generally fall into two groups: (a) smaller randomized trials, some of which were funded by pharmaceutical firms and others of which were funded by federal granting agencies such as the National Institutes of Health, and (b) a handful of large multicenter studies funded by the pharmaceutical industry. Although the goals of these types of protocols certainly overlap, the emphasis is often somewhat different in that the former group of studies attempt to answer interesting new research questions, whereas the latter are often designed to prove a level of efficacy and safety necessary to satisfy the Food and Drug Administration (FDA). Therefore, one must approach this literature with the foreknowledge that some of the largest, best-funded studies available have not necessarily been designed to answer what might be the most interesting questions scientifically.

A third point concerns progress in the field. Although it may be relatively easy to find fault with trials conducted more than a decade ago when judging them by contemporary standards, the fact is that the earlier and perhaps more primitive studies served as the basis for the more sophisticated studies that followed, and therefore it is much more useful to judge studies by the criteria appropriate to the time they were conducted.

Certain issues in treating patients with eating disorders are somewhat unique, given the medical sequelae of these illnesses. For example, low-weight patients with anorexia nervosa can be intolerant of medication side effects. The agents that can be used in patients with bulimia nervosa also at times are limited, given their fluid and electrolyte status.

Issues that have been dealt with indirectly in this literature, but perhaps not to the extent they deserve, are comorbidity and what constitutes "good outcome." Researchers tend to think of outcomes in terms of certain target symptoms in patients with bulimia nervosa (e.g., frequency of binge eating and vomiting) and in terms of weight in patients with anorexia nervosa. However, pharmacotherapy may target comorbid conditions such as obsessive–compulsive disorder, depression, or anxiety and only secondarily affect the eating disorder per se. Because comorbidity is such a common phenomenon among eating disorders, it is conceivable that a pharmacological approach might benefit other symptoms without significantly affecting eating disorders and is still worthy of consideration.

Although the dropout rate in certain reported trials has been high, in other studies the rate has been modest. Therefore, of interest are the nature of the investigation, the drug being studied, and in particular the therapeutic environment in which the study is conducted (e.g., the nature of the medication management, the attitudes of the staff involved).

The fact that most studies have relatively brief duration requires emphasis. It is known from clinical experience that drug therapy, if effective, needs to be continued for a long period of time, at least 6 months and often 1 year, yet the data on chronic use of medication are limited. Much of this can be attributed to the expense and difficulties involved in conducting longitudinal studies with medications. Nonetheless, this lack of data is problematic in assessing the role of drug therapy in the treatment of patients with eating disorders.

CONTROLLED DRUG TRIALS OF EATING DISORDERS

Anorexia Nervosa

Several classes of compounds have been used experimentally in the psychopharmacological treatment of anorexia nervosa. An overview of the trials is shown in Table 10.1. The class that has been studied most extensively are antidepressants, beginning with the use of tricyclic drugs about 20 years ago and progressing to more recent studies using the serotonin reuptake inhibitors (SSRIs). As can be seen, in some of the early trials, researchers found negative results, often using agents that were not well tolerated by patients with anorexia nervosa, with the side effects of constipation, sedation, and hypotension commonly seen with the tricyclic compounds. Of particular interest are several recent studies, including the relapse prevention trial by Kaye (1996) and the trial looking at the efficacy of SSRIs in low-weight patients with anorexia nervosa by Attia, Haiman, Walsh, and Flater (1998). The former trial suggests a markedly attenuated rate of relapse in weight-restored patients with anorexia nervosa who were also receiving other outpatient treatments. This study has led to considerable enthusiasm for using SSRIs in weight-restored or partially weight-restored patients with anorexia nervosa, usually in combination with other treatments. The study by Attia et al. suggests that low-weight patients with anorexia nervosa may not be able to generate an adequate serotonergic response to SSRI therapy, an interesting observation both clinically and theoretically. We know that patients with anorexia nervosa have low tryptophan to large neutral amino acid ratios (tryptophan being the precursor of serotonin), which compete with other large neutral amino acids for saturable uptake sites into the central nervous system (Kaye, Gendall, & Strober, 1998). Therefore, the lack of available precursor may impair the effectiveness of the drugs.

In a second group of studies, researchers have examined the efficacy of cyproheptadine, a serotonin antagonist, which has been associated with increased appetite and weight gain. The third such study, the largest and highest dose study, by Halmi, Eckert, LaDu, and Cohen (1986), suggests some efficacy for cyproheptadine in improving the rate of weight gain in hospitalized patients with anorexia. The results were not dramatic in clinical terms, however, and cyproheptadine has never been widely accepted as a pharmacological treatment for this group of patients.

Several other types of agents have been used, most without clear evidence of efficacy. Note that the researchers of two studies tested antipsy-

TABLE 10.1
Placebo-Controlled Drug Trials for Anorexia Nervosa

Category and study	N	Duration (weeks)	Treatment (dosage)	Outcome
Antidepressants				
Lacey & Crisp (1980)	16	Variable	Clomipramine (50 mg)	No difference
Gross et al. (1981)	16	4	Lithium (variable dose)	No difference
Biederman et al. (1985)	25	5	Amitriptyline (M = 160 mg)	No difference
Halmi et al. (1986)	72	4	Amitriptyline (M = 175 mg)	Amitriptyline > placebo
Kaye et al. (1998)	7	52	Fluoxetine (variable dose)	Fluoxetine > placebo
Attia et al. (1998)	31	7	Fluoxetine (M = 56 mg)	No difference
Cyproheptadine				
Vigersky & Loriaux (1977)	24	8	Cyproheptadine (12 mg)	No difference
Goldberg et al. (1979)	81	Variable	Cyproheptadine (variable dose)	No difference
Halmi et al. (1986)	72	4	Cyproheptadine (32 mg)	Cyproheptadine > placebo (weight gain)
Antipsychotics				
Vandereycken & Pierloot (1982)	18	6	Pimozide (6 mg)	No difference
Vandereycken (1984)	18	6	Sulpiride (400 mg)	No difference
Other				
Gross et al. (1981)	16	4	Lithium (variable dose)	No difference
Gross et al. (1983)	11	4	Tetrahydrocannabinol (30 mg)	No difference
Casper et al. (1987)	4	8	Clonidine (0.5–0.7 mg)	No difference
Stacher et al. (1993)	12	12	Cisapride (30 mg)	No difference

chotic drugs using the older dopamine-blocking agents available at the time (Vandereycken, 1984; Vandereycken & Pierloot, 1982). There is considerable interest now in using the new atypical neuroleptic agents with treatment-resistant patients with anorexia nervosa, although they have not been systematically studied. Also although their efficacy has not been fully established in double-blind trials, gastric peristaltic agents were commonly used clinically when patients had a great deal of gastric discomfort early in the course of refeeding. However, Cisapride, the agent usually used, was recently withdrawn from the market because of cardiac toxicity.

In summary, most recent results suggest that antidepressants of the SSRI type may be useful in helping to prevent relapse in those with anorexia nervosa (although this finding requires replication), that low-weight patients with anorexia nervosa may not respond adequately to SSRIs, and that additional work needs to be done studying gastric peristaltic agents and atypical neuroleptics in this group of patients.

Bulimia Nervosa

Soon after the delineation of bulimia nervosa as a distinct diagnostic entity by Russell in 1979, it became a common observation that many patients with bulimia nervosa were depressed; the thinking was that this disorder might represent a variant of an affective disorder or at least have a high comorbidity with affective disorders. Therefore, it was postulated that treatments for affective disorders might help many of these patients. This led to a series of open-label and later double-blind placebo-controlled trials, the latter of which using antidepressants are summarized in Table 10.2. As can be seen, most of the researchers of the available studies have found some degree of efficacy in terms of improvement in eating symptoms, mood, or both.

The agent that has been studied most extensively is fluoxetine hydrochloride, which has been shown to be efficacious at a dose of 60 mg in two multicenter trials (Fluoxetine Bulimia Nervosa Collaborative Study Group, 1992; Goldstein et al., 1995) and to be more powerful than placebo in preventing relapse during a 1-year maintenance multicenter study, although the dropout rate was high among both drug and placebo patients (Romano, 1999). Fluoxetine currently remains the only FDA-approved drug for this disorder. Note that fluoxetine is used at high doses in this group of patients (e.g., in the first multicenter study, 60 mg was clearly preferable to 20 mg). Of interest, results concerning fluoxemine are inconsistent, with researchers in one study finding evidence of a relapse prevention effect in patients who had received inpatient treatment for bulimia nervosa (Fichter, Krüger, Reif, Holland, & Dohne, 1996), whereas the researcher in another study failed to find evidence of efficacy in outpatients with bulimia nervosa (Freeman, 1999). The main limitation to the use of antidepressants is the observation that the abstinence rates from core bulimic symptoms are frequently disappointingly low, with an average of fewer than 1 in 4 participants so treated achieving remission.

In a series of studies, researchers have also examined the relative efficacy of antidepressant therapy versus cognitive–behavior therapy (CBT), the best established form of psychotherapy for bulimia nervosa. One of these studies (Goldbloom, 1996) is difficult to interpret because of a high dropout rate, whereas researchers of another study aborted early because of a high

TABLE 10.2
Placebo-Controlled Antidepressant Drug Studies for Bulimia Nervosa

Study	N	Duration (weeks)	Treatment (dosage)	Outcome ↓ BE (%)	AB (%)
Pope et al. (1983)	36	8	Imipramine (≤200 mg)		0
Sabine et al. (1983)	19	8	Mianserin (60 mg)		
Mitchell & Groat (1984)	32	8	Amitriptyline (150 mg)	72	19
Hughes et al. (1986)	22	6	Desipramine (200 mg)	91	68
Agras et al. (1987)	22	16	Imipramine (M = 167 mg)	72	30
Horne et al. (1988)	81	8	Bupropion (≤450 mg)	67	30
Barlow et al. (1988)	24	6	Desipramine (150 mg)	4	
Blouin et al. (1988)	10	6	Desipramine (150 mg)	45[a]	
Kennedy et al. (1988)	18	13	Isocarboxazid (60 mg)		33
Walsh et al. (1988)	50	12	Phenelzine (60–90 mg)	64	35
Pope et al. (1989)	42	4	Trazadone (≤400 mg)	31	10
Fichter et al. (1991)	40	35 (days)	Fluoxetine (60 mg)		
Kennedy et al. (1993)	36	8	Brofaromine (≤200 mg)	62	
FBNC (1992)	387	12	Fluoxetine (20, 60 mg)	67	
Goldstein et al. (1995)	398	16	Fluoxetine (60 mg)	50	
Romano (1999)	150	52	Fluoxetine (60 mg)		

Note. BE = binge eating; AB = abstinence; FBNC = Fluoxetine Bulimia Nervosa Collaborative Study Group.
[a]Vomiting frequency.

dropout rate in the medication cell (4 of 7 participants; Leitenberg et al., 1994). The other three studies have all proved informative, and the results in two of the studies suggest that CBT is superior to drug therapy on most outcome variables, although the combination may provide the best outcome on certain variables (Agras et al., 1992; Mitchell et al., 1990). In the third study, researchers found similar efficacy for CBT and antidepressant treatment used alone, but in a post hoc analysis, the best results were obtained with a combination of CBT and drug therapy (Walsh et al., 1997).

A few other agents have been used experimentally in the treatment of bulimia nervosa, as summarized in Table 10.3. d-Fenfluramine appears not to add to the effectiveness of outpatient counseling for those with bulimia nervosa (Fahy, Eisler, & Russell, 1993; Russell, Checkley, Feldman, & Eisler, 1988). Lithium is apparently ineffective as well (Hsu, Clement, Santhouse, & Ju, 1991). The results concerning the efficacy of phenytoin were confounded by continued improvement following the crossover from active drug to placebo; unfortunately, this study has never been replicated

TABLE 10.3
Other Placebo-Controlled Drug Studies for Bulimia Nervosa

Study	N	Duration (weeks)	Treatment (dosage)	Outcome
Wermuth et al. (1977)	19	12 (crossover)	Phenytoin (variable)	Unclear
Russell et al. (1988)	42	12	d-Fenfluramine (30 mg)	No difference
Ingoin-Apfelbaum & Apfelbaum (1987)			Naltrexone (120 mg)	No difference
Hsu et al. (1991)	91	8	Lithium (variable)	No difference
Mitchell et al. (1989)	16	6 (crossover)	Naltrexone (50 mg)	No difference
Fahy et al. (1993)	43	8	d-Fenfluramine (45 mg)	No difference

(Wermuth, Davis, & Hollister, 1977). Controlled trials using narcotic antagonists, such as naltrexone, have for the most part been negative (Ingoin-Apfelbaum & Apfelbaum, 1987; Mitchell et al., 1989), although open-label studies using higher dose therapy (e.g., 200–300 mg/day) do suggest efficacy (Jonas & Gold, 1986, 1987, 1988). There are concerns, however, that the drug may be hepatotoxic at this dosage.

In summary, the available literature suggests that antidepressants are effective in suppressing the frequency of binge eating and vomiting as well as improving core psychopathology in patients with bulimia nervosa. In general, the results obtained with drug therapy alone are inferior to those obtained with CBT, although for some patients the combination appears to represent the best treatment alternative. The best-established drug therapy for bulimia nervosa at this time is fluoxetine hydrochloride at a dose of 60 mg/day, which is generally well tolerated. The main problems with antidepressant therapy are the low abstinence rates achieved and the lack of compliance with chronic therapy.

Binge-Eating Disorder

In the examination of the literature on binge-eating disorder, it is important to remember that some studies focus on weight loss (which most people with binge-eating disorder desire because many are overweight), binge eating, or both. The pharmacotherapy trials involving patients with binge-eating disorder are summarized in Table 10.4. As can be seen, the number of trials completed to date is limited, but the results suggest some degree of efficacy for agents that have also been found to have efficacy for patients with bulimia nervosa. d-Fenfluramine was effective in suppressing binge eating but has been withdrawn from the market because of cardiac toxicity (Stunkard, Berkowitz, Tanrikut, Reiss, & Young, 1996). A multicen-

TABLE 10.4
Placebo-Controlled Drug Studies for Binge-Eating Disorder

Study	N	Duration (weeks)	Treatment (dosage)	Outcome
Marcus et al. (1990)	11[a]	52	Fluoxetine + BT (60 mg)	(Weight loss) fluoxetine + BT > placebo + BT
McCann & Agras (1990)	23[b]	12	Desipramine (≤300 mg)	(Binge eating) 63% ↓ BE, 15% abstinence; desipramine > placebo
de Zwaan et al. (1992)	15[c]	18	Fluvoxamine + CBT (100 mg)	(Weight loss) fluvoxamine = placebo
Agras et al. (1994)	84	36	CBT/weight loss/desipramine (M = 285 mg)	(Weight loss) Adding desipramine → ↑ weight loss
Hudson et al. (1998)	67	9	Fluvoxamine (M = 260 mg)	75% ↓ BE, 45% abstinence; fluvoxamine > placebo
Stunkard et al. (1996)	24	8	d-Fenfluramine (30 mg)	(Binge eating) 80% abstinence; fenfluramine > placebo

Note. BT = behavior therapy; BE = binge eating; CBT = cognitive–behavioral therapy. [a]Binge-Eating Scale score > 29. [b]BN nonpurging. [c]Overeating + loss of control.

204 JAMES E. MITCHELL

ter fluvoxamine trial in binge-eating disorder did show evidence of efficacy compared with a placebo (Hudson et al., 1998).

THE ROLE OF PHARMACOTHERAPY

There are two important conclusions related to the role of drug therapy in the treatment of patients with eating disorders. First, in the treatment of those with anorexia nervosa, drug therapy has never been seen as the sole treatment but as an ancillary to other types of interventions, primarily inpatient treatment or outpatient counseling. In the treatment of those with bulimia nervosa, when drug therapy has been compared directly with a structured form of effective psychotherapy such as CBT, the results in general suggest superior efficacy for CBT, whereas the addition of drug therapy appears to improve outcome on some variables. Therefore, the role of drug therapy in patients with eating disorders is ancillary. However, that being said, many important questions remain as to when these ancillary treatments should be used.

1. When CBT is available for those with bulimia nervosa, should drug therapy also be used? As mentioned, some work suggests that the combination of CBT and drug therapy is probably superior to CBT alone, although other work suggests only marginal additional benefit. Also when questions of cost efficacy arise in the treatment for bulimia nervosa, treatment with an SSRI such as fluoxetine over the course of 1 year adds a considerable expense to treatment with CBT. Therefore, it would seem important to identify those patients who do better with the combination and in particular those patients who should have drug therapy added if they fail to initially respond to CBT. One such model would be a stepped care approach, wherein individuals who fail to evidence a likelihood of response to CBT early in treatment would also receive treatment with fluoxetine hydrochloride. Such a trial will soon be under way. However, currently, no one can say who will need the combination; in an ideal situation in which both CBT and high-dose fluoxetine are available, one can argue that both should be used.

2. Do specific symptoms suggest the need for ancillary pharmacotherapy in anorexia nervosa? SSRIs, for example, are known to be useful in terms of improvement in obsessive–compulsive symptoms in those with anorexia nervosa (e.g., Kaye, 1996), and such symptoms are common and severe in these patients

(e.g., Kaye et al., 1998). Might this serve as a marker for those who would do better with ancillary treatment? Might those with significant levels of depression do better? Further work is needed that targets not only diagnoses but also symptom clusters, given the heterogeneity of patients with these diagnoses.

DIRECTIONS FOR FUTURE RESEARCH

In considering possible directions for treatment research in eating disorders, many of the questions that come up concern psychotherapy approaches rather than drug therapy, given the fact that by consensus psychotherapy is important in the treatment of both anorexia nervosa and bulimia nervosa. However, particularly effective forms of psychotherapy for anorexia nervosa are not well established, and although CBT clearly is effective for many patients with bulimia nervosa, some do not respond, and there are significant rates of relapse among those who initially do respond. Therefore, further pharmacological questions must be posed to parallel the psychotherapy questions.

What would be the logical next questions to ask concerning anorexia nervosa? Three issues come to mind:

1. An attempt must be made to replicate the use of SSRIs to help prevent relapse in patients with anorexia nervosa, given the high relapse rate for those with this condition and the limited availability of accepted treatments. This clearly is a pressing issue.
2. Anecdotally, there has been much discussion about the use of atypical neuroleptics such as olanzapine in the treatment of anorexia nervosa, targeting the severe obsessionality, the body distortion that at times reaches delusional proportions, and the mood disturbance. Studies need to be done in which atypical neuroleptic drug therapy is tested embedded in other types of interventions.
3. A logical question arises concerning the use of SSRIs in low-weight patients with anorexia nervosa. If an inadequate precursor is available to allow for sufficient serotonin synthesis, would the provision of the precursor in the form of tryptophan or tryptophan-rich foods improve outcome? Such a study is currently in progress, and the results should prove both clinically and theoretically interesting.

In relation to the treatment of bulimia nervosa, several important issues also come to mind.

1. Augmentation strategies, which are commonly used in other areas of psychiatry, have really not been adequately explored in the treatment of bulimia nervosa. These might include combinations of SSRIs plus tricyclics, SSRI plus lithium (a drug that may be difficult to use in this population given their fluid and electrolyte abnormalities), and SSRIs plus buspirone hydrochloride, to name three.

2. Because pharmacotherapy alone usually does not result in remission after treatment, the possibility exists that a greater number of patients could experience abstinence on drug therapy if given additional but fairly minimal treatment, such as the use of a self-help manual, a supervised self-help approach, or a group psychoeducational approach. In one such study, researchers found improved outcome but not higher abstinence rates in those treated with drug and self-help (Mitchell et al., in press), but further work should be done to attempt to enhance the efficacy of such combinations.

In relation to binge-eating disorder, the literature here is too new to draw any firm conclusions. Unfortunately, the amount of weight loss accomplished with SSRIs is usually minimal, which may limit their value for this condition. Additional possibilities include the following:

1. Two new medications marketed for weight loss in the last few years, the serotonin and norepinephrine reuptake inhibitor sibutramine and the lipase inhibitor orlistat, have not been studied empirically in those with binge-eating disorder. The former may be useful because the combination of serotonergic and noradrenergic effects may result in increased energy production, decreased appetite, and increased satiety, with the suppression of binge eating and weight loss. The latter may be useful in improving compliance with a lower fat diet. Both drugs should be evaluated for binge-eating disorder.

2. Another possibility that needs to be examined is the use of opiate antagonists, such as naltrexone. Although such drugs appear to have limited applicability in the treatment of bulimia nervosa, there is growing evidence that the endogenous opioid system is involved in modulating the hedonics of preferred substances (Mitchell et al., 1999). Because the hedonics of binge eating may differ among those with binge-eating disorder

compared with those with bulimia nervosa, opiate antagonists may prove more useful for this group of patients.

CONCLUSION

Pharmacotherapy plays an important albeit ancillary role in the treatment of patients with eating disorders. Namely, pharmacotherapy clearly provides an useful adjunct in the treatment of those with bulimia nervosa. The best established agent, studied in the largest number of participants, is fluoxetine hydrochloride, which is usually dosed at 60 mg/day. Pharmacotherapy plays a more limited role in the treatment of those with anorexia nervosa, but results do suggest the possibility of the important role of a relapse prevention agent when used in combination with other treatments. Pharmacotherapy for binge-eating disorder is just now being studied, but given the current available agents and the likelihood that many new agents for obesity will be introduced over the next decade, pharmacotherapy appears to offer the potential for a considerable benefit for these patients as well. There are numerous interesting possibilities for new research; it is clear that pharmacotherapy should remain a significant research focus in the treatment of eating disorders in the years ahead.

REFERENCES

Agras, W. S., Dorian, B., Kirkley, B. G., Arnow, B., & Bachman, J. (1987). Imipramine in the treatment of bulimia: A double-blind controlled study. *International Journal of Eating Disorders*, 6, 29–38.

Agras, W. S., Rossiter, E. M., Arnow, B., Schneider, J. A., Telch, C. F., Raeburn, S. D., Bruce, B., Perl, M., & Koran, L. M. (1992). Pharmacologic and cognitive–behavioral treatment for bulimia nervosa: A controlled comparison. *American Journal of Psychiatry*, 149, 82–87.

Agras, W. S., Telch, C. F., & Arnow, B. (1994). Weight loss, cognitive–behavioral, and desipramine treatments in binge eating disorder: An additive design. *Behavior Therapy*, 25, 225–238.

Attia, E., Haiman, C., Walsh, B., & Flater, S. R. (1998). Does fluoxetine augment the inpatient treatment of anorexia nervosa? *American Journal of Psychiatry*, 155, 548–551.

Barlow, J., Blouin, J., Blouin, A., & Perez, E. (1988). Treatment of bulimia with desipramine: A double-blind crossover study. *Canadian Journal of Psychiatry*, 33, 129–133.

Biederman, J., Herzog, D. B., Rivinus, T. M., Harper, G. P., Ferber, R. A., Rosenbaum, J. F., Hamartz, J. S., Tandorf, R., Orsulak, P. J., & Schildkraut, J. J.

(1985). Amitriptyline in the treatment of anorexia nervosa: A double-blind, placebo study. *Journal of Clinical Psychopharmacology, 5,* 10–16.

Blouin, A. G., Blouin, J. H., Perez, E. L., Bushnik, T., Zuro, C., & Mulder, E. (1988). Treatment of bulimia with fenfluramine and desipramine. *Journal of Clinical Psychopharmacology, 8,* 261–269.

Casper, R. C., Schlemmer, R. F., Jr., & Javaid, J. I. (1987). A placebo-controlled crossover study of oral clonidine in acute anorexia nervosa. *Psychiatry Research, 20,* 249–260.

de Zwaan, M., Nutzinger, D. O., & Schönbeck, G. (1992). Binge eating in overweight females. *Comprehensive Psychiatry, 33,* 256–261.

Fahy, T. A., Eisler, I., & Russell, F. M. (1993). A placebo-controlled trial of d-Fenfluramine in bulimia nervosa. *British Journal of Psychiatry, 162,* 597–603.

Fichter, M. M., Krüger, R., Reif, W., Holland, R., & Dohne, J. (1996). Fluvoxamine in prevention of relapse in bulimia nervosa: Effects on eating-specific psychopathology. *Journal of Clinical Psychopharmacology, 1,* 9–18.

Fichter, M. M., Leibl, K., Reif, W., Brunner, E., Schmidt-Auberger, S., & Engel, R. R. (1991). Fluoxetine versus placebo: A double-blind study with bulimic inpatients undergoing intensive psychotherapy. *Pharmacopsychiatry, 24,* 1–7.

Fluoxetine Bulimia Nervosa Collaborative Study Group. (1992). Fluoxetine in the treatment of bulimia nervosa. *Archives of General Psychiatry, 49,* 139–147.

Freeman, C. P. L. (1999, November). *The treatment of bulimia nervosa with fluvoxamine.* Paper presented at the annual meeting of the Eating Disorders Research Society, San Diego, CA.

Goldberg, S. C., Halmi, K. A., Eckert, E. D., Casper, R., & Davis, J. M. (1979). Cyproheptadine in anorexia nervosa. *British Journal of Psychiatry, 134,* 67–70.

Goldbloom D. (1996, May). *Fluoxetine versus CBT in the treatment of bulimia nervosa.* Paper presented at the annual meeting of the American Psychiatric Association, New York, NY.

Goldstein, D. J., Wilson, M. G., Thompson, V. L., Potuin, J. H., Rampey, A. H., & Fluoxetine Bulimia Nervosa Research Group. (1995). Long-term fluoxetine treatment of bulimia nervosa. *British Journal of Psychiatry, 166,* 660–666.

Gross, H. A., Ebert, M. H., Faden, V. B., Goldberg, S. C., Kaye, W. H., Caine, E. D., Hawks, R., & Zinberg, N. (1983). A double-blind trial of D^9-tetrahydrocannabinol in primary anorexia nervosa. *Journal of Clinical Psychopharmacology, 3,* 165–171.

Gross, H. A., Ebert, M. H., Faden, V. B., Goldberg, S. C., Nee, L. E., & Kaye, W. H. (1981). A double-blind controlled trial of lithium carbonate in primary anorexia nervosa. *Journal of Clinical Psychopharmacology, 51,* 378–382.

Halmi, K. A., Eckert, E., LaDu, T. J., & Cohen, J. (1986). Anorexia nervosa: Treatment efficacy of cyproheptadine and amitriptyline. *Archives of General Psychiatry, 43,* 177–181.

Horne, R. E., Fergusen, J. M., Pope, H. G., Hudson, J. I., Lineberry, C. G., Ascher, J., & Ceto, A. (1988). Treatment of bulimia with bupropion: A multicenter controlled trial. *Journal of Clinical Psychiatry, 49*, 262–266.

Hsu, L. K., Clement, L., Santhouse, R., & Ju, E. S. (1991). Treatment of bulimia nervosa with lithium carbonate: A controlled study. *Journal of Nervous and Mental Disorders, 179*, 351–355.

Hudson, J. I., McElroy, S. L., Raymond, N. C., Crow, S., Keck, P. E., Carter, W. P., Mitchell, J. E., Strakowski, S. M., Pope, H. G., Coleman, B., & Jonas, J. M. (1998). Fluvoxamine in the treatment of binge eating disorder: A multi-center placebo-controlled double blind trial. *American Journal of Psychiatry, 155*, 1756–1762.

Hughes, P. L., Wells, L. A., Cunningham, C. J., & Ilstrup, D. M. (1986). Treatment of bulimia with desipramine. *Archives of General Psychiatry, 43*, 182–186.

Ingoin-Apfelbaum, L., & Apfelbaum, M. (1987). Naltrexone and bulimic symptoms. *Lancet, 2*, 1087–1088.

Jonas, J. M., & Gold, M. S. (1986). Naltrexone reverses bulimic symptoms. *Lancet, 1*, 807.

Jonas, J. M., & Gold, M. S. (1987). Treatment of antidepressant-resistant bulimia with naltrexone. *International Journal of Psychiatry in Medicine, 16*, 305–309.

Jonas, J. M., & Gold, M. S. (1988). The use of opiate antagonists in treating bulimia: A study of low-dose versus high-dose naltrexone. *Psychiatry Research, 24*, 195–199.

Kaye, W. H. (1996, November). *The use of fluoxetine to prevent relapse in anorexia nervosa.* Paper presented at the annual meeting of the Eating Disorders Research Society, Pittsburgh, PA.

Kaye, K. H., Gendall, K., & Strober, M. (1998). Serotonin neuronal function and selective serotonin reuptake inhibitor treatment in anorexia and bulimia nervosa. *Biological Psychiatry, 44*, 825–838.

Kennedy, S. H., Goldbloom, D. S., Ralevski, E., Davis, C., D'Souza, J. D., & Lofchy, J. (1993). Is there a role for selective monoamine oxidase inhibitor therapy in bulimia nervosa? A placebo-controlled trial of brofaromine. *Journal of Clinical Psychopharmacology, 13*, 415–422.

Kennedy, S. H., Piran, N., Warsh, J. J., Prendergest, P., Mainprize, E., Whynot, C., & Garfinkel, P. (1988). A trial of isocarboxazid in the treatment of bulimia nervosa. *Journal of Psychopharmacology, 8*, 391–396.

Lacey, J. H., & Crisp, A. H. (1980). Hunger, food intake and weight: The impact of clomipramine on a refeeding anorexia nervosa population. *Postgraduate Medical Journal, 56*, S79–S86.

Leitenberg, J., Rosen, J. C., Wolf, J., Vara, L. S., Detzer, M. J., & Srebnik, O. (1994). Comparison of cognitive–behavior therapy and desipramine in the treatment of bulimia nervosa. *Behavioral Research Therapy, 32*, 37–46.

McCann, U. D., & Agras, W. S. (1990). Successful treatment of non-purging bulimia nervosa with desipramine: A double-blind, placebo-controlled study. *American Journal of Psychiatry, 147*, 1509–1513.

Marcus, M. D., Wing, R. R., Ewing, L., Kern, E., McDermott, M., & Gooding, W. (1990). A double-blind, placebo-controlled trial of fluoxetine plus behavior modification in the treatment of obese binge-eaters and non-binge-eaters. *American Journal of Psychiatry, 147,* 876–881.

Mitchell, J. E., Christenson, G., Jennings, J., Huber, M., Thomas, B., Pomeroy, C., & Morley, J. (1989). A placebo-controlled, double-blind crossover study of naltrexone hydrochloride in patients with normal weight bulimia. *Journal of Clinical Psychopharmacology, 9,* 94–97.

Mitchell, J. E., Fletcher, L., Hanson, K., Mussell, M. P., Seim, H., Al-Banna, M., Wilson, M., & Crosby, R. (in press). The relative efficacy of fluoxetine and manual-based self-help in the treatment of outpatients with bulimia nervosa. *Journal of Clinical Psychopharmacology.*

Mitchell, J. E., & Groat, R. (1984). A placebo-controlled, double-blind trial of amitriptyline in bulimia. *Journal of Clinical Psychopharmacology, 4,* 186–193.

Mitchell, J. E., Mussell, M. P., Peterson, C. B., Crow, S., Wonderlich, S. A., Crosby, R. D., Davis, T., & Weller, C. (1999). Hedonics of binge eating in women with bulimia nervosa and binge eating disorder. *International Journal of Eating Disorders, 26,* 165–170.

Mitchell, J. E., Pyle, R. L., Eckert, E. D., Hatsukami, D., Pomeroy, C., & Zimmerman, R. (1990). A comparison study of antidepressants and structured intensive group psychotherapy in the treatment of bulimia nervosa. *Archives of General Psychiatry, 47,* 149–157.

Pope, H. G., Jr., Hudson, J. I., Jonas, J. M., & Yergelun-Todd, D. (1983). Bulimia treated with imipramine: A placebo-controlled, double-blind study. *American Journal of Psychiatry, 140,* 554–558.

Pope, H. G., Keck, P. E., McElroy, S. L., & Hudson, J. I. (1989). A placebo-controlled study of trazadone in bulimia nervosa. *Journal of Clinical Psychopharmacology, 9,* 254–259.

Romano, S. (1999, November). *Fluoxetine maintenance therapy for bulimia nervosa.* Paper presented at the annual meeting of the Eating Disorders Research Society, San Diego, CA.

Russell, G. F. M. (1979). Bulimia nervosa: An ominous variant of anorexia nervosa. *Psychological Medicine, 9,* 429–448.

Russell, G. F. M., Checkley, S. A., Feldman, J., & Eisler, I. (1988). A controlled trial of d-Fenfluramine in bulimia nervosa. *Clinical Neuropharmacology, 11,* S146–S159.

Sabine, E. J., Yonace, A., Farrington, A. J., Barra, H. K. H., & Wakeling, A. (1983). Bulimia nervosa: A placebo-controlled, double-blind therapeutic trial of mianserin. *British Journal of Clinical Pharmacology, 15,* S195–S202.

Stacher, G., Abatzi-Wentzel, T. A., Wiesnagrotzki, S., Bergmann, H., Schneider, C., & Gaupmann, G. (1993). Gastric emptying, body weight, and symptoms in primary anorexia nervosa: Long-term effects of cisapride. *British Journal of Psychiatry, 162,* 398–402.

Stunkard, A., Berkowitz, R., Tanrikut, C., Reiss, E., & Young, L. (1996). d-Fenfluramine treatment of binge eating disorder. *American Journal of Psychiatry, 153*, 1455–1459.

Vandereycken, W. (1984). Neuroleptics in the short-term treatment of anorexia nervosa: A double-blind placebo-controlled study with sulpiride. *British Journal of Psychiatry, 144*, 288–292.

Vandereycken, W., & Pierloot, R. (1982). Pimozide combined with behavior therapy in the short-term treatment of anorexia nervosa. *Acta Psychiatrica Scandinavica, 66*, 445–450.

Vigersky, R. A., & Loriaux, D. L. (1977). The effect of cyproheptadine in anorexia nervosa: A double-blind trial. In R. A. Vigersky (Ed.), *Anorexia nervosa* (pp. 187–210). New York: Raven Press.

Walsh, B. T., Gladis, M., Roose, S. P., Stewart, J. W., Stetner, F., & Glassman, A. H. (1988). Phenelzine vs. placebo in 50 patients with bulimia. *Archives of General Psychiatry, 45*, 471–475.

Walsh, B. T., Wilson, G. T., Loeb, K. L., Devlin, M. J., Pike, K. M., Roose, S. P., Fleiss, J., & Waternaux, C. (1997). Medication and psychotherapy in the treatment of bulimia nervosa. *American Journal of Psychiatry, 154*, 523–531.

Wermuth, B. M., Davis, K. L., & Hollister, L. E. (1977). Phenytoin treatment of the binge eating syndrome. *American Journal of Psychiatry, 134*, 1249–1253.

III

PREVENTION

Efforts to prevent eating disorders may represent the fastest growing area of research in the field, with novel, creative approaches being evaluated in Australia, Europe, Canada, and the United States (Piran, Levine, & Steiner-Adair, 1999; Vandereycken & Noordenbos, 1998). Few areas engender more debate and passion. Yet it seems clear that treatment alone cannot eliminate eating disorders. There simply are not enough therapists; many sufferers do not seek help; recovery, especially in anorexia nervosa, can be a protracted process; and treatments do not exist that can help everyone. However, current efforts to prevent eating disorders or their precursors have met with mixed success and, of greater concern, are sometimes associated with negative effects.

There is a fundamental dilemma in that, on the one hand, eating disorders prevention is often aimed at accepting one's body and body fat, whereas, on the other hand, obesity is a serious health problem that should not be considered innocuous. How does one educate the public that a fear of fat or excessive weight concerns may place one at risk and a lack of concern with being very overweight may also raise one's risks of negative health outcomes? Leslie Heinberg, J. Kevin Thompson, and Jonas Matzon (chapter 11) address this extraordinarily difficult issue by considering whether a degree of realistic body dissatisfaction might be good because it may motivate weight loss efforts. Their position is sure to be controversial, yet their commitment to identifying testable hypotheses should foster the research that is needed to answer these questions.

Michael Levine and Niva Piran (chapter 12) then discuss some of the existing evaluations of prevention programs. They, too, identify gaps in the knowledge that require empirical evidence. More important, they clearly demonstrate that there is evidence that prevention can work. Their participatory ecology model, which has already received some empirical support, offers a new way to conceptualize and design prevention efforts. Research concerning this model will be challenging to many eating disorder researchers because it relies on more qualitative methods than we typically use.

Finally, this is the 21st century. C. Barr Taylor, Andy Winzelburg, and Angela Celio (chapter 13) make this evident by considering how interactive computer technology might be used in prevention efforts for eating disorders. They describe an ongoing research program that has resulted in the development of computer and Internet-based technologies. This program has already been successful with a few groups of college students and offers an imaginative way to reach a large group of people. Their ideas as to how to build on this program provide an approach to prevention that is very different from that being suggested by Levine and Piran. Yet research may well indicate that there are important uses for both approaches. It is clear that the time to investigate such prevention techniques has arrived.

REFERENCES

Piran, N., Levine, M. P., & Steiner-Adair, C. (1999). *Preventing eating disorders: A handbook of interventions and special challenges.* Philadelphia: Brunner/Mazel.

Vandereycken, W., & Noordenbos, G. (1998). *The prevention of eating disorders.* London: Athlone Press.

11

BODY IMAGE DISSATISFACTION AS A MOTIVATOR FOR HEALTHY LIFESTYLE CHANGE: IS SOME DISTRESS BENEFICIAL?

LESLIE J. HEINBERG, J. KEVIN THOMPSON, AND JONAS L. MATZON

Body image dissatisfaction is pervasive and steadily increasing (Cash & Henry, 1995), with a majority of people reporting dissatisfaction with weight or body shape. The research literature focuses on not only the "disturbed" aspects of body image (e.g., body image disturbance evidenced by patients with eating disorder or those with body dysmorphic disorder) but also the "normative" aspects of appearance-based body image (e.g., dissatisfaction seen in nonpsychiatric populations; Thompson & Heinberg, 1999). Clearly delineating where normal concerns with appearance or dissatisfaction approach or reach psychological disturbance is extremely difficult, and much of the literature "muddies" these distinctions. As a result, nonprofessionals may assume that any degree of body image dissatisfaction is injurious (Thompson & Heinberg, 1999). It has been suggested that individuals lie on a continuum of "normative discontent," with the minority of individuals reporting no body image distress while those at the other extreme evidence distress so severe that it is associated with significant impairment in daily functioning (e.g., eating disorders; Rodin, Silberstein, & Striegel-Moore, 1985). We previously conceptualized body image disturbance as a multifaceted construct consisting of subjective dissatisfaction, cognitive characteristics, behavioral components, and, possibly, perceptual aspects (Thompson, Heinberg, Altabe, & Tantleff-Dunn, 1999). In this chapter, we confine our discussion to the subjective component, which we refer to as *body image dissatisfaction*.

We have previously asserted (Heinberg, Haythornthwaite, Rosofsky, McCarron, & Clarke, 2000; Thompson et al., 1999) and argue in this chapter that some level of body image dissatisfaction may conceivably be beneficial because it may lead to healthy exercise and eating behaviors. Although the vast majority of the extant literature on body image disturbance suggests that higher levels of body dissatisfaction are associated with higher levels of eating disturbance, depression, and low self-esteem (Thompson et al., 1999), a few investigations show possible positive effects of body dissatisfaction (Cash, Novy, & Grant, 1994; Heinberg et al., 2000). Before presenting these data and a tentative theoretical model explaining emerging hypothesis, we describe our argument.

We hypothesize in this chapter that body image dissatisfaction is not always a negative process. Rather, some degree of dissatisfaction may be helpful and necessary to motivate individuals to engage in healthy behaviors, such as exercise and restricting fats and calories. We question the assumption that dissatisfaction with weight is universally deleterious. Rather, we suggest that to further analyze the role of body image dissatisfaction in eating disorders, one might examine how body dissatisfaction interacts with motivation and participation in healthy behaviors.

For individuals at low body mass indexes (BMIs; indicating relative thinness), body image dissatisfaction and its role as a motivator for weight loss are clearly injurious. Indeed, this problematic level of distress is what led to body image disturbance being considered among the necessary criteria for both eating disorders, anorexia nervosa and bulimia nervosa (American Psychiatric Association, 1994). In contrast, for individuals at average or above-average BMIs, body image dissatisfaction may serve an important motivating function regarding the decision to engage in healthy behaviors related to exercise, food consumption, or both. We do not believe that the continuum of body image dissatisfaction in populations with no eating disorder is simply linear, with greater distress leading to greater eating disturbance. Instead, we assert that the relationship between body image dissatisfaction and healthy dieting and exercise behaviors can best be illustrated by an inverted U-shaped curve (see Figure 11.1). When body image distress is very low, individuals may not engage in healthy dieting and exercise—even if necessary to improve health outcomes. When body image distress is very high, individuals may engage in unhealthy or even dangerous dieting behaviors (e.g., fasting or purging) or may fail to engage in any diet or exercise behaviors because of their perceived inability to overcome their body image deficits (or, possibly, excessive weight). Mild to moderate levels of distress may be beneficial for average to above-average BMIs because it serves as a constant motivator to continue a healthy lifestyle.

This chapter offers an overview of the theoretical background and empirical support for these hypotheses. We review the following issues: the relationship between body image dissatisfaction and dieting behavior; the public health problem of obesity, body image, and dieting behavior in overweight and obese populations; the research examining the possible

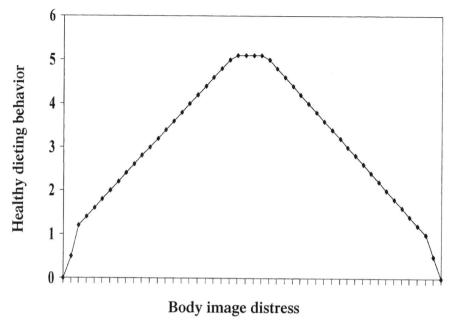

Figure 11.1. Interaction of body image distress and healthy eating behavior: An inverted U-shaped curve.

beneficial aspects of body image dissatisfaction in predicting weight loss and exercise behavior; and the theories from the health psychology literature supporting the notion that distress may serve as a motivating factor for engaging in healthy behaviors. Finally, we offer implications for this reconceptualization of the hazards of body image dissatisfaction and discuss specific research directions that might provide a fuller test of the model.

BODY IMAGE DISSATISFACTION AS A MOTIVATOR FOR WEIGHT LOSS AND EXERCISE

The body image literature often contains reports of the prevalence of dieting practices as evidence of a society's normative discontent with appearance. In a recent, very large survey sample of over 100,000 adults, Serdula et al. (1999) reported that 35.1% of men and 43.6% of women were dieting to maintain weight, and 28.8% of men and 34.4% of women were currently dieting to lose weight. Thus, fewer than 20% of women were not purposefully monitoring their food intake and exercise with the goal of managing their weight. Attempts to lose weight were higher for women than men within every sociodemographic and weight category. Although these numbers initially seem troubling and excessive, large epidemiological studies (Must et al., 1999) suggest that approximately half of American men and women have a BMI of 25 kg/m^2 or higher (a typical cutoff used to categorize someone as overweight). Serdula et al. (1999) found that weight loss efforts were significantly higher in overweight and obese populations. However, more interesting, weight loss attempts were reported by only 60% of obese men and 70% of obese women, indicating that a sizable minority had possibly either accepted their weight or lacked the self-efficacy to engage in weight loss efforts. In addition, despite increasing prevalence of obesity with age (Mokdad et al., 1999), attempts to lose weight steadily declined across increasing age groups for women (Serdula et al., 1999).

Although dieting may be a behavior driven by concerns other than dissatisfaction with current appearance (e.g., health reasons), body image dissatisfaction appears to be a clear and consistent motivator. Striegel-Moore, Wilfley, Caldwell, Needham, and Brownell (1996) evaluated a large number of attitudes and behaviors of 324 dieting African American and White women. They assessed nine different reasons for participating in weight loss efforts, including a desire to improve appearance, concerns about health, pressures from others, and the desire to feel more physically comfortable. No significant differences were found for race on any of the nine reasons for undertaking weight loss. However, if the absolute strength of these ratings is examined, desire to improve appearance and a desire to feel better about oneself were the highest rated in terms of importance (Striegel-Moore et al., 1996). For instance, on the 1–5 scale (*not at all important* to *extremely important*), for the item "wanted to improve appearance," the ratings were 4.47 for African American women and 4.41 for White women. The numbers for "concerns about health" were 3.81 and 3.82, respectively.

It is also informative from other research that people may not exercise so much for health reasons as body image ones (Cash et al., 1994; MacDonald & Thompson, 1992). McDonald and Thompson evaluated reasons for exercising among college-age men and women. They demonstrated that women were significantly more likely to exercise for weight and toning reasons than were men and that these motivators were significantly correlated with body dissatisfaction and eating disturbance. Exercising for fitness was negatively connected with eating disturbance in men. Exercising for health reasons was positively related to self-esteem for both genders (MacDonald & Thompson, 1992). Cash et al. developed an instrument to assess women's reasons for exercise. A subscale assessing appearance–weight management reasons for exercise was significantly associated with body image disturbance (rs = .40–.47), even after controlling for BMI. Furthermore, appearance–weight management reasons were the only ones to significantly predict women's reported exercise frequency. Other potential reasons, such as health management, stress management, and socializing, did not predict exercise frequency

(Cash et al., 1994). Results of both studies may be interpreted as evidence that body image distress motivates individuals to exercise, whereas health concerns do not. All individuals, not just those who are overweight, benefit from regular exercise. However, subjective satisfaction with body image may decrease a potentially potent source of motivation to engage in an activity that is time consuming and not universally enjoyable.

An important question and one not yet sufficiently addressed by the available research is the degree to which motivation to lose weight that is based on health factors is associated with different weight loss behaviors than motivation driven by body image dissatisfaction. It certainly could be hypothesized that body image concerns (especially extreme disparagement) may produce excessive and unhealthy restrictive eating patterns, bulimic behaviors, excessive exercise, or some combination. Even if these "un-healthy" weight loss strategies fall short of constituting an eating disorder, they may be detrimental to the psychological and physical well-being of the individual and should thus be discouraged as a route to weight loss.

OBESITY

Dramatic increases in obesity have led to one out of every two adults in the United States being identified as overweight or obese (defined by a BMI = 25 or higher; Must et al., 1999). This reflects an increase of 49% during the past decade (Mokdad et al., 1999). Recent data suggest that obesity prevalence (i.e., BMI = 30 or higher) increased from 12.0% in 1991 to 17.9% in 1998 (Mokdad et al., 1999). Steady increases have been observed in all states, in both sexes, and across all age groups, races, and educational levels (Mokdad et al., 1999).

This steadily increasing prevalence is associated with enormous burdens of morbidity and mortality. It has been estimated that the average yearly cost of obesity in the United States is $45.8 billion (Oster, Thompson, Edelsberg, Bird, & Colditz, 1999) and accounts for 6.8% of U.S. health care costs. Although all groups are at increasing risk, minority populations, especially African, Mexican, and Native American women, are particularly vulnerable to obesity (Kuczmarski, Flegal, Campbell, & Johnson, 1994).

Obesity poses a high risk for morbidity and mortality because of numer-ous deleterious health consequences, including hypertension, cardiovascular disease, diabetes, stroke, some cancers, osteoarthritis, sleep apnea, and gall-stones (Folsom et al., 1991; Jung, 1997; Rosenbaum, Leibel, Rudolph, & Hirsch, 1997). Obese individuals have higher mortality rates from all causes, and morbidity risks are generally linear, increasing proportionately with degree of obesity (Soloman & Manson, 1997). In regards to attributable risk, Allison, Fontaine, Manson, Stevens, and Van Itallie (1999) found that

53% of all deaths of women with a BMI of 29 or higher could be attributed to obesity. Other recent work suggests that 325,000 deaths in the United States each year are attributable to obesity.

Clearly, obesity is a major public health threat affecting an estimated 50 million people in the United States (Kuczmarski et al., 1994). The prevalence of obesity-related disease strongly suggests the need to prevent and treat obesity rather than just address its associated sources of morbidity (Must et al., 1999). Surprisingly, weight losses of as little as 10% of body weight can substantially reduce morbidity, mortality, and lifetime medical care costs (Blackburn & Kanders, 1987; Goldstein, 1992; Oster et al., 1999). Thus, even small, realistic goals for weight loss may be beneficial. Unfortunately, the treatment of obesity has been largely unsuccessful (National Task Force on Prevention and Treatment of Obesity, 1994). Although various methods, including dietary restriction, increased physical activity, behavior modification, and pharmacologic interventions, have been demonstrated as successful in the short term, no treatment has been shown to reliably sustain weight loss in the long term (National Task Force on Prevention and Treatment of Obesity, 1994; Rosenbaum et al., 1997). Strikingly, 95% of those entering weight loss programs return to their baseline weight within 5 years (Jung, 1997).

Unfortunately, concern about the health effects of obesity may not be motivating enough for many overweight individuals to engage in lifestyle change. Heinberg et al. (2000) found that for older African American men and women, health concerns were not predictive of weight loss at either 6- or 15-month follow-up. That is, individuals reporting more concern and focus on their health were not any more successful in initially losing weight or maintaining weight loss. Additional recent evidence also suggests that physicians may not be advising their obese patients to lose weight (Galuska, Will, Serdula, & Ford, 1999) or counseling patients of any size to exercise (Wee, McCarthy, Davis, & Phillips, 1999). In a study of over 12,000 obese men and women (BMI > $30kg/m^2$), only 42% had been advised by their health care professional to lose weight. Women as well as middle-aged, better educated, more obese people and those in poorer health were more likely to receive weight loss advice (Galuska et al., 1999). Similarly, only 34% of a national population-based sample (N = 9,299) had been advised to exercise during their last physician visit (Wee et al., 1999). Women and individuals who are middle-aged, of higher socioeconomic status, better educated, and more obese were more likely to be counseled on the importance of exercise (Wee et al., 1999). More interesting, those with an already higher level of physical activity were more likely to get exercise advice. Clearly physicians may not be optimizing prevention strategies for reducing the health consequences of obesity. For individuals without body image distress and without physician advice, motivators to engage in healthy lifestyle change may be almost entirely absent.

The previously reviewed numbers reflect a striking epidemic of obesity, and the health care consequences are staggering, yet some researchers have suggested that it is dieting rather than obesity that leads to increased morbidity and mortality (Cogan & Ernsberger, 1999; Miller, 1999; Rothblum, 1990, 1992) and that medical problems associated with obesity may be better treated directly rather than through weight loss (Ernsberger & Koletsky, 1999). Additionally, it has been argued that ideal weights based on actuarial data are invalid (Rothblum, 1990) and that obese individuals do not consume more calories than nonobese individuals (Rothblum, 1990). The antidieting movement has fostered self-help organizations to advance fat acceptance (e.g., National Association for the Advancement of Fat Acceptance) and an outpouring of scholarly activity attacking dieting and the mass marketers who purvey unrealistic models for emulation and profit (Cogan & Ernsberger, 1999). In fact, we (Thompson et al., 1999) have also fallen into the trap of narrowly focusing on a singular aspect of body image dissatisfaction (i.e., its malevolency) to the exclusion of hardly any consideration of a different view (in our recent book, 331 of 332 pages were devoted to the nefarious side of body image dissatisfaction).

In summary, it appears that the public health literature and general philosophical thrust of its researchers are at odds with much of the body image and eating disorder work and writings. The latter literature is replete with examples of correlational and prospective studies in which researchers find body image disturbances predictive of eating problems in adults and children–adolescents (Shisslak & Crago, in press; Thompson et al., 1999; Thompson & Smolak, in press). The public health literature, as noted earlier in this section, clearly focuses on the negative aspects of not limiting food intake and increasing energy expenditure (i.e., obesity). A third group, or faction, has promoted the idea that individuals, of all weights, should be encouraged to forgo dieting and restrictive eating and, in fact, should attempt to accept a large body size (or at least a nonideal body size; McFarlane, Polivy, & McCabe, 1999; Rothblum, 1992). In addition, one of the most active research and clinical areas in the entire field of eating disorders is the early intervention and prevention work with children and adolescents (Piran, Levine, & Steiner-Adair, 1999). Much of the work in this area promotes acceptance of a variety of body shapes and discourages dieting behavior. Yet obesity is much more prevalent in children and adolescents (approaching 20%) than eating disorders, which perhaps affects less than 2%–3% of this population (Thompson & Smolak, in press).

In addition, although body image has been extensively explored among eating-disordered populations, researchers have just begun to examine the important role of body image among overweight populations (Thompson, 1996). In general, research strongly supports the commonsense observation that overweight individuals are dissatisfied with their appearance and that greater body image distress is associated with increases in dieting behavior (Stice, Mazotti, Krebs, & Martin, 1998; Thompson, 1990; Thompson et al., 1999). Furthermore, obese individuals tend to overestimate their whole body size to a larger degree than do normal-weight controls, are more dissatisfied and preoccupied with their appearance, and avoid more social situations because of their physical appearance (Cash, 1990; Collins et al., 1987; Fisher, 1986). However, an extremely important question regarding the body image concerns of overweight and obese individuals is whether their dissatisfaction is, in fact, a robust motivating force for weight and health changes and whether the actual level of their dissatisfaction is commensurate with their weight (i.e., BMI). We noted earlier that Serdula et al. (1999) found that 40% of obese men and 30% of obese women were not trying to lose weight. Is it possible that size acceptance is too high or that dissatisfaction is too low for some individuals? Are the wrong people (i.e., those overweight or obese) at the front end of the inverted U?

OBESITY, BODY DISSATISFACTION, AND WEIGHT LOSS

Studies of older African Americans (Heinberg et al., 2000) and predominantly White college-age sorority women (Schulken, Pinciaro, Sawyer, Jensen, & Hoban, 1997) suggest that BMI and body dissatisfaction do not increase in a linear manner—the majority of obese individuals identify as being in a normal or acceptable body size range. For example, the actual BMIs of overweight elderly African American women who self-reported their weight status as "very underweight" did not differ significantly from those who described themselves as "very overweight" (Heinberg et al., 2000). Rather, a more bimodal distribution of BMIs was shown, with those reporting "normal weight" having the lowest BMIs (see Figure 11.2). Similarly, 84% of college-age women with a BMI above 27.4 described their current size as "acceptable," with only 15.8% correctly identifying themselves as "overweight" (Schulken et al., 1997).

In addition to the literature examining body image among the obese (Rosen, 1996; Rosen, Orosan, & Reiter, 1995), body image has been examined in individuals undergoing treatment for weight loss (Foster, Wadden, & Vogt, 1997). The role of body image in outcome has been mixed. For instance, individuals who later dropped out of a weight loss treatment program were more likely to overestimate their body size than were individuals who completed treatment (Collins et al., 1987), suggesting a negative prognostic role of perceptual body image disturbance. In another study,

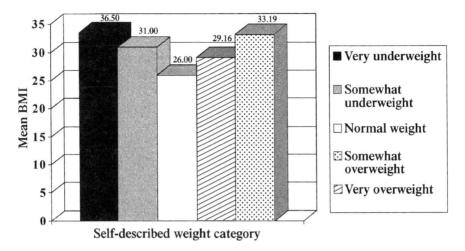

Figure 11.2. Self-described weight category by body mass index (BMI) for elderly African American women.

dropouts from a very low-calorie diet program were less actively invested in physical fitness than were those who remained in treatment; however, no differences were found on measures of body image (Cash, 1994). Such findings suggest a potential role for body image or related constructs in predicting adherence and clinical outcomes. However, these investigators examined weight loss regimens designed solely for reducing weight.

Many individuals seek to lose weight not only for appearance concerns but also for health benefits. They may be told to lose weight by their physicians and may even be placed on diets to reduce weight-related morbidity. For instance, Heinberg et al. (2000) examined 68 (59% women, 41% men) older (mean age = 66.26 years) African Americans with hypertension randomly assigned either to participate in a 15-month weight loss program (weight reduction or weight reduction and sodium reduction) or to control conditions (sodium reduction or no treatment). Heinberg et al. also evaluated, for the first time, the effects of body image on weight loss efforts.

Compared with the control groups, individuals in the weight loss intervention groups demonstrated a 6.23-pound versus a 1.22-pound loss at 6 months and a 6.43-pound loss versus a 0.41-pound gain at 15 months. Baseline weight was a significant predictor at 6-month follow-up. In addition, an interaction between gender and self-ideal discrepancy contributed an additional 13% of the variance. Men low on self-ideal discrepancy gained an average of 0.8 pounds, whereas men high on self-ideal discrepancy lost an average of 8.33 pounds. In contrast, women in the two groups lost an equivalent amount of weight. The treatment group was a significant predictor of weight loss at 15 months, accounting for 22% of the variance at 15 months. The addition of body image variables significantly contributed to the prediction of weight loss, accounting for an additional 24% of variance in weight loss. Significant independent prediction was provided by appearance evaluation at 15 months ($R^2 = .22$), which demonstrated a negative relationship; that is, individuals with higher satisfaction in their appearance evidenced less weight loss at 15 months. The interaction between gender and self-ideal discrepancy contributed an additional 8% of the variance. Men low on self-ideal discrepancy gained an average of 2.3 pounds ($SD = 8.39$), whereas men high on self-ideal discrepancy lost an average of 10.89 pounds ($SD = 8.01$), but no significant differences between women high and low on self-ideal discrepancy were found.

These results suggest that subjective body image dissatisfaction appears to play a beneficial role in weight loss, with self-ideal discrepancy being especially important for men. Participants who were more satisfied with their appearance prior to randomization to treatment demonstrated a tendency to lose less weight in the short term and were significantly less likely to lose weight in the long term, that is, over 15 months. Indeed, those who were most satisfied were likely to gain as much as 2.4 pounds. Those most dissatisfied with their appearance lost 7.25 pounds over the 15-month period, resulting in almost a 10-pound difference (and 5% of total body weight) between the two extremes. It was concluded that some degree of body image dissatisfaction is necessary to maintain the countless, daily changes necessary for long-term lifestyle change, including daily vigilance to calorie consumption and expenditure (Heinberg et al., 2000). Given the impact of even small amounts of weight change on blood pressure and other health outcomes (Kuczmarski et al., 1994), the differences between satisfied and dissatisfied participants in weight-loss management appear to be clinically significant.

The discrepancy between one's ideal size and current perceived size demonstrated a more complex relationship. A significant interaction between self-ideal discrepancy and gender was demonstrated. Men who described a larger discrepancy between how they currently feel and how they would like to be lost a significant amount of weight, whereas those men with a smaller discrepancy tended to gain weight during the trial. No such relationship occurred for women. It is unclear why satisfaction alone is important for women, whereas satisfaction as well as a comparison with an idealized self is salient for men. Future research should explore this distinction further.

The previous study and others (Striegel-Moore et al., 1996) suggest that body image dissatisfaction may be important in weight loss efforts and may motivate exercise behavior (Cash et al., 1994; McDonald & Thompson, 1992). Perhaps body image dissatisfaction should not be conceptualized solely as a deleterious state. Rather some distress may motivate one to engage in potentially healthy behaviors. In the next section, we conceptualize body image dissatisfaction as an important variable in predicting health behavior change.

HEALTH PSYCHOLOGY MODELS WITH BODY IMAGE DISSATISFACTION AS PREDICTOR OF BEHAVIOR CHANGE

The health psychology literature has produced numerous theories to help predict and explain engagement in health behaviors, including stages of change, protection motivation theory, and decisional balance theory. One such theory is the health belief model (Becker & Maiman, 1975), which has been used to predict compliance with preventive health recommendations. It emphasizes four conditions that are assumed to precede an individual's decision to change his or her health behavior: (a) perceived vulnerability to disease, (b) perceived severity of the disease's consequences, (c) perceived benefit (effectiveness) of the health action against the threat of the disease, and (d) self-efficacy to overcome physical or psychological impediments to behavior change. For example, using the concept of vulnerability, Ransford (1986) demonstrated that worry about heart disease predicted engagement in diet and exercise health behaviors for lower socioeconomic African Americans but not for White people at any socioeconomic level. Educational attainment for White people was the sole predictor of engaging in a heart healthy lifestyle. It may be argued that better educated individuals and those with higher socioeconomic status levels may engage in a healthier lifestyle normatively and independently of heart disease worry. For others, anxiety about heart disease may provide an important motivator to engage in healthy dieting and exercise.

Similar assumptions may be made for dieting and exercise by individuals interested in reducing or maintaining their weight. If individuals do not perceive their body size to be problematic, they may be less likely to view themselves as vulnerable to disease. Conversely, if they experience a very high level of distress, they may lack the self-efficacy to believe they can change or that minor daily changes in diet and exercise are efficacious in decreasing their distress.

Numerous studies in other medical populations suggest that fear of disease, or its opposite denial of risk, is an important predictor of health-related behavior (Hailey, 1991, Howell & Talley, 1999; Kreitler, 1999). Preliminary results, however, suggest that health concerns do not consistently predict engagement in diet, exercise, weight loss initiation, or maintenance (Heinberg et al., 2000; Ransford, 1986).

We hypothesize that the relationship between body image dissatisfaction and healthy dieting behaviors is not a linear one as previous studies would suggest. Rather, as researchers in other investigations of health behaviors have demonstrated (e.g., cancer screening behavior), an inverted U-shaped curve (see Figure 11.1) best describes the relationship between body image dissatisfaction and dieting behavior.

Almost a hundred years ago, Yerkes and Dodson (1908) described the relationship between cognitive efficiency and stress as it related to arousal. These researchers found improvement in the performance of easy tasks with increasing stress. However, with more difficult cognitive tasks, they found an inverted U-shaped function of higher performance with medium stress and worse performance with low or high stress (Mandler, 1993). One could certainly argue that dieting behavior is a more complex task that entails the maintenance of countless, daily changes necessary for long-term lifestyle change, including daily vigilance to calorie consumption and expenditure (Heinberg et al., 2000).

One of the clearest examples of adapting the notion of a U-shaped curve to health behavior is in relation to a family history of breast cancer and screening behavior (Hailey, 1991). Hailey's review of 13 studies examines the association between breast cancer risk factors and early detection and screening behaviors. Because evidence suggests that early detection increases the survival rate of women with breast cancer, one would predict that a linear relationship exists between risk status and screening behavior. However, this was not always the case. Hailey argued that anxiety or fear associated with a family history of breast cancer may mediate the relationship between risk factor status and screening behavior, similar to the manner in which anxiety or fear operates in many complex behavioral–cognitive tasks. This results in a curvilinear relationship, with a moderate degree of anxiety facilitating compliance with screening but too much anxiety inhibiting it. Although the hypothesis of diminishing returns from increasing fear intensities (i.e., engagement in screening behaviors) was not directly tested, 13 studies were analyzed according to the inverted U-shaped hypothesis and provide indirect support.

This hypothesis could explain the findings of Heinberg et al. (2000). Individuals in that sample who did not report baseline disturbance were likely to gain weight after 15 months of a healthy lifestyle change intervention. Perhaps these participants fell on the left side of the U-shaped curve (see Figure 11.1) and did not have the necessary distress to substantially change their behavior. Although not empirically tested, perhaps when distress is too high, individuals do not believe that their behavior can change appearance. That is, they fall on the far right side of the U-shaped curve. In future studies, researchers should evaluate whether a bimodal distribution best describes weight loss or exercise engagement findings. Perhaps previous work, testing only for a linear relationship, fails to recognize this U-shaped distribution.

IMPLICATIONS AND RESEARCH DIRECTIONS

The current thin ideal promulgated by Western culture is unrealistic, often unhealthy, and generally unachievable for the majority of individuals. Internalizing these exacting standards is not necessary for incorporating a healthy lifestyle, and we in no way argue that body image distress should be used to facilitate the attainment of a waifish, anorexiclike appearance. The acceptance of a variety of body sizes by U.S. culture is a laudable goal, and it is likely that such approval may provide "protection" from eating disorders. However, a general lack of concern in personal assessments of weight, including the evaluation of obesity, may limit the efficacy of self-initiated dieting, exercise, or behavioral interventions for weight loss. We asserted earlier in this chapter that some degree of body image concern is helpful, but the point at which concern becomes distress and motivation becomes preoccupation is not known.

Future work should explore which factors might moderate or even mediate the relationship between body dissatisfaction and healthy weight loss behaviors (or its obverse, unhealthy weight loss behaviors). For instance, the issue of biological sex (male, female) or gender role orientation could be examined as a moderating variable. Perhaps men and women who do not identify with the traditional "feminine" gender role engage in relatively higher levels of exercise and healthy dietary restriction, as opposed to extreme dietary restriction, excessive exercise, or purging behaviors. Also ethnicity is a key potential moderator that should be examined. In addition, dispositional factors such as self-esteem or internalization of societal values of attractiveness might moderate or even mediate the relationship between body dissatisfaction and weight loss behaviors. For instance, a high level of internalization has been found in numerous studies to predict body image and eating disturbances (e.g., Thompson et al., 1999; Thompson & Stice, in press). Conceivably, if internalization is high, individuals with body dissatisfaction may be differentially driven to meet societal appearance standards (i.e., media icons) and thus engage in more excessive and unhealthy dieting and weight loss practices.

It is clear that our argument should not be used to advocate interventions designed to increase body image distress. Rather clinicians working with weight loss populations may want to consider assessing body image dissatisfaction as part of their regular evaluation to better identify individuals at risk for poorer long-term outcome. In future studies, researchers should examine potential interventions to motivate those satisfied with their body image. For example, individuals satisfied with their appearance may benefit more from interventions that emphasize the specific health benefits of weight loss.

A further concern, if one accepts the proposed hypothesis that some degree of body dissatisfaction may be desirable, is whether (or how) this should affect the design of early intervention and prevention programs for eating disorders (Piran et al., 1999). Typically, these programs are predicated on the idea that body dissatisfaction is "bad" and that strategies designed to counteract media messages and enhance body acceptance are indicated. The onesidedness of this content should not be modified at this point, especially given the limited research available, even with adults, to support the heuristic model presented in this chapter. However, one possible potential modification might prove worthy of study. If one separates weight dissatisfaction from overall appearance satisfaction, conceivably the messages used in prevention programs might differ, especially given the increasing prevalence of obesity in childhood and adolescence. Fostering acceptance of diversity of nonweight-related features is difficult to assail at any level. Facial features, skin color, height, muscularity, and other nonweight features are not risks for the health consequences of obesity. Weight dissatisfaction, however, if it is paralleled by an objective elevation in weight, may require alternative prevention techniques. For these individuals, strategies designed to foster acceptance of overweight or obesity, in essence, trying to improve their body satisfaction, may be inadvisable and may potentially contribute to future health risks. The goal, albeit a sensitive one, is to encourage healthy self-esteem and a self-evaluation that is not dominated by appearance, while reinforcing the veracity of an overweight status and its concomitant body image dissatisfaction, with the goal of increasing healthy weight control strategies.

Americans are at high risk for obesity, and obesity-related morbidity and mortality have been identified as major threats to public health (Brownell & Wadden, 1992; Must et al., 1999). The challenge that lies ahead is to encourage weight reduction and develop strategies to increase long-term weight loss maintenance in a population that is relatively tolerant to a variety of body shapes and sizes. Rather than inducing body image dissatisfaction or unrealistic body image perceptions and an unhealthy preoccupation with weight, educational or behavioral interventions on the health consequences of obesity must be developed that help increase long-term compliance with weight loss for individuals satisfied with their physical appearance.

This chapter has been much more speculative than we would prefer, primarily owing to the lack of studies in which researchers have examined the premise. Future research and reanalyses of extant data sets may necessarily determine if the hypotheses are supported. We encourage researchers to include measures of motivation for healthy behaviors and actual participation in such endeavors, along with the usual indexes of body image, eating disturbance, and psychological functioning. In addition, the examination of ethnic, gender, sociodemographic, and age effects are suggested. Finally, it seems imperative to clearly evaluate the effects of BMI. If participant samples are clearly subclassified by weight–height ratios, researchers might be able to more fully determine whether body dissatisfaction, at a particular level of weight category, is a productive driving force for healthy behaviors, a maladaptive driving force for extreme eating-disordered behaviors, or possibly a factor that lacks any predictive ability.

REFERENCES

Allison, D. B., Fontaine, K. R., Manson, J. E., Stevens, J., & Van Itallie, T. B. (1999). Annual deaths attributable to obesity in the United States. *Journal of the American Medical Association, 282,* 1530–1538.

American Psychiatric Association. (1994). *Diagnostic and statistical manual of mental disorders* (4th ed.). Washington, DC: Author.

Becker, M. H., & Maiman, L. A. (1975). Sociobehavioral determinants of compliance with health and medical care recommendations. *Medical Care, 13,* 10–24.

Blackburn, G. L., & Kanders, B. S. (1987). Medical evaluation and treatment of the obese patient with cardiovascular disease. *American Journal of Cardiology, 60,* 55g–58g.

Brownell, K. D., & Wadden, T. A. (1992). Etiology and treatment of obesity: Understanding a serious, prevalent, and refractory disorder. *Journal of Consulting and Clinical Psychology, 60,* 505–517.

Cash, T. F. (1990). The psychology of physical appearance: Aesthetics, attributes, and images. In T. F. Cash & T. Pruzinsky (Eds.), *Body images: Development, deviance and change* (pp. 51–79). New York: Guilford Press.

Cash, T. F. (1994). Body image and weight changes in a multisite comprehensive very-low-calorie diet program. *Behavior Therapy, 25,* 239–254.

Cash, T. F., & Henry, P. E. (1995). Women's body images: The results of a national survey in the U.S.A. *Sex Roles, 33,* 19–28.

Cash, T. F., Novy, P. L., & Grant, J. R. (1994). Why do women exercise? Factor analysis and further validation of the reasons for exercise inventory. *Perceptual and Motor Skills, 78,* 539–544.

Cogan, J. C., & Ernsberger, P. (1999). Dieting, weight and health: Reconceptualizing research and policy [Special issue] . *Journal of Social Issues, 55,* 187–206.

Collins, J. K., Beumont, P. J. V., Touyz, S. W., Krass, J., Thompson, P., & Philips, T. (1987). Variability in body shape perception in anorexic, bulimic, obese and control subjects. *International Journal of Eating Disorders, 6,* 633–638.

Ernsberger, P., & Koletsky, R. J. (1999). Biomedical rationale for a wellness approach to obesity: An alternative to a focus on weight loss. *Journal of Social Issues, 55,* 221–260.

Fisher, S. (1986). *Development and structure of the body image.* Hillsdale, NJ: Erlbaum.

Folsom, A. R., Burke, G. L., Byers, C. L., Hutchinson, R. G., Heiss, G., Flack, J. M., Jacobs, D. R., & Caan, B. (1991). Implications of obesity for cardiovascular disease in Blacks: The CARDIA and ARIC studies. *American Journal Clinical Nutrition, 53,* 1604S–1611S.

Foster, G. D., Wadden, T. A., & Vogt, R. A. (1997). Body image in obese women before, during and after weight loss treatment. *Health Psychology, 16,* 226–229.

Galuska, D. A., Will, J. C., Serdula, M. K., & Ford, E. S. (1999). Are health care professionals advising obese patients to lose weight? *Journal of the American Medical Association, 282,* 1576–1578.

Goldstein, D. J. (1992). Beneficial health effects of modest weight loss. *International Journal of Obesity, 16,* 397–415.

Hailey, B. J. (1991). Family history of breast cancer and screening behavior: An inverted U-shaped curve. *Medical Hypotheses, 36,* 397–403.

Heinberg, L. J., Haythornthwaite, J. A., Rosofsky, W., McCarron, P., & Clarke, A. (2000). Body image and weight loss compliance in elderly African-American hypertensives. *American Journal of Health Behavior, 24,* 163–173.

Howell, S., & Talley, N. J. (1999). Does fear of serious disease predict consulting behaviour amongst patients with dyspepsia in general practice? *European Journal of Gastroenterology and Hepatology, 11,* 881–886.

Jung, R. T. (1997). Obesity as a disease. *British Medical Bulletin, 53,* 307–321.

Kreitler, S. (1999). Denial in cancer patients. *Cancer Investigation, 17,* 514–534.

Kuczmarski, R. J., Flegal, K. M., Campbell, S. M., & Johnson, C. L. (1994). Increasing prevalence of overweight among US adults: The National Health and Nutrition Examination Surveys, 1960 to 1991. *Journal of the American Medical Association, 272,* 205–211.

McDonald, K., & Thompson, J. K. (1992). Eating disturbance, body image dissatisfaction, and reasons for exercising: Gender differences and correlational findings. *International Journal of Eating Disorders, 11,* 289–292.

McFarlane, T., Polivy, J., & McCabe, R. E. (1999). Help, not harm: Psychological foundation for a nondieting approach toward health. *Journal of Social Issues, 55,* 261–270.

Mandler, G. (1993). Thought, memory and learning: Effects of emotional stress. In L. Goldberger & S. Breznitz (Eds.), *Handbook of stress: Theoretical and clinical aspects* (pp. 40–55). Toronto, Ontario, Canada: Free Press.

Miller, W. C. (1999). Fitness and fatness in relation to health: Implications for a paradigm shift. *Journal of Social Issues, 55,* 207–220.

Mokdad, A. H., Serdula, M. K., Dietz, W. H., Bowman, B. A., Marks, J. S., & Koplan, J. P. (1999). The spread of the obesity epidemic in the United States, 1991–1998. *Journal of the American Medical Association, 282,* 1519–1522.

Must, A., Spadano, J., Coakley, E. H., Field, A. E., Colditz, G., & Dietz, W. H. (1999). The disease burden associated with overweight and obesity. *Journal of the American Medical Association, 282,* 1523–1529.

National Task Force on Prevention and Treatment of Obesity. (1994). Towards prevention of obesity: Research directions. *Obesity Research, 2,* 571–584.

Oster, G., Thompson, D., Edelsberg, J., Bird, A. P., & Colditz, G. A. (1999). Lifetime health and economic benefits of weight loss among obese persons. *American Journal of Public Health, 89,* 1536–1542.

Piran, N., Levine, M. P., & Steiner-Adair, C. (1999). *Preventing eating disorders.* New York: Brunner/Mazel.

Ransford, H. E. (1986). Race, heart disease worry and health protective behavior. *Social Science in Medicine, 22,* 1355–1362.

Rodin, J., Silberstein, L. R., & Striegel-Moore, R. H. (1985). Women and weight: A normative discontent. In T. B. Sonderegger (Ed.), *Psychology and gender: Nebraska Symposium on Motivation, 1984* (pp. 267–307). Lincoln: University of Nebraska Press.

Rosen, J. C. (1996). Improving body image in obesity. In J. K. Thompson (Ed.), *Body image, eating disorders, and obesity: An integrative guide for assessment and treatment* (pp. 425–440). Washington, DC: American Psychological Association.

Rosen, J. C., Orosan, P., & Reiter, J. (1995). Cognitive behavior therapy for negative body image in obese women. *Behavior Therapy, 26,* 25–42.

Rosenbaum, M., Leibel, R., Rudolph, L., & Hirsch, J. (1997). Medical progress: Obesity. *New England Journal of Medicine, 337,* 396–407.

Rothblum, E. D. (1990). Women and weight: Fad and fiction. *Journal of Psychology, 124–24.*

Rothblum, E. D. (1992). Women and weight: An international perspective. In U. P. Gielen, L. L. Adler, & N. A. Milgram (Eds.), *Psychology in international perspective* (pp. 271–280). Amsterdam, The Netherlands: Swets & Zeitlinger.

Schulken, E. D., Pinciaro, P. J., Sawyer, R. G., Jensen, J. G., & Hoban, M. T. (1997). Sorority women's body size perceptions and their weight-related attitudes and behaviors. *Journal of American College Health, 46,* 69–74.

Serdula, M. K., Mokdad, A. H., Williamson, D. F., Galuska, D. A., Mendlein, J. M., & Heath, G. W. (1999). Prevalence of attempting weight loss and strategies for controlling weight. *Journal of the American Medical Association, 282,* 1353–1358.

Shisslak, C. M., & Crago, M. (in press). Risk and protective factors in the development of eating disorders. In J. K. Thompson & L. Smolak (Eds.), *Body image, eating disorders, and obesity in children and adolescents.* Washington, DC: America Psychological Association.

Solomon, C. G., & Manson, J. E. (1997). Obesity and mortality: A review of the epidemiologic data. *American Journal of Clinical Nutrition, 66*(Suppl.), 1044S–1050S.

Stice, E., Mazotti, L., Krebs, M., & Martin, S. (1998). Predictors of adolescent dieting behaviors: A longitudinal study. *Psychology of Addictive Behaviors, 12,* 195–205.

Striegel-Moore, R. H., Wilfley, D. E., Caldwell, M. B., Needham, M. L., & Brownell, K. D. (1996). Weight-related attitudes and behaviors of women who diet to lose weight: A comparison of Black dieters and White dieters. *Obesity Research, 4,* 109–116.

Thompson, J. K. (1990). *Body image disturbance: Assessment and treatment.* Elmsford, NY: Pergamon.

Thompson, J. K. (1996). Body image, eating disorders, and obesity: An emerging synthesis. In J. K. Thompson (Ed.), *Body image, eating disorders, and obesity: An integrative guide for assessment and treatment* (pp. 1–20). Washington, DC: American Psychological Association.

Thompson, J. K., & Heinberg, L. J. (1999). The media's influence on body image disturbance and eating disorders: We've reviled them, now can we rehabilitate them? *Journal of Social Issues, 55,* 339–353.

Thompson, J. K., Heinberg, L. J., Altabe, M., & Tantleff-Dunn, S. (1999). *Exacting beauty: Theory, assessment, and treatment of body image disturbance.* Washington, DC: American Psychological Association.

Thompson, J. K., & Smolak, L. (in press). (Eds.). *Body image, eating disorders, and obesity in children and adolescents.* Washington, DC: American Psychological Association.

Thompson, J. K., & Stice, E. (in press). Thin-ideal internalization: Mounting evidence for a new risk factor for body image disturbance and eating pathology. *Current Directions in Psychological Science.*

Wee, C. C., McCarthy, E. P., Davis, R. B., & Phillips, R. S. (1999). Physician counseling about exercise. *Journal of the American Medical Association, 282,* 1583–1588.

Yerkes, R. M., & Dodson, J. D. (1908). The relation of strength of stimulus to rapidity of habit-formation. *Journal of Comparative and Neurological Psychology, 18,* 459–482.

12

THE PREVENTION OF EATING DISORDERS: TOWARD A PARTICIPATORY ECOLOGY OF KNOWLEDGE, ACTION, AND ADVOCACY

MICHAEL P. LEVINE AND NIVA PIRAN

Ideally, prevention involves translating theory and research about risk factors and resilience into policies, programs, and individual practices designed to (a) keep large groups of people who are well from developing that disorder in the first place (*primary* or *universal* prevention); (b) identify people who are either at high risk (*secondary* or *selective* prevention) or well along the path to disorder (*secondary* or *indicated* prevention) and help them before their problems become serious and chronic; and (c) systematically evaluate the success or failure of these universal and targeted efforts (Mrazek & Haggerty, 1994). Somewhere between universal and selective prevention are programs applied to a large group of people (e.g., girls) who are at risk because they are facing a stressful transition, such as early adolescence (Durlak & Wells, 1997). There is tension in the field as to whether the goal of prevention is reducing the incidence of new "cases" of a clearly defined disorder (Mrazek & Haggerty, 1994) or general avoidance of dysfunctions and diseases through "health promotion" (Cowen, 1997).

The prevention of eating disorders has a short but complicated and controversial history (see, e.g., Carter, Stewart, Dunn, & Fairburn, 1997). Significant progress has been made in identifying risk factors (see Stice, chapter 3, this volume), and some progress has been made in developing innovative programs and systematically evaluating larger scale projects (see, e.g., Franko & Orosan-Weine, 1998; Piran, Levine, & Steiner-Adair, 1999). However, progress has been slow and, in our opinion, impeded by a lack of appreciation for the larger field of prevention and by a reluctance to explore participatory models that operate outside the social learning and problem-behavior theories guiding many of the prominent programs for prevention of substance abuse and cardiovascular disease (Perry, 1999).

We agree with the longstanding contention that prevention is not a luxury waiting for full clarification of multiple pathways to disordered eating and complete development of effective therapy. Rather, prevention is the only reasonable and complete answer to reducing the incidence of disorder, to replacing risk and vulnerability (for various disorders) with health and resilience, and to establishing variables as risk factors, not correlates (Albee & Gullotta, 1997; Durlak, 1997). This chapter extends our ongoing attempts to disentangle the complexities of prevention (Levine & Smolak, in press; Piran, 1995; Piran et al., 1999). The first section reviews prevention outcome studies, many of them very recent, that are controlled and have a follow-up period. Second, we consider the implications of those studies in light of mainstream prevention and health promotion research. Finally, we offer conclusions and recommendations for developing a relational–ecological paradigm that incorporates the many positive aspects of current curricular prevention programs while addressing their theoretical, empirical, and methodological limitations.

PREVENTION OF DISORDERED EATING: A RESEARCH UPDATE

Table 12.1 summarizes the essential components and findings of 22 outcome studies that meet two basic criteria: (a) experimental or quasiexperimental design containing at least one comparison, control, or no-treatment group and (b) repeated assessment with at least a 1-month follow-up. Four studies appear to be evaluations of selective prevention programs in that participants were designated a priori as "high risk" on the basis of self-reported elevated "body image concerns" (Olmsted, Daneman, Rydall, Lawson, & Rodin, 1999; Stice, Chase, Stormer, & Appel, in press; Stice, Mazotti, Weibel, & Agras, 2000; Zabinski et al., in press). A fifth study is probably an example of indicated prevention because participants were chosen who had partial-syndrome bulimic symptoms and psychopathology (Kaminski & McNamara, 1996).

Two models dominate the choice of content for eating disorders prevention programs. The disease-specific pathways (DSP) model emphasizes the role and determinants of negative body image, weight and shape concerns, calorie-restrictive dieting, and, to some extent, negative affect (Killen et al., 1993; Stice, chapter 3, this volume). All of the programs in Table 12.1 emphasize body image, including weight and shape concerns. In addition, for each study, Table 12.1 rates how many of the following program elements

TABLE 12.1
Findings of 22 Outcome Studies

Study	Sample	Program	FU(month)[a]	DSP[b]	NSVS[c]	Ecology[d]	K	A	B	Comment
			Universal programs							
Outwater (1990/91)	25 U.S. boys, 25 girls, ages 11–12	10 units 45 min each	1	3	2	1	NM	N	N	Body image, self-esteem scores improved significantly in both IG and control
Killen et al. (1993)	931 U.S. girls, ages 11–13	18 units 50 min each	7, 14, and 24	5	0	0	Y	N	N	Trend toward positive intervention effect for HR participants
Moreno & Thelen (1993), two studies	104 and 115 U.S. girls, ages 12–14	6.5-min video + 30 min discussion	1	4	0	0	Y	Y	NM	IG had more positive behavioral intentions; attrition was a problem
Paxton (1993)	136 Australian girls, ages 14–15	5 units 90 min each	11	4	0	0	NM	N	N	Focus on nutrition, dieting, emotions and eating, and determinants of body size
Neumark-Sztainer et al. (1995)	341 Israeli girls, M age = 15.3	10 units 60 min each	6, 24	4	1	1	Y-6 N-12	N	Y-6 N-12	Many engaging activities; final lesson promotes student activism
Mann et al. (1997)	379 U.S. women, M age = 18	90-min presented by 2 ED patients	3	1	0	0	NM	N	N	IG reported more symptoms at posttest; attrition was a problem
McVey & Davis (1998)	263 Canadian girls, M age = 10.9	6 units 55 min each	6,12	3	4	0	NM	N	Y-6 N-12	Extensive manual includes material on media literacy and gender socialization
Winzelberg et al. (1998)	45 U.S. women, M age = 19.7	Interactive software	3	2	0	0	N	Y	N	Includes email support group; program fidelity was low for both aspects
McVey et al. (1999)	286 Canadian girls, M age = 11.2	6 units 55 min each	6	3	4	1	NM	N	N	One 3-hr evening session for parents; parent participation was very low *(continued)*

TABLE 12.1
(Continued)

Study	Sample	Program	FU(month)[a]	DSP[b]	NSVS[c]	Ecology[d]	K	A	B	Comment
Neumark-Sztainer et al. (1999)	226 U.S. Girl Scouts, M age = 10.6	6 units 90 min each	3	3	2	3	Y	Y	N	Troop leaders with 3 hr training, implemented a media literacy program; parents participated; randomized design
Santonastaso et al. (1999)	308 Italian girls, M age = 16.1	4 units 120 min each	12	4	1	0	NM	Y	N/Y	Low-risk girls had lower body dissatisfaction + less increase in bulimic behavior–attitudes
Winzelberg et al. (2000)	53 U.S. women, M age = 20	8-week interactive software	3	2	1	0	NM	Y	N	Includes email support; HR group appeared to achieve greatest benefits; compliance was a problem
Celio et al. (2000)	59 U.S. women, M age = 19.6	Same as Winzelberg et al.	6	4	2	0	NM Effects were greatest for HR group	Y	Y	Compared *Student Bodies program plus Body Traps* (Springer et al., 1999) with *Body Traps* and to wait-list control; *Body Traps* program was ineffective; high dropout rate
O'Dea & Abraham (2000)	170 Australian boys, 295 girls, ages 11.5–14	9 units 50–80 min each	12	1	4	1	NM	Y	N	*Everybody's Different* focuses extensively on self-esteem, self-image, and relationship skills through cooperative, student-centered discovery-based learning
Smolak & Levine (in press)	248 U.S. boys, 252 U.S. girls, ages 11–13	10 units 50 min each	24	4	1	2	Y	Y	Y	Parents of IG received 9 newsletters; significant effects involved IG vs. new control; IG effect on body esteem for girls only

			6	5	1	0	Y	N	N	
Stewart et al. (in press)	752 U.K. girls, M age = 13.4	6 units 45 min each	6	5	1	0	Y	N	N	Dieters in IG had lower restraint scores at FU; intervention had many positive effects at posttest, but none were maintained significantly or comparatively at FU

Selective programs

Kaminski & McNamara (1996)	25 U.S. women, M age = 18.3	8 units 90 min each	1+	3	2	N	NM	Y	Y	IG also had increased self-esteem reduced fear of negative evaluation
Olmstead et al. (1999)	71 Canadian girls, M age = 16, Type 1 diabetes, and parents	P&P-6 units, 90 min each	1, 6, and 12	4	2	1	NM	6-Y 12-Y	6-Y 12-N	Psychoeducation focused on nondieting, communication skills approach to diabetes, and its implications for disordered eating
Stice, Mazotti, et al. (2000)	30 U.S. women, ages 18–22	3 units 60 min each	1	2	0	2	NM	Y	Y	Dissonance-based program focused on helping other adolescent women avoid internalization of the slender ideal
Stice, Chase, et al. (in press)	78 U.S. women, ages 17–29	3 units 60 min each	1	2	0	2	NM	Y	N	Dissonance-based program; significant improvement but only one Group × Time interaction was significant

(continued)

TABLE 12.1
(Continued)

Study	Sample	Program	FU(month)[a]	DSP[b]	NSVS[c]	Ecology[d]	K	A	B	Comment
Zabinski et al. (in press)	56 U.S. women, $M = 19.3$	Software + e-mail support	2.5	2	1	0	NM	N	N	Moderate intervention effect sizes for a number of measures, but Group × Time interactions were not significant

Notes. K = improvements in knowledge; A = improvements in attitudes; B = improvements in behavior. In this regard, Y = yes on at least one variable; N = no on any of the dependent variables; NM = not measured; IG = intervention group; HR = high risk; ED = eating disorder; P&P = patients and parents. FU = length of time, in months, between posttest and follow-up assessments. [a]Age refers to age at the onset of the intervention. [b]DSP = number of elements of disease specific pathways model. Possible elements are (1) nutrition and exercising for healthy weight control; (2) nature and dangers of calorie-restrictive dieting; (3) individual strategies for analyzing and resisting unchanging cultural factors; (4) nature and dangers of eating disorders; and (5) developmental factors such as pubertal weight gain. [c]NSVS = number of elements of nonspecific vulnerability stressor model. Possible elements are (1) nutrition and exercising as part of a healthy lifestyle; (2) life skills, such as relaxation and assertion; (3) development of social support; (4) critical thinking about gender; and (5) improvement of general self-esteem and sense of competence. [d]Ecology = number of elements: (1) changing attitudes and behaviors of parents, teachers, and other significant adults; (2) collective efforts to transform sociocultural influences (e.g., media); and (3) creating healthier values and norms in, for example, peers or community.

are present; in keeping with the DSP model, each is geared specifically to eating and to issues in weight and shape management: (a) nutrition and exercising for healthy weight control; (b) dangers of calorie-restrictive dieting; (c) individual strategies for analyzing and resisting fixed cultural factors, such as media and weight-related teasing; (d) the nature and dangers of eating disorders themselves; and (e) developmental factors, such as pubertal weight gain, in the context of a culture that idealizes thinness and vilifies fat and fat people.

The nonspecific vulnerability-stressor (NSVS) model focuses on the well-established, general relationship between various forms of psychopathology and increased life stress, poor health, lack of coping skills, and lack of social support (Albee & Gullotta, 1997). Consequently, Table 12.1 also rates how many of the following elements of the NSVS model the program contains: (a) nutrition and exercising as part of a healthier, more vigorous lifestyle (vs. for weight management); (b) life skills, such as relaxation, assertion, and decision making; (c) critical thinking about the meaning and social construction of gender; and (d) improvement of the participants' general self-esteem and sense of competence (Shisslak, Crago, Renger, & Clark-Wagner, 1998). Finally, to evaluate the application of an ecological perspective (Neumark-Sztainer, 1996; Perry, 1999; Smolak, 1999), Table 12.1 rates how many of the following elements are present: (a) changing the attitudes and behaviors of parents, teachers, or significant adults in the lives of students; (b) collective efforts to transform negative sociocultural influences, such as media; and (c) emphasis on creating new, healthier norms and values (Levine, Piran, & Stoddard, 1999; Piran, 1999a, 1999b, in press).

Although Table 12.1 simplifies prevention effects to an extreme, it is important to acknowledge the sheer complexity of prevention outcomes. For example, O'Dea and Abraham (2000) evaluated a nine-lesson program ("Everybody's Different") that used group-oriented, cooperative activities to foster a positive body image and to promote life skills in young adolescent boys and girls. At posttest, body satisfaction increased for boys and for girls. For girls, there was also a true pre-to-post prevention effect: The number in the experimental group currently trying to lose weight rose only 2% compared with 8% in the control group. However, there were no significant changes in the Eating Disorders Inventory–Drive for Thinness, and the relative improvement in body satisfaction dissipated at the 12-month follow-up. Moreover and more troubling, there was a significant pre-to-follow-up increase of 9% in the number of girls in the intervention group trying to lose weight, whereas the comparable figure for the control group was 6% (a nonsignificant increase). With this important caveat in mind, Table 12.1 suggests a number of conclusions about the current state of affairs in the prevention of disordered eating, which we discuss below.

Universal Prevention Affects More Than Just Knowledge

Recent researchers are not particularly interested in the acquisition of knowledge, although five of the seven universal prevention programs that measured change in knowledge reported statistically significant long-term increases. In contrast to the often-heard contention that knowledge is all that can be modestly increased by such programs, Table 12.1 indicates that it is possible to improve healthy attitudes (and reduce unhealthy attitudes) over periods between 3 and 24 months. There was at least one significant attitudinal effect in 9 of the 17 studies (53%).

However, long-term prevention effects pertaining to behavior remain an elusive accomplishment. Only 3 of the 15 universal studies (20%) that measured behavior reported positive behavioral effects: Smolak and Levine (in press; 24 months); Santonastaso et al. (1999; 12 months); and Celio et al. (2000; 6 months). Moreover, in Celio et al.'s study, the effect was greatest for participants identified post hoc as high risk. Several well-crafted programs produced significant improvements over the pre-to-posttest period, which then dissipated over the follow-up period (McVey & Davis, 1998; Neumark-Sztainer, Butler, & Palti, 1995; Stewart, Carter, Drinkwater, Hainsworth, & Fairburn, in press).

Mainstream Prevention Research Provides Reasons for Optimism

Several researchers (e.g., Stice, Chase, et al., in press; Stice et al., 2000) have vocally chosen to concentrate on high-risk groups because they see little evidence that universal prevention works. Although Table 12.1 offers some justification for this perspective, this conclusion is too pessimistic because it ignores not only the successful studies (e.g., Santonastaso et al., 1999; Smolak & Levine, in press) but also a large body of research on the successful prevention of a variety of problems (Albee & Gullotta, 1997; Durlak, 1997; Perry, 1999). Durlak and Wells (1997) conducted a meta-analysis of 177 prevention studies published before 1992. Each was controlled and "directed primarily at children's and adolescents' behavioral and social functioning" (p. 120). Effect sizes ranged from −0.45 to 2.36, with a mean of .34. Durlak and Wells (1997) found that "the average participant in a primary prevention program surpasses the performance of 59–82% of those in a control group" (p. 137).

Drug use, like the continuum of disordered eating, is a health issue that is widespread, serious, and embedded in deeply held and ambivalent cultural values concerning gender, control, and indulgence. The Life Skills Training Program (LST; Botvin, 1996) combines three basic elements of successful curricular drug abuse prevention: (a) skills to resist social and cultural inducements to use tobacco and other drugs, (b) skills to resist the false normative expectancy that "everybody is doing it," and (c) development of effective communication, problem solving, and other behaviors emphasized in the NSVS model. A 6-year follow-up of nearly 4,500 students clearly demonstrated LST's efficacy in preventing the initiation of drug use (Dusenbury & Falco, 1997). Attempts to change norms have long been a standard feature of substance use prevention programs, but only recently have eating disorder prevention programs focused on changing peer and family expectations for weight and shape concerns, dieting, and teasing. As seen in Table 12.1, these programs have produced encouraging results (Neumark-Sztainer, Sherwood, Coller, & Hannan, 1999; O'Dea & Abraham, 2000; Smolak & Levine, in press; see also Piran, 1999a).

Prevention Requires Multidimensional Changes in the Ecology of Participants

Sociocultural factors help establish and reinforce the values, beliefs, and behaviors that constitute disordered eating (Stice, chapter 3, this volume; J. K. Thompson, Heinberg, Altabe, & Tantleff-Dunn, 1999). A number of successful or partially successful programs have attempted to change the values and practices of peers, parents, or other adults (Neumark-Sztainer et al., 1999; O'Dea & Abraham, 2000; Smolak & Levine, in press). Still, it is odd that although theorists have long advocated the need to work simultaneously with families, peers, and media (Piran, 1995; Smolak & Levine, 1994), none of the studies reviewed in Table 12.1 (with the possible exceptions of Neumark-Sztainer et al., 1999; and Smolak & Levine, in press) did this in any depth. Piran's participatory-relational approach, discussed at length later, emphasizes ecological intervention and has been very successful (Piran, 1999a, 1999b, in press).

Changing the multiple environments that influence healthy and unhealthy behavior is, in fact, another prominent current in the mainstream of prevention. For example, the Social Competence Promotion Program for Young Adolescents (SCPP–YA; Weissberg, Barton, & Shriver, 1997) blends 27 sessions of instruction in life skills oriented toward social problem solving (e.g., decision making, effective communication) with a 9-session substance abuse module (e.g., resistance skills) and a 9-session module on AIDS and pregnancy prevention. Engaging, action-oriented classroom lessons, designed to make social competence the norm, are systematically reinforced by (a) training teachers to model problem solving in their daily behavior and as they implement the curriculum, (b) working with parents, and (c) implementing systemwide changes in the policies and practices of the school and the broader community. Compared with controls, students participating in the SCPP–YA have improved problem-solving skills, better relationships with peers, and fewer conduct problems, and they are less inclined to use alcohol and other drugs (Weissberg et al., 1997).

These findings strongly suggest that the prevention of disordered eating will be facilitated when lesson plans designed to change norms (e.g., toward acceptance of diversity in weight and shape) are integrated with daily lessons in the classroom and with efforts to change the behavior of teachers, the policies of the staff, and the environments of the school and community.

More Attention Needs To Be Paid to the Construct Validity of Primary Prevention

Eating disorder prevention researchers need to follow the lead of mainstream prevention researchers in articulating the relationship among theory, program development, and evaluation methodology (Perry, 1999). At a minimum, prevention programs should strive for the following (for more details, see Perry, 1999; and Valente & Dodge, 1997; for good examples in the eating disorders field, see Killen et al., 1993; Neumark-Stzainer et al., 1999; Stice, Chase, et al., in press; and Stice et al., 2000):

1. *Precision in theory and program definition:* Researchers should specify how their model of prevention guides development of program elements and the processes of learning and environmental change. The program should be clear in distinguishing its participants, its objectives, and its programs in terms of universal, selective, or indicated prevention.
2. *Randomization:* Randomization prior to program implementation guarantees that control groups are comparable with the experimental group, especially in regard to willingness to participate.
3. *Fidelity:* Steps should be taken to ensure that the program has been implemented as planned by the agents of change, whether they are professionals, teachers, peers, parents, or others.
4. *Psychometrics:* Changes in knowledge, attitudes, motives, behavior, and environments should be assessed with reliable and valid instruments.
5. *Necessary proximal changes:* Prevention involves reducing risk factors and increasing resilience factors. Consequently, over the period of the program (i.e., from pretest to posttest or extending to some reasonable period beyond), researchers need to determine whether this indeed happens, in relation to both baseline levels and the control condition.

6. *Sufficient follow-up and true prevention*: Researchers need to assess whether the experimental group, in comparison with the control group, has either a lower incidence of the problem (rate of new "cases") or better health status on the continuum of disordered eating. This follow-up assessment should be conducted at a point well along in the period of risk (e.g., ages 18–20 if the prevention program targets girls ages 12–14).

Selected or Targeted Prevention Is Recommended

The empirical and theoretical foundations of universal prevention programs in no way diminish the demonstrated value of selective or indicated prevention programs for reducing unhealthy attitudes and behaviors over the short follow-up periods applied thus far (see Table 12.1). The type of program that has been effective is diverse, including structured psychoeducational groups with cognitive–behavior training (Kaminski & McNamara, 1996; Olmsted et al., 1999), counterattitudinal role playing and discussion to develop materials ostensibly designed to help younger adolescents resist the slender ideal (Stice, Chase, et al., in press; Stice et al., 2000), and an interactive computer program that combines psychoeducation and anonymous bulletin board discussion (Zabinski et al., in press).

The Potential Contribution of Participatory Ecological Approaches Should Be Recognized

Participatory ecological approaches to universal health promotion differ from structured, top-down preventative programs in their emphasis on dialogical processes, context-specific understanding and solutions, systemic interventions and social transformations, empowerment and activism, and the reliance on a matrix of relationships for change. For example, the World Health Organization's model of a "Health Promoting School" (O'Dea & Maloney, 2000) describes the development of context-specific, school-based programs through a participatory process of dialogue with all stakeholders, including parents, teachers, school administration, students, health professionals, and other community members.

Dialogical, Context-Specific Emphasis

Most risk factor research follows large-scale positivistic paradigms that ignore variables, such as ethnocultural or racial group membership, socioeconomic status, or gender. Experts then use these studies to construct prevention programs that are expected to be universally applied (Piran, 1995). However, critics (e.g., Gerstein & Green, 1993) have questioned the "robustness" of prevention or health promotion programs across varied social contexts. For example, it has been recognized that gender is an important social variable to attend to in the construction of widely applied prevention programs for smoking or AIDS (Greaves, 1996). It has also been demonstrated that an understanding of the impact of contextual variables on health-related target behaviors best emerges from qualitative inquiries into the meaning of particular behaviors directed at individuals from varied cultural contexts (see, e.g., Greaves, 1996, for the prevention of smoking among women; Anderson, Blue, & Lau, 1991, for health maintenance among diabetic women; and Gerstein & Green, 1993, in the area of substance abuse). These inquiries can inform health promotion work at all levels, and they can also guide larger scale quantitative risk factor research.

Within the field of eating disorders, both "universal" and "context-specific" approaches to risk factor research and to prevention programs have been represented. For example, pressures for thinness and weight concerns have been examined in different large-scale positivistic studies (see Stice, chapter 3, this volume), whereas the impact of sexual harassment, racism, or poverty on the social construction of women's bodies and body images has been explored through qualitative paradigms (see, e.g., Larkin, Rice, & Russell, 1999; Piran, 1999a, in press; B. Thompson, 1994). Most prevention programs to date rely exclusively on positivist risk factor studies (Piran, 1995).

Participatory approaches incorporate participants' experienced-based knowledge into the content and process of prevention and hence tend to be more context specific (Piran, 1995, 1999a, in press). Inviting members of a school community to examine their own understanding of body weight and shape preoccupation in the school generates new knowledge that is anchored in students' daily life experiences and that can produce context-specific solutions. Piran (1999a, in press) invited girls and young women ages 10–18 years attending an elite coed dance school to examine in focus groups their own body weight and shape preoccupation. This process of inquiry led to a complex understanding of the social experience of living in a young woman's body. This knowledge highlighted the adverse impact on body image of (a) disruptions in girls' and young women's sense of respectful ownership of their bodies, (b) people's use of the female body as a site for expression of sexism and racism as well as weightism, and (c) the constricting effects of stereotypical images of femininity on body image. These three dimensions were experienced by the girls and young women as related to issues of social equity and power. Their emergent understanding was strikingly divergent from, and much more complex than, the exclusive "pressures-for-thinness" factor that was hypothesized, in a positivistic quasi-experimental study conducted earlier in the same dance school (Garfinkel

& Garner, 1982), to account for that school's high prevalence rate of eating disorders.

Piran (1999b, in press) found that disruptive (negative) and protective (positive) processes related to body image may vary greatly between schools. In one school, sexual harassment and other violations of girls' sense of ownership of their bodies were experienced as overwhelming and devastating by girls going through puberty; this awareness guided participants and their mentors to request and implement schoolwide antiharassment policies and staffing changes. In another school, extreme pressures created by intense academic competition resulted in girls feeling out of place and self-conscious because of repeated disparaging comments about their female bodies. This necessitated clarification of sexist prejudice and establishment of more constructive peer norms. In yet a third school, racial issues had to be addressed because they contributed to disordered eating among minority group members of the school community. This intense process—combining dialogue, enhanced communication between all stakeholders of the school community, and shared endeavors toward change—benefits the school as a whole, beyond the stated issues of body image.

Transformation of Social Environments

Our literature review highlights the often-neglected importance of multidimensional changes in the ecology of program participants. Participatory approaches to prevention allow for fuller and more context-specific alterations of social environments. Although adult experts may suggest particular plans for environmental changes, program participants themselves guide desirable transformations in their particular social environments by identifying the most relevant disruptive and protective conditions. Students in the residential dance school study (Piran, 1999a, in press) worked toward and requested changes in the following domains of school life: young women's peer norms; cross-gender peer norms; student–staff behavior norms; schoolwide policies and norms; and the curriculum, staffing, and the physical environment of the school. These changes created a safer and more equitable social subsystem that respected students' experiences in the body domain. These systemic changes have allowed for maintenance of gains over time with limited facilitator involvement (Piran, 1999a, 1999b).

As a general principle, Piran (1999c) found it advisable to conduct educational and dialogical forums with teachers, coaches, and parents before intervening with students. These discussions convey important information about body image and adolescent development, help adults to examine their own prejudices and experiences in the body domain, and identify challenging and protective aspects of that particular school system. Parents may be more open to educational discussions that focus on the healthy development of body and self-image than to presentations about eating disorders. These sessions enable adults to respond in a more constructive and open manner when approached by students about challenges in the area of body image. In turn, constructive responses by adults enhance further communication and suggestions by students. Thus, in participatory projects, parents and other adults are enlisted as informative and active partners in the process of change.

Piran (1999c) found that teachers' strong weightist attitudes were reduced following participation in a day-long workshop about body image development. In that school, teachers themselves felt vulnerable to pervasive weightist attitudes and disclosed their occasional tendency to transmit these values to the students. These shared discoveries started a shift toward the creation of a more constructive environment for teachers themselves and greater awareness on their part about norms conveyed to their students. On the basis of their experiences inside and outside the classroom, students in a participatory prevention program may now approach staff directly about expressions of weightist or sexist attitudes that students feel are hurting their body image and self-image.

Examination and alteration of peer group norms comprise another important area for contextual change (Piran, 1999b, 1999c; see also Piran et al., 1999). Students involved in participatory projects were found to first focus on and repair unhealthy peer norms regarding body and self-image, before uniting to address adverse issues outside of their peers (Piran, 1999a, 1999b, in press). These norms include sexist, racist, or harassing behaviors; teasing about body shape; or colluding with restrictive images of women and men. In line with Smolak's (1999) suggestions about working on normative peer issues at the elementary school level, Piran found that establishing constructive peer group norms during Grades 3 to 5, prior to the onset of puberty, has a powerful effect. Peer-level interventions continue to be an important target of contextual interventions throughout and following puberty.

Literacy and Activism

The information gathered (constructed) in participatory approaches to prevention is subject to critical contextual analysis by participants, who then derive a critical "theory" or understanding of social and economic factors that affect their experience (Freire, 1981). This emergent understanding leads to action through strategic group planning for mobilizing support, communicating key messages, and advocating for change. This process involves multiple interpersonal, communication, and advocacy skills, so implementation of successful changes enhances participants' competence ("life skills") in various areas and their experience of their social power. Examining events that caused their weight and shape dissatisfaction, students in the dance school arrived at a critical understanding that led to actions that transformed all facets of the school environment, including acceptable norms, policies, training, staffing, and the physical environment. This process of dialogue, reflection, and action transforms the body from an untrustworthy container of private hungers and anxieties into a site of collective and personal knowledge power—a foundation for multiple constructive actions (Freire, 1981; Piran, in press).

Empowering participatory processes can occur in the context of programs that develop particular skills, such as media literacy. The "Five As" of media literacy (Levine & Smolak, in press) refer to an expanding cycle of *awareness* of media use; *analysis* of media content and motives pertaining to entertainment, business, and politics; *activism* (e.g., praise or protest communicated to advertisers and other businesses); *advocacy* (based on use if not exploitation of the media) of healthy alternative messages (e.g., size acceptance); and an understanding, through participation, of who has *access* to mass media and how this is obtained. Ideally, this collaborative process produces more critical knowledge and a greater sense that citizens in a democracy have the power to understand their lives, envision healthier alternatives, and take collective action to change "sociocultural factors." Studies of brief programs that encourage media awareness, media analysis, and critical resistance of unhealthy messages have produced promising improvements in media knowledge, media skepticism, and internalization of the thin standard of beauty in high school students (see Levine et al., 1999, for a review).

Relational Contexts of Change

Given that experience-based knowledge, activism, and change occur within the context of interpersonal relationships, addressing experiences in the body domain may be particularly demanding. According to social critics such as Foucault (1979), the body reflects and expresses one's power and privilege in a particular society. The unconscious nature of this process requires that the construction of embodied knowledge take place in a supportive, validating, and amplifying context, similar to the process of consciousness raising in groups, as described by MacKinnon (1989): "Consciousness raising socializes women's knowing and thus transforms it, creating a shared reality that clears a space in the world within which women can begin to move in a substantial, embodied way" (p. 101).

The domains of the body (e.g., appearance, sexuality, anger, hunger) have been particularly problematic experiences for women. Unchanged rates of sexual harassment, use of women's bodies as commodities, and pressures for extreme thinness are just a few of the diverse, multiple, and interlocking expressions that oppress women as they experience and define their bodies (see Smolak & Murnen, chapter 5, this volume). Within the context of new social and physical opportunities for young women in Western countries (e.g., athletics), the body remains a territory that "weighs" women down and a central target for constraining women's progress (Bordo, 1993). For young women, the great disparity between new opportunities for economic and social equity versus unchanged inequity in the body domain may be particularly poignant and toxic (Silverstein & Perlick, 1995). The deepening of relationships, and therefore the dialogues, among young women and between young women and adult facilitators helps to clarify problematic experiences involving the body and body image (Piran, 1999b, in press). The ultimate effect of this process of connection and communication is a deepening of critical consciousness about sociocultural determinants of negative body image, shame, anxiety, and so forth. This constitutes a major way in which strong relational groups allow for activism and change. Forming supportive peer group norms around body-anchored experiences may afford young women the power to demand change in particular aspects of a school environment (Piran, 1999a, 1999b). This process is enhanced when adults committed to the same causes provide supportive connections and important role modeling (Shisslak et al., 1998).

CONCLUSION

Our literature review and our personal experiences in prevention leave us confident and optimistic about several conclusions. First, prevention of eating disorders is possible, and it is not a luxury waiting for refinement of the treatment or full clarification of etiology. Second, classroom instruction is limited in its power to effect meaningful, long-term changes, but this does not mean that selective or indicated prevention is the only or even the best answer. Rather, classroom "lessons," whether they be top down (Smolak & Levine, in press) or constructed by students (O'Dea & Abraham, 2000), need to be combined with participatory, ecological programs designed to change (a) the behavior of teachers, parents, and other adults and (b) the policies, values, and norms operating within the school system and within larger communities and cultures. Third, the passion, knowledge, and skills of experts must be blended with participatory approaches that nurture reflection, dialogue, critical analysis, and activism by students, parents, and other community members. Fourth, gender and the inscribed body, as well as race, class, and weight prejudice, need to be a focus of this developmental sequence. Finally, the larger field of prevention and health promotion, embodied in the work of scholars such as Cowen (1997), Durlak (1997), and Perry (1999), must be brought into the dialogue among specialists in the prevention of eating disorders. Recent media literacy work by Neumark-Sztainer et al. (1999) with Girl Scout troops and their leaders and by Levine et al. (1999) offer a glimpse of what an effective blend of approaches and research strategies might look like.

REFERENCES

Albee, G. W., & Gullotta, T. P. (1997). Primary prevention's evolution. In G. W. Albee & T. P. Gullotta (Eds.), *Primary prevention works* (pp. 3–22). Thousand Oaks, CA: Sage.

Anderson, J. M., Blue, C., & Lau, A. (1991). Women's perspectives on chronic illness: Ethnicity, ideology and restructuring of life. *Social Science and Medicine, 33,* 101–113.

Bordo, S. (1993). *Unbearable weight: Feminism, Western culture, and the body.* Berkeley: University of California Press.

Botvin, G. J. (1996). Substance abuse prevention through Life Skills Training. In R. D. Peters & R. J. McMahon (Eds.), *Preventing childhood disorders, substance abuse, and delinquency* (pp. 215–240). Thousand Oaks, CA: Sage.

Carter, J., Stewart, D., Dunn, V., & Fairburn, C. (1997). Primary prevention of eating disorders: Might it do more harm than good? *International Journal of Eating Disorders, 22,* 167–173.

Celio, A. A., Winzelberg, A. J., Wilfley, D. E., Eppstein, D., Springer, E. A., Dev, P., & Taylor, C. B. (2000). Reducing risk factors for eating disorders: Comparison of an Internet- and a classroom-delivered psychoeducation program. *Journal of Clinical and Consulting Psychology, 68,* 650–657.

Cowen, E. L. (1997). On the semantics and operations of primary prevention and wellness enhancement (or will the real primary prevention please stand up?). *American Journal of Community Psychology, 25,* 245–255.

Durlak, J. A. (1997). *Successful prevention programs for children and adolescents.* New York: Plenum Press.

Durlak, J. A., & Wells, A. M. (1997). Primary prevention mental health programs for children and adolescents: A meta-analytic review. *American Journal of Community Psychology, 25,* 115–152.

Dusenbury, L., & Falco, M. (1997). School-based drug abuse prevention strategies: From research to policy and practice. In R. P. Weissburg, T. P. Gullotta, R. L. Hampton, B. A. Ryan, & G. R. Adams (Eds.), *Healthy Children 2010: Enhancing children's wellness* (pp. 47–75). Thousand Oaks, CA: Sage.

Foucault, M. (1979). *Discipline and punish.* New York: Vintage Books.

Franko, D. L., & Orosan-Weine, P. (1998). The prevention of eating disorders: Empirical, methodological and conceptual considerations. *Clinical Psychology: Science and Practice, 5,* 459–477.

Freire, P. (1981). *Pedagogy of the oppressed* (M. B. Ramos, Trans.). New York: Continuum.

Garfinkel, P., & Garner, D. M. (1982). *Anorexia nervosa: A multidimensional perspective*. New York: Brunner/Mazel.

Gerstein, D. R., & Green, L. W. (1993). *Preventing drug abuse: What do we know?* Washington, DC: National Academy Press.

Greaves, L. (1996). *Smokescreen: Women's smoking and social control*. Halifax, Nova Scotia, Canada: Fernwood Press.

Kaminski, P. L., & McNamara, K. (1996). A treatment for college women at risk for bulimia: A controlled evaluation. *Journal of Counseling and Development, 74*, 288–294.

Killen, J. D., Taylor, C. B., Hammer, L. D., Litt, I., Wilson, D. M., Rich, T., Hayward, C., Simmonds, B., Kraemer, H., & Varady, A. (1993). An attempt to modify unhealthful eating attitudes and weight regulation practices of young adolescent girls. *International Journal of Eating Disorders, 13*, 369–384.

Larkin, J., Rice, C., & Russell, V. (1999). Sexual harassment and the prevention of eating disorders: Educating young women. In N. Piran, M. P. Levine, & C. Steiner-Adair (Eds.), *Preventing eating disorders: A handbook of interventions and special challenges* (pp. 194–207). Philadelphia: Brunner/Mazel.

Levine, M. P., Piran, N., & Stoddard, C. (1999). Mission more probable: Media literacy, activism, and advocacy as primary prevention. In N. Piran, M. P. Levine, & C. Steiner-Adair (Eds.), *Preventing eating disorders: A handbook of interventions and special challenges* (pp. 3–25). Philadelphia: Brunner/Mazel.

Levine, M. P., & Smolak, L. (in press). Primary prevention of body image disturbance and disordered eating in childhood and adolescence. In J. K. Thompson & L. Smolak (Eds.), *Body image, eating disorders, and obesity in youth*. Washington, DC: American Psychological Association.

MacKinnon, C. (1989). *Towards a feminist theory of the state*. Cambridge, MA: Harvard University Press.

Mann, T., Nolen-Hoeksema, S., Huang, K., Burgard, D., Wright, A., & Hanson, K. (1997). Are two interventions worse than none? Joint primary and secondary prevention of eating disorders in college females. *Health Psychology, 16*, 1–11.

McVey, G., Davis, R., & Shaw, B. F. (1999, April). *Primary prevention of eating disorders: Preliminary findings of a program which targets Grade 6 girls and their parents*. Paper presented at the biennial meeting of the Society for Research in Child Development, Albuquerque, NM.

McVey, G., & Davis, R. (1998). *A long-term controlled evaluation of an elementary school prevention program for eating problems*. Unpublished manuscript, Department of Psychology, Hospital for Sick Children, Toronto, Ontario, Canada.

Moreno, A. B., & Thelen, M. H. (1993). A preliminary prevention program for eating disorders in a junior high school population. *Journal of Youth and Adolescence, 22*, 109–124.

Mrazek, P. J., & Haggerty, R. J. (Eds.). (1994). *Reducing risks for mental disorders: Frontiers for preventive intervention research*. Washington, DC: National Academy Press.

Neumark-Sztainer, D. (1996). School-based programs for preventing eating disturbances. *Journal of School Health, 66*(2), 64–71.

Neumark-Sztainer, D., Butler, R., & Palti, H. (1995). Eating disturbances among adolescent girls: Evaluation of a school-based primary prevention program. *Journal of Nutrition Education, 27*(1), 24–30.

Neumark-Sztainer, D., Sherwood, N., Coller, T., & Hannan, P. J. (1999). *Promoting media literacy and advocacy skills: A community-based intervention to enhance body acceptance and prevent unhealthy weight control behaviors among preadolescent girls*. Manuscript submitted for publication, University of Minnesota, Minneapolis.

O'Dea, J., & Abraham, S. (2000). Improving the body image, eating attitudes and behaviors of young and behaviors of young male and female adolescents: A new educational approach which focuses on self esteem. *International Journal of Eating Disorders, 28*, 437–457.

O'Dea, J., & Maloney, D. (2000). Preventing eating and body image problems in children and adolescents using the Health Promoting Schools Framework. *Journal of School Health, 70*, 18–21.

Olmsted, M. P., Daneman, D., Rydall, A. C., Lawson, M. L., & Rodin, G. M. (1999). *The effects of psychoeducation on disturbed eating attitudes and behaviors in young women with Type 1 diabetes mellitus*. Manuscript submitted for publication, Department of Psychiatry, Toronto General Hospital, Toronto, Ontario, Canada.

Outwater, A. D. (1991). An intervention project to improve body image and self-esteem in 6th-grade boys and girls as a potential prevention against eating disorders (Doctoral dissertation, The Union Institute, 1990). *Dissertation Abstracts International, 51*, 4029.

Paxton, S. J. (1993). A prevention program for disturbed eating and body dissatisfaction in adolescent girls: A 1 year follow-up. *Health Education Research: Theory and Practice, 8*, 43–51.

Perry, C. L. (1999). *Creating health behavior change: How to develop community-wide programs for youth*. Thousand Oaks, CA: Sage.

Piran, N. (1995). Prevention: Can early lessons lead to a delineation of an alternative model? A critical look at prevention with schoolchildren. *Eating Disorders: Journal of Treatment and Prevention, 3*(1), 28–36.

Piran, N. (1999a). Eating disorders: A trial of prevention in a high risk school setting. *Journal of Primary Prevention, 20*, 75–90.

Piran, N. (1999b). The reduction of preoccupation with body weight and shape in schools: A feminist approach. In N. Piran, M. P. Levine, & C. Steiner-Adair (Eds.), *Preventing eating disorders: A handbook of interventions and special challenges* (pp. 148–159). Philadelphia: Brunner/Mazel.

Piran, N. (1999c, February). *The whole-school approach to the prevention of eating disorders*. Paper presented at the Second Annual Conference for Educators, Harvard Eating Disorders Center, Boston.

Piran, N. (in press). Re-inhabiting the body from the inside out: Girls transform their school environment. In D. L. Tolman & M. Brydon-Miller (Eds.), *Transforming psychology: Interpretive and participatory research methods*. New York: New York University Press.

Piran, N., Levine, M. P., & Steiner-Adair, C. (Eds.). (1999). *Preventing eating disorders: A handbook of interventions and special challenges*. Philadelphia: Brunner/Mazel.

Santonastaso, P., Zanetti, T., Ferrara, S., Olivetto, M. C., Magnavita, N., & Favaro, A. (1999). A preventive intervention program in adolescent schoolgirls: A longitudinal study. *Psychotherapy and Psychosomatics, 68*, 46–50.

Shisslak, C. M., Crago, M., Renger, R., & Clark-Wagner, A. (1998). Self-esteem and the prevention of eating disorders. *Eating Disorders: Journal of Treatment and Prevention, 6*, 105–117.

Silverstein, B., & Perlick, D. (1995). *The cost of competence: Why inequality causes depression, eating disorders, and illness in women*. New York: Oxford University Press.

Smolak, L. (1999). Elementary school curricula for the primary prevention of eating problems. In N. Piran, M. P. Levine, & C. Steiner-Adair (Eds.), *Preventing eating disorders: A handbook of interventions and special challenges* (pp. 85–104). Philadelphia: Brunner/Mazel.

Smolak, L., & Levine, M. P. (1994). Toward an empirical basis for primary prevention of eating problems with elementary school children. *Eating Disorders: Journal of Treatment and Prevention, 4*, 293–307.

Smolak, L., & Levine, M. P. (in press). A two-year follow-up of a primary prevention program for negative body image and unhealthy weight regulation. *Eating Disorders: The Journal of Treatment and Prevention*.

Stewart, D. A., Carter, J. C., Drinkwater, J., Hainsworth, J., & Fairburn, C. G. (in press). Modification of eating attitudes and behaviour in adolescent girls: A controlled study. *International Journal of Eating Disorders*.

Stice, E., Chase, A., Stormer, S., & Appel, A. (in press). A randomized trial of a dissonance-based eating disorder prevention program. *International Journal of Eating Disorders*.

Stice, E., Mazotti, L., Weibel, D., & Agras, W. S. (2000). Dissonance prevention program decreases thin-ideal internalization, body dissatisfaction, dieting, negative affect, and bulimic symptoms: A preliminary experiment. *International Journal of Eating Disorders, 27*, 206–217.

Thompson, B. (1994). *A hunger so wide and so deep*. Minneapolis: University of Minnesota Press.

Thompson, J. K., Heinberg, L., Altabe, M., & Tantleff-Dunn, S. (1999). *Exacting beauty: Theory, assessment, and treatment of body image disturbance*. Washington, DC: American Psychological Association.

Valente, E., Jr., & Dodge, K. A. (1997). Evaluation of prevention programs for children. In R. P. Weissburg, T. P. Gullotta, R. L. Hampton, B. A. Ryan, & G. R. Adams (Eds.), *Healthy Children 2010: Establishing preventive services* (pp. 183–218). Thousand Oaks, CA: Sage.

Weissberg, R. P., Barton, H. A., & Shriver, T. P. (1997). The social-competence promotion program for young adolescents. In G. W. Albee & T. P. Gullotta (Eds.), *Primary prevention works* (pp. 268–290). Thousand Oaks, CA: Sage.

Winzelberg, A. J., Eldredge, K. L., Wilfley, D., Eppstein, D., Dasmahapatra, R., Dev., P., & Taylor, C. B. (2000). Effectiveness of an Internet-based program for reducing risk factors for eating disorders. *Eating Disorders, 27,* 206–217.

Winzelberg, A. J., Taylor, C. B., Sharpe, T., Eldredge, K. L., Dev, P., & Constantinou, P. S. (1998). Evaluation of a computer-mediated eating disorder intervention program. *International Journal of Consulting and Clinical Psychology, 68,* 346–350.

Zabinski, M. F., Puung, M. A., Wilfley, D. E., Eppstein, D. L., Winzelberg, A. J., Celio, A., & Taylor, C. B. (in press). Reducing risk factors for eating disorders: Targeting at-risk women with a computerized psychoeducational program. *International Journal of Eating Disorders.*

13

THE USE OF INTERACTIVE MEDIA TO PREVENT EATING DISORDERS

C. BARR TAYLOR, ANDREW J. WINZELBERG, AND ANGELA A. CELIO

Within the next decade or so, interactive multimedia technology may help reduce the incidence of eating disorders. In this chapter, we present an overview of issues related to the use of interactive technology to reduce the incidence of eating disorders, discuss a series of studies evaluating one interactive approach, suggest how future changes in technology will enhance the effectiveness and availability of interactive programs, and provide a model that uses technology to integrate risk factor reduction with clinical treatment.

As used in this chapter, *interactive technology* refers to computer- and Internet-based multimedia systems that deliver computer-assisted psycho-educational programs (CAPP). Similar to live treatment, CAPP can be tailored to users' needs. Intervention programs can be used privately, providing an atmosphere of comfort and safety. CAPP can query for comprehension and repeat the presentation of information that may have been misunderstood. The computer also can protect the patient who is uncomfortable disclosing personal information, a particularly important feature in the treatment of disordered eating where secretiveness is a predominant feature. Like bibliotherapy and video training, CAPP can be used anytime, without scheduling problems; is inexpensive; can be used frequently; and can be inexpensively disseminated. Finally, interactive multimedia programs have become a part of U.S. culture. About 60% of homes in the United States now have computers, and most of these are or will be linked to the Internet.

The number of CAPP written and evaluated has increased dramatically since the advent of the low-cost personal computer. In a meta-analysis, Kulik and Kulik (1991) found that computer-assisted instruction is an effective method of education. The literature on the use of computer software by health care providers in the delivery of psychoeducational interventions is expanding and suggests that computers may be useful in this area. Several

255

controlled studies in clinical samples show, for instance, that computer-aided interventions can be effective in treating depression (Selmi, Klein, Greist, & Sorrell, 1990) and anxiety disorders (Newman, Consoli, & Taylor, 1997) and in helping with weight regulation (Taylor, Agras, Losch, & Plante, 1991) and a variety of medical problems (Gustafson et al., 1999; Lewis, 1999; Noell & Glasgow, 1999). Overall, however, few controlled long-term studies are available on this technology (Noell & Glasgow, 1999).

PRELIMINARY STUDIES DEMONSTRATE FEASIBILITY AND EFFECTIVENESS

To reduce the incidence of eating disorders, one must reduce the risk factors that are strong contributors to the onset of eating disorders. As reviewed elsewhere, numerous cross-sectional and clinical studies identify potential risk factors for eating disorders (e.g., Striegel-Moore, Silberstein, & Rodin, 1986). Excessive weight concerns, a drive for thinness, and related factors (e.g., poor body image) appear to be common risk factors across populations. More recently, longitudinal studies link excessive weight concerns with subclinical and clinical eating disorders. In our first longitudinal, prospective study, we followed a school-based sample of young adolescent girls (ages 11–12 years at baseline) for up to 3 years (Killen et al., 1994). Over the 3-year interval, 3.6% (32/887) of the sample became symptomatic. One factor, a measure developed for the study and identified as Weight Concerns, was significantly associated with symptom onset. In the course of follow-up, about 12% of the girls scoring in the highest quartile on the Weight Concerns measure became symptomatic compared with 2% of the girls in the lowest quartile. We replicated and extended these findings in a longitudinal, prospective study of 9th–10th-grade girls (ages 13–16 years at baseline) who were followed for up to 3 years (Killen et al., 1996). About 10% of girls in the upper quartile developed partial or full-syndrome eating disorders in the course of the follow-up, whereas no girls in the lowest quartile developed such disorders. Although a high Weight Concerns score is not the only risk factor for eating disorders, it is clearly an important one.

In our early prevention studies in college women, we decided to focus on body image, rather than weight or shape concerns, because we felt the former addressed a broader set of issues. In later studies, we shifted our focus to changes in weight or shape concerns because of the data from our prospective studies showing that high scores on weight–shape predict the onset of subclinical–clinical eating disorders (Killen et al., 1994, 1996). However, Weight Concerns is significantly correlated with other standard measures of eating disorder attitudes, such as the overall Eating Disorders Inventory (EDI; Killen et al., 1994), and with the Body Shape Questionnaire

(BSQ; Winzelberg et al., 2000). In unpublished data collected on 20 college-age women at an East Coast university participating in an eating disorders prevention class, weight concerns was significantly correlated ($r = .72$, $p < .000$) with body weight–shape concerns as measured by the self-report on the Eating Disorders Examination Questionnaire (EDE–Q). Thus, BSQ, EDI Weight Concerns, and the EDE–Q Weight/Shape subscales all measure a common factor.

With the help of Stanford University Medical Media and Information Technologies, a research group at Stanford University's Medical School has spent the past 5 years developing a program called *Student Bodies*. Four iterations of this program have been evaluated so far using a wait-list control group for comparison and using a 3- or 4-month follow-up (see Exhibit 13.1). In each iteration, the program lasted 8 weeks and had the primary goal of reducing body dissatisfaction and excessive weight concerns. The program draws strategies and concepts from "The Road to Recovery" program for bulimia (Davis et al., 1989), cognitive–behavior therapy exercises suggested by Cash (1991) for improving body image, Fairburn et al.'s work on binge eating (Fairburn & Carter, 1996; Fairburn et al., 1995), and prevention and healthy weight regulation guidelines by Taylor and Altman (1997) and Taylor et al. (1991). Each week, participants were expected to read a section of the program covering a variety of topics, such as nutrition, exercise, body image, and eating disorders; participate in a moderated on-line discussion group with other participants; and complete interactive or cognitive–behavior exercises. The structure of the program can be seen in Exhibit 13.1.

Study 1: Evaluation of *Student Bodies* (CD-ROM)

In the first study (Winzelberg et al., 1998), 57 Stanford women were recruited and randomized to use *Student Bodies* (CD-ROM version) with an electronic discussion group or no intervention (see Table 13.1). Both intervention and control groups exhibited a significant reduction in body dissatisfaction and eating disorder behaviors, and both groups maintained their weight. Compared with the control group, the intervention group demonstrated a significantly greater reduction in body dissatisfaction, even with no change in weight. The effect sizes of the intervention (adjusted for changes in the control group) were as follows: EDI Bulimia Scale = 0.27; EDI Drive for Thinness Scale = 0.29; EDE–Q Weight Scale = 0.48; EDE–Q Shape Scale = 0.51; and BSQ = 0.56.

Study 2: Evaluation of *Student Bodies* (Internet)

The program was revised on the basis of information obtained from Study 1 and was placed on an Internet server to improve access (Winzelberg

EXHIBIT 13.1
Outline of *Student Bodies* Assignments

Week	Mandatory assignments	Optional assignments
1	Beliefs about my body (BI)	Nutrition: Food myths
	Self-esteem (BI)	Nutrition basics and pyramids
	Body Image Survey (BI)	What are eating disorders? (ED)
	Getting a historical perspective:	Eating disorders: Are you at
	Exercise (BI)	risk? (ED)
	Body image journal (BI)	Sample student diary
	Common reactions to starting this	
	program	
	What to do if you have a technical	
	problem	
	Academic readings	
	Future assignments	
2	Cultural images of beauty (BI)	Causes of eating disorders (ED)
	Challenging negative thoughts (BI)	Dorm food (nutrition)
	Letter to my body: Exercise (BI)	Snaking (nutrition)
	Body image journal (BI)	Sample student diary
	Academic readings	
3	Changing how I feel about my body (BI)	Nutrition: Food myths, fat guide,
	Quick feel-good body tips (BI)	food cravings, and off-campus
	Exercise: Benefits and getting started	eating
	(exercise)	Am I overexercising? Survey
	One size does not fit all: Exercise (BI)	(exercise)
	Body image journal	Consequences and treatment of
	Academic readings	eating disorders (ED)
		Sample student diary
4	Developing an exercise program	Nutrition information and access
	(exercise)	to the entire nutritional menu
	Getting a perspective (BI)	Sample student diary
	My body in action: Exercise (BI)	
	Body image journal	
	Academic readings	
5	Monitoring my exercise journal	Nutrition information and access
	(exercise)	to the entire nutritional menu
	Diet mentality (nutrition)	
	Dealing with critical comments (BI)	
	Mirror, mirror: Exercise (BI)	
	Diet check: Survey (nutrition)	
	Body image journal (BI)	
	Academic readings	
6	Monitoring my exercise journal	
	(exercise)	
	Knowing when I'm full (nutrition)	
	Clothes make the woman: Exercise (BI)	
	Body image journal (BI)	
	Academic readings	

(continued)

EXHIBIT 13.1
(Continued)

Week	Mandatory assignments	Optional assignments
7	Body image journal (BI) Monitoring my exercise journal (exercise) Academic readings	Review of all body image exercises (BI)
8	Body image journal (BI) Body image quiz–survey (BI) Academic readings	

Note. BI = the focus is on body image; ED = the focus is on eating disorders; nutrition = the focus is on nutrition; exercise = the focus is on exercise.

et al., 2000). The content of the program remained the same as for the first pilot project, but the weight loss aspect of the program was deemphasized. Students were recruited through the same channels as in Study 1. Sixty-one students at a public California university were randomized to *Student Bodies* or to a no-treatment, wait-list control group (see Table 13.1). Students were evaluated pre- and postintervention (following 8 weeks of program use) and 3 months later. Adherence to the program was measured as the percentage of assigned screens viewed per week.

At follow-up, intervention participants, compared with control participants, reported a significant improvement in body image and a decrease in drive for thinness. The baseline to postintervention and baseline to follow-up effect sizes on BSQ for the intervention group were 0.4 and 0.7, respectively. Although these results were promising, the sample size was relatively small, the follow-up short, and mean adherence under 50% for the final 4 weeks of the program. We felt that the program could have been more effective if adherence had been increased.

Study 3: Comparison of *Student Bodies* With a Psychoeducational Class

The next study (Celio et al., 2000) was designed to enhance the outcome of the Internet-based intervention by increasing adherence through incentives (class grades) and adding a course reader (see Table 13.1). We were also interested in comparing an Internet-based program with a traditional class.

Participants were again female undergraduate students recruited primarily through fliers posted on campus advertising for a study to help women improve their body image. Participants were excluded if they were currently diagnosed with bulimia or anorexia (self-report) or had a body mass index

TABLE 13.1

Evolution of the *Student Bodies* (SB) Program and Intervention

Program variable	Study 1	Study 2	Study 3	Study 4
Time period	All of 1995	January–March 1997	April–June 1998	April–June 1998
Institution	University A	University B	University B	University A
No. of participants (SB, control)	27, 30	31, 30	31, 31	27, 24
Participants	High-weight concern	High-weight concern	High risk (BSQ score = 110+)	High-weight concern
Software	CD-ROM	Web	Web	Web
Newsgroup	Email list	Web newsgroup	Web newsgroup	Web newsgroup
Interface	On-line and floppy disk	On-line only	On-line only	On-line, readings, meetings, written reflections
Intervention	"Grazing" approach	Recommendations	Structured with requirements	Structured with requirements
Newsgroup moderator	Clinical psychologist	Graduate student	Graduate student	Master's student
Privacy	Anonymity	Anonymity	Anonymity	Profile on the Web; group meetings
Personal contact	None	None	None	Three group meetings
Approach	CBT-guided self-help	CBT-guided self-help	CBT-guided self-help	CBT-guided self-help and academic
Reminders	None	Phone	Phone	Email
Payment	$10	$25	$25	Course credit

Note. BSQ = Body Shape Questionnaire; CBT = cognitive–behavior therapy.

(BMI) < 18. Participants were randomly assigned to one of three groups: *Student Bodies* (Internet program), *Body Traps* (psychoeducational class), or wait-list control. Participants were offered 2 units of ungraded academic credit contingent on the completion of the program requirements.

To enhance group cohesion and familiarity with the other group members participating in the moderated discussion group, participants had a link to "profiles" of each of the group members. Each profile comprised a photograph of the participant and a personal statement introducing herself and stating her personal goals for the program. Face-to-face sessions, lasting 1–2 hours, were held during the 1st, 2nd, and 6th week of the intervention. These meetings were used to orient the participants to the program and to enhance the group's cohesion. Face-to-face sessions were led by a moderator, who ensured proper use of the on-line discussion group, facilitated discussion, and addressed any problems participants had with the software. Each week participants were also required to read one article from the *Body Traps* course reader (Springer, Winzelberg, Perkins, & Taylor, 1999) and to write a 1-page critical reflection paper on a reading of their choice. These papers were sent via email to the moderator.

During the treatment phase (baseline to posttest), significant group differences were found for the EDE–Q Weight/Shape subscale and the EDI Drive-for-Thinness subscale, all favoring the *Student Bodies* over the wait-list control group. From baseline to follow-up, significant group differences were found for the EDE–Q Weight/Shape subscale, EDE–Q Eating Concerns, EDE–Q Restraint, and EDI Drive-for-Thinness, with all post hoc analyses favoring the *Student Bodies* group. Intention-to-treat analyses produced similar results. (There were no significant differences between the *Body Traps* and the *Student Bodies* or the wait-list control group.)

On average, the *Student Bodies* participants read 71% of the assigned on-line screens and posted 64% of the required discussion group messages. Compliance with the discussion group was higher in the early weeks of the program, with postings becoming less frequent over time. Overall, the discussion group was used frequently, with participants posting an average of about two messages each week. On average, participants submitted 74% of the required written reflections and attended 63% of the face-to-face sessions. The effect sizes of the *Student Bodies* group, compared with the control group ranged from 0.28 to 0.76 from baseline to posttest and from 0.21 to 0.76 from baseline to follow-up, depending on the measure.

At posttest, participants in the *Student Bodies* group reported receiving a moderate amount of social support from the other members in their group. Computer-generated logs of participants' interactions with the *Student Bodies* program showed that participants tended to log on to the program most often between the hours of 6 p.m. and 7 p.m. A surprising number of log ons occurred between 10 p.m. and 3 a.m.

Study 4: Effect of *Student Bodies* on Students With High BSQ Scores

We next examined the effects of *Student Bodies* on students with high BSQ scores (see Table 13.1; Zabinski et al., in press). Fifty-six college women were recruited on the basis of BSQ scores > 110. We chose this BSQ score on the basis of studies that suggest that individuals with probable bulimia score $M = 129 \pm 17$ compared with the mean for college students without eating disorders who score around 72 ± 23 (Cooper, Taylor, Cooper, & Fairburn, 1987). Students were then randomized to the *Student Bodies* or the no-treatment control group. All participants improved over time on most measures, and there were no significant differences between the two groups. However, effect sizes suggested that *Student Bodies* participants experienced greater reduction in excessive concerns with weight and shape, as measured by the EDE–Q, and a reduction of disordered eating behaviors and attitudes as measured by the EDI.

Study 5: Evaluation of a Synchronous, On-Line-Moderated Discussion Group

Student Bodies is designed for students who do not meet the criteria for clinical or subclinical eating disorders. In our study, we decided to examine an Internet-based intervention designed to reduce eating disorder symptoms and attitudes in students with subclinical eating disorders but who are not in need of traditional clinical treatment. In this small pilot study, 4 students who did not meet criteria for a clinical eating disorder but had some clinical features of bulimia participated only in a 6-week synchronous on-line-moderated discussion group. (Note that *Student Bodies* uses an *asynchronous* group, meaning students can participate in the group whenever they wish. Also this study did not use the *Student Bodies* program, so it is not included in Table 13.1.) The participants were enthusiastic about the group and reported improvement in their attitudes toward weight or shape (Zabinski et al., 1999). The next step is to evaluate the effectiveness of this discussion group in a controlled study.

All of these studies are limited by small sample size and short-term follow-up. However, we believe that our studies demonstrate that college students are interested in programs that address body image concerns. Multimedia programs combined with electronic discussion groups can reduce potential risk factors for eating disorders. The intervention was most effective for students with very high scores on a measure of weight or shape concerns in two of the studies (Celio et al., 2000; Winzelberg et al., 2000), although in a third study the control group high-risk students improved as much as did the intervention students on many measures. Synchronous discussion groups may enhance the effect for students with subclinical eating disorders.

Our optimistic projection that interactive technology will help reduce the incidence of eating disorders is predicated on the assumptions that the risk factors for eating disorders can be identified, that these risk factors can be modified, and that modification of risk factors can lead to a reduction in the incidence of the disorders. Our work focuses on one set of risk factors (excessive weight or shape concerns), but many other risk factors—and protective factors—have been identified that may prove equally or more important.

THE FUTURE OF TECHNOLOGY

In this section, we speculate on how changes in Internet-connected technology might affect interactive programs to prevent eating disorders over the next year or so. It is always risky to speculate on the course and speed of advances in technology, but the following three advances in technology seem certain: Bandwidth (the amount of information that can be conveyed electronically over a "line") will increase dramatically, communication computer devices will be interconnected, and microprocessor speed will continue to increase.

Current interactive programs are limited by the speed of transmission of digital information. For instance, today it may take several minutes or longer to download even a short video presentation that might otherwise enhance a program. Advances in bandwidth will dramatically increase the types of data that can be efficiently delivered. Interventions will no longer be constrained to a primary text-based system, and developers and users will have greater access to audio, video, and interactive graphics, including three-dimensional avatars (visual "handles" or display appearances used to represent oneself on-line). For example, members of an on-line psychoeducational or support group may pick a three-dimensional avatar to represent themselves (or create an actual three-dimensional image of themselves) as they interact with other group members and the group facilitator.

In a virtual psychoeducational group, the facilitator may alter the background depending on the topic addressed to enhance the salience of the discussion topic. For instance, if the discussion topic was eating in public, the moderator could create a restaurant background for the discussion with all the relevant ambient sounds and images. Group members could change their avatar for personal expression and role-playing purposes.

The concept of a solitary computer connected via telephone line to the Internet will fade as more and more electronic devices are interconnected and computer technology becomes ubiquitous. In the future, software programs will easily communicate with telephone, paging devices, video wristwatches, and personal digital assistants (PDAs). Programs will incorporate more push technology to provide a more comprehensive intervention. (Push technology occurs when the program ostensibly "pushes" information to the user rather than waiting until the user specifically requests it.) This enhanced connectivity allows for the collection of more real-time data, such as journaling of behavior, affect, and cognitions. Already PDAs, which can readily download information to personal computers, have been used to increase the use of cognitive–behavior interventions outside of the office (Newman et al., 1997).

Greater connectivity will go beyond the devices used by a single user to the ability to connect to a larger community of simultaneous users. User groups will be able to form anywhere in cyberspace and comprise members living in a variety of locations with different cultural backgrounds. The community of users may also include parents and peers. In the future, parents will be able to take an active part in the treatment by both participating in their own structured intervention and interacting with younger women (including their children). Forums will be created in which parents and children can communicate anonymously and discuss relevant issues (e.g., dieting, family pressures). Male peers will also be able to participate in discussions of cultural beauty and peer pressure. In this forum, young men may be able to increase their understanding of the pressures women experience and how they, along with their partners, suffer from holding unrealistic and limiting standards. Users may benefit from interactions with diverse participants as they learn how other members cope with different standards of beauty (e.g., hairstyle, clothing, makeup regimens). Groups will be able to discuss regional and cultural differences, share coping strategies, and enhance their ability to understand and challenge the cultural influences on their standard of beauty. By a broadening of the perspective of young women, it is possible that fewer will succumb to cultural pressures and avert their development of eating disorders and body image dysphoria. Such "communities" could also be mobilized to resist standard media and cultural messages that endorse the "thin-body" ideal and in other ways to become more active in redefining cultural standards.

Technology is not without its downside, however; the developments that could facilitate personal change and awareness could also be used in just the opposite fashion. Commercial interests already dominate many aspects of Internet activity and are likely to increase. Diet programs and products are likely to be endorsed in many subtle ways. For instance, a company could hire a person as a "plant" to participate in eating disorder programs with the purpose of the plant endorsing their product.

Additionally, Internet multimedia interventions raise a number of important ethical and professional issues, including those of privacy, safety, and professional practice. Although some safeguards can be instituted to protect participants' privacy, a dedicated "hacker" is likely to gain access to any data retained by the program. It is simply not possible to ensure total privacy, and users should be so informed. Safety is another issue. Participants have access to these programs at any time and may report suicidal or other information that requires immediate action. Members may inaccurately assume that all postings are reviewed on an ongoing basis and experience undue distress if their postings are not promptly addressed. It is important that the participants are reminded on a regular basis that participation in the intervention is not a substitute for psychotherapy or medical treatment and that urgent messages may not be responded to. Incorrect information is also likely to be posted in chat rooms and newsgroups. For instance, Winzelberg (1997) found that 12% of medical information posted on an Internet-based eating disorder chat room was inaccurate.

The technology also has the potential of creating an impersonal, "virtual" society in which virtual rather than "real" human connections can be made. (However, the difference between real human connections and virtual ones may lessen as technology changes.) As technology changes and new, innovative programs are developed, the line between psychoeducation and therapy will become blurred. Prevention and intervention activities can be conducted or provided by untrained or unscrupulous individuals intent on personal gain at the expense of program users. Research is urgently needed in this area to evaluate the strengths, limitations, and even dangers of these approaches.

POPULATION-BASED MODELS AND PREVENTION

The development of databases on capitated populations, such as those served by a university or a health care system, the use of algorithms to determine treatment sequencing, and new advances in CAPP will begin to blur the lines between prevention and treatment. In recent years, some researchers have begun to focus on this issue in an area sometimes described as population-based psychotherapy. *Population-based psychotherapy* considers the provision of services to a population at risk for or already affected with a disease or disorder (Katon et al., 1997). Thus, it incorporates elements of secondary (selective) and tertiary (indicated) prevention. Population-based psychotherapy uses data from epidemiology, risk factor identification and modification, and clinical treatment outcome to determine preventive and treatment approaches for the targeted population. Although the focus of this chapter is on risk factor reduction, in the future, interventions are likely to focus on a spectrum of risk factors as well as subclinical and clinical disorders screening. The ready access of technology will permit interventions to be individualized, so that the users' progress may become more relevant than epidemiologically derived risk factors. For instance, assuming a female participant with high weight or shape concerns is providing data on her weight–shape attitudes and behaviors, it may become apparent that she has increased her weight under a condition of being very stressed and begins to diet and binge. This change in behavior, coupled with other risk factors, may indicate a need for an intervention.

A population-based intervention might follow a stepped care CAPP approach. In providing a population-based intervention to a college student population, all female students would take a short screening test to determine if they are at high risk for an eating disorder or have an eating disorder. Students identified as being at high risk could then receive a relatively inexpensive intervention such as Student Bodies, and those with subclinical–clinical eating disorders could receive a stepped care intervention (except for students with anorexia, who would be referred to individual assessment and treatment as needed). Winzelberg et al.'s (1998) multimedia intervention (or some other low-cost psychoeducational program proven to be equally effective and safe) would be applied to approximately 25% of the female students at a college on the basis of screening into the high-risk group for eating disorders. Assuming that students recruited to the intervention through screening would experience similar outcomes as self-referred students and that students in any university would achieve the same results as those who participated in Winzelberg et al.'s study, then risk might be reduced in over half of the participating students. The students who failed this intervention might benefit from simply being monitored, with more active interventions applied when and if they reached a subclinical level of the disorder.

The elegant research strategies that have evolved to examine treatment outcome efficacy among individuals in narrowly defined populations of treatment volunteers are only partly relevant to the effectiveness of these interventions as applied to populations with the goal of reducing incidence or providing cost-effective care to everyone in the population who may benefit from it. Furthermore, from the standpoint of linking prevention and intervention, psychopathology often exists on a continuum of disorder not only from clinical to subclinical populations but perhaps even from high-risk to subclinical–clinical groups. The application and monitoring of effects of standardized interventions on defined populations would help elucidate these continua. For instance, are there characteristics of individuals with subclinical disorders that predispose them to develop more serious psychopathology? Are treated participants no longer at risk for even subclinical problems? Standardized and stepped care interventions applied across populations might be a better way to identify nonresponsive subpopulations of patients requiring different or new treatments and of examining the ecological validity of defined population studies.

CONCLUSION

Studies undertaken by our research group and by others suggest that interactive multimedia interventions may have an impact on altering attitudes and behaviors that predispose young women to eating disorders. Advances in computer technology are likely to make such interventions more effective, and as advanced multimedia technology becomes more widely available, such approaches may be used to help reduce the onset of subclinical and clinical eating disorders. Yet the use of this technology poses important ethical, privacy, and practice issues. Research on the effectiveness of these approaches, with consideration of possible negative effects, is urgently needed.

REFERENCES

Cash, T. F. (1991). *Body image therapy: A program for self-directed change*. New York: Guilford Press.

Celio, A. A., Winzelberg, A. J., Wilfley, D. E., Eppstein, D., Springer, E. A., Dev, P., & Taylor, C. B. (2000). Reducing risk factors for eating disorders: Comparison of an Internet- and a classroom-delivered psychoeducation program. *Journal of Consulting and Clinical Psychology. 68*, 650–657.

Cooper, P., Taylor, M., Cooper, Z., & Fairburn, C. (1987). The development and validation of the Body Shape Questionnaire. *International Journal of Eating Disorders, 6*, 485–494.

Davis, R., Dearing, S., Faulkner, J., Jasper, K., Olmsted, M., Rice, C., & Rockert, W. (1989). *The road to recovery: A manual for participants in the psychoeducation group for bulimia nervosa*. Toronto, Ontario, Canada: Toronto Hospital, Toronto General Division.

Fairburn, C. G., & Carter, J. C. (1996). Self-help and guided self-help for binge eating problems. In D. M. Garner & P. E. Garfinkel (Eds.), *Handbook of treatment for eating disorders* (pp. 494–499). New York: Guilford Press.

Fairburn, C. G., Norman, P. A., Welch, S. L., O'Connor, M. E., Doll, H. A., & Peveler, R. C. (1995). A prospective study of outcome in bulimia nervosa and the long-term effects of three psychological treatments. *Archives of General Psychiatry, 52*, 304–312.

Gustafson, D. H., Hawkins, R., Boberg, E., Pingree, S., Serlin, R. E., Graziano, R., & Chan, C. L. (1999). Impact of a patient-centered, computer-based health information/support system. *American Journal of Preventive Medicine, 16*, 1–9.

Katon, W., Von Korff, M., Lin, E., Unutzer, J., Simon, G., Walker, E., Ludman, E., & Bush, T. (1997). Population-based care of depression: Effective disease management strategies to decrease prevalence. *General Hospital Psychiatry, 19*, 169–178.

Killen, J. D., Hayward, C., Taylor, C. B., Litt, I., Hammer, L. D., Wilson, D. M., & Miner, B. (1994). Factors associated with symptoms of bulimia nervosa in a community sample of 6th and 7th grade girls. *International Journal of Eating Disorders, 15*, 357–367.

Killen, J. D., Taylor, C. B., Hayward, C. H., Haydel, K. F., Wilson, D., Hammer, L., Kraemer, H., Blair-Greiner, A., & Strachowski, D. (1996). Weight concerns influence the development of eating disorders: A four-year prospective study. *Journal of Consulting and Clinical Psychology, 64*, 936–940.

Kulik, C., & Kulik J. (1991). Effectiveness of computer based instruction: An updated analysis. *Computers in Human Behavior, 7*, 75–94.

Lewis, D. (1999). Computer-based approaches to patient education: A review of the literature. *Journal of the American Medical Informatics Association, 6*, 272–282.

Newman, M. G., Consoli, A., & Taylor, C. B. (1997). Computers in assessment and cognitive behavioral treatment of clinical disorders: Anxiety as a case in point. *Behavior Therapy, 28*, 211–235.

Noell, J., & Glasgow, R. E. (1999). Interactive technology applications for behavioral counseling: Issues and opportunities for health care settings. *American Journal of Preventive Medicine, 17*, 269–274.

Selmi, P., Klein, M., Greist, J., & Sorrell, S. (1990). Computer-administered cognitive–behavioral therapy for depression. *American Journal of Psychiatry, 147*, 51–56.

Springer, E. A., Winzelberg, A. J., Perkins, R., & Taylor, C. B. (1999). Effects of a body image curriculum for college students. *International Journal of Eating Disorders, 26*, 13–20.

Striegel-Moore, R. G., Silberstein, L. R., & Rodin, J. (1986). Toward an understanding of risk factors for bulimia. *American Psychologist, 41*, 246–263.

Taylor, C. B., Agras, W. S., Losch, M., & Plante, T. G. (1991). Improving the effectiveness of computer-assisted weight loss. *Behavior Therapy, 22*, 229–236.

Taylor, C. B., & Altman, T. M. (1997). Priorities in prevention research for eating disorders. *Psychopharmacology Bulletin, 33*, 413–417.

Winzelberg, A. (1997). The analysis of an electronic support group for individuals with eating disorders. *Computers in Human Behavior, 13*, 393–407.

Winzelberg, A. J., Eppstein, D., Eldredge, K. L., Wilfley, D., Dasmahapatra, R., Dev, P., & Taylor, C. B. (2000). Effectiveness of an Internet-based program for reducing risk factors for eating disorders. *Journal of Consulting and Clinical Psychology, 68*, 346–350.

Winzelberg, A. J., Taylor, C. B., Altman, T. M., Eldredge, K. L., Dev, P., & Constantinou, P. S. (1998). Evaluation of a computer-mediated eating disorder intervention program. *International Journal of Eating Disorders, 24*, 339–349.

Zabinski, M. F., Pung, M. A., Wilfley, D. E., Eppstein, D. L., Winzelberg, A. J., Celio, A., & Taylor, C. B. (in press). Reducing risk factors for eating disorders: Targeting at-risk women with a computerized psychoeducational program. *International Journal of Eating Disorders*.

Zabinski, M., Wilfley, D., Pung, M., Winzelberg, A., Eldredge, K., & Taylor, C. B. (1999, December). *An interactive psychoeducational program (chat room) for women at risk of eating disorders*. Poster presented at Computer Support for Collaborative Learning, Institute for Research on Learning, Stanford University, Stanford, CA.

14

CONCLUSION: IMAGINING THE FUTURE

RUTH H. STRIEGEL-MOORE AND LINDA SMOLAK

The past two decades have seen an explosion of theory and research in the area of eating disorders. This is illustrated in Figure 14.1 for anorexia nervosa and Figure 14.2 for bulimia. These figures show the cumulative number of citations (in English, human participants) found by searching PsycINFO, an electronic database of scientific journal articles and book chapters published from 1967 to 1999. (*Bulimia nervosa* was initially called *bulimia* in the *Diagnostic and Statistical Manual of Mental Disorders* [3rd ed., American Psychiatric Association, 1980]; therefore, "bulimia" was the search term used.) Binge-eating disorder was introduced in 1991 by Spitzer et al., and, not surprisingly a search for "binge-eating disorder" did not identify any citations until 1991. Up till 1994, there were only 30 citations, but from 1995 to 1999 there were 165 citations when searching for binge-eating disorder. This rapid and extensive growth in research has been paralleled by the founding of two journals, *International Journal of Eating Disorders* and *Eating Disorders: Journal of Treatment and Prevention*, dedicated to publishing work about eating disorders. A further indication of how active this field has become is the fact that within the past 10 years, two new organizations have been established in the United States that aim to advance research, treatment, and prevention of eating disorders: the Academy for Eating Disorders (an international organization of professionals working in the field) and the Eating Disorder Research Society (membership requires an active publication record).

It is clear that eating disorders have become the focus of coherent, sustained scholarship and clinical activity. As it happens in any field, certain paradigms have come to dominate the published work with a hegemonic approach gradually taking form. As an "established" field of research, there are, ironically, decreasing opportunities to explore new research ideas and clinical techniques. The contributors to this volume were invited to use

271

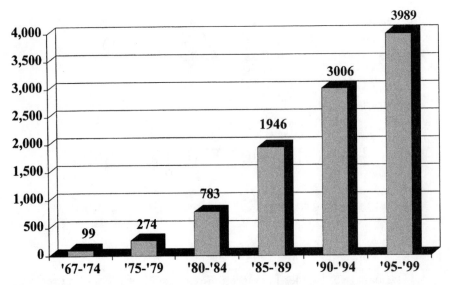

Figure 14.1. Cumulative number of citations in the PsycINFO database (1967–1999), using the search term *anorexia nervosa*.

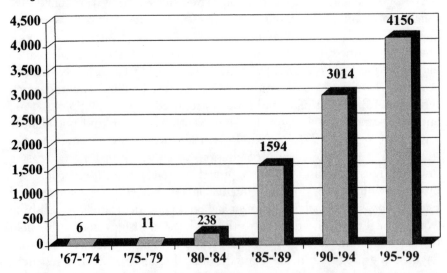

Figure 14.2. Cumulative number of citations in the PsycINFO database (1967–1999), using the search terms *bulimia* and *bulimia nervosa*.

their chapters as a forum for reflecting on the advances in a particular topical area and to put forth bold, provocative suggestions for future directions. We asked our colleagues to highlight gaps in knowledge and to shine light on possible new paths toward advancing knowledge.

From this collection of chapters, several themes emerged. As is evident from Herzog and Delinski's chapter on classification (chapter 2), a major shift is needed in the approach to eating disorders not otherwise specified (NOS). It represents the largest number of individuals seeking treatment for an eating disorder, yet to date this "catch-all" category is poorly defined and poorly understood. The public health impact of the various suggested syndromes embedded within eating disorder NOS has yet to be studied. Binge-eating disorder is an example of such a syndrome and has become the focus of considerable research activity. Early data suggest that, indeed, binge-eating disorder may be distinguishable in some clinical parameters and in clinical course from bulimia nervosa (Fairburn, Cooper, Doll, Norman, & O'Connor, in press; Striegel-Moore et al., in press). However, studies show that treatments of proven efficacy for bulimia nervosa also work for binge-eating disorder (for a review, see Wilfley & Cohen, 1997), suggesting that regardless of the differences in clinical presentation and course, treatments for these two syndromes may be comparable. Clearly, the intense research activities over the past few years that have focused on binge-eating disorder specifically have produced rapid advancement in the understanding of and therapeutic approach to this particular eating disorder NOS syndrome.

These advances notwithstanding, other symptom clusters, most notably night-eating syndrome (Birketvedt, et al., 1999; Stunkard, Grace, & Wolff, 1955), have been introduced and warrant further study. At the threshold to a new century of eating disorder research, technological advances (e.g., powerful computers that can handle large datasets and complex mathematical computations), decades of progress in diagnostic assessment technologies (e.g., standardized, validated diagnostic interviews), and sophisticated sampling technologies should provide ideal setting conditions for establishing in representative samples the clusters of clinical syndromes present in the community, their distribution patterns, and the clinical significance of these disturbances. Hence, eating-disorder researchers are in a position of moving the classification of eating disorders away from a patient sample approach to an epidemiologic, empirically based approach. Given that a majority of people suffering from psychiatric symptoms do not seek treatment for these mental health problems, this will be an important advance. The need for such research is made even more pressing by the fact that treatment seeking shows biases across ethnic and socioeconomic groups. If experts are to truly serve all citizens, they must develop a nomenclature that represents all of their needs.

The chapters on classification and etiology render salient the tension between the genetic (nature) and cultural (nurture) perspective. Genetic studies suggest that biological factors may contribute to the development of eating disorders, but researchers have not yet examined the role of the environment in fostering the expression of any potential genetic vulnerability. Even though the split between biology and culture is untenable from an epistemological viewpoint, in practice research has not yet conceptualized fully how "nature and nurture" converge to contribute to the development of eating disorders. As Smolak and Murnen (chapter 5) describe, genetic and biochemical studies often are devoid of emphasis on cultural factors, and cultural studies do not incorporate hypotheses about biological vulnerability. Moreover, the contribution of genetically transmitted risk factors, such as obesity, to the risk for development of eating disorders needs to be explored more fully in multivariate models.

The chapters by Stice on risk factors (chapter 3) and Crago, Shisslak, and Ruble on protective factors (chapter 4) illustrate the critical distinction between correlates and risk factors. Etiological research as described in these chapters is at the brink of major breakthroughs. Prospective studies such as the McKnight project or experimental studies such as Stice's research program hold exciting promise for an improved understanding of the causes of eating disorders. As Stice notes, it is time to move beyond testing the "same old" risk factors and begin to imagine new variables. Smolak and Striegel-Moore (chapter 6) discuss acculturation and racially based discrimination as examples of such "new" risk factors. Similarly, Crago et al. provide an example of this approach by looking at protective factors that have been defined in developmental psychopathology literature that looks at disorders other than eating problems.

Two decades ago, Striegel-Moore, Rodin, and Silberstein (1986) raised three broad questions about eating disorders: Why do they affect women more so than men? Which women in particular are affected? Why is this happening now? The first question not only remains unanswered but is rarely even the focus of etiological research or theory. Smolak and Murnen demonstrate that gender may prove to be the key to identifying relevant new variables or mechanisms that explain risk. By deconstructing (biological) sex and gender, we as researchers enrich our theories because we are forced to consider a broader range of biological and cultural factors than might be apparent from the largely gender-neutral approach to risk factor research that has been characteristic of many studies of risk and protection. Smolak and Murnen illustrate how objectification theory can become an organizing framework for new scholarship in this area.

Smolak and Murnen are clearly adopting a sociocultural approach, outlining how the cultural experience of being female might contribute to the development of eating disorders. This approach is central to answering the question of "Why is this happening now?" We (Smolak & Striegel-Moore, chapter 6) adopt a similar perspective in our chapter concerning ethnicity. The chapter underscores the aforementioned argument that researchers' focus on White women may have distorted the categories they currently use to diagnose and do research concerning eating disorders. Furthermore, the deconstruction of ethnicity will also provide new variables to investigate in etiological studies.

Taken as a whole, the etiological chapters in this volume offer many leads to answering the question of "which women in particular are affected." They further suggest that many contributing factors, risk and protective, might be amenable to intervention. It is clearly the perspective of these authors that multiple environmental characteristics and experiences contribute to the development of eating disorders, their subclinical variants, and their symptoms. A part of the challenge is to identify which factors are amenable to intervention; a related challenge is to focus preventive efforts both on the individuals at risk and on their broader social context that exposes the individuals to risk. Furthermore, researchers need to identify the timing that may be crucial in effective intervention. For example, reducing dieting may have a more salutary effect at some points in development (e.g., elementary school) than in others.

We have assembled several chapters on challenges and new directions in the clinical treatment of eating disorders. Several themes emerge. First, progress in treatment research has been considerable, and cognitive–behavior therapy clearly dominates the psychotherapeutic approach to the treatment of eating disorders (Whittal, Agras, & Gold, 1999). Second, despite the availability of proven treatments, only a minority of individuals appear to access such care. Third, major changes in how health services are allocated raise the question of whether resources are adequate for offering proven treatments to all who need them. Such pressures have been instrumental in promoting the search for more cost-effective treatments. In each of these areas, major questions remain.

A major concern in the United States is that despite the availability of efficacious treatments, few individuals appear to have access to such care. Obtaining clear estimates of who needs treatment and who seeks care for eating disorders has proved difficult. The dearth of data is paralleled by the lack of epidemiologic data. Moreover, the absence of systematic data of services use, rehabilitation, and treatment outcome in relation to service characteristics makes it difficult to advocate effectively for better treatment resources. Health services research represents a fertile research area in other fields yet has received only minimal attention in the eating disorders field. As Garvin and Striegel-Moore (chapter 7) suggest, there are numerous opportunities for creative forms of collaborations that need to be realized.

The chapter by Garvin, Striegel-Moore, Kaplan, and Wonderlich (chapter 8) addresses an important area of research: minimal interventions. In the current climate of cost containment and enthusiasm for brief interventions, a careful consideration of the ethical and procedural issues of minimal therapeutic interventions is overdue. Garvin et al. encourage researchers and clinicians to realize more fully the potential of self-help by returning to its roots and original aims of empowerment, personal growth, and political action.

The psychosocial treatment of eating disorders has been dominated by the cognitive–behavior model. Given the fact that cognitive–behavior therapy does not seem to benefit a large subset of individuals with eating disorders, increasingly alternative models have been sought. Wonderlich, Mitchell, Peterson, and Crow (chapter 9) give a tour de force introduction to their innovative clinical work that draws from a broad theoretical and empirical foundation of scholarship in cognitive psychology and neuroscience. An important component of this program is its attention to emotional and interpersonal functioning. Their treatment approach fits well with the theoretical work on risk and protection described in the earlier chapters in the section on etiology. Wonderlich et al. offer the fresh, innovative thinking that will shift the treatment paradigm away from more narrowly defined approaches to a richer, integrative approach to treatment.

As Mitchell (chapter 10) illustrates, pharmacological treatments of eating disorders have been studied with considerable scientific rigor. It seems apparent that "no stone has been left unturned" in the efforts to find a pharmacological cure. Yet to date, there is no drug treatment of choice for eating disorders. This may change as new findings about the biochemical causes or maintainers of disordered eating become available. Moreover, the need to look at eating disorder NOS is evident. For example, researchers of binge-eating disorder now pursue pharmacological treatment on the basis of theoretical models of appetite and satiety regulation.

Prevention long has been the stepchild of research on eating disorders. As the contributions to the section on prevention research illustrate, this is beginning to change. Heinberg, Thompson, and Matzon (chapter 11) provide a fresh look at the important question of the relationship between body image dissatisfaction and weight loss efforts. This relationship has been treated far too simplistically in many studies as well as in treatment and prevention efforts, with body dissatisfaction always casts as problematic. As Heinberg et al. illustrate, a simplistic approach obscures the possibly important function of body dissatisfaction as a motivating factor to engage in health-promoting behaviors. Relatedly, their chapter highlights the need to integrate research of obesity and eating disorders. Such an integration is long overdue, yet the two fields have been at odds particularly regarding the benefits and risks of dieting to lose weight. This provocative chapter asks readers to take a fresh look at body image dissatisfaction and offers suggestions for new empirical efforts.

The chapter by Taylor, Winzelberg, and Celio (chapter 13) provides a compelling model both for how to build systematically a successful research program in prevention and a specific intervention approach. The use of modern technology for dissemination is an important, novel feature of this work. We predict that rapid advances will occur in this area, and the resulting success will help shift the debate in prevention away from the tired but often-used excuse that prevention does not work to a discussion of who to target for preventive interventions.

Levine and Piran (chapter 12) offer a comprehensive framework for prevention that shifts the paradigm from an isolationist view of these disorders to a contextual, ecology-based approach. These pioneers in theory and research of prevention offer a framework that is highly consistent with the themes that emerged from earlier chapters in this volume: Progress will be made if researchers can grasp with the theories and intervention the complexity of the etiology of eating disorders, including giving more attention to contextual factors.

The prevention chapters clearly indicate that prevention is possible and it is possible right now. One does not need to wait to understand every aspect of the etiology of eating disorders to have some salutary effects. However, it is clear from these chapters that much more research is needed on prevention per se. One needs to understand audiences, delivery systems, teaching methods, and much more to intervene effectively to prevent or reduce eating disorders and their symptoms. Indeed, the differences between Taylor et al.'s Internet-based approach and Levine and Piran's feminist focus group–based orientation could not more dramatically frame the importance of investigating prevention methods themselves.

Taken together, the treatment and prevention chapters not only point to the need for a shift in paradigm in terms of theory and clinical practice but also point to the need to shift the paradigm of how research is accomplished. There is a definite need for greater collaboration both among experts with similar subspecialties (e.g., multicenter treatment studies) and across specialty areas. There is a pressing need to integrate scholarship of biological (genetic and biochemical) and cultural (proximal and distal) mechanisms. There is an important need to coordinate treatment research and health services research. There is a need to intensify efforts to approach prevention within the broader framework of a continuum of interventions that spans the range from prevention to treatment to rehabilitation. Of course, all of this needs to be coordinated with research on etiological factors. This relationship should be reciprocal, with the etiological work shaping treatment and prevention efforts but with the treatment and prevention work equally informing the risk and protective factors research.

Finally, the gaps in knowledge highlighted in this volume point with urgency to the need to advocate for greater resources that will then enable an infrastructure and support for innovative research. This will facilitate tests of the new theories and intervention that have been proposed so elegantly by our colleagues in this volume.

REFERENCES

American Psychiatric Association. (1980). *Diagnostic and statistical manual of mental disorders* (3rd ed.). Washington, DC: Author.

Birketvedt, G. S., Florholmen, J., Sundsfjord, J., Osterud, B., Dinges, D., Bilker, W., & Stunkard, A. (1999). Behavioral and neuroendocrine characteristics of the night-eating syndrome. *Journal of the American Medical Association, 282,* 657–663.

Fairburn, C. G., Cooper, Z., Doll, H. A., Norman, P. A., & O'Connor, M. E. (in press). The natural course of bulimia nervosa and binge eating disorder in young women. *Archives of General Psychiatry.*

Spitzer, R. L., Devlin, M., Walsh, B. T., Hasin, D., Wing, R., Marcus, M., Stunkard, A., Wadden, T., Yanovski, S., Agras, S., Mitchell, J., & Nonas, C. (1991). Binge eating disorder: To be or not to be in *DSM–IV? International Journal of Eating Disorders, 10,* 627–629.

Striegel-Moore, R. H., Cachelin, F. M., Dohm, F. A., Pike, K. M., Wilfley, D. E., & Fairburn, C. G. (in press). Comparison of binge eating disorder and bulimia nervosa in a community sample. *International Journal of Eating Disorders.*

Striegel-Moore, R. H., Silberstein, L. R., & Rodin, J. (1986). Toward an understanding of risk factors for bulimia. *American Psychologist, 41,* 246–263.

Stunkard, A. J., Grace, W. J., & Wolff, H. G. (1955). The night-eating syndrome: A pattern of food intake among certain obese patients. *American Journal of Medicine, 19,* 78–86.

Whittal, M. L., Agras, W. S., & Gold, R. A. (1999). Bulimia nervosa: A meta-analysis of psychosocial treatments and pharmacological treatments. *Behavior Therapy, 30,* 117–135.

Wilfley, D. E., & Cohen, L. R. (1997). Psychological treatments of bulimia nervosa and binge eating disorder. *Psychopharmacological Bulletin, 33,* 437–454.

AUTHOR INDEX

Numbers in italics refer to listings in reference sections.

Beutler, L., 155, 165, *169*
Bhugra, D., 122, *128*
Biebl, W., 41, *48*
Biederman, J., *208*
Bigler, R., 104, *105*
Bilker, W., 46, *278*
Bird, A. P., 219, *231*
Bird, H. R., 88
Birketvedt, G. S., 40, *46*, 273, *278*
Bishop, E. R., Jr., 178, *190*
Black, A. E., *71*
Blackburn, G. L., 220, *229*
Blaine, B., 104, *105*
Blair-Greiner, A., 69, *268*
Blais, M. A., *48*
Blake, W., 164, *169*
Blake Woodsie, D., *47*
Blakley, T., 93, *108*
Blouin, A., *208, 209*
Blouin, J., *208, 209*
Blue, C., 244, *249*
Blum, R., *127*
Blum, R. W., 77, 83, 85, 88, 120, *131*
Boberg, E., *267*
Boney-McCoy, S., 75, *85*
Bonsch, C., 161, *170*
Bordo, S., 103, *105*, 111, *127*, 248, *249*
Borowiecki, J., 91, *108*
Boskind-Lodahl, M., 94, *105*
Bosworth, K., 85, *85*
Botvin, G. J., 240, *249*
Bowers, W., 141, *149*
Bowlby, J., 180, *190*
Bowman, B. A., *230*
Bradburn, I. S., 51, *69*
Braiman, S., *73, 152*
Braithwaite, R., 162, *170*
Bramlette, J., 16, *24*
Brassington, G. S., 16, *24*
Braun, D. L., 41, *46*
Brewerton, T., 98, *110*, 136, 137, *149*, 178, *190, 194*
Broadnax, S., 104, *105*
Bronfenbrenner, U., 80, 81, 82, 85, *86*
Brooks-Gunn, J., 53, 55, 58, 60, 67, 68, 119, *127*
Brown, L., 92, *105*
Brownell, K., 38, *49*, 92, *105*, 118, *132*, 218, 228, *229, 232*
Brozek, J., 92, *107*
Bruce, B., 136, 137, *148, 150, 190, 208*

Bruch, H., 14, *22*, 94, *105*
Brumberg, J., 17, *22*, 99, *105*, 111, *127*
Brunner, E., *209*
Bryant, A., 98, 99, 101, *105*
Bryant-Waugh, R., 137, *148*
Buck, R., 180, *190*
Bulik, C., 5, 7, 42, *46*, 178, *190, 192*
Bunnell, D. W., 37, *46*
Burgard, D., 24, 87, *250*
Burke, G. L., *230*
Burke, J., *151*
Burns, C. D., 38, *48*
Burwell, R. A., *48*
Bush, T., *267*
Bushnik, T., *209*
Butler, R., 240, *251*
Button, E., 79, *86*
Buysse, W. H., 75, *86*
Byers, C. L., *230*

Caan, B., *230*
Cachelin, F., 28, 29, 34, *46*, 122, 126, 127, *278*
Caine, E. D., *209*
Calam, R., 58, 59, *67*
Caldwell, M. B., 118, *132*, 218, *232*
Callahan, E. J., 65, *67*
Camargo, C., 47, 54, 68, 138, *149*
Cameron, R., 51, 55, *71, 72*
Campbell, S. M., 115, *128*, 219, *230*
Carlat, D., 138, *149*
Carroll, D., 154, 155, *171*
Carter, J., 19, *22*, 163, 166, *169*, 233, 240, *249, 252, 257, 267*
Carter, W. P., *210*
Cash, T. F., 215, 216, 218, 219, 222, 223, 224, *229, 257, 267*
Casper, R., 11, *22*, 33, 43, *46, 209*
Caspi, A., 53, 68, *70*
Cattarin, J., 53, 54, 58, *67*, 119, *127*
Cavell, T. A., 76, *87*
Ceci, S. J., 80, 81, 85, *86*
Cederblad, M., 77, *86*
Celio, A., 240, *249*, 253, 259, 262, *267, 268*
Ceto, A., *210*
Chaiken, S., 179, *193*
Chan, C. L., *267*
Change, J., 122, *130*

Dohne, J., 201, *209*
Dolan, B., 16, *23*
Dolinsky, A., *73, 152*
Doll, H., 15, *23,* 35, 36, 46, 47, 67, 68, 119, *127,* 140, *149, 178, 191, 267, 273, 278*
Dong, Q., 118, *127*
Dorer, D. J., 43, *48*
Dorian, B., *208*
Dorian, B. J., 18, *23*
Dorr, T., 78, *87*
Douchinis, J., 7, 111, 114, 115, *127*
Dowling, H., *70*
Downes, B., *127*
Downs, K., 98, *108*
Drinkwater, J., 240, *252*
D'Souza, J. D., *210*
Dubbert, B. K., 38, *50*
Duchman, E. G., 12, *23*
Dumont, M., 153, 154, *169*
Dunn, V., 233, *249*
Durlak, J. A., 83, 84, 86, 233, 234, 240, 248, *249*
Dusenbury, L., 241, *249*

Eagly, A., 94, *106*
Early-Zald, M. B., 53, *70*
Eaves, L., *24,* 69, *128, 150, 192*
Ebert, M. H., *209*
Eckert, E., 11, *22,* 43, 46, *192,* 199, *209,* 211
Edelsberg, J., 219, *231*
Edelstein, C., 139, *152*
Edlund, *150*
Eisler, I., 9, *25,* 202, *209, 211*
Ekeblad, E., *48*
Elder, K. A., 38, *49*
Eldredge, K., 26, 38, *46,* 253, 268, *269*
Ellis, A., 154, *169*
Engbloom, S., *49, 170*
Engel, R. R., *209*
Eppstein, D., *249,* 253, 267, *268*
Epstein, L. H., 65, *67*
Ernsberger, P., 221, *229*
Estes, L. S., 15, *22,* 37, *49,* 79, 86, 114, *127*
Evans, K., 141, *149*
Ewald, L., 175, *194*
Ewing, L., *211*

Faden, V. B., *209*
Fahy, T. A., 202, *209*
Fairburn, C., 9, 15, 19, *22, 23,* 25, 35–39, *45–47,* 50, 51, 59, 66, 67, 68, *92–94, 105, 106, 110,* 115, 119, 120, *127, 131, 132,* 137, 140, *149,* 151, 162, 163, 166, *169, 171,* 172–174, 176, 178–180, 182, 187, *190, 191, 194,* 233, 240, 249, 252, 257, 262, *267, 273, 278*
Fairman, B., 99, *108*
Falco, M., 241, *249*
Fallon, P., 92, *106*
Faludi, S., 164, *169*
Farrington, A. J., *211*
Faulkner, J., *267*
Favaro, A., 39, 49, 55, *71, 252*
Fear, J., 42, *46*
Federal Bureau of Investigation, 123, *127*
Feighner, J. P., 31, *46*
Feldman, J., 202, *211*
Ferber, R. A., *208*
Fergusen, J. M., *210*
Ferguson, C. P., 5, *7*
Ferrara, S., 39, *49, 252*
Fichter, M., 10, 16, *23,* 201, *209*
Field, A. E., 40, 47, 48, 54, 55, 58, 68, *230*
Finkelhor, D., 98, *107*
Fischer, J., 35, *48*
Fisher, M., *47*
Fisher, S., 222, *229*
Fitzgibbon, M., 114, *131, 139, 149*
Flack, J. M., *230*
Flater, S. R., 199, *208*
Flegal, K. M., 115, *128,* 219, *230*
Fleiss, J., *212*
Fleming, C., 161, *169*
Fletcher, L., *170, 211*
Flores, A. T., 42, *48*
Florholmen, J., *46, 278*
Fluoxetine Bulimia Nervosa Collaborative Study Group, 201, *209*
Fluoxetine Bulimia Nervosa Research Group, *209*
Foa, E., 185, *191*
Folsom, A. R., 219, *230*
Fontaine, K. R., 219, *229*
Ford, C., 183, *191*
Ford, E. S., 220, *230*

Ford, K., 15, 24
Foreyt, J. P., 56, 68
Foster, G. D., 56, 73, 222, 230
Foucault, M., 247, 249
Frank, R., 146, 150
Franklin, M., 94, 110
Franko, D. L., 78, 83, 86, 233, 250
Frazier, A. L., 47
Frederickson, B., 92, 101, 102, 106
Freeman, C. P. L., 201, 209
Freeman, R., 33, 49
Freeman, R. J., 174, 190
Freire, P., 246, 247, 250
French, S. A., 56, 68, 120, 127, 131
Friederici, S., 55, 71
Friedman, B., 111, 128
Friedman, S., 104, 106
Fulkerson, J. A., 53, 69, 70, 78, 87
Funsch, C. L., 73
Furnham, A., 14, 23

Galuska, D. A., 220, 230, 231
Garcia Coll, C., 112, 128
Gardner, C. D., 119, 132
Gardner, R., 111, 128
Garfield, S., 155, 165, 169
Garfinkel, P., 10–12, 14, 18, 21, 23, 24,
        32, 34, 36–38, 40, 41, 43, 44, 46,
        47, 51, 55, 68, 115, 128, 137,
        149, 161, 169, 210, 244, 250
Garmezy, N., 76, 87
Garner, D. M., 11, 14, 23, 35, 40, 41, 43,
        46, 47, 55, 59, 68, 116, 128,
        174, 176, 190, 191, 245, 250
Garner, M. V., 43, 47
Garthe, R., 171
Garvin, V., 114, 131, 133, 134, 138,
        140, 151, 164, 166, 169, 172
Gaupmann, G., 211
Gauvin, L., 181, 193
Gendall, K., 199, 210
George, G. C. W., 11, 22
Gerrard, M., 75, 85
Gerstein, D. R., 243, 244, 250
Gest, S. D., 87
Gibbons, F. X., 75, 85
Gilbert, S., 97, 100, 101, 106
Gilligan, C., 99, 109, 113, 132
Gillman, M. W., 47
Gladis, M., 212

Glasgow, R., 154, 169
Glasgow, R. E., 256, 268
Glassman, A. H., 212
Glenberg, A. M., 179, 193
Glowinski, H., 122, 128
Goering, C., 149
Goering, P., 23, 47, 68, 128, 149, 169
Gold, M. S., 203, 210
Gold, R. A., 275, 278
Goldberg, G. R., 71
Goldberg, S. C., 11, 22, 43, 46, 209
Goldbloom, D., 23, 47, 68, 128, 149,
        169, 201, 209, 210
Golden, N. H., 47
Goldsmith, H., 93, 107
Goldstein, D. J., 209, 220, 230
Gooding, W., 211
Goodman, S., 88
Goodrick, G. K., 56, 68
Gordon, J. R., 187, 192
Goreczny, T., 12, 22
Gorey, K., 147, 150
Gorman, P. W., 180, 193
Gowen, L. K., 122, 128
Graber, J. A., 53, 55, 58, 60, 68
Grace, P. S., 179, 193
Grace, W. J., 40, 50, 273, 278
Gralen, S., 58, 60, 71
Grant, J. R., 216, 229
Grave, R., 170
Gray, J., 15, 24
Graziano, R., 267
Greaves, L., 244, 250
Green, L. W., 243, 244, 250
Greenberg, L., 176, 180, 183, 191
Greenberger, E., 118, 127
Greeno, C. G., 192
Greenwood, D. N., 48
Greist, J., 256, 268
Griffing, A., 44, 50
Griffing, S., 44, 50
Griffith, J. R., 79, 87
Grilo, C., 103, 105
Grinspoon, S. K., 16, 22, 135, 148
Grisset, N. I., 180, 191
Groat, R., 211
Gross, H. A., 209
Grossman, P. B., 76, 87
Gruber, A., 91, 108
Gruenberg, E., 151
Guidano, V. F., 175, 176, 191

Gullion, C. M., *194*
Gullotta, T. P., 234, 239, 240, *249*
Guo, M., 118, *127*
Gustafson, D. H., 256, *267*
Gustavson, C. R., 15, *25*
Gustavson, J. C., 15, *25*
Guze, S. B., *46*
Gyorky, Z., 154, *170*

Habermas, T., 33, *47*
Haggerty, R. J., 75, 76, 77, 82–84, 87,
    233, *251*
Hagnell, O., 77, *86*
Hailey, B. J., 225, 226, *230*
Haiman, C., 199, *208*
Hainsworth, J., 240, *252*
Hall, S. K., 119, *128*
Halmi, K., 11, 22, 41, 43, 46, 141, *149*,
    199, *209*
Hamartz, J. S., *208*
Hamburg, P., 17, *22*
Hammer, L., 24, 68, 69, *130*, 250, *268*
Hand, L. D., 178, *190*
Hannan, P. J., 241, *251*
Hanson, K., 24, 87, *170*, 211, *250*
Hansson, K., 77, *86*
Hardy, B. W., *194*
Harper, G. P., *208*
Harris, D., 113, 122, *128*
Harris, K. M., *88*
Harris, T. R., *72*
Harrison, P., 93, *106*
Hart, K., 96, *106*
Harter, S., 80, 87, 102, *106*
Hartley, P., *170*
Hasin, D., 49, *171*, *278*
Hatsukami, D., 192, *211*
Hawkins, J. D., *86*
Hawkins, R., *267*
Hawks, R., *209*
Hawley, D., 178, *190*
Hay, P., 35–39, 41, *47*, 67, *127*, 137,
    149
Haydel, K., 24, 68, 69, 122, *130*, *268*
Hayden, H., 96, 103, *105*, *107*, 111, 119,
    127, *129*
Hayes, A. M., 175, 176, *193*
Haynes, S. N., 188, *191*
Haythornthwaite, J. A., 215, *230*

Hayward, C., 24, 51, 55, 58, 60, 68, 69,
    71, *72*, 122, *128*, *130*, 250, *268*
Heath, A., 24, 69, *128*, *150*, *192*
Heath, G. W., *231*
Heatherton, T. F., 40, 41, 48, 53, 55, 57,
    60, 68, 69, *72*, 173, 180, 182,
    191
Heinberg, L., 54, 68, *72*, 103, *110*, 111,
    132, 215, 216, 220, 222–226,
    230, 232, 241, *252*
Heiss, G., *230*
Helmreich, R., 95, *109*
Helzer, J., *151*
Henry, B., 53, *68*
Henry, P. E., 215, *229*
Henschel, A., 92, *107*
Herman, C. P., 55, 57, 61, *71*, 118, *130*
Herman, P., 92, 100, *108*
Herrling, S., 100, *104*
Herzog, D., 16, 22, 36, 38, 42, 43, 48,
    51, 69, 135, 138, *148*, *149*, 180,
    192, *208*
Heshka, S., *70*
Hessen, L. D., 60, *70*
Heymsfield, S. B., *70*
Hicks, R. A., 16, *24*
Higgins, E. T., 179, 183, *191*, *193*
Hill, C., 135, *152*
Hill, K., 135, 145, *149*
Hirsch, J., 219, *231*
Ho, T. P., 33, *48*
Hoban, M. T., 222, *231*
Hoberman, H. M., *47*
Hodges, E. L., 137, *149*
Hoek, H., 37, *48*, 115, *132*, 135, 139,
    143, *149*
Hohlstein, L. A., 66, *69*
Holden, N. L., 178, *191*
Holland, R., 201, *209*
Hollister, L. E., 203, *212*
Hollon, S. D., 175, *191*
Honda, K., 25, *129*
Hope, R. A., 36, 46, 173, *190*
Hopkins, J. D., 38, *48*
Hops, H., 115, *129*, 136, *150*
Horne, R. E., *210*
Hoshino, Y., *129*
Hoven, C., *88*
Howard, K., 137, 140, *151*
Howard, W., 141, 144, 145, *149*
Howell, S., 225, *230*

Hsu, L. K., 33, *48*, 202, *210*
Huang, K., *24*, *87*, *250*
Hubbard, J. J., *87*
Huber, M., *211*
Hudson, J. I., 205, *210*, *211*
Hughes, J. N., 76, *87*
Hughes, P. L., *210*
Hugo, P., 143, *149*
Humphrey, L. L., 178, 185, *191, 194*
Huon, G., 111, *128*
Huston, A., 94, *106*
Hutchinson, R. G., *230*

Iancu, I., *22*
Ilstrup, D. M., *210*
Ingoin-Apfelbaum, L., 203, *210*
Ingram, R. E., 175, *191*
Ireland, M., *88*
Irving, L. M., 54, *69*
Irwin, C. E., 14, *24*
Isbell, T. R., 56, *69*

Jackman, L. P., *73*
Jacobs, D. R., *230*
Jacobson, M. S., 37, *46*
Jacobson, R., 180, *192*
Jarrell, M. P., 137, *149*
Jasper, K., *267*
Javaid, J. I., *209*
Jeffery, R. W., 56, *68*
Jennings, J., *211*
Jensen, J. G., 222, *231*
Jensen, P. S., *7*, *69*, *87*, *88*
Jocic, Z., 98, *110*, 178, *194*
Johnson, C., 140, *149*, 179, 180, *192*
Johnson, C. L., 115, *128*, 219, *230*
Johnson, J., *73*, *151, 152*
Johnson, J. L., 83, *89*
Johnson, S., 183, *191*
Johnson, W., 91, *106*
Johnson-Sabine, E., 14, *25*, 55, *70*
Joiner, T. E., 4, *7*, 53, 57, *69*, 72, 179, *192*
Jonas, J. M., 203, *210, 211*
Jones, J., *88*
Jones, R., 36, *46*, 173, *190*
Jordan, J., 164, *170*
Ju, E. S., 202, *210*
Jung, R. T., 219, 220, *230*

Kahn, A., 96, *106*
Kahn, C. B., 31, *50*
Kalikow, K., 73, *152*
Kaminski, P. L., 234, 243, *250*
Kanders, B. S., 220, *229*
Kaplan, A., 21, 23, *24*, 32, 36, *47*, 68, 128, 143, *149, 150, 169*, 187, *193*
Kappius, R. E., 180, *193*
Kashubeck-West, S., 4, 5, *7*
Kaslow, N., 94, *107*
Katon, W., 265, *267*
Katz, A., *170*
Katz, S., *150*
Katzman, D. K., *47*, *92*
Katzman, M., *106*, 122, *127*
Kay, R., *172*
Kaye, K. H., 199, 206, *210*
Kaye, W., 5, *7*, 43, 49, *92*–94, *106*, 143, 144, *150*, *152*, 178, *190, 192*, 199, 205, *209, 210*
Kazdin, A., *7*, 52, *69*, 75, 79, *87*, 155, *170*
Kearney-Cooke, A., 97, 98, *106, 109*, 176, *192*
Keck, P. E., *210, 211*
Keel, P., 10, *24*, 35, 40, 41, *48*, 53, 57–59, 64, *69*, 78, *87*, 145, *150*
Keilen, M., *171, 172*
Keller, M. B., 43, *48*, 51, *69*
Kelly, L., 15, *24*
Kenardy, J., 96, *105*, 124, *127*
Kendall-Tackett, K., 98, *107*
Kendler, K., 14, *24*, 53, *69*, 115, *128*, 136–138, *150, 152*, 178, *192*
Kendrick, A., 143, *149*
Kennedy, S., 23, 32, 36, *47*, 68, 100, *106*, 128, *149*, 169, *210*
Kenny, M., 96, *106*
Kern, E., *211*
Kessler, R., *7*, *24*, *69*, 75, *87*, *128*, 139, 146, *150, 151, 192*
Keys, A., 92, *107*
Kilbourne, J., 101, *107*
Killen, J., 14, 19, *24*, 51, 53, 55, 57–61, 64, 65, 68–72, 122, *128*, 130, 234, 242, *250*, 256, *268*
Kilpatrick, D., 136, *149*
Kimball, K. T., 56, *68*
King, M., 122, *128*
Kinzl, J. F., 41, *48*

Kirkley, B. G., 208
Kirschenbaum, D., 139, *149*
Klein, M., 185, *195*, 256, 268
Kleinman, A., 44, *45*
Klesges, L. M., 56, 69
Klesges, R. C., 56, 69
Klibanski, A., 16, *22*, 135, *148*
Klinnert, M., 93, *107*
Kobak, R., 178, 180, *190*
Koeske, R., 65, 67
Koletsky, R. J., 221, *229*
Koplan, J. P., *230*
Koran, L., 144, *150*, 190, 208
Korman, L., 183, *191*
Kouzis, A., 139, *150*, 152
Kraemer, H., 5, 7, *24*, 51, 52, 56, 68, 69, 75, 76, 87, *150*, 250, 268
Krass, J., *229*
Krebs, M., 54, 72, 222, *231*
Kreipe, R. E., *47*
Kreitler, S., 225, *230*
Kristjanson, A. F., *72*
Krüger, R., 201, *209*
Kuba, S., 113, 122, *128*
Kuczmarski, R. J., 115, 119, *128*, 219, 220, 224, *230*
Kulik, C., 255, *268*
Kulik, J., 255, 268
Kumpfer, K. L., 77, 83, *87*
Kuperminc, G., 100, *104*
Kupfer, D., 7, 52, 69, 75, 87

Lacey, J., 143, *149*, 210
LaDu, T. J., 199, *209*
Lake, A., 122, *128*
Lambert, M., 155, *170*
Lancelot, C., 94, *107*
Landsverk, J., 139, *152*
Langley, J., 53, 68
Larkin, J., 99, *107*, 113, 124, *128*, 244, *250*
Larson, R., 179, 180, *192*
Lask, B., 137, *148*
Lau, A., 244, *249*
Lavori, P. W., 43, 48, 51, 69
Lawson, M. L., 234, *251*
Leaf, P., 139, *150*, 152
Leahy, R., 176, 186, *192*
Lee, A., *172*
Lee, A. M., 16, *24*, 116, *128*

Lee, S., 16, *24*, 32, 33, 48, 116, *128*
LeGrange, D., 9, 25
Lehoux, P. M., 181, *193*
Leibel, R., 219, *231*
Leibl, K., *209*
Leitenberg, J., 202, *210*
Lemery, K., 93, *107*
Leo, R., 96, *110*
Leon, G. R., 53, 55, 57–59, 64, 69, 70, 78, 87
Leslie, D., 133, *134*, 140, *151*
Lester, J., 118, *127*
Letizia, K. A., 56, 73
Leung, T., 116, *128*
Levine, M., 27, 29, 54, 58, 60, 70, 71, 79, 82, 84, 87, 91, 93, 95–98, *107–109*, 111, 119, 120, *129*, *131*, 213, 214, 221, *231*, 233, 234, 239–241, 247–250, *252*
Lewczyk, C. M., *7*
Lewinsohn, P., 58, 68, 115, *129*, 136, 138, *150*
Lewis, B. A., *72*
Lewis, C., 114, *131*
Lewis, D., 256, 268
Lewis, L., 140, *149*
Liben, L., 104, *105*
Lichtman, S. W., 64, 70
Licinio, J., 141, *149*
Lilenfeld, L. R., 5, 7, 178, *192*
Lin, B., *23*, 47
Lin, E., 36, 41, *47*, 68, *128*, *149*, 169, 267
Lineberry, C. G., *210*
Linehan, M. M., 184, 189, *192*
Linton, J., 65, 67
Liotti, G., 176, *191*
Litt, I., *24*, 68, 69, *130*, 250, 268
Loan, P., 79, 86
Loeb, K. L., *212*
Lofchy, J., *210*
Loggie, J., 119, *130*
Long, B., 86
Loriaux, D. L., *212*
Losch, M., 256, 268
Lowe, M., 55, 57, 62, 70, 175, *193*
Luborsky, L., 143, *150*, 157, *170*
Lucas, A. R., 115, *132*
Lucero, K., 16, *24*
Ludman, E., 267
Luhtanen, R., 104, *105*
Luthar, S. S., 77, 87

Mulder, E., *209*
Mumford, D. B., 16, *24*
Mundray, K., 54, *70*
Munoz, R., *46*
Muran, J. C., 175, *193*
Murdock, M. V., *194*
Murgatroyd, P. R., *71*
Murnen, S., 78, 88, 94–96, 98, 99, 101,
    102, *107, 109*, 118, *129*
Mussell, M., 39, *49, 170, 211*
Must, A., 218–220, 228, *230*

Nagata, T., 43, *49*
Nagy, L., *192*
Nakamura, K., 122, *129*
Nakamura, Y. H., 16, *25*
Nasser, M., 16, *25*
National Center for Education Statistics,
    123, *129*
National Heart, Lung, and Blood Insti-
    tute Growth and Health Study
    Research Group, *129*
National Task Force on Prevention and
    Treatment of Obesity, 220, *231*
Neale, M., *24, 69, 128, 150, 192*
Nee, L. E., *209*
Needham, M. L., 118, *132*, 218, *232*
Neighbors, H., 162, *170*
Nelson, J. E., 38, *50*
Nemeroff, C., 94, 97, *107, 109*
Netermeyer, R. G., *73*
Neufeldt, S., 155, *169*
Neumark-Sztainer, D., 81, 82, 88, *127*,
    239, 240–242, 249, *251*
Newell, A., 143, *150*
Newman, D. L., 51, *70*
Newman, M. G., 256, 264, *268*
Newsholme, E., 94, *105*
Nichols, P., 40, *48*
Nichter, M., 97, *108*, 126, *129, 130*
Niego, S. H., 35, *49*
Niwa, S., *25, 129*
Noell, J., 256, *268*
Nolen-Hoeksema, S., *24, 87, 250*
Nonas, C., *49, 278*
Noordenbos, G., 213, *214*
Norcross, J., 164, *170*
Norman, D. K., 36, *48*, 180, *192*
Norman, P., *23, 68, 140, 149, 191, 267,
    273, 278*

Norvell, N. K., 180, *191*
Novwell, T., *172*
Novy, P. L., 216, *229*
Nugent, S., *49, 170*
Nussbaum, M. P., 37, *46*
Nutzinger, D. O., *209*

Obarzanek, E., *131*
Oberklaid, F., *107*
O'Connor, M., 15, *23*, 67, 68, 119, *127*,
    140, *149*, 173, 178, *190, 191,
    267, 273, 278*
O'Dea, J., 239, 241, 243, 248, *251*
O'Donohue, W., 98, 100, *108*
Offenbacher, E., *70*
Offord, D., *7*, 52, 69, 75, *87*
Ogden, J., 54, *70*
Ogg, E., 135, 143, 145, *150*
Oldman, A., 94, *110*
Olfson, M., 135, 139, 140, *150*
Olivardia, R., 91, *108*
Olivetto, M. C., *252*
Olmsted, M., 14, *23*, 40, *47*, 59, 68, 116,
    128, 187, *193*, 234, 243, *251,
    267*
O'Neil, P., 136, *149*
Orenstein, P., 125, *129*
Orosan, P., 222, *231*
Orosan-Weine, P., 78, 83, 86, 233, *250*
Orsulak, P. J., *208*
Orvaschel, H., *151*
Osimo, F., 165, *170*
Oster, G., 219, 220, *231*
Osterud, B., *46, 278*
Outwater, A. D., *251*

Paikoff, R. L., 53, *68*
Palmer, R. L., 21, *25*
Palti, H., 240, *251*
Parker, S., 117, 126, *129, 130*
Parry-Billings, M., 94, *105*
Patton, G. C., 14, *25*, 53, 55, 60, *70*
Pavetto, C., 144, *152*
Pawluck, D., 147, *150*
Paxton, S., 19, *25*, 98, *108, 251*
Pederson, Mussell, M., *49*
Pepose, M., 36, *48*
Perez, E., *208, 209*
Perkins, R., 19, *25*, 261, *268*

Perl, M., *150, 208*
Perlick, D., 94, 100, *108,* 248, *252*
Perrin, L. A., 78, 89
Perry, B., 93, *108*
Perry, C. L., 53, *70,* 234, 239, 240, 242,
    249, *251*
Pestone, M., *70*
Peterson, C., *49,* 135, 140, 142, *150,*
    163, *170,* 173, 176, *193, 195,*
    211
Petrill, S., 133, *134,* 140, *151*
Pettit, A., *151*
Petty, F., *194*
Peveler, R. C., *23, 36, 46, 68,* 173, *190,*
    191, 267
Philips, T., *229*
Philliber, S., 100, *104*
Phillips, R. S., 220, *232*
Phinney, J., 113, 121, 123, 124, *130*
Pickering, A., 42, 46
Pierloot, R., 200, *212*
Pigott, T. A., 5, 7
Pike, K., 15, *25,* 115, 119, *131, 132,*
    137, 138, *151,* 162, *171,* 176,
    191, 212, 278
Pinciaro, P. J., 222, *231*
Pincus, H., 135, 139, 140, 147, *150, 151*
Pingree, S., *267*
Piran, N., 79, 81, 82, 84, 85, 87, 88, 92,
    99, 100, 104, *108,* 111, *130, 210,*
    213, *214,* 221, 228, *231,* 233,
    234, 239, 241, 243–248, *250–252*
Pisarska, K., *70*
Plante, T. G., 256, *268*
Platts, M., 16, *24*
Plotnicov, K., *192*
Polivy, J., 40, *47,* 55, 57, 59, 60, 61, 68,
    71, 92, 100, *108,* 118, *130,* 221,
    230
Pollard, R., 93, *108*
Pollice, C., *192*
Pomeroy, C., *192, 211*
Pope, H., 91, 97, 103, *108, 210, 211*
Posavac, E. J., 54, *71*
Posavac, H. D., 54, *71*
Posavac, S. S., 54, *71*
Poston, W. S., 56, 68
Potuin, J. H., *209*
Power, T. G., 119, *128*
Pratt, E. M., 35, *49*
Prendergest, P., *210*

Prentice, A. M., 63, *71*
Prineas, R., 119, *130*
Prior, M., *107*
Prochaska, J., 164, *170*
Pruitt, J. A., 180, *193*
Pryor, T., 42, 43, *49*
Pumariega, A. J., 15, *25*
Pung, M., 268, 269
Pusztai, E., 135, *150*
Puung, M. A., *253*
Pyle, R. L., *192, 211*

Quadflieg, N., 10, *23*
Quintero-Howard, C., 141, *149*

Rabalais, J. Y., *73*
Raeburn, S., *150,* 173, *189, 190, 208*
Ralevski, E., *210*
Ramey, S. L., 86
Ramirez, M., 87
Rampey, A. H., *209*
Ransford, H. E., 225, *231*
Rao, R., 43, *49, 192*
Rapoport, J., *73, 152*
Rathner, G., 161, *170*
Ravelski, E., 100, *106*
Raymond, N. C., 39, *49, 210*
Rees, J., *47*
Reeves, R. S., 56, 68
Regier, D., *151*
Reid, F., 143, *149*
Reid, G., 77, 88
Reif, W., 201, *209*
Reiss, D., *25*
Reiss, E., 203, *212*
Reiter, J., 222, *231*
Renger, R., 83, 88, 100, *108,* 239, *252*
Resnick, M., 78, 88, 120, *127, 131*
Rice, C., 99, *107,* 244, *250, 267*
Rich, T., *24, 250*
Richards, M. H., 58, *72*
Richins, M. L., 54, *71*
Riessman, F., 154, 155, *171*
Rigotti, N. A., 36, *48*
Ritenbaugh, C., *130*
Rivinus, T. M., *208*
Robbins, C. J., 180, *192*
Robbins, W. M., *48*
Roberts, R., 124, *130,* 136, *150*

Shaw, B. F., *250*

Shaw, H., 54, *72*, 94, *109*

Sheffield, C., 99, *108*

Shelton, R. C., 175, *191*

Shenker, I. R., 37, *46*

Sherwood, N., 241, *251*

Shew, M., 88

Shimai, S., *25*, *129*

Shisslak, C., 15, 16, 19, *24*, *25*, 69, 100, *108*, 114, 122, *129*

Shisslak, C. M., *22*, 37, *49*, 75, 78, 79, 83, 86, 88, *127*, 221, *231*, 239, 248, *252*

Shore, R., 19, *24*

Shriver, T. P., 241, *253*

Shuman, M. D., 60, *70*

Shure, M. B., 86

Sieving, R. E., 88

Sifneos, P., 155, 157, 162, *171*

Sigman, G., *47*

Silberstein, L., 6, 7, 94, 95, 97, *108–110*

Silberstein, L. R., 40, *49*, 54, *72*, 76, 88, 111, *130*, 215, *231*, 256, 268, 274, *278*

Silva, P. A., 53, 68, *70*

Silverstein, B., 94, 100, *108*, 248, *252*

Simmonds, B., *24*, 69, *250*

Simon, G., *267*

Sims, C., *130*

Smart, D., *107*

Smart, D. E., 11, *22*

Smilack, K., 97, *107*

Smith, D. E., 114, 120, *131*

Smith, G. T., 66, 69

Smith, R. S., 77, 83, 89

Smolak, L., 27, *29*, 54, 58, 60, *70*, 71, 78, 82, 87, 88, 91, 93–99, 101, 102, 104, *107–109*, 111, 112, 118–120, 126, *129*, *131*, 137, *151*, 174, *194*, 221, 232, 234, 239–241, 246–248, *250*, *252*

Sobhan, M., 124, *130*

Sokol, M. S., 43, *49*

Sollner, W., 161, *170*

Solomon, C. G., 219, *231*

Sonuga-Barke, E. J. S., 79, 86

Sorrell, S., 256, 268

Sorter, R., 111, *128*

Sourdi, L., 16, *23*

Sourdi, Z., 16, *23*

Spadano, J., *230*

Spangler, D., 54, *72*

Specker, B., 96, *107*

Spegg, C., *23*, *47*, 68, *128*, *149*, *169*

Spence, J., 95, *109*

Spitzer, R., 162, *171*

Spitzer, R. L., 38, 39, *49*, *50*, 271, *278*

Springer, E. A., 19, *25*, *249*, 261, *267*, 268

Spurrell, E. B., 38, *50*

Stacher, G., *211*

Staiger, P., 122, *128*

Staley, J., *48*

Stanton, W. R., *70*

Stebnik, O., *210*

Steiger, H., 181, *193*

Stein, R., 97, *107*

Stein, R. I., 5, *7*

Steiner-Adair, C., 95, 96, *109*, 183, *193*, 213, *214*, 221, *231*, 233, *252*

Stern, T., 154, *170*

Stetner, F., *212*

Stevens, J., 219, 229

Stewart, D., 19, *22*, 233, 240, *249*, *252*

Stewart, J. W., *212*

Stewart, M., 77, 83, 88

Stice, E., 51–57, 60–62, 64, 65, 69–72, 81, 88, 94, *109*, 111, 121, *131*, 222, 227, *231*, 232, 234, 240, 242, 243, *252*

Stoddard, C., 239, *250*

Stolley, M., 139, *149*

Stormer, S., 54, *71*, 234, *252*

Story, M., 120, *127*, *131*

Strachowski, D., 69, 268

Strakowski, S. M., *210*

Strauman, T. J., 179, 183, *193*

Strickler, P. M., 12, *23*

Striegel-Moore, R. H., 6, 7, 15, *25*, 28, 29, 38–40, *49*, 54, 61, *72*, 76, 88, 92, 94, 95, 97, 98, *106*, *108–110*, 111, 112, 114–116, 118–122, 124, 126, *127*, *130–134*, 137, 138, 140, 141, *151*, 162, 164, *169–172*, 174, 176, 183, *192*, *194*, 215, 218, 224, *231*, *232*, 256, 268, 273, 274, *278*

Strober, M., 5, *7*, 33, 38, *49*, 58, *72*, 92–94, *106*, *109*, 178, *192*, *194*, 199, *210*

Strong, K., 111, *128*

Strupp, H., 163–165, 167, *169*, *171*

Wright, D., *131*, *132*
Wu, L., 139, 140, *152*

Yager, J., 139, 140, *152*
Yamamoto, M., *25*, *129*
Yanovski, S., 38, *49*, *50*, 56, 64, *73*, 120,
    132, *171*, *278*
Yeater, E., 98, *108*
Yeh, C., 43, *48*
Yergelun-Todd, D., *211*
Yerkes, R. M., 226, *232*
Yoder, J., 96, *106*
Yonace, A., *211*

Young, J. E., 176, *195*
Young, L., 203, *212*
Yuker, H., 95, 97, *110*

Zabinski, M., 243, *253*, 262, 268, 269
Zanetti, T., *252*
Zarin, D., *151*
Zhao, S., *150*
Zimmerman, R., *192*, *211*
Zinberg, N., *209*
Zucker, M., 143, *150*
Zucker, N. L., 78, 89
Zuro, C., *209*

SUBJECT INDEX

Body dissatisfaction, *continued*
  in models of eating disturbances, 60–61, 225–226
  possible beneficial aspects, 216–217
  as risk factor, 55
  and weight loss, 217–219, 222–224
Body dysmorphic disorder, gender and, 91, 97
Body image, 115, 120
  and prevention programs, 244–247, 256
Body image dissatisfaction. *See* Body dissatisfaction
Body mass, as risk factor, 53
Body Shape Questionnaire, 256–257
Body shape–weight, 40, 111, 183, 256–257
  See also Body dissatisfaction; Thin ideal
Bowlby, J., 180
Bronfenbrenner, U., 80–82, 85
Brownell, K. D., 218
BSRI. *See* Bem Sex Roles Inventory
Bulik, C., 5
Bulimia nervosa, 3, 31–32, 34–36, 115, 120, 135, 137, 216, 271
  and anorexia nervosa, 5, 41–42
  and binge-eating disorder, 38–39, 273
  cost effectiveness of treatments, 144–145
  dropout rates from treatment, 142
  duration of treatment, 141
  and eating disorder NOS, 38
  and ethnicity, 114
  and gender, 91
  integrative cognitive therapy, 182–187
  models, 173–174, 176–182, 188
  pharmacotherapy, 201–203, 205–207
  risk factors, 178–182
  self-help interventions, 157–160
  subtyping, 44
  and treatment seeking, 139–140
Button, E. J., 79

Caldwell, M. B., 218
CAPP. *See* Computer-assisted psychoeducational programs
Cash, T. F., 218, 257

CBT. *See* Cognitive–behavior therapy
Ceci, S. J., 80–81, 85
Celio, A., 7, 213–214, 240, 276
Child sexual abuse, 101
  as risk factor, 59, 98
Circumplex model of interpersonal behavior, 185
Cisapride, for treatment of anorexia nervosa, 200
Clark, D. A., 174–175
Classification issues, 31, 42–45
Clinical myths, 59
Clinical severity, diagnosis of, 40–41
Cloninger, C. R., 178
Cognitive–behavior model, 276
Cognitive–behavior therapy (CBT), 133, 275–276
  critiques, 175–176
  and self-help interventions, 157–160
  for treatment of bulimia nervosa, 173, 201–203, 205
  See also Integrative cognitive therapy
Cognitive style, and bulimia nervosa, 180–181
Cognitive theory, 174–176
Cohen, J., 199
Community, and bioecological model, 82
Community mental health movement, 153, 163
Comorbidity, 138–139, 141, 147, 161, 198
Computer-assisted psychoeducational programs (CAPP), 255–256
  future, 263–265
  and population-based intervention, 266
  preliminary studies, 256–263
  users of, 264
Computer use. *See* Technology
Context specificity, in prevention programs, 243–245
Control issues, as risk factor, 59
Coping skills, in integrative cognitive therapy for bulimia nervosa, 184–185
Cost containment, health services, 156, 167–168
Cost effectiveness, health services, 144–146
Cowen, E. L., 248
Crago, M., 5, 28, 274

Crossover, 5, 41–42
Crow, S., 6, 133, 141, 176, 276
Cultural factors, 111–112, 183
Cultural influences, 111–112, 122
Cultural specificity, 33, 44
Cumulative stressor model, 60
Cyproheptadine, for treatment of
    anorexia nervosa, 199

Dancyger, I. F., 37
Data bases, existing, 140, 148
Deihl, L. M., 81
Deike, R. C., 81
Delinksi, S. S., 5, 27–28, 272
Demand characteristics, and research on
    ethnic group differences, 117
Denial, as barrier to treatment seeking,
    139–140
Depression, 55, 57, 175, 201
d-Fenfluramine
    for treatment of binge-eating
        disorder, 203
    for treatment of bulimia nervosa,
        202
Diagnosis
    of anorexia nervosa, 32–34
    of binge-eating disorder, 38–40
    of bulimia nervosa, 34–36
    of clinical severity, 40–41
    and ethnicity, 125–126
    and provider characteristics, 143
Diagnostic and Statistical Manual of Mental
    Disease, third edition (DSM-III),
    31–32, 36
Diagnostic and Statistical Manual of Mental
    Disease, third edition, revised
    (DSM-III-R), 34, 36
Diagnostic and Statistical Manual of Mental
    Disease, fourth edition (DSM-IV),
    32, 34–36, 38, 41–44, 114, 157,
    161
Dietary restraint model, 61
Dieting, 40, 217–219
    biochemical effects, 93–94
    and bulimia nervosa, 181–182
    and ethnicity, 120
    and gender, 91, 97
    in models of eating disturbances,
        60–61
    as risk factor, 55–57, 65, 94, 173

See also Body dissatisfaction; Weight
    loss
Discrimination, racial, as risk factor, 123–
    125, 274
Disease-specific pathways (DSP) model,
    234–239
Dodson, J. D., 226
Dorian, B., 5
Dropout rate, for drug trials, 198,
    201–202
Drug abuse prevention, 240–241
Drug therapy. *See* Pharmacotherapy
Drug trials, controlled, 199–205
DSM-III. See Diagnostic and Statistical
    Manual of Mental Disease (third
    edition)
DSM-III-R. See Diagnostic and Statistical
    Manual of Mental Disease (third
    edition, revised)
DSM-IV. See Diagnostic and Statistical
    Manual of Mental Disease (fourth
    edition)
DSP. *See* Disease-specific pathways model
Dual diagnosis, of anorexia nervosa and
    bulimia nervosa, elimination of,
    42
Dual pathway model, 61–62
Durlak, J. A., 240, 248
Dysfunctional family systems, as risk
    factor, 59

Eating Attitude Test, 96, 116
Eating Disorder Inventory, 116, 256–
    257
Eating disorder not otherwise specified
    (NOS), 27–28, 34, 36–38, 137–
    138, 273, 276
Eating Disorder Research Society, 271
Eating disorders, 4, 27, 51, 92, 122, 136–
    137, 140–141
    atypical, 37
    biological explanations, 92–94
    and ethnicity, 114–118
    and gender, 91–92, 94–101, 103–
        104, 138
    and pharmacotherapy, 199–206
    and protective factors, 78–82
    public image, 3–4, 54
    and self-help, 157–160
    timing and crossover, 41–42

Herzog, D., 5, 27–28, 272
Hill, K., 145
Ho, T. P., 33
Howard, W., 145
Hsu, L. K. G., 33

ICD. See *International Classification of Diseases*
ICT. *See* Integrative cognitive therapy
Impulsivity, as risk factor, 58
Independence, and "superwoman" role, 96
Individual pathology model, 160
Ineffectiveness, feelings of, as risk factor, 59
Institute of Medicine, 76, 82–84
Integrative cognitive model, for bulimia nervosa, 176–182
Integrative cognitive therapy (ICT)
    for bulimia nervosa, 182–187
    development of, 174
Internalization
    of objectification, 101–103
    of thin ideal, 54, 61, 118–119, 227
International Classification of Diseases (ICD), 157, 161
International Journal of Eating Disorders, 271
Internet. *See* Computer-assisted psychoeducational programs
Interoceptive awareness, as risk factor, 59
Interpersonal distress, and bulimia nervosa, 181–182
Interpersonal factors, and bulimia nervosa, 180–181
Interpersonal patterns, in integrative cognitive therapy for bulimia nervosa, 185–187
Interpersonal relationships, as context for change, 247–248
Intervention
    with ethnic minority groups, 125–126
    Internet based, 262–263
    minimal, 275
    See also Computer-assisted psychoeducational programs; Self-help interventions; Treatment intervention programs
    "Road to Recovery," 257

Student Bodies, 257–262
Isolation, feelings of, and "superwoman" role, 96

Japanese, 119
Jordan, J., 164

Kaplan, A., 6, 133, 275
Kashubeck-West, S., 5
Kaye, W. H., 5, 199
Kazdin, A. E., 79
Keel, P., 145
Kirschenbaum, D., 139
Knowledge acquisition, and prevention programs, 240
Koran, L., 144
Kraemer, H., 5
Kulik, C., 255
Kulik, J., 255

LaDu, T. J., 199
Lapse, and relapse, 187
Latina Americans, as ethnic minority group, 113, 115
Latina American women, 118–120, 122, 124
Lee, S., 33
Leslie, D., 140
Levine, M., 7, 79, 84, 213, 277
Levine, M. P., 60, 82, 96, 98, 240, 249
Lichtman, S. W., 64
Life skills training, 83
    as protective factor, 79
Life Skills Training Program (LST), 240–241
Life skills training program model, 80–82
Lifestyle management, in integrative cognitive therapy for bulimia nervosa, 187
Lilenfeld, L. R., 5
Lin, E., 41
Lithium, for treatment of bulimia nervosa, 202
Long-term effects, 92
Loss of control, 35, 96
Loss of voice, women and, 99, 125
Lowe, M., 62
LST. *See* Life Skills Training Program

MacKinnon, C., 247
Maki, D., 141
Maloney, M., 145
Managed care, 133, 143–144, 147–148
Mann, T., 85
Manson, J. E., 219–220
Martin, G., 93
Masculinity. *See* Gender roles
Mastery experiences, as protective factor, 81
Matoba, M., 116
Matzon, J., 6, 213, 276
McDonald, K., 218
McKnight Risk Factor Study, 119
Measures of eating pathology, 64, 116–117
Media, 3–4, 54, 82, 96–97
Media literacy, in participatory prevention programs, 246–247
Mediation, 52
Medline, 157
Men, 91, 93, 97, 137–138, 141, 223–224
    See also Gender
Mentoring, 83
Miller, G., 154
Miller, J., 116
Minority status, 113–114
Mintz, L. B., 5
Mitchell, J., 6, 133–134, 141, 145, 147, 276
Mitchell, J. E., 176
Moderating factors, 65
Morrell, W., 33–34
Motivation, 161–162, 164, 182–184, 217–219
Motivational interviewing, 182
Mukai, T., 119
Multivariate etiologic models, 59–63, 66
Murnen, S., 6, 28, 94–95, 124, 274
Murnen, S. K., 78
Muscle dysmorphia, gender and, 91

Naltrexone
    for treatment of binge-eating disorder, 207
    for treatment of bulimia nervosa, 203
National Association for the Advancement of Fat Acceptance, 221

National Heart, Lung, and Blood Institute (NHLBI) Growth and Health Study Research Group, 116
National Institute of Mental Health, 76
National Institutes of Health, 198
National Women's Study, 136
Native Americans, as ethnic minority group, 113, 115
Needham, M. L., 218
Negative affectivity, 60–61, 121, 124, 179–180, 186
    as risk factor, 57, 174
Neumark-Sztainer, D., 82, 249
New Jersey Adolescent Study, 136
NHLBI. *See* National Heart, Lung, and Blood Institute
Night eating syndrome, 40, 273
Nonspecific vulnerability-stressor (NSVS) model, 239
Nontreatment, cost of, 145–146
Normalization of eating, in integrative cognitive therapy for bulimia nervosa, 184–185
NOS. *See* Eating disorder not otherwise specified
NSVS. *See* Nonspecific vulnerability-stressor model

Obese individuals, 56, 139, 218, 222
    and binge-eating disorder, 38–39
    and night eating syndrome, 40
    and self-report data, 63–64
Obesity, 51, 220, 276
    and ethnicity, 119–121
    as health problem, 213, 219–222, 228
Objectification theory, 101–104
O'Dea, J., 239
Ogg, E., 145
Oregon Adolescent Depression Study, 136
Orenstein, P., 125
Orlistat, for treatment of binge-eating disorder, 207
Outcomes, 143, 145, 161–162, 198
    criteria, 166–167
    See also Research

PAQ. *See* Personal Attributes Questionnaire

Parental affection, deficits in, as risk factor, 59
Parents, and prevention programs, 81–82
Parker, S., 117
Participatory ecology model, 213, 243–248. *See also* Ecological perspective
Participatory-relational approach, 241
Peer relationships, 119
Peers, and reinforcement of thin ideal, 97–98
Perfectionism, 61, 95–96, 120
    as risk factor, 57–58
Perry, C. L., 248
Persistence, factors in, 66
Personal Attributes Questionnaire (PAQ), 95
Personality characteristics, 93
Peterson, C., 6, 133, 176, 276
Petrill, S., 140
Pharmaceutical companies, and research funding, 197–198
Pharmacotherapy, 134, 140, 198, 205–207
    ancillary, 205–206, 208
    for anorexia nervosa, 199–201, 205–206
    for binge-eating disorder, 203–205, 207–208
    for bulimia nervosa, 201–203, 205–207
Phenytoin, for treatment of bulimia nervosa, 202
Pigott, T. A., 5
Piran, N., 7, 79, 81–82, 84–85, 213, 241, 244–246, 277
Polivy, J., 60
Population-based models, and prevention, 265–266
Potency, as methodological issue, 64
Prejudice, racial. *See* Discrimination, racial, as risk factor
Prentice, A. M., 63–64
Prevention, 4, 233–234, 265–266, 276–277
    and ethnic minority groups, 112–114, 125–126
    and objectification theory, 102–103
    and population-based models, 265–266
    primary–universal, 84–85, 233, 240–243

and protective factors, 82–83
    secondary–selective, 84–85, 233, 243, 265
    tertiary–indicated, 265
    See also Risk factor reduction
Prevention programs
    "Everybody's Different," 239
    outcome studies, 234–239
    recommended aims, 242–243
    Student Bodies, 257–262
Privacy, and computer-assisted psychoeducational program, 255, 264–265
Program evaluation, for self-help interventions, 166–167
Protective factors, 28, 52, 75–76, 78–82, 274
    general, 76–78, 82–84
    high self-esteem as, 100–101
    and intervention, 275
    life skills training as, 79
    mastery experiences as, 81
    and prevention, 82–83
    sports participation as, 78–79, 100–101
    See also Risk factors
Proximal processes, 80–82
Psychodynamic psychotherapy, short term, 157, 161–162, 164–165
Psychoeducation, in treatment of bulimia nervosa, 182–184
Psychoeducation programs
    Body Traps, 259–261
    See also Computer-assisted psychoeducational program
Psychotherapy, 140
    population based, 265–266
PsycLIT, 157
Puberty, timing of, as risk factor, 58
Purging, 36, 182
    and subtyping, 43–44

Ransford, H. E., 225
Recovery, defining, 92
Relapse prevention
    for anorexia nervosa, 199, 206, 208
    for bulimia nervosa, 187, 201
Research
    computer-assisted psychoeducation program preliminary studies, 256–263

guided, 154, 156–160, 163–164
interpersonal aspects, 163–165
See also Computer-assisted psycho-
educational programs
Self-help groups, 153–154, 163
Self-help interventions, 133, 154–155
current context, 155–156
new paradigm, 157–160
research agenda, 161–167
Self-ideal discrepancy, men and, 223–224
Self-neglect, and bulimia nervosa, 181–
182, 186
Self-objectification, women and, 101–103
Self-report data, use of, 63
Self-silencing, 125
Serdula, M. K., 217–218, 222
Serotonin levels, reduced, 94
Serotonin reuptake inhibitors (SSRIs)
for treatment of anorexia nervosa,
199, 201, 206
for treatment of bulimia nervosa,
205, 207
Service delivery, mode of, for self-help
interventions, 162–163, 165
Sexual abuse, gender and, 98–100. *See
also* Child sexual abuse
Sexual harassment, gender and, 98–101
Sexual potency, male loss of, 34
Shame, as barrier to treatment seeking,
139–140
Shisslak, C., 5, 28, 274
Sibutramine, for treatment of binge-
eating disorder, 207
Silberstein, L., 6, 274
Silberstein, L. R., 76
Smolak, L., 6, 28, 60, 78, 82, 94–96, 98–
99, 124, 240, 246, 274
Social Competence Promotion Program
for Young Adolescents
(SCPP-YA), 241–242
Social environments, in participatory pre-
vention programs, 245–246
Social status, and research on ethnic
group differences, 117
Social support, 83
as protective factor vs. risk factor, 75
Sociocultural approach, 61, 111–112, 274
Sociocultural factors, 241–242
Sociocultural pressures for thinness, as
risk factor, 54
Spiral model, 60–61

Sports participation, as protective factor,
78–79, 100–101
SSRIs. *See* Serotonin reuptake inhibitors
Stages of change model, 164
Stakeholders, and program evaluation,
167
Stanford Study, 137
Stanford University Medical Media
and Information Technologies,
257
Stein, R. I., 5
Steiner-Adair, C., 95
Stepped care approaches, 141, 162, 205,
266
Stevens, J., 219–220
Stice, E., 5, 28, 81, 274
Stolley, M., 139
Striegel-Moore, R. H., 6, 28, 76, 119–
120, 133, 140, 218, 274–275
Strober, M., 5, 33–34, 38
Strupp, H., 164
Student Bodies, 262, 266
CD-ROM, 257
Internet, 257–259
and psychoeducational class,
259–261
Stunkard, A. J., 40
Submission pattern, of interpersonal
relations, 180–181
Substance abuse prevention, 240–241
Subtyping, 42–44
Suicide, risk of, 43
Supervision, in self-help interventions,
165–166
"Superwoman," 95–96
Symptom reduction, as goal of self-help
intervention, 160

Taylor, C. B., 7, 213–214, 257, 276
Taylor, J., 125
Technology
and dissemination of treatment protocols, 156
and eating disorder classification, 40,
45
and ethical standards, 165–166
interactive, 255, 263–265
and prevention, 214
push, 264

Technology, *continued*
    See also Computer-assisted psycho-
        educational programs
Teenagers. *See* Adolescents
Telch, C. F., 55–57
Temperament, and bulimia nervosa, 178
Therapist, lay, 165
Therapist–client relationship, and self-
        help interventions, 163–165
Therapist factors, 143, 163
Thin ideal, 95–98, 227
    and ethnicity, 118–119
    internalization, 54, 61, 118–119, 227
Thinness, culture of, 96–98
Thinness schema, 98
Thompson, B., 124
Thompson, J. K., 6, 61, 213, 218, 276
Thompson, K., 179
Three-way interactive model, 61
Tiet, Q. Q., 77
Timing, 41–42
    and computer-assisted psychoeduca-
        tional program, 255, 262
    of self-help intervention, 162
Trait impulsivity, and bulimia nervosa,
        181
Treasure, J., 164
Treasure, J. L., 81
Treatment, 4, 140–141, 275–276
    dropout rates, 142
    duration, 141, 143–144
    effectiveness, 145, 155
    of obesity, 220
    and prevention, 265–266
    See also Health services; Interven-
        tion; Pharmacotherapy
Treatment approaches, and ethnicity, 126
Treatment matching, for self-help inter-
        ventions, 161–162
Treatment modality, in self-help interven-
        tions, 162–163
Treatment protocols, 155–156
    of integrative cognitive therapy for
        bulimia nervosa, 182–187
Treatment safeguards, for self-help inter-
        ventions, 166
Treatment seeking, 139–140, 145–146,
        275
Treatment sequencing, 141
Troop, N. A., 81
Turnbull, S., 164

U.S. Equal Employment Opportunity
        Commission, 123
U.S. Food and Drug Administration, 198
Ustun, T., 148

Van Itallie, T. B., 219–220
Via, M., 145
Vicary, J. R., 81
Virginia Twin Study, 136
Vohs, K. D., 61

Waller, G., 116
Walsh, B., 199
Ward, A., 164
Waters, P., 80–81
Weight, defining typical vs. pathological, 40
Weight dissatisfaction. *See* Body dissatis-
        faction
Weight loss, and body dissatisfaction,
        217–219, 222–224
Weight loss criterion, 32
Weight phobia, 33
Wells, A. M., 240
Wentzel, K. R., 81
Whitesell, N. R., 80–81
Wiederman, M., 139
Wilfley, D., 120
Wilfley, D. E., 218
Winzelberg, A., 7, 265, 276
Winzelberg, A. J., 266
Winzelburg, A., 213–214
Withdrawal patterns, of interpersonal
        relations, 180–181
Wolff, H. G., 40
Women
    and body image, 247–248
    and internalization of objectification,
        101–103
    "lived experiences" of, 92, 96–101, 104
    loss of voice, 99, 125
    See also Gender
Wonderlich, S., 6, 133, 147, 275–276
Wonderlich, S. A., 176
World Health Organization, 243

Yerkes, R. M., 226

Zucker, N. L., 78

ABOUT THE EDITORS

Ruth H. Striegel-Moore, PhD, is a professor of psychology at Wesleyan University in Middleton, CT. Dr. Striegel-Moore received her diploma in psychology from the Eberhard-Karls-Universitat in Tuebingen, Germany, and her PhD in clinical psychology from the University of South Carolina, Columbia. For her work in epidemiology of eating disorders, she has received major funding from the National Institute of Mental Health and the National Institute of Diabetes, Digestive, and Kidney Disease of the National Institutes of Health. Dr. Striegel-Moore is past president of the Academy for Eating Disorders and current president of the Eating Disorder Research Society. She is a Fellow of the American Psychological Association.

Linda Smolak, PhD, received her doctoral training at Temple University, obtaining her degree in 1980. She has been at Kenyon College in Gambier, OH, since 1980 and is a professor in the Departments of Psychology and of Women's and Gender Studies. Her research specialty is the developmental psychopathology of eating disorders, with an emphasis on gender issues. She has coedited two other books in the area of body image and eating disorders—*The Developmental Psychopathology of Eating Disorders* (1996) and *Body Image, Eating Disorders, and Obesity in Youth: Assessment, Prevention, and Treatment* (American Psychological Association, 2001)—and is coauthoring a book on the prevention of eating disorders—*The Prevention of Eating Problems and Eating Disorders: Theory, Research, and Practice.* She has served as a consultant to the McKnight Risk Factor Study, the U.S. Office on Women's Health, and the Harvard Eating Disorders Center.